GO SUCCESS MANTRAS

THE FIFTEEN MANTRAS THAT LEAD YOU TO SUCCESS

GOLDEN SUCCESS MANTRAS

THE FIFTEEN MANTRAS THAT LEAD YOU TO SUCCESS

RAMASHISH

Notion Press

Old No. 38, New No. 6
McNichols Road, Chetpet
Chennai - 600 031

First Published by Notion Press 2016
Copyright © Ramashish Yadav 2016
All Rights Reserved.

ISBN 978-93-86073-02-0

This book has been published with all efforts taken to make the material error-free after the consent of the author. However, the author and the publisher do not assume and hereby disclaim any liability to any party for any loss, damage, or disruption caused by errors or omissions, whether such errors or omissions result from negligence, accident, or any other cause.

No part of this book may be used, reproduced in any manner whatsoever without written permission from the author, except in the case of brief quotations embodied in critical articles and reviews.

© Ramashish Yadav, 2016

All rights reserved. No part of this publication may be reproduced, stored in or introduced into retrieval system, or transmitted, or permitted, in any form, or by any means(electronic, mechanical, photocopying, recording or otherwise) without the prior written permission of the author and publisher. Any person who does any unauthorized act in relation to this publication may be liable to criminal prosecution and civil claims for damages.

Disclaimer

The thoughts, views and contents in this book are solely of the author based on his vast experiences supported by many stories and famous quotations of imminent persons. This book has been written only as a recipe, guideline, self-help, and not as a guarantee; and based on this condition, this book is being sold in the market as neither the author nor publisher or printers or sellers are engaged in rendering legal, accounting or other professional service with reference to its contents.

Further, the author, publisher and printer disclaim any liability for any loss, damage, risk, injury, distress, pain, etc. suffered by any person, whether or not as purchaser of this book, as a consequence whether direct or indirect any action taken or not on the basis of the contents of this book.

It is the belief of the author and publisher that the contents of this book do not violate any existing copyright/intellectual property of others in any manner whatsoever. However, in the event the author has been unable to track any source and if any copyright has been unintentionally violated, infringed, kindly write to the publisher and author for corrective measures as we respect the copyright of any person in real spirit.

Dedication

I dedicate this book to the Almighty God for His creation of this extremely beautiful and infinite universe with a massive mystery; for running the show of the universe; and for showering blessings on all creatures of the universe. I also dedicate this book to all the children of God who will shape this world into a better place to live in, by His blessings and through their sincere and honest efforts.

Contents

Preface	*xi*
Acknowledgments	*xiii*
1. Success is at Your Doorstep-Through the Fifteen Mantras	1
2. Have Imagination, Dream and Desire	29
3. Practice Determination, Dedication and Discipline (3 Ds)	39
4. Build A Positive Attitude	48
5. Practice Motivation For Yourself and Others	77
6. Develop Self – Esteem and Self – Confidence (2 Ss)	92
7. Build Character, Courage, Conviction, Commitment and Concentration (5 3Cs)	109
8. Develop Passion, Patience, Persistence and Perspiration (4 Ps)	131
9. Practice Cooperation, Harmony, Wisdom and Forgiveness	144
10. Avoid Fear, Procrastination and Bad Habits	160
11. Have Eagerness for Education, Learning, Research and Innovation	172
12. Do Goal-Setting and Planning	189
13. Take Decision and Action	198
14. Practice Values and Spirituality	212
15. Develop Leadership Qualities	225
16. Maintain Stress Free Life and Good Health	262

Preface

"Resolve to perform what you ought;
Perform without fail what you resolve"

—*Benjamin Franklin*

Success is a fascination of life, a dream of life, a desire of life, an elixir of life; hence, everybody wishes to achieve it in reality for themselves. As a result, a large number of motivational or self-help books have become available on this topic. Since success is the progressive realization of one's dream, it is but natural that many books will be written on this topic depicting various mantras in new ways. The present book **"GOLDEN SUCCESS MANTRAS"** is an attempt to fill up the space using new ways to rejuvenate and passionate the heart, mind, soul and body to achieve golden success. This book is a unique, uplifting, unbeatable, and unparalleled recipe in the form of mantras supported by appropriate quotes, real life anecdotes and stories as well as the messages they convey for achieving success in life.

Though everyone wishes to succeed, the fact is that, either most people are not well equipped with the mantras, or they don't have the required desire, determination and are not ready to put in the necessary effort and time to succeed. This book will put them on the glorious path and in the right gear to succeed.

What motivated me to pen this book? I have an experience of about forty-five years in engineering teaching and research profession, including being the head of three institutions. During this period, I found that some students with a lot of talent were not able to succeed to even fifty percent of their potential. I used to motivate them, guide them and help them reach their potential. This inspired me to read a lot of books in this field and in the last ten years I have devoted sufficient time on this. Moreover, I attended some lectures of experts on such topics. Though, I am an author of six Mechanical Engineering text books for B. Tech. course in the field of Thermal Engineering, due to my new found passion in the fields of self-help, human resource development and management, motivation, inspiration and mythology (not course oriented), I decided to write down my experiences of forty-five years for the benefit of people ranging from the age of fifteen to seventy-five years. Moreover, it is also God's will, I believe.

The special features of this book include the following:

- It offers sixteen chapters incorporating the fifteen groups of Success Mantras and every group (except three) consists of related sub-mantras. The sixteen chapters symbolize with sixteen arts (Kala) of Lord Krishna.
- The style is unique in the sense that every mantra begins with two highly suitable famous quotations befitting the topic and is given in italic with bullets, instead of a single quotation as found in currently available books.

- It also consists of more quotes in the write-up at suitable places to reinforce the message and the mantras.
- Further, I have included my own quotes, a new concept which I coined, during writing and have been given in italic under bullets in the passage to strengthen the thought.
- I have included many real and fictional stories to strengthen the mantras followed by the theme of the stories. As a result, the book encompasses a basket of ideas, thoughts and wisdom.
- The idea behind including more quotes lies in the fact that sometimes one word, one sentence or one expression depending on the person changes one's attitude and destiny in an unprecedented way as human life is nothing but the self-management of mind.
- The fifteen groups of success mantras cover a wide spectrum and ecosystem of a beautiful human life symbolizing the mystery of pearl formation in an oyster, the blossoming of beautiful flowers of different colors in the garden of success and act as fascinating and bewildering agents to face the challenges of human life.

This book is for those persons who ask: "What is success? What is the taste of success? What is happiness in life? What is peace in life? What is the way to a meaningful life for which God has sent us in this world? What are the Mantras to succeed?"

- This book is also meant for those persons who are frustrated, who are failures, who are having low dreams, who are not passionate about their dreams, who have no dreams at all, who are pessimists, who are procrastinators, who do not believe in contribution, who are not hard working and persistent and also for those who want to succeed further and further achieving many milestones.
- To supplement the Mantras to a practical shape, suitable real and fictional stories have been included wherever necessary in most of the chapters followed by themes and messages of the story which add beauty to the Mantras.
- The book is a treasure of experience, wisdom, inspiration, motivation, leadership, glory, values and success mantras. Such a book may act as a companion throughout life as a guide to the soul which people may like to read many times and may treasure it for life long.

I hope the book will help in meeting the aspirations of readers in a big way and the world will see more successful people, more winners, more history creators, more nation builders, more contributors through goodness and righteous approach, more compassionate people, more happy and prosperous people.

"Four basic factors are involved in successful outcomes:
Goal-Setting, Positive thinking, Visualizing and Believing."

—*Dr. A. P. J. Abdul Kalam*

Acknowledgments

Any venture, any dream, and any goal cannot be completed without the cooperation of many people, either directly or indirectly. This present venture is no exception either. I am indebted to many authors whose books and articles on the Internet enriched my knowledge, wisdom and experience. The list of authors is too long to list and I acknowledge all of them from the bottom of my heart. During my teaching profession, I have addressed many students and teachers. Their interaction and feedback have enriched my knowledge and experience. I thank and acknowledge all of them.

I am very fond of quotes and meaningful messages and I have been writing these in my notebook for the last ten years on a large scale which I have included in this book. I have noted the author's name but not the source. I have also included a large number of quotes and some data from websites on the Internet, from books and newspapers. Further, I have included many stories available on various websites, in various children's books and told by parents and teachers to children; but I have written all of them in my own ways followed by the themes of the stories. I sincerely acknowledge all of them for adding wisdom, value, reality and beauty to my book directly or indirectly.

I have taken some references on Stress and Health Management from websites on Internet and from my discussion with doctors but I have written them in my own way. I acknowledge all of them in the passage in the brackets as my sources.

I thank, from the bottom of my heart, the team members of Notion Press Media Pvt. Ltd. for their excellent work, as without their cooperation, help, passion, hard work and dedication, this book could not have seen the light of the day in such a beautiful form. I also thank the team of marketing officials for the promotion of the book to reach out to the readers in a big way.

I wholeheartedly thank my nephew Kapil Deo for typing the first hand-written manuscript and for his encouragement. I thank my wife, Meera Yadav who is the source of my biggest inspiration. I thank my sons- Dr Sanjay and Er Rajay, my grandchildren, my daughters-in-law, my nephews, and all my friends and well-wishers for their constant encouragement during its writing and their curiosity to see this book in the market and in the hands of the readers.

—*Ramashish*

Chapter 1

Success is at Your Doorstep-Through the Fifteen Mantras

"Nothing succeeds like success."

—*Oscar Wilde*

"Successful people in this world are those who get up and look for circumstances they want. If they can't find them, they make them."

—*George Bernard Shaw*

WHAT IS SUCCESS?

An eminent preacher was asked by someone from the audience in a congregation to speak to us of success. He replied: Success! Success! Success! Everyone's dream. Everyone's goal. Everyone's desire. An elixir for everybody. How fascinating it is? How alluring it is? How beautiful it is? How elusive it is? How slippery it is? How hilarious it is? How challenging it is? You can only assess these when you try to achieve your golden success. One person says: Oh! I missed the golden chance to succeed but I will try again with new vigor, new zeal. Other person says: Oh! I could have struggled more and won. If success is the craze and buzzword of everybody, then the question arises: What really is success? What does success mean to you?

In simple words, success may be defined as the attainment of one's desired goal. The desired goal may vary from person to person. The goal of a student is to pass examinations with flying colors and to get an excellent job of his or her choice with a high pay package. A singer's choice is to become famous in the cinema world having a lot of fans, fame and wealth. An artist from the movie business desires to become a great artist (hero/heroine) with a lot of name, fame, fans and wealth. The aim of a sports player is to become a top player in the country or the world with a lot of name, fame, fans and wealth. An entrepreneur or a businessman desires to achieve great heights in his business by expanding his business empire throughout the country or the world, and earning a lot of wealth while contributing greatly to the building of the nation. A service holder aims to achieve a high position in the organization with a lot of contributions to his or her credit having name and fame giving him or her satisfaction. The goal of a social worker is to serve the maximum number of needy, downtrodden persons which will give him or her great satisfaction and happiness. The aim of a politician is to become a minister or chief minister or prime minister or president, in order to acquire the power to contribute to the building of the nation giving him or her name, fame, wealth and satisfaction.

Similarly, persons engaged in other professions may view success in different ways, such as recognition, satisfaction, good health, peace of mind, happiness, freedom, liberty, social service, constantly evolving for the better, changing things for the better, etc. So, success means different things to different people and it is a relative term. Every success in the pursuit of a worthy goal is a golden success or a part of golden success. Napoleon Hill advocated, "Whatever the mind of man can conceive and believe, it can achieve."

"Success is the story of succeeding by overcoming the fear of failures, accepting responsibilities, achieving goals and making the world a better place to live in."

A BROADER VIEW OF SUCCESS

At present, in the world, there are more than 7.4 billion people. Everybody has their own view of success. So, in this respect, a broader view of success needs to be discussed. The words of Thomas S. Monson present a broader view of success in the following line:

"Success is the progressive realization of a worthy ideal."

—*Thomas S. Monson*

This quote is like an entire ocean contained in a small pot. Success is a continuous journey, a voyage and not the final destination. The moment we achieve one of our goals, we decide to go on to another and so on. It is a non-stop journey in the ocean of success, crossing many milestones and facing many hardships while achieving the worthy ideal- a pious goal, a value based goal which is different for every person.

Another broader view of success may be conceptualized by the famous poem of Bessie Anderson Stanley (supplement):

Poem of Bessie Anderson Stanley(Supplement)

"He has achieved success who has lived well, laughed often, and loved much;
Who has enjoyed the trust of pure women, the respect of intelligent men, and the love of little children;
Who has filled his niche and accomplished his task;
Who has never lacked appreciation of Earth's beauty or failed to express it;
Who has left the world better than he found it;
Whether an improved poppy, a perfect poem, or a rescued soul;
Who has always looked for the best in others and given them the best he had;
Whose life was an inspiration;
Whose memory a benediction."

(Source:www.goodreads.com; Bessie Anderson Stanley, More Heart Throbs, Volume Two, in prose and verse Dear to the American People and by them contributed as supplement to the original USD 10,000 Prize Book HEART THROBS)

This is an ideal and may be called the golden definition of success, as it covers a wide spectrum and ecosystem of humanity. Though in the material world, possessing wealth, power, name and fame constitute the main ingredients of success, if it is achieved along with the ingredients of the Stanley supplement, then it becomes fulfilling. The Stanley supplement emphasizes mainly on the human aspects: "The contributions for a better world, maintaining the values, systems and a good lifeare the real success." The effective social workers, people who seek happiness, wisdom seekers, natural beauty seekers and persons of good character with a lot of contributions come under this category.

Deepak Chopra has also postulated a broader view of success: "There are many aspects to success; material wealth is only one component. But success also includes good health, energy and enthusiasm for life, fulfilling relationship, creative freedom, emotional and psychological stability; a sense of well-being, and peace of mind." "Success is in making a meaningful positive difference in the life of self and others, leading a beautiful life and shaping the world a better place to live in through right, progressive and innovative actions."

The following stories of some famous people will further give a broader view of success including the qualities they possessed.

Service to Downtrodden and Sick People Offers Immense Satisfaction and Happiness: Mother Teresa was a nurse in Albania. Once, she visited Calcutta and saw the suffering of the downtrodden and sick people – men, women and children that moved her. An intense desire entered her mind to serve the sick people of Calcutta. She came back to India and started serving the sick people and the downtrodden. She started a mission and brought smiles on the faces of millions of people. She got many awards from all over the world. She became a great and successful person in serving the downtrodden and sick people as it was her desire and mission. It gave a great sense of satisfaction to her soul.

The **moral** of this story is: "Success is not only about earning a lot of wealth, acquiring a high position, or getting high awards but also about making a difference in the lives of people, especially, the downtrodden through a spiritual quest."

Success in Innovative Products Makes You a Legend: When Bill Gates was a second-year student of Mechanical Engineering at Harvard University, USA, an idea cropped up in his mind to develop an operating system for a desktop/personal computer which did not exist in the market then. He dropped out from the university and started a company called Microsoft with his friend. He developed the operating system 'Windows' which revolutionized the personal computers industry. For many years, he remained the richest person in the world with a fortune worth more than USD 60 billion. Later on, he started a foundation- Bill and Melinda Gates Foundation to which he donated half of his wealth (about USD 28 billion)saying, "It is the society which gave me wealth that I am returning partly to serve humanity worldwide in the health sector."

The **moral** of this story is: "It is your decision at the right time to work with passion, persistence and perspiration for your innovative dream, ignoring risks which make you successful in many respects-as an innovative technology provider, a great wealth creator and a great philanthropist."

Success in Freedom Struggle Made Him a National Icon: Mahatma Gandhi was a simple lawyer from Gujarat (India). He went to South Africa to practice there as a lawyer. At that time, both India and South Africa were under the British Rule. He met with social discrimination from the British on the train and at other places. He also observed a high degree of social discrimination against Indians settled there and the original inhabitants, from the British. Seeing the pitiable condition, he decided to fight against this. He raised the issue of social discrimination there and fought. Later on, he returned to India on 15th January, 1915 to join the freedom struggle. In this process, he toured all over India and started a freedom struggle by using a new tool Satyagraha and Ahimsa. Many times, he was sent to jail along with others, and finally, the British had to give freedom to India on 15th August, 1947. He struggled, worked hard and suffered a lot for the freedom of India for about thirty-two years. He was a great successful person for his resolve- stopping of social discrimination, achieving the rights of Indians and the freedom of India. He is a role model for many people in the world, as a highly successful person in his mission, as a leader of the highest caliber and as a great freedom fighter who enabled India to achieve freedom.

The **moral** of the story is: "Success demands many trials and tribulations, a lot of patience, great perseverance, a lot of wisdom and lots of hard work. Success is not a mystery, but it is the result of consistently applying some fundamental principles such as a great dream, strong willpower, excellent character, unflinching courage, high enthusiasm, strong determination and whole-hearted actions."

In the journey of success, failures will come. Failure is the route to success and greatness. Winston Churchill opined, "Success is not final, failure is not fatal: it is the courage to continue that counts." It is not at all important as to how many times you have failed, but the most important thing is whether you are trying hard to succeed after every failure or not. The world salutes such winners. Confucius said, "Our greatest glory is not in never falling, but in rising every time we fall."

IGNITE THE FIRE IN YOUR BELLY

Unless and until you ignite the fire in your belly to succeed, to win, success will not be achieved. This fire will create a great passion in you for success towards your goal. There is a need to acquiring a winning edge to become a winner and be successful in any competitive pursuit. It is nothing but to strive for excellence with a fire in your belly and an unflinching determination. "Nobody can be successful and great unless and until one wants to, earnestly enough, becomes highly positive, and gets ready to pay the price for it in the form of hard work and sacrifice." Take the case of an athlete for a 100 metres or a 200 metres race. One has to practice hard, to empower oneself with stamina, and to find out the strategies to be a winner. What does one need finally? All that is needed is the winning edge for the fraction of a second. One doesn't have to be many times smarter than the other top athletes. Take the example of Usain Bolt, who is an Olympic gold medalist in 100 metres and 200 metres race clocking 9.58 seconds and 19.19 seconds respectively. It is the practice, stamina and winning edge in the last second that made him a gold medalist.

Similarly, in horse racing, a winning edge has to be achieved. For finding winning edge, one has to do research in every segment of the pursuit with reference to his or her strength and weakness and the capability required for winning. So, wherever there are competitions in any field, the requirements for a winning edge matter and these are developed by improving in every segment of winning, be it just one to ten percent. "Acquiring a winning edge is the cornerstone of success."

Success comes through sincere involvement and hard work. The words of Theodore Roosevelt elucidate this beautifully, "It is hard to fail, but it is worse never to have tried to succeed." Your success depends upon your intensity of desire over your fear of failure. A winning team always plays to win. A team which plays not to lose is generally a loser. The words of Bill Cosby showcase this beautifully, "In order to succeed, your desire for success should be greater than your fear of failure."

WHAT LIES BEHIND A SUCCESS? STRUGGLES!

Behind every success story, there are stories of gigantic struggles. For getting success in life, one has to struggle at various stages in the journey of success. The whole life is full of struggles and if anybody stops struggling, one cannot be a winner and be successful. "Struggling bravely against the odds and overcoming them is winning."

For getting success, your association with different types of people matters a lot. If you associate with a great visionary, you would be like that. The words of Steve Maraboli confirm this eloquently, "If you hang out with chickens, you are going to cluck and if you hang out with eagles, you're going to fly."

"Wings don't matter much. It is the enthusiasm that matters in flying."

The following are the stories of winners and successful people who struggled immensely and finally succeeded.

Dream, Courage and Struggles Make You a History Maker in Mountaineering: After years of dreaming about the Mount Everest and seven weeks of climbing, New Zealand's Edmund Hillary and Nepal's Tensing Norgay reached the top of the Mount Everest, the highest mountain in the world at 11:30 am, on May 29, 1953. They were the first people to reach the summit. The Mount Everest had long been considered insurmountable by some, and the ultimate climbing challenge by others due to severe cold, freezing weather, mountain sickness, danger of falling from the cliff into deep crevasses, snow storms, etc. At that time, the accessories were also not advanced. In spite of all odds, both of them showed courage, patience and overcame all obstacles in the way to become the first climbers to climb the highest mountain in the world.

The **theme** of the story is: "A high degree of courage, enthusiasm and passion in life will enable you to overcome great hardships and finally make you a winner and history maker."

"Even gigantic obstacles are not able to defeat great winners. They face Himalayan hardships in the journey of success, but they defeat these hardships and become successful. Fear doesn't touch them." The words of B. C. Forbes confirm this: "History has demonstrated that the most notable winners usually encountered heartbreaking obstacles before they triumphed. They won because they refused to become discouraged by their defeats."

Struggle Provides Strength to the Wings to Fly: The story of a caterpillar turning into a butterfly is a very interesting one to showcase the importance of struggle in life. This is a common story told to children by parents and teachers. A biology teacher was demonstrating to his students that in a couple of hours the butterfly would struggle to come out of the cocoon through a small hole in the cocoon. After advising the students that no one should help the butterfly in her struggle, he left the scene.

The students were watching the struggle of the butterfly to come out of the small hole in the cocoon very curiously. However, against the advice of the teacher, one student showed pity seeing the pain and the struggle of the butterfly and decided to help her by breaking the cocoon. Though the butterfly came out, it had a swollen body and small, shriveled wings. It could not fly but crawled for some time and later on died.

After sometime, the teacher returned to the scene and the students told him about the events that happened in his absence. The teacher explained to his students that as per natural law, the struggle of the butterfly to come out from the cocoon helps in developing the strength in its wings. The butterfly died because the help provided by the student, which deprived the butterfly of struggling and gaining strength.

In human life also, the principle of struggling and gaining strength is valid. If parents or well-wishers stop any child from struggling to gain strength, they are simply spoiling the life of the child and making him meek and weak- both physically and mentally.

The **theme** of this story is: "We all can gain stronger wings and enthusiasm through struggle to fly high in the world of success."

Willpower Makes You a Great Winner Despite Adversity: Franklin D. Roosevelt is regarded as one of the greatest American presidents by citizens of the world. A misfortune occurred in his life when he contracted an illness at the age of thirty-nine that left him paralyzed from the waist down for the rest of his life. But one can imagine his willpower, courage and self-esteem to run for the presidency of USA being paralyzed. He was elected four times president of America – making him the only American President to be elected more than twice.

The **theme** of the story is: "Your colossal willpower, unwavering courage and high self-esteem will take you to greater heights in spite of severe adversities."

Struggle and People Skills Make You Highly Successful: Richard Branson has become the fourth richest person in the United Kingdom overcoming all obstacles in his life. He owns the Virgin group of brands, an airline and a mobile phone company. He also owns an island in the Caribbean. In childhood, he struggled with dyslexia and was poor in studies at school. His teachers and school authorities took it for granted that he wouldn't go very far but Branson defied all the odds and obstacles in his life and reached his present height proving his entire destiny's forecasters totally wrong. He mainly attributes his success to his decisive power and interpersonal (people) skills - proving that street smarts can take you far ahead.

The **gist** of the story is: "It is your persistent struggle defying all odds, decisive power, street smartness and people skills that ensure a great success."

Do you know the importance of your own resolution? It is amazing. It is your conviction. All the winners, all the great people have their own resolution, and that is why they succeeded. Abraham Lincoln once said, "Always bear in mind that your own resolution to succeed is more important than any other thing."

You can't attain greatness by leading a cozy life, without facing obstacles, without facing an opposite current or an opposite wind. Greatness is achieved by facing great hardships and overcoming them. The words of Winston Churchill elucidate this very beautifully: "Kites rise high against the wind, not with it."

Defying All Odds and Using Willpower Makes a National Icon: Stevie Wonder has proved to be an iconic singer by receiving twenty-two Grammy awards – highest ever by a single male. It is worthy to note that he was blind since birth but he defied his blindness and released more than thirty numbers of hits which placed him as one of the greatest performers who had ever lived. He spearheaded many political campaigns and became an American cultural icon.

The **theme** of the story suggests that: "If you have passion and willpower, no physical disability will be a hindrance to achieve unparalleled success in life and become a national icon."

"Success is realized when you care about your project like a baby and perspire hard relentlessly."

All Odds are Small before Passion: Marlee Matlin was deaf from childhood. But her deafness did not deter her. By overcoming all hardships, she received an Academy Award for Best Actress for her role in the 1986 movie –'Children of a lesser God.' She was also awarded Hollywood Walk of Fame in 2009.

The **theme** behind this story showcases that: "Success is about defying all odds and obstacles, working hard for your passion using your talent, and then expecting a miracle."

The proverb, "A smooth sea cannot produce a tough sailor" fully justifies all the above stories.

"Passion, patience, perseverance and perspiration overcome all hardships and stumbling blocks of life and finally make you a great winner and history creator."

A Slow Mind at Childhood Couldn't Stop Him From Becoming a Great Scientist: Albert Einstein proved himself to be one of the most intelligent persons of the world but there was no sign of it during his childhood. He didn't speak till he was four and didn't read till seven. His parents and teachers thought he was a mentally challenged boy. But he turned out to be one of the greatest physicists of the world. He gave the world "Theory of relativity" and "$E = mc^2$" of nuclear physics. He won the Nobel Prize and is called as the face of modern physics.

The **moral** of the story is: "One can rise above the perception of a mentally challenged child and can be a great scientist of the world through character, discipline, patience, persistence and perspiration."

GREAT FAILURES ARE THE GOLDEN WAYS TO SUCCESS:

"Success is stumbling from failure to failure with no loss of enthusiasm."

–*Winston Churchill*

"Behind every success story, there are stories of great failures. Failure is the stepping stone to success. There are a lot of slips between the cup and the lips. Failure offers experience and gives direction to succeed. The fact that you've failed is proof that you're not finished and may bounce back with more vigor and zeal. Failures and mistakes are a bridge, not a barricade, to success." Sven Goran Eriksson opined, "The greatest barrier to success is the fear of failure." Worldwide, successful people believe that mistakes are just feedback. It is not important how low you fall but how high you bounce back, that makes all the difference. If the end is good, everything is good. "Forget what you have lost; rather focus on what is left with you."

Experience suggests that failures can offer you either weight or wings. The only way to make a comeback is to go on with full enthusiasm. The following stories will reveal this fact:

A Great Success after a Series of Failures Shows the Supreme Substance in A Person: The life history of Abraham Lincoln is really interesting and provides a testimony that behind every success story, there are stories of great failures. Lincoln was born in a poor family on Feb.12, 1809 in the USA and got less chances to have a good education. When he was nine years old, his mother died and he had to work hard for a living. With his step mother, he bonded well and she encouraged him to study. For getting reading materials, he had to walk a lot. He failed in almost all his ventures he tried, but he never gave up. He started his business at the age of twenty-one but failed; ran for state legislature at the age of twenty-two but lost; lost his job at the age of twenty-two; he again tried business by borrowing money from friend at the age of twenty-four but failed with heavy debt which he paid back in many years; he lost his sweetheart at the age of twenty-six which devastated him and he got nervous breakdown and was in bed for a year; he tried to become an elector at the age of thirty-one, but got defeated; at the age of thirty-four, he ran for congress but lost; he again ran for congress at the age of thirty-seven and this time he won and did a good job in Washington; at age of thirty-nine, he ran for re-election for congress but lost; he ran for senate of the United States at the age of forty-three but lost; at the age of forty-seven, he sought for vice-presidential nomination of Republican party but lost miserably; he ran for U.S. Senate at the age of forty-nine but again he lost; and finally at the age of fifty-one, he was elected as the sixteenth President of United States.

Being the president, he led the United States through its greatest constitutional, military and moral crisis- the American civil war- preserving the union, abolishing slavery, strengthening the national government and modernizing the economy.

The **moral** of this story is: "The story of Lincoln is the best example of unparalleled success after a series of failures without losing hope, without giving up the pursuits through qualities such as patience, persistence, enthusiasm, conviction, decisive power and courage."

> *"Standing firmly against adversities without losing hope, and working persistently with renewed vigor is the DNA of success."*

> *"Success is the story of trying again and again with renewed zeal after each failure till you achieve it."*

EvenTen Thousand Failures Didn't Deter a Persistent Success Seeker: The story of Thomas Edison is full of failures and full of success. He was born in 1847 in USA. Edison was declared slow student in studies and so his parents decided to drop him out from school after three months of schooling and her mother taught him at home. "He was a geek and a crazy person for invention." He first developed the telegrapher. Then, he dreamed of inventing an electric bulb. Despite more than a 10,000 failures, he never gave up, but worked hard until he finally invented the electric bulb and demonstrated. He is a symbol of great persistence and perspiration who saw his dream turn into a reality. Due to his various inventions, he got many awards and appreciations by the government of USA.

The **theme** of this story is better illustrated by the quote of Thomas Edison: "People are not remembered by how few times they failed, but how often they succeeded. Every wrong step can be another step forward."

> *"Roses have thorns, so success has failures. Be an achiever by overcoming thorns of failures through a great zeal and persistent efforts."*

Hey, sons and daughters of God! Get up, wake up and take up the challenges of life. Success is awaiting you with arms open to embrace you, to hug you through the thorns of failures. This has also been advocated by Colin Powell: "There is no secret to success. It is the result of preparation, hard work and learning from the failure."

Making Persistent Efforts even after a Series of Rejections Brings Historical Success: J.K. Rowling was an unknown lady till she became the author of the famous book "Harry Potter." While speaking to the graduating students at Harvard University in June, 2006, she talked about failures instead of success. While addressing the audience, she said: "You might never fail on the scale I did, but it is impossible to live without failing at something, unless you live so cautiously that you might as well not have lived at all – in which case, you fail by default."

She got divorced when she had a child. While raising her child on her own living on welfare she wrote her first "Harry Potter" book and typed on an old manual type writer. She used to sit and write in a coffee house to save electricity bill. Twelve publishers rejected the manuscript. A year later, Barry Cunningham from Bloomsbury published the book saying: "There is no earning in children books." But the book proved to be a blockbuster. What if she stopped at the first rejection? The fifth? Or the tenth? After the success of the first Harry Potter novel, she wrote a series of Harry Potter books. Presently, she is one of the richest ladies in the world.

Her story conveys a **message** to us that: "The measure of historical success can be shown by how many times someone keeps going despite hearing NO all the way."

"Hardships and failures in life make you stronger, tougher and wiser. Take it as God's gift, swallow it, digest it, don't give up, be persistent and finally, you will be a great winner."

Self-confidence Defeats Failures and Makes You a Mogul: At the age of twenty-two, Oprah Winfrey, the new TV mogul was fired from her job as a television reporter because she was declared unfit for TV. She was terminated from her post as a co-anchor of the 6 'o'clock weekday news on Baltimore's WJZ TV after the show received a low rating. Winfrey called it the first and the worst failure of her TV career.

She was then demoted to the morning TV. There she found her voice and met a fellow newbie Gayle King, who later on became her producer and editor of O, the Oprah Magazine. Seven years later, she moved to Chicago, where her self-titled talk show went on to dominate daytime TV for twenty-five years, and ultimately headed her own channel, OWN.

The great **lesson** we learn from her story is: "Not giving up, believing in yourself and persistent efforts always pay and ultimately you become a winner. Success is not an instant coffee. One has to put in heart and soul to achieve it."

Not Giving up Despite Failures Makes You a Great Winner: The story of Michael Jordan, the basketball superstar is an eye-opener for achieving success after setbacks. After being removed from his high school basketball team, a young Michael

Jordan went home and cried in the privacy of his bed room. But Jordan didn't let this early-life setback stop him from playing the game and he gives all the credit of his success to his failures- missing 900 shots, losing 300 games, missing 26 winning shots.

The **lesson** of the story is: "The story of Michael Jordan is a motivational lesson for those who give up after initial failures and remain deprived of grand success."

> *"Failures are the stepping stones to success, by offering you experience and making you tough."*

Persistence Defeated Constant Rejection and Made Him an Icon: Colonel Sanders is famous as the founder of KFC. At the age of sixty-five, he made his dream come true! He got a social security amount of only USD105 which jolted him. But he did not complain to anybody and instead he did something about it.

As per his dream, he thought: "Restaurant owners would love his fried chicken recipe, would relish it, then sales would increase, and he would get a percentage of it." In this process, he drove around the country knocking on doors, sleeping in his car wearing his white suit to save some money. Do you know how many times people said no till he got one yes? 1009 times! Later on, he founded KFC and turned it into a multi-national company.

What patience! What persistence! The **message** is: "The power of persistence is enormous to garner success despite failures."

> *"Success passes through a thread of failures."*

Legend Emerges after a Series of Failures: Walt Disney is the man who gave us Disney World and Mickey Mouse. His first animation company went bankrupt. He was fired by a news editor stating that he lacked imagination. He was turned down 302 times before he got the funds for creating Disney World.

"His story **proves** that: "If you have self-confidence and possess imagination, courage and conviction for your dream, no failure, however big, can stop your success wheel."

Steven Spielberg has been regarded as an unparalleled legend of movie direction. Spielberg was interested in film-making and so he applied to the prestigious University of Southern California Film School but was denied admission twice. But this failure didn't deter him and he went to Cal State University in Long Beach. He went on to direct some of the biggest movies turning them into blockbusters -the history of movies. Now, he's worth USD 2.7 billion and in 1994, he got an honorary degree from the film school that rejected him twice.

His life history teaches us the **lesson** that: "You can be both a legend and a billionaire, despite failures." "Think of becoming victors, not victims. Be fearless and get fair success."

> *"Successful people treat failures as festivals of future which give them high positive energy in the journey of success to achieve goals."*

CHOICE, NOT CHANCE MAKES YOU SUCCESSFUL

God has created all the creatures of the world. There are some similarities among all creatures. They include hunger, food, sex, rest, sleep, entertainment and fears. A great gift to human beings is the sense to discriminate and make a choice. It gives the mind numerous capacities which make them superior to all creatures. With the capacity of mind, human beings are able to control all the mighty animals- tigers, lions, elephants, etc. This suggests that we must use our choices wisely to achieve our goals. But most of the people do not use the option of choice wisely to achieve their goals.

It is to be noted that there is no free lunch in the world. You have to pay the price to get anything. If you want to achieve a goal, to get success, you have to work hard using your positive energy and passion. Kahlil Gibran took more than eleven years to formulate and perfect his world famous book- 'The Prophet,' – a poetic essay which runs into just 126 pages.

"Choice, not chance determines destiny."

Nothing great was ever done without an act of decision. It is true that too many people go through life not knowing what they want but feeling sure that they don't have it. Deepak Chopra opined, "When you make a choice, you change the future. "It is your choice and desire that matter in the success story. Destiny is not a matter of chance but of choice, don't wait for it, and instead achieve it. In choosing the course of life, strong decision is a must otherwise the relentless drift of events will decide it for you. A concept of "fake it until you make it" can be adopted and many achievers have used this technique in the past to condition their mind, to raise their self-esteem, and to see success as a reality. Actor Jim Carrey, before becoming an actor on the big screen had faked himself by writing a cheque for USD 10 million for his acting service and carried it in his pocket for seven years till he became a big star.

Success and excellence can be achieved only through strong willpower, desire and inner passion. The words of Confucius eloquently testify this, "The will to win, the desire to succeed, the urge to reach your full potential, these are the keys that will unlock the door to personal excellence."

Every choice has its own consequences. If the choice is wrong, you may be doomed. If you do everything wrong, such as catching a train when it has picked up some speed at the station, you may get hurt or even killed. If you drink heavily for a long period, your kidneys and liver may get damaged. If you like to smoke heavily, you may get cancer. If you drive after drinking heavily, your car may meet with an accident and you or any other passenger may even get killed in the accident. If the choice is right and good, it may give you excellent results provided you act right.

Human life can be compared to a potter, who shapes clay into any form, as per his wish or choice. In the same manner, we can mold our life for betterment, for excellence or even prepare for the worst. "We, human beings often are like wheelbarrows, trailers or canoes. We need to be pushed, pulled or paddled for getting good work done. Either you lead or be a follower." Decide to do something now as per your choice to make your life better. The choice is yours. "You achieve half the success the moment you have the will to win. If you don't, then you have achieved half your failure."

Success depends upon your choice of people in your surroundings. If they are smarter than you, vibrant and ready to take challenges in life, you also will try to follow their footsteps. Success is a habit and you have to put all your might, irrespective of the size of the endeavor. Swami Sivananda opined, "Put your heart, mind, intellect, and soul even to your smallest acts. This is the secret of success."

> *"Make your choice sincerely, chase your inner spirit and churn your positive energy to achieve success."*

Thought process is a great tool to turn any event or situation in a positive or negative way. Choice is derived from the thinking process. The following golden poem by Walter D. Wintle conveys a lot of situations where the effect of thought process prevails and it is up to you to follow the way you want.

Poem on "THINKING"-A Recipe for Success

> *"If you think you are bitten, you are.*
> *If you think you dare not, you don't,*
> *If you like to win, but think you can't,*
> *It's almost a cinch you won't.*
> *If you think you all lose, you're lost,*
> *For out in the world we find*
> *Success begins with a fellow's will,*
> *It's all in the state of mind.*
> *If you think you are outclassed you are,*
> *You've got to think high to rise,*
> *You've got to be sure of yourself before*
> *You can ever win a prize.*
> *Life's battles don't always go*
> *To the stronger and faster man,*
> *But sooner or later the man who wins*
> *Is the man WHO THINKS HE CAN."*

The above poem by Walter D. Wintle showcases human thought process and its consequences. Remodel your choice towards positive aspects and come out as a winner and a historymaker.

"'I CAN' Concept is the Soul of Success."

Each letter of the word 'SUCCESS' stands for something special where **S**: stands for Sincerity; **U**: stands for Understanding; **C**: stands for Character; **C**: stands for Courage; **E**: stands for Empathy; **S**: stands for Self-esteem;**S**: stands for Self-confidence. Try to acquire these seven qualities for achieving success in your life.

CAUSES OF FAILURE

"The true measure of success is how many times you can bounce back from failure."

—*Stephen Richards*

Nobody in the world wishes to fail, but many people fail in their missions and goals. Failure brings many bad effects on the psychology of a person. Some break down; some develop suicidal tendencies, some even commit suicide; some become alcoholic and some bounce back with great vigor and eventually win. "Behind all these failures, one of the common ingredients is the lack of sufficient efforts put in, due to the ignorance of various mantras of success." Here the question arises: what are the reasons for failure? The answers lie in the *thirty reasons* given below:

THE THIRTY MAJOR REASONS FOR FAILURE

"It's fine to celebrate success but it is more important to heed the lessons of failure."

—*Bill Gates*

The greatest tragedy of life is that a lot of men and women who earnestly try, fail! As per data collected, the tragedy lies in the fact that majority of people have failed, as compared to the few who have succeeded. There is something wrong with the civilization, education system, grooming of children, culture, governance, shortcomings of individuals, wisdom of individual and society at large which are not conducive for success and they permit many to fail. One has to locate one or more reasons for his failures out of the thirty reasons of failure given below and accordingly correct them to succeed.

"Success is a dream, desire and elixir of one's life. Try! Try! And try till you achieve it!"

1. Lacking a Definite Aim to Achieve

A person who lacks a definite aim or goal to achieve success is like a rudderless ship which sails aimlessly far from the destination. There is no hope of success for a person who has no definite aim in life. It is worthy to note that whatever definite aim a person sets, it should be according to one's potential, liking and temperament, otherwise one will not be able to give his or her 100 % effort to achieve success. "Potential of a person increases with hard work."

Many students, either after tenth class or twelfth class choose wrong streams in the absence of a definite aim. They fail miserably or perform poorly in examinations. Similarly, many graduate students don't compete in high level competitive examinations due to the absence of a definite aim.

> *"Success without definite aim will never be realized like the arrow released without definite aim will never hit the target."*

2. Lack of Risk-Taking Capability

> *"No pain, no gain.*
> *No thorns, no throne.*
> *No gale, no glory.*
> *No cross, no crown."*
>
> —*William Penn*

There is a common saying: No pain, no gain. In every step of the decision process, there is a risk of failing. This does not mean that one should not take risk. Success will only come when one takes a calculated risk. Risk-taking is not gambling but a courageous step on the path of success.

Risk-taking capability varies from person to person. For an experienced business man, taking a risk in any new venture is comparatively easier, whereas for a beginner, it is quite a difficult task due to the fear of failure, the lack of experience and so on.

> *"Life is full of risks and wonders. There is a close relation between taking risk and greatness. Learn to take risk, of course judiciously and with an open mind for great accomplishments, otherwise, your future will be doomed."*

The courage for taking risks comes from many factors such as knowledge, positive attitude, unwavering mind, etc. There is a saying: No decision, no mistake. If one takes this approach, his or her life will be doomed. Indecision and wrong decision will lead you to the brink. "Success is plagued by indecision and wrong decision." So everyone has to be careful about these two, but indecision is the greatest enemy as the effect of a wrong decision can be corrected to a large extent. Many countries, many organizations and many individuals have suffered a lot due to these two.

Paulo Coelho said, "There is only one thing that makes a dream impossible to achieve: The fear of failure." If an individual or a family or a nation is poor, it means that they have not taken risks for betterment. Be proactive to take risk in life otherwise, you will be at the lower rung on the ladder of success.

3. Lacking in Discipline in Life (Refer Chapter 3)

> *"Discipline is necessary to curb the mind, otherwise there is no peace."*
>
> —*J. Krishnamurti*

If we go to the history of a large number of unsuccessful, frustrated, and troubled people, we will find that most of them were lacking self-discipline. People engaged in games, sports, academia, business, show/movie business, music, dance, spirituality, agriculture, politics and other activities cannot excel in their respective profession without maintaining discipline in their lives. Many topmost players and athletes spoiled their careers, lost their medals and fell from grace by getting involved in the banned drugs and spot fixings. (Refer Chapter 3)

"Discipline is the foundation of success. Without discipline, the mind is uncontrolled, and all undesirable activities are possible, leading to chaos and troubles in life."

Without self-discipline, one has to face a lot of problems in life and his or her success becomes a distant dream. "Discipline acts as a bridge between goals and accomplishment. Without the bridge in the form of discipline, your success will sink."

4. Lacking in Persistence (Refer Chapter 8)

"My greatest point is my persistence. I never gave up in a match. However down I am, I fight until the last ball. My list of matches shows that I have turned a great many so-called irretrievable defeats into victory."

—*Bjorn Borg*

The human life is full of problems, anxieties and tensions. While solving life's problems, some people think of quitting as the best option. Perhaps, they forget to realize that the solution and success might be only an extra mile away, but they quit. If they had stayed for more time and struggled for a while longer, they could perhaps be winners. The words of Thomas A. Edison confirm this: "Many of life's failures are people who did not realize how close they were to success when they gave up."

"Patience and persistence offer a magical effect which helps in removing difficulties, overcoming obstacles and bringing success in life. Failing is not due to the lack of knowledge and talent but because people quit."

"Persistence is the magical mother which nullifies all failures with its smooth consistent touch and makes you victorious and successful."

Without being persistent in the chosen venture, one cannot be successful. (Refer Chapter 8)

5. Lacking in Hard Work and Concentration (Focus)

There is no substitute for hard work. No person in the world has ever achieved any success without hard work. Success kisses those who work hard. Intense heat and energy at a certain point is achieved by the concentration of a light beam through laser. The analogy of laser beam holds good in the case of concentration of our efforts on a particular pursuit. If your energy is utilized in many areas, say like in jack of all trades, the desired result will be unsatisfactory. If your effort is concentrated on one definite goal, the desired result will be obtained. (Refer Chapter 9)

"Concentrated effort acting like a laser beam raises your output and efficiency to a higher level which in turn makes you winner and successful."

6. Habit of Enjoying Instant Pleasure

A wrong habit of enjoying instant pleasure is currently prevailing throughout the world. Many youngsters below forty desire to become rich by the midnight with minimum effort and wish to enjoy after midnight. They want perfect lives, a lot of money, and excellent relationship which are utopian. This habit is not a horse of big racea one will be lost in middle of the race of life, inviting frustration, anxiety and depression.

"Instant pleasure is like a mirage to allure you, for trapping you in the small wins and preventing you from the big wins."

Many people get involved in lottery and betting, and lose a lot of money in the process. Some people with the habit of instant gratification get involved in wrong businesses such as gambling and such, and spoil their careers. "A short vision, a small dream cannot produce a long vision and a big dream."

7. Lacking in Enthusiasm

"Nothing great was ever achieved without enthusiasm."

—*Ralph Waldo Emerson*

Enthusiasm is an outcome of passion that produces fire in the belly to accomplish a great task. In dealing with life's problems, one may get demotivation and lose interest in the work. Enthusiasm in one's life vanishes because of sheer disappointment. Such people feel life as dull. In the success of any venture, if you lack enthusiasm, the results will be poor and you may even fail. All the great achievements of people are the result of constant enthusiasm in their lives, undeterred by hardships and failures. "Potential in a person doesn't matter, unless it is fueled by enthusiasm and hard work in the success story."

"Enthusiasm acts as a great catalyst which awakens the sleeping energy and sleeping spirit of human beings to a colossal level for great accomplishments."

8. Lacking in Tolerance

Intolerance is the result of a closed mind and one cannot go far in life with this. Intolerance implies that one has stopped acquiring knowledge and wisdom. Victor Hugo said, "Tolerance is the best religion." Wisdom suggests that if you wish to succeed in life, you have to be tolerant; otherwise a lot of gigantic obstructions will come in your way. Intolerance is more predominant and in damaging forms in matters related to religion, race and politics, which lead to a loss of many lives and severe sufferings. "Tolerance acts as a lubricating enhancer and takes out the friction from our life."

"Intolerance produces friction in the society and even small work gets derailed and it takes damaging forms beyond imagination."

In all religions, emphasis has been made on tolerance and peace (Shanti). In all Sanskrit hymns and prayers related to worshipping, many times the word Shanti (peace) comes:Shanti! Shanti! Shanti! "Humanity thrives on tolerance and cooperation."

9. Lacking in Cooperation (Refer Chapter 9)

"We all do better when, we work together, our differences do matter, but our common humanity matters more."

—*Bill Clinton*

In most of our working environment - offices, industries, corporate houses, homes, playground for games and sports, societies, states, nations, etc., work cannot be completed without cooperation from others. It is the quality of leadership which gets the work done by others. Many people lose their high positions in the work environment due to their non-cooperative attitude. Team spirit is a must in the work environment. In games and sports, team spirit is the buzzword and without cooperation of all team members, no team can win.

"Cooperation is a great tool to successfully complete a big job with a small contribution from many and forms the basis of unity and harmony in human relations."

It is a universal truth that you will get cooperation from others when you will cooperate with them. It is an attitude which has to be developed by one and all. Even a house of four persons cannot run successfully and cannot progress if there is no cooperation from each member. Bertrand Russell opined, *"The only thing that will redeem mankind is cooperation."* If you want to succeed, you have to extend a cooperative hand to others, and in return, you will get cooperation when the need arises.

10. Incapability to Recognize Opportunity

"A pessimist sees the difficulty in every opportunity; and an optimist sees the opportunity in every difficulty."

—*Winston Churchill*

Everyone is born to excel in life through opportunity. But opportunities do not have any distinct pleasure icon to recognize. They always come in disguised form as obstacles, crisis, failures and that is why most people do not recognize them and curse their fate instead. Welcome those crisis-ridden complicated problems and obstacles, as they contain your biggest and most powerful opportunities. From my experience,

I can say that: "Bigger the obstacles, better are the opportunities." Some people have a sixth sense and they grab the opportunities that are in the form of obstacles. "A crisis creates an opportunity." In Hindu mythology, it is said that "Goddess Laxmi (wealth) always comes in every house in a disguised form." "An obstacle adorns a hidden opportunity."

"Opportunities are inherently imbedded in every crisis, obscured in the form of obstacles, anxieties, hard work and fear. Grab, face and solve the crisis boldly and become a great winner."

Opportunity-Grabber Achieves Greatness: Margaret Thatcher was appointed Britain's first woman prime minister in May 1979. The country was facing several problems such as recession and labor problems in the industries, especially by the miner's union. She saw and grabbed the opportunities in these problems. She did massive privatization of social housing and public transport and came out of recession and labor problems. When Argentina invaded the Falkland Island, she sent her troops immediately and won. Because of solving such severe problems, she was known as the Iron Lady of UK.

The **theme** of the story is: "Greatness lies in grabbing the problems and solving them."

11. Lack of Having the Right Priorities in Life

Our life is full of challenges and one has to set one's priorities right to get success. In the cut-throat competitive environment, anybody hardly has time. "Work-life balance is a must in the success story." Note that priorities continually shift and demand attention which can be taken care by evaluation, elimination and estimation.

Among priorities many aspects come into picture such as money, power, fame, position, properties, maintaining relationship, health, entertainment, and quality time to children, wife and parents. For getting success, it is necessary to understand the correct priorities and to set them right, otherwise problems will keep arising, which may eventually result in failure.

"Having correct priorities in life is a balanced and righteous act which brings happiness and prosperity in life."

12. Lack of Honesty (Refer Chapter 15)

"Confidence thrives on honesty, on honor, on the sacredness of obligations, on faithful protection and on unselfish performance. Without them it cannot live."

—*Franklin D. Roosevelt*

In human interactions, there is no substitute to honesty. In all professions and working environments, maintaining honesty is essential because through it, you can achieve great success and sustain for a long time. Benjamin Franklin said, "Honesty is the best policy." It is said that this is a world of deceit where one can easily be attracted towards dishonesty as this brings easy money. But this mindset is not going to help in the long run, but will bring disastrous. Zig Ziglar opined, "The foundation stones for a balanced success are honesty, character, integrity, faith, love and loyalty." Many top companies of the world are thriving on honesty and the companies that followed the path of dishonesty went bankrupt. Similar is the case with individuals. One may thrive on dishonest methods, but once caught, by various agencies of government he or she may be in deep trouble and may lose all success and honor.

"Honesty is the horse of long race of great success and great honor."

Involvement in Scandal Ruins Life: The Enron scandal, revealed in October 2001, eventually led to the bankruptcy (loss of USD74 billion) of the Enron Corporation, an American Energy Company based on Houston, Texas. There was a *de facto* dissolution of Arthur Anderson which was one of the five largest audit and accountancy partnership in the world. About 85,000 employees lost their jobs. Kenneth Lay, Jeffrey Skilling and others got heavy sentences by the court. There were a large number of serious cases of dishonest methods adopted in companies, in government, and in individual interactions all over the world, but everybody faced the consequences.

The **theme** of the story is: "Dishonesty derails and ruins life in the long run."

13. Habit of Overindulgence

Excess of everything is bad. It has been observed that when money comes in the pockets of people, they lose their minds over enjoyment. They get heavily indulged in eating, heavy drinking and sex. Overindulgence in any of these is fatal, either through failure of kidney, liver or heart. When one is seriously ill or no more, the question of happiness and success does not exist.

14. Habit of Procrastination (Refer Chapter 10)

"Procrastination is one of the most common and deadliest of diseases and its toll on success and happiness is heavy."

—*Wayne Gretzky*

Procrastination is a common cause of failure in life. Most of the people are in the habit of postponing today's work to be done later, when one is at ease or when the proper time arrives. Some persons are in the habit of waiting for the "time to be right" to start doing something worthwhile. There is no need to wait as any time is the right time to start a good work. So, as and when work comes, he/she should finish the work.

"Procrastination, being a prime bad habit leads to self-destruction, like a slow poison."

Due to the habit of procrastination, office work suffers as files remain pending for months together, students fail in examinations, agriculture and business works suffer and so on.

Charles Dickens said, "Procrastination is the thief of time, collar him."(Refer Chapter 10)Many students become victims of procrastination and as a result they fail miserably in examinations. Many employees in private companies lose their jobs due to procrastination.

"Procrastination invites failures and poverty."

15. Insufficient Education and Knowledge (Refer Chapter 11)

"Education is a progressive discovery of our own ignorance."

—*Will Durant*

Advancement in civilization has come through education and knowledge. In the modern world, knowledge and skills are the real wealth. Whatever profession you choose - be it service, business, consultancy, art, technology, etc., knowledge and skills are definitely required. If anyone has insufficient knowledge and skills, it is difficult for him or her to go on to the higher rung in the ladder of success. You are paid not merely for what you know, but more particularly for what you do with what you know. (Refer Chapter 11) Socrates advocated, "Education is the kindling of a flame, not the filling of a vessel."

"True education kindles the flame in mind, improves thought process, removes ignorance, and prepares us fully competent for life- intellectually, skillfully, emotionally, socially and spiritually."

It is our ignorance that we think we have sufficient education and knowledge. The more you learn, the more you realize how ignorant you have been. Aristotle said, "Learning is an ornament in prosperity, a refuse in adversity and a provision in old age." Knowledge, skill and wisdom help in making decisions and completion of work, as everywhere you have to take a decision and act to succeed.

16. Living by the Short-cut Attitude

"To succeed in life, there is no short-cut;only a difficult path."

Some people are always in the habit of looking out for short-cut methods in life. But these short-cut methods are not everlasting. A person with such short-cut attitude is dangerous, for himself and the society, as such methods do not create wealth, instead spread a wrong message. Many people lose their lives while crossing a railway track near the railway stations, to find a short-cut route. Many people resort to stealing, and robbing, instead of working hard to earn money. They are caught sometimes and put behind bars. JRR Tolkien said, "Short-cuts make long delay."

17. Lacking in Conviction (Refer Chapter 7)

"A leader has the vision and conviction that a dream can be achieved. He inspires the power and energy to get it done."

—*Ralph Nader*

People without conviction are like pendulums. They can't take a stand on any issue. They adopt the approach of the middle path. Everybody knows what happens to such people. They are likely to be crushed! Isn't it?

During meetings, whether at society level, office level, assembly level or parliament level, people lacking in conviction do not take any stand on a right issue and as a result a wrong decision detrimental to the society or the office or the nation, is taken. By not taking a stand on a right issue implies that you support the persons with vested interest. Denis Waitley opined, "You must stick to your conviction, but be ready to abandon your assumptions." A man lacking in conviction means a man without faith. Mahatma Gandhi, Nelson Mandela had great conviction to free their countries from British Rule and they ultimately got freedom. "If you lack in conviction in any aspect, in any right thing, no miracle can be expected from your contribution."

"Conviction in anything produces an unshakable force and an unflinching courage in the subconscious mind to get the desired result in the endeavor, despite many hardships." "Have strong conviction in the right thing and win the world convincingly."

"Conviction brings confidence to succeed."

18. Attitude of Egotism and Vanity

"Every man of action has a strong dose of egoism, pride, hardness and cunningness, but all those things will be regarded as high qualities if he can make them the means to achieve great ends."

—*Charles de Gaulle*

People who possess egotism and vanity serve as a red alert that warns others to keep away from them. These qualities are very fatal to success. Most of the work is the team work, which requires support from others. If the person in charge is having egotism and vanity, he can't get work done by others. Further, they create many enemies, who will strike at the appropriate time against them.

"Through the attitude of egotism and vanity you don't get support from others, resulting in a distant dream of success."

19. No Planning and Preparation

"Action without planning is the cause of all failure. Action with planning is the cause of all success."

—*Brian Tracy*

Execution of every work in an efficient manner with quality content needs a detailed planning. Some people are not in the habit of planning and so they start executing their work haphazardly. As a result, such people fail to execute their work successfully, or if they execute, the quality of the work is very poor. It is a waste of time, energy and money, if there is no planning.

"Planning is the route to vision while preparation is the soul of mission."

In every sphere of life, extensive preparation and planning is a must. Preparation comes from practice. It is said that better preparation means better practice. In any competitive environment such as games, sports and examinations, you need a strong preparation to excel. (Refer Chapter 12)

Delhi Metro, a world-class and an ultra-modern facility, under the leadership of E. Sreedharan got completed before time, which happens to be a world record. It was the result of excellent planning, preparation and execution. E. Sreedharan is also known as the "Metro Man" worldwide.

20. Attitude of Selfishness and Greed

"It was not curiosity that killed the goose who laid the golden egg, but an insatiable greed that devoured common sense."

—E.A. Buchianean

You might have heard people saying that Mr. X is a very selfish and greedy person and stay away from him. Though, this attitude is spreading in this world at a fast rate, it will never allow you to be successful.

"Selfishness and greed emanate from the man of mean mindset for unjust, unfair gain which results in losing self-esteem and great achievements."

There is no end to selfishness and greed. A person with this attitude takes the other's share and as a result he is not respected in the society. "Greed is a great destroyer of relationships." "The need of a person can be satisfied but not his greed; as there is no end to it." With a greedy person, nobody wants to do business or keep relationships. In all the great achievements of a person, society plays an important role and greedy people get cornered by the society. Gautama Buddha said, "There is no fire like passion, there is no shark like hatred, there is no snare like folly, and there is no torrent like greed."

Greed Finally Brings a Fatal End: This story is common in Indian villages. A greedy, rich man for land got a wish from the king to get all land he can cover from the sunrise to the sunset. Due to greed he went on running from the sunrise to cover as much land as possible. When he returned to back running despite tiredness at the starting point by the sunset, he died due to tiredness and exhaustion. He was buried in a land coffin of just five square metres. There was no use of the land he covered.

The **theme** of the story is: "Greed can put you in the gear of destruction and even may lead you to a fatal end."

21. The Habit of Indiscriminate Spending

It is said that the more you earn, more you will try to spend. This is true up to a certain limit. Indiscriminate spending is the crossing of certain limits beyond which your decline begins. In a success story of most professions especially business, you need a certain amount of money to invest. If you spend indiscriminately on unimportant things, then you will be short of money to invest in the business. Bank loans have certain limitations and interest rate is very high. Indiscriminate spending should be avoided; otherwise you may fall in a heavy debt trap. The failure of King Fisher Airlines is a fitting example of this. Many such people lost all their properties. Abraham Lincoln said, "You cannot bring about prosperity by discouraging thrift. You cannot keep out of trouble by spending more than you earn."

22. Uninterested to Learn from Mistakes

"It's failure that gives you the proper perspective on success."

—*Ellen De Geners*

When you work, it is certain that you will commit some mistakes. These mistakes are your experience, your torch lights that help you later in life. If you are careless to learn from your mistakes, then even God may not be able to help you on the journey of success. History is full of achievements and failures. Those who do not learn from history, they are bound to be doomed. "Failure is not a defeat but simply a delay in the delivery of success. It has come to you to give you a lesson to learn, to make you tough." Are you ready to learn?

"Mistakes are valuable experiences. If you are not learning from mistakes, you are bound to fail."

23. A Wrong Mindset of Fear (Refer Chapter 10)

"Tell your heart that the fear of suffering is worse than the suffering itself. And no heart has ever suffered when it goes on in search of its dream."

—*Paulo Coelho*

Fear is a state of mind. It emanates from the feeling of insecurity and lack of understanding. Living in the environment of fear is highly dangerous in many respects. Once fear crops up in mind, it lowers the potential and ability of a person and may cause stress and depression. It ruins many relationships; it may affect your health and deprive you success. "Fear is a great de-motivator and a deadly hindrance to decision making and achievements. Fight your fear by using wisdom and developing courage for fulfilling your dreams." Gautama Buddha said, "The whole secret of existence is to have no fear. Never fear what will become of you, depend on no one. Only the moment you reject all help, are you freed."

"The only way to get out of fear is to increase understanding, develop courage and immediately thrash fear when it comes in mind to garner success."

24. Lacking in Self-esteem (Refer Chapter 6)

"Believe in yourself! Have faith in your abilities! Without a humble and reasonable confidence in your OWN powers you cannot be successful or happy."

—*Norman Vincent Peale*

Why do you have a poor self-esteem? Have you ever thought over the causes of poor self-esteem? It is due to your lack of self-confidence, self-respect and self-worth. You are valuable in the market on the basis of your self-esteem. Just recall the fees charged by stars of Bollywood or Hollywood who have high self-esteem, and that will verify my statement. When one has poor self-esteem, one's ego will take a leading role to hide it and whatever decision one takes, it will only be to justify the ego, without any fruitful results.

"Self-esteem is the power of your positive personality. Higher your self-esteem better is your price tag."

The only way to improve self-esteem is to develop the potential in your field of work. Nobody can give you self-esteem, but you have to create it. Thomas Carlyle advocated, "Nothing builds self-esteem and self-confidence like accomplishment." The root cause of poor self-esteem is the habit of laziness and procrastination and this duo act like rust that eats into the human mind and eclipses the intelligence and the potential of an individual. Are you ready to come out of the world of poor self-esteem?

25. Luck Oriented Attitude and Negative Personality

"Don't build roadblocks out of assumptions."

—*Lorii Maers*

Some people do not believe in hardwork and they attribute their success and failure to luck, horoscope and the stars. They submit themselves to their fate, ignoring the real fact of life. Such attitude is fatal to success. "Luck is the outcome of myth while success is the outcome of effort." Many people associate their failure to luck, which is not true at all.

"It is not your luck that makes you successful but your persistent efforts with patience and passion."

Some of the dubious god-men and fortune tellers are thriving by fooling people who believe in luck, through their sermons and solutions, embedded with rituals. It is worthy to note that the Almighty God removes about ninety-nine percent problems of people as natural phenomena with the passage of time, if you keep patience and go on working judiciously. Luck is not written but created. The successful people create their luck through sheer hard work, judicious planning, courage, wisdom and positive attitude. Half-hearted involvement based on luck in any pursuit is bound to fail and whatever the energy, time and money invested will definitely be wasted."

Negative personality oriented persons create disharmony in any society and nobody is ready to cooperate with such people. They are not growth oriented. They always criticize the performers and try to de-motivate them through various means. Negative personality oriented persons are basically a curse for the society. "Build bridges among people instead of putting a barricade."

26. Lacking in Courage (Refer Chapter 7)

"One man with courage is a majority."

—*T. Jefferson*

If you take the statistical data of successful people in any field from the world over, you will find that all of them were courageous and overcame the various obstacles and fears that came in their way. They did not believe in miracles for success, but worked hard with courage and conviction. Success is the result of courage and lack of it leads to failure.

"Courage is standing up in the favor of right cause, and standing against the unjust, obstacles and fears."

Nobody can do anything in this world without courage. It is the greatest quality of the mind. Everybody should develop the sense of courage in their subconscious mind. Mark Twain opined, "Courage is resistance to fear, mastery of fear, not the absence of fear." Be courageous and win the world. All the sea swimmers, rafters, mountaineers, decision makers are courageous.

27. Lacking in Purpose and Direction

"The secret of success is consistency of purpose."

—*Benjamin Disraeli*

There are two types of people – one with mere wishes and without purpose and direction; and the other, with a burning desire and a great purpose. The lack of purpose and direction can't lead you anywhere. Statistical data obtained from all over the world showed that success belonged to those who had a burning desire to succeed. In their burning desire, there was purpose and direction which made them winners. When opportunity is at the doorstep, a person without purpose and direction does not recognize it.

"The lack of purpose and direction is like a closed road, without any destination."

There are a large number of people who are healthy and fit. But due to the lack of purpose and direction, they do not accomplish any great task. In contrast to that, the first amputee, Arunima Sinha from Ambedkar Nagar (UP, India) with one artificial leg had climbed the Mount Everest in 2013.

The **theme** of the story is: "A burning desire with great purpose and direction will lead you to a great victory overcoming all adversities."

28. Failing to Capitalize Talent

With reference to the mind, there goes a saying: "Use or lose." Mind is a like a razor. If you do not use, it will rust. If you use, it will sharpen. A large number of people are unaware of their potential because they never get involved in various activities and as a result, their potential does not come out upfront. In many countries, especially the underdeveloped and developing ones, the schooling systems are in a pathetic condition. Some do not get the chance to even go to a school. Those that get the chance, their grooming in most of the institutions are pathetic and as a result they are unable to use their talents. Even in developed countries, some people are failing to use the talents they possess.

Human mind has enormous potential. Human beings, in general are able to use only up to ten percent of the potential of their mind. Even Albert Einstein could hardly use twenty-five percent of his intellectual capability. Those who have the desire, conviction and determination to do something extraordinary, they try to recognize their talents and become successful. A large number of people do not know what their talents and they do not get any opportunity to showcase their talents and as a result their talents remained hidden and unutilized.

Even after recognizing their talent and getting selected in the national team, some players fail to convert it into a success story, due to the lack of support, discipline, hard work, practice, persistence, patience, passion, and concentration.

29. Having Superstitions and Prejudiced Notion

"Fear is the main source of superstitions and of the main source of cruelty. To conquer fear is the beginning of wisdom."

—*Bertrand Russell*

Superstition is a form of fear. Even highly educated people from all over the world are in the grasp of superstitions and as a result these affect the productivity of persons. Edmund Burke opined, "Superstition is the religion of a feeble mind." In some places, people have a superstition that no new work should be started on a

Saturday and many people religiously follow that. As a result, productivity on a Saturday is jeopardized. Some people do not go on a trip on Tuesday, out of a superstitious belief. It is to be noted that it takes 365 days and 6 hours for our planet earth to take a revolution around the sun, which defines a year. God has created every day as a good day with a new hope for every creature. Superstition is a sign of ignorance. Successful people have open minds and do not believe in such superstitions.

"Some incidents will always happen irrespective of days or dates, either due to natural phenomena or worldly affairs, and affect anyone under the multi-dynamics mode."

Prejudice is a wrong notion for anyone, which does not help you when you are seeking success. The person with whom you are prejudiced may be a good person, talented and may help you in your venture. Your success always depends upon the cooperation of others.

30. Living with Ill Health

Those who desire for success and to enjoy the life, they should be health conscious and must be away from causes of illhealth as with poor health you cannot do work effectively and efficiently. (Refer Chapter 16)

THE FIFTEEN MANTRAS FOR SUCCESS

The fifteen mantras outlined in this book can help one to get success in their chosen pursuits –be it a better job and position, better academic result, greater financial gain, better contribution in the world, a glorious achievement, a better person, better spirituality, better relationship, more happiness, more joy, better leadership, better health, better philanthropy, more meaningful social works, etc. It is necessary to follow each mantra in letter and in spirit.

***

Chapter 2

Have Imagination, Dream and Desire
THE 1ST MANTRA

IMAGINE LIKE AN INNOVATOR TO SUCCEED

"I am enough of an artist to draw freely upon my imagination. Imagination is more important than knowledge. Knowledge is limited. Imagine encircles the world."
—*Albert Einstein*

"Logic will get you from A to Z; imagination will get you everywhere."
—*Albert Einstein*

A famous innovator-cum-speaker was asked by a student from the audience in a symposium to speak to us of imagination, dream and desire. He replied in sequence: Imagination! An outcome of an intelligent mode of mind. An attempt of invention or innovation. A curiosity of everyone. A route to nation building. The craze of every soul. Are you an imaginative person? If not, you are missing something great. Be an imaginative person for your glorious success, wealth creation, greatness and nation building.

"Imagination is the primary source of an idea for creating a fresh new or a change in existing one which is to be transformed into a reality." Let us look at the various scenarios and realities around us. "We realize that before any invention or innovation ever created, any building or bridge ever constructed, any new product ever made, any song ever sung, any film ever made, any industry or corporate house or company ever established, any university ever established, any monument ever constructed, any mode of governance ever thought of and implemented, any book ever written, any music ever created, any painting ever made, taking part in any competition ever decided, taking part in any election ever decided, any development ever made and or any change that was ever made, it first appeared in someone's imagination. "It is the imagination which is the major source of desire and motivation." All the achievers get what they want by utilizing the power of their imagination in a much planned way. John Dewey opined, "Every great advance in science has issued from a new audacity of imagination."

"The capacity of imagination is developed by churning the mind, by brain storming the mind in the direction of imagination. It depends upon the culture, the necessity, the methodology and the quality of education, and the craze to lead a decent life." "Every moment offers a fabulous opportunity to direct our attention to ideas that inspire us." In a certain culture such as European, American and Japanese, people are more imaginative and more innovative. Necessity is the mother of invention, which is the outcome of imagination. "The quality education through better teaching methodology develops creativity, critical thinking, and imagination among students, and nurtures their talents. Rote learning is not going to help you to develop the capacity of imagination but it is the education that allows creativity to flourish in a big way." "The craze to lead a decent life forces one to work hard; to take risks; to imagine, dream and desire more and to achieve more success in life." Are you ready to develop the capacity of imagination?

"The source of all achievements in any field lies in the imagination and takes the physical form after desire, decision, goal-setting, planning and action."

It is the power of imagination through which people made various inventions and innovations such as aeroplanes, rockets, space vehicles, cars, buses, trucks, trains, submarines, ships, electricity, telephones, mobiles, Internet, computers, camera, washing machines, refrigerators, air-conditioners, motor cycles, laptops, smart phones, tablets, CT scanners, etc. which modernized the society. Too many developments have taken place in the field of medicine which has increased the life span of human beings to a great extent. Naturally, there was a tremendous rise in the wealth of companies engaged in these developments. The major developments took place in USA, UK, Germany, Japan, France, and some other European countries and as a result their GDP and per capita income of the citizens rose to a very high level. The quality of life increased immensely. The per capita income of USA is USD 53,101 while the per capita income of India is USD 1505 i.e. about 35.28 times less than USA (in 2013).

The **message** of the above cited examples is: "The origin of success in every respect lies in the imagination. A nation takes a giant leap in success, prosperity and growth if it houses a large number of imaginative people with decisive power and action-oriented."

Just ponder over the unimaginable feat achieved by human beings in the exploration of outer space, which includes spacewalk, space laboratory, landing on the Moon, landing of space vehicle on Mars, sending the Chandrayaan-1 to know more about the Moon, sending the Mangalyaan (MOM) to know more about Mars, satellites used for weather forecasting and communication, etc. These achievements are the result of imaginations by some people that modernized the society in many ways and a lot of wealth has been created in the process by developers.

With the power of imagination, Bill Gates created Microsoft, a leader in the Information Technology sector with a revenue of USD73.723 billion in 2012, Ray Kroc created McDonalds, a great empire in food-chain restaurants, Steve Jobs created Apple Computers which completely changed the scenario of mobile phones, tablets and music players, Narayana Murthy created Infosys, Tata created TCS, Walt

Disney created the Mickey Mouse, Wright brothers invented the aero-plane, Larry Page created Google, Hewlett and Packard created H.P., Larry Ellison created Oracle, Mark Zuckerberg created Facebook, Koum and Acton created WhatsApp, etc.

Constructions of big dams, big canals, great highways, skyscrapers, big industries, power plants, etc. are the result of someone's imagination. The creation of great epics, famous poetries, famous paintings, famous novels, various forms of music, various forms of dance, various games, and various famous movies made are the result of imaginations of some genius persons. Dr. APJ Abdul Kalam, the former President of India was a man of great imagination. He was the father of missiles in India and known as the "Missile Man." Similarly, there are million other persons who turned their imaginations into realities and helped the society. Mahatma Gandhi once said, "Find purpose and the means will follow."

The importance of imagination can be understood by the message given by Steve Jobs, the founder of 'Apple Computers' in a conversation with an industrialist: "It's like when I walk into a room, and I want to talk about a product that hasn't been invented yet. I imagine that I am seeing the product kept right on the table and I have to simply materialize it and bring it into life for the use of human beings." What an imagination! Only a genius can imagine like this! All the seven wonders of world are a result of imaginations of some persons. All the start-ups are the imaginations of their founders. As per data, only about 0.2% people are innovators in any organization, so there is a great need to transform more people into innovators.

Research and innovation in any field are the result of imaginations of some persons. All the Noble Prize winners in any field, all top leaders of any field, all top inventors, all top innovators, all top scientists, all top poets, and all top philosophers are the great thinkers and imaginative people. "A society, an organization, an institution, and a nation can only thrive when they house a large number of imaginative people. Any country which banks on mediocrity cannot progress. Many underdeveloped and developing countries including India lack much in imagination in political class at present and instead of focusing on real issues; they go off-track and focus on petty issues. Nation building here takes a back seat."

"Mediocrity breeds insecurity that leads to dishonesty resulting in a chaos and decline in the growth of a nation. In any field including the most vital politics, any nation needs intelligent (not clever) and imaginative people with good character, integrity and leadership qualities for achieving grand success, high inclusive growth, peace, prosperity and pleasure." Verify this fact in the case of underdeveloped, developing and developed nations and you will find the truth. G-7 countries, South Korea, and Singapore are examples of this. Charles F. Kettering, inventor with 140 patents once said, "Believe and act as if it were impossible to fail". It is necessary that you should condition your mind to achieve what you want to achieve.

"Note that working all the time will not help you imagine and get new ideas. All the inventors got the big ideas when they were either relaxing, or chilling, or making fun. In a burnout mode, no new ideas can generate in mind. Creativity comes in your mind when you are relaxed, chilled, happy and enjoying the moment." So go, have fun, relax, take a vacation, chill out, and finally you will be more creative, more productive, and more successful. The world needs more big imaginations and much greater ideas to enrich customers with exciting products, to improve people's lives, to elevate the planet, to bring innovative change in the governance of a country for prosperity and happiness.

"The art to operate from your imagination is one of the greatest tools through which you can produce the results you want. This is possible by using the subconscious mind." The subconscious mind stores emotions, experiences, knowledge, skills, images, etc. and "makes you act like you" in harmony with the stored information. Whatever picture you imagine, or phrases you repeatedly speak, will eventually be imprinted in your subconscious mind and finally your mind will be conditioned to those matters which you repeat and thus you will act accordingly. "Give wings to your imagination and miracles will happen."

Dr. APJ Abdul Kalam, the former President of India who was adored by Indians as the 'People's President' administered a pledge to students in a college while addressing students: "I am born with potential. I am born with goodness and truth. I am born with ideas and dreams. I am born with greatness. I am born with confidence. I have wings, so I am not meant for crawling. I have wings. I will fly. I will fly. I will fly…" If students follow this pledge covering ideas, imagination, big dreams, potential, confidence and goodness in real spirit, their destiny and their nation's destiny will be very bright. Are you ready to follow this beautiful pledge in real spirit? If yes, a bright future is awaiting to kiss and hug you. If not, you will be at a lower rung of success or you may even fail in your endeavors. Charles Chaplin said, "Imagination means nothing without doing."

Through imagination of successful outcomes (I can do it, I am unstoppable, I will win, etc.) repeatedly, you not only reduce the negative emotions associating with taking actions, but you can also eliminate them. Further, your mind will be conditioned for successful outcomes and you will start visualizing and initiating for these to happen in reality. Oscar Wilde said, "Anyone who lives within their means suffers from a lack of imagination." "The poor countries are poor, in general, due to the lack of imagination of their leaders, their scientists, their professors, their students." Lloyd Alexander beautifully expressed this: "I think imagination is the heart of everything we do. Scientific discovery couldn't have happened without imagination. Art, music and literature couldn't exist without imagination. And so anything that strengthens imagination and reading certainly does that, can help us for the rest of our lives."

The scope of imagination is unlimited. Whatever field you choose, there is an enough scope of imagination to make a great difference towards betterment, towards contribution. One has to orient one's mind towards imagination as an imaginative mind can do wonders. Make our planet beautiful and better place to live, to enjoy using your power of imagination.

The physical reality passes through many phases such as imagination, dream, desire, visualization, goal-setting, planning and finally putting into action using all our virtues.

Visualization is the detailed process in the mind about how the imagined idea will take various shapes till the final reality is achieved and how it will look like in a final shape.

Some psychologists believe that seven hours of visualization is equal to one hour of actual experience. Other group of psychologists claims that visualization accompanied with emotion is sixty times as powerful as a real event. This is based on the psychological fact that before getting any desired thing, there is a lot of excitement in achieving it. When you achieve the goal the excitement goes down for that thing.

Are you a person who loves your imagination? Do you imagine? Develop a habit of imagination for yourself and society, and translate it into a reality for the benefit of all and be successful. Make a commitment for one innovation every month in your field of work. "Imagination is your innovation for success. Have it! Have it! Have it!"

HAVE A GREAT DREAM AND DESIRE TO SUCCEED

"The future belongs to those who believe in the beauty of their dreams."

—*Eleanor Roosevelt*

"I prefer to be a dreamer among the humblest with visions to be realized than loser among those without dreams and desires."

—*Kahlil Gibran*

Dream and desire! An integral part of human life for betterment and glory. The colossal craze of every soul. A hope of happiness, joy and a meaningful life. How vibrant is your dream and desire? Do you live with your dream and desire? If not, live with it for your allround development and success.

"Dreams are successions of images, ideas, emotions and sensations that occur involuntarily in mind during certain stages of sleep. Some may be forgotten but some remain in mind. So, we can say that dream is something you hope for, while desire is something you want." "The real dream is one that keeps you on your toes for success, for greatness." In the common discussion, people don't differentiate between a dream and a desire. In fact, the real journey of success starts only when dream gets converted into a burning desire. The world needs more dreamers, more visionaries to change people's lives for betterment. History is a great witness to the fact that all dreamers and innovators are initially laughed at- be it the Wright brothers, Christopher Columbus, Thomas Elva Edison, etc. Dr. APJ Abdul Kalam said, "Dreams transform into thoughts and thoughts into actions. Dreams are not those which come while we are sleeping, but dreams are those when you don't sleep before fulfilling them."

"When imagination and dream get converted into burning desire, then it forms the foundation of success."

In a general sense, the word dream gives more impact on the readers and listeners as compared to desire that carries a similar meaning. The starting point of any achievement is the dream and intense desire. The words of Bertrand Russell verify this in the subsequent line: "All human activity is prompted by desire." The words of Napoleon Hill also support this view: "Desire is the starting point of all achievements, not a hope, not a wish, but a keen pulsating desire which transcends everything." If your desire is intense and great, you can achieve anything. Abraham Lincoln said, "You can have anything you want if you want it badly enough. You can be anything you want to be, do anything you set out to accomplish if you hold on to that desire with the singleness of purpose." Salvador Dali said, "Intelligence without ambition is like a bird without wings." "Ambition, dream and desire take a leading role in your success story, so own these, act on these persistently and success will kiss you."

If we account the life history of successful people, we find that they immensely desired a defined goal and placed all their energy, all their willpower, all their efforts with full concentration into achieving that goal. They created a plan by which they attained the desired goal. They used to burn all bridges behind them and stood by desire until it became the dominating obsession of their lives and finally a fact i.e. success. Malcolm Forbes said, "When you cease to dream you cease to live."

The Rig Veda (Hymn of Creation) says, "In the beginning there was desire, which was the first seed of mind......" In spiritual terms, as advocated by Deepak Chopra, the law of intention and desire is one of the seven spiritual laws of success. "In every burning desire, there are inherent mechanics of organizing power to achieve the goals." Intention holds the real power behind desire as desire may be without attachment or with attachment. In most of the cases, desire is observed with the attachment of outcome. Desire without attachment is superior to desire with attachment as in the former case enormous energy of nature with great organizing power is released to fulfil such desire. There is virtually no chance of failure in such desire. However, desire with detachment from the outcome is difficult to follow in this materialistic world, but it is not impossible.

"Burning desire is like a high intensity reaction which produces immense energy, motivation, passion and courage to achieve the desired success."

The following stories showcase the impact of a burning desire in the success stories of people.

A Burning Desire Makes You a Winner in the Battle Field: A great army general had decided to get victorious in a battle with a neighboring country that was separated by a small sea. The problem before him was his small number of armies as against a powerful foe whose number was just the double of his own. He loaded his soldiers and war equipment into the ships, and sailed to the enemy's country. After reaching the shore, he unloaded the soldiers and the war equipment, and ordered to burn the ships that had carried them. During address to his armies before the first battle, he said, "Let us see the burning of ships which brought us. It means that we can't leave these shores alive unless and until we win! Winning is the only solution! We have only two choices – we win or we perish!" Even with half the size of the enemy's armies, they won.

The **theme** of this story is: "Every person who desires to win in any venture must burn his ships and cut all the resources to retreat which will force him to use all his energy to win."

"Extraordinary desires under extraordinary circumstances require extraordinary responses to achieve goals."

Every person wishes to be successful in his venture. Wishing alone will not bring success. But desiring success with obsessive mind, then planning definite ways and means to acquire success, and backing these with strong action, great will, great passion and persistence efforts ignoring obstacles and failures will bring success in life.

Observe the following:

The desire of success creates the prospect of success.

The prospect of success creates the possibility of success.

The possibility of success creates the probability of success.

The probability of success creates the passion for success.

The passion for success creates the perspiration for success.

The perspiration for success creates the surety of success.

The unparalleled rise of China in the last thirty years is the result of the burning desire of its leaders to succeed. For about ten years, growth rate of India was also appreciable due to the burning desire of its leaders. It was the burning desire of Singapore's founding father Lee Kuan Yew who transformed a tiny poor island into one of the wealthiest and least corrupt countries in Asia in thirty years. The per capita income of Singapore rose from USD 400 in 1959 to USD 55,000 in 2014. The impact of the burning desire of leaders could be seen in the highest growth rate (15%) of Bihar, a poor state of India as compared to other states during 2012-13. This shows that any person, any organization, any state, any country can improve at a rapid rate if there is a burning desire among stakeholders. Nothing in this world is constant. Either it is improving or decaying. So, develop a desire to improve, to grow, to excel otherwise you will find yourself decaying.

History tells that those who have achieved success have gone through the various phases of dreaming, hoping, wishing, desiring, planning, extensive hard work, failures, and disappointments before they got success. It is the practical dreamers who put dreams into action. They have been the pattern makers of civilization from the very beginning. It is they who have converted their ideas into realities like all the development in the world, such as type of governance, skyscrapers, cities, factories, aeroplanes, cars, air-conditioners, TV, mobiles, computers, better health care facilities and other consumer products which make life easier and pleasant. So, if you want to succeed, you have to live by the spirit of the great practical dreamers and pioneers of the past who overcome all obstacles and failures. Practical dreamers are not deterred by failures as they know that: "Every failure brings with it the seed of an equivalent opportunity for success."

Many people in the world, who became successful in their chosen professions working as entrepreneurs, movie stars, singers, music directors, film directors, dancers, script writers, players, athletes, academicians, doctors, nurses, businessmen, officers, peasants, politicians, business leaders, social workers, etc., are the result of their intense desire to succeed. The dreams of poor are as beautiful and as important as that of the rich. This is obvious from the fact that many top rich persons in the world were very poor before they reached to that top position and this was possible due to their great dreams and burning desires and actions on it.

"When you desire something from the core of your heart, the whole universe conspires to help you make it happen."

The following stories further reveal that those who had burning desires succeeded in spite of many hurdles, severe personal adversities, many failures and un-conducive environment.

A Great Willpower Defeats Adversity and Turns You a Winner: Double Amputee Mark Inglis scaled the Mount Everest, won cycling silver medal, turned to be a great global speaker and a wine maker. His achievements are a great inspiration for all.

The **message** from his story is: "No personal adversity and challenges in the chosen pursuits are big enough that can't be defeated and overcome by great dreams, desires, resilience, positivity and strong willpower and finally enable one to become a great winner."

"Defeating one's mind is defeat but defeating other's mind is winning. Winning one's mind is winning and winning other's mind is also winning."

Imagination, Dream and Desire can Make an International Brand: Ray Kroc was a salesman of the milkshake mixer. He visited the McDonald Brothers food outlet that purchased eight mixers. Seeing the sales, he advised him to open a chain outlet to earn some big money. The McDonald brothers used his idea and opened an outlet and then a chain of outlets, and later on Ray Kroc bought the company and made it international.

The **message** of this story is: "It is the efficient implementation of your imagination, dream and desire that can make your venture an international brand and a household name."

A Great Dream Defeats Blindness and Turns You into a Legend: Milton was blind but he became a great poet. His name will last forever as he imagined, dreamed and translated his dreams into a great thought.

The **message** is: "No blindness is big enough to defeat a great dream and desire and power of imagination."

A Serial Dreamer Wears Many Hats: Arnold Schwarzenegger dreamed of many things in his life. He first became Mr. Universe, a glorified weight-lifter. He wrote an autobiography, Arnold: "The Education of a Body- builder" which became a bestseller book and started a company to produce body-building events. Next, he became a famous movie star. After that, he entered into real estate business and earned a lot. He entered into politics and became the governor of California.

His life history **shows** that: "The better implementation of dream and desire with great passion enables one to achieve an unparalleled feat in many fields."

"Never stop dreaming as dreams are the torch- bearers of vibrant life, happiness, glory and success."

Spiritual Curiosity Makes You a Winner in Mountaineering: Santosh Yadav was having an intense desire with spiritual curiosity to climb the Mount Everest. She became a member of an Indo-Nepalese women's expedition and scaled the Everest twice, thus setting a record as the only women to have scaled the Mount Everest twice in a year.

The **message** of her story is: "The intense dream and desire with spiritual curiosity enables one to climb the Mount Everest twice in a year- a double winner."

A Beautiful Dream Shapes Your Destiny: Shahnaz Hussain was just a high school pass and got married early at the age of sixteen and was blessed with a daughter. She dreamed of opening abeauty parlor with herbal products during the period when her husband was working in Iran. She started a company, Shahnaz Herbal with just Rs.35,000 which became a brand. At present, the company produces 400 herbal beauty products and has 400 franchisee clinics across the world covering over 138 countries.

The **theme** of story is:" It is the generation of idea and dream that changes your destiny and the course of action, if it is implemented with patience, courage, conviction and faith."

A Burning Desire Clubbed with Self-esteem Defeats Severe Adversityand Inspires Millions: Linda Down and her twin sister were born with cerebral palsy. Both ran in the 1982 New York City Marathon and covered the entire 26.2 miles with the help of their special crutches. Such persons cannot walk even one metre without special crutches. Though, they came last and took eleven hours and fifty-four seconds to finish the marathon but both inspired the Americans much more than the gold medalist of the marathon. After getting such inspiration, many depressed people got cured. What a burning desire! What conviction! What self-esteem! What self-confidence!

The **message** of this story is: "An unparalleled feat achieved by severe adversity-affected people, out of burning desire inspires even the depressed minds to a colossal level which acts as an unparalleled medicine that cures them."

The great companies of the world such as Apple, Google, Microsoft, Berkshire Hathaway, General Electric, Johnson & Johnson, Wal-Mart, Nestle, IBM, Facebook, TCS, Infosys, Petro- China, Samsung, Toyota, Honda, Ford, Boeing, Airbus, Sony, Alibaba, Foxconn, etc. saw the light of the day due to dreams and desires of their founders. All these achievements fully satisfy the words of William Arthur Ward, who said: "If you can imagine it, you can achieve it. If you can dream it, you can become it." Bertrand Russell once said, "All human activity is prompted by desire". Before desire, everything is little. Without desire, we are an empty vessel, directionless. In the words of Willa Cather, "The world is little, people are little, human life is little. There is only one big thing-desire."

"Success is achieved by those whose dreams are live and vibrant. Wings don't matter; enthusiasm enables you to fly."

Hey, young men and women! Are you imagining? Are you dreaming? What is your level of dream? How is it great and practical? Do you want to give wings to your imagination, dreams and desire to fly in the world of success after giving the real shapes on the ground? If you are ready, then you are a man of contribution, enthusiasm, character, courage, and commitment. Come on, get up, and give a concrete shape to your imagination, dream and desire. It's never too late to follow your dreams. It is your prime duty to make the world a better place to live through your dream, desire and actions. God is already ready to help you and bless you at all junctures. "Vibrant dream and desire designs your victory. Have it! Have it! Have it!"

STEPS TAKEN BY YOURSELF

After going through this chapter, I (as a reader) will do the following for having imagination, dream and desire and giving them the real shape:

   i. _____
   ii. _____

***

Chapter 3

Practice Determination, Dedication and Discipline (3 Ds)

#THE 2ND MANTRA

DETERMINATION DECIDES YOUR DESTINY

"A dream doesn't become reality through magic; it takes sweat, determination and hard work."

—*Colin Powell*

"An invincible determination can accomplish almost anything and in this lies the great distinction between great men and little men."

—*Thomas Fuller*

A monk-cum-speaker was asked by an athlete from the audience in a congregation to speak to us of determination, dedication and discipline. He said in sequence: Determination! A Himalayan firmness. Stability like the tallest tower. Firmness like the hardest solid steel. An invincible vow. A colossal will to win. Are you ready to have strong determination in life? If not, think of having strong determination in life to excel.

Once decision is taken about the desire, then its hundred percent accomplishments have to be ensured through determination. The impact of determination is great. "Your determination remains stable and gets enhanced only through self-motivation. Many hardships appear in the journey of success of chosen ventures and one overcomes these only through firm determination and finally succeeds."

"Your determination decides and ensures the fulfilment of your dream irrespective of obstacles through the route of persistence and perspiration."

The following stories depict the impact of determination on the lives of successful people:

Your Invincible Determination Serves Your Passion and Shapes Your Destiny: Amish Tripathi worked as a banker in an MNC for fourteen years after graduating from IIM Calcutta. He was having affinity in literature, history, philosophy and mythology. He decided and determined to leave the banker's monotonous job after writing his firstbook of the *Shiva* Trilogy. He later published the second and third volume of the *Shiva* Trilogy and all the three volumes became blockbuster. He was offered an advance of Rs.50 million for a new unnamed book by his publisher. It is a nice comment from Business World that "Amish.... is well on to becoming the Paulo Coelho of the East."

Chetan Bhagat is an IITD and IIMA alumnus. After working as a banker for about ten years in a multi-national company, he took determination to serve his passion as a novelist and resigned from the job after the first book. He wrote many famous fiction books. At present, he is among the most famous novelists of India. His one book was chosen for a movie screened in the name of '3 Idiots' that turned out to be a blockbuster. His book 'Two States' has also been made into a movie. His latest book 'Half Girlfriend' has also been chosen for a movie now.

The **theme** of these stories is: "Nobody knows what future holds for you. It is you who can make that determination."

These stories are also a testimony of what George Eliot said once, "It is never too late to be what you might have been."

Strong Determination and Willpower Makes You a History Maker Despite Severe Adversity: Glenn Cunningham was horribly burned in a schoolhouse fire at the age of eight. Doctors predicted he would never walk again. Though, he was on the wheelchair, but was determined to walk. In this process, he used to throw himself out of the wheelchair. Twenty-two months later, he took his first step and through his sheer determination he learned to run despite the pain. In 1932 Olympics, he finished fourth due to the severe cold. On June 16, 1934, he ran the mile in 4.068 minutes breaking the world record and became a history maker. He went on to earn a Master's degree from University of Iowa and later on earned a doctorate from New York University. He was declared as the most popular athlete. What a colossal determination!

The **moral** of this story is: "As long as you desire anything strongly enough, remain highly determined and allow your will to guide you, you can achieve unparalleled success despite any severe adversity."

The **lessons** of the above stories are also a testimony to what Stephen Covey opined, "Deep within each one of us there is an inner longing to lead a life of greatness and contribution."

The **gist** of the above stories satisfies what Oliver Wendell Holmes said, "What lies behind us and what lies before us are tiny matters compared to what lies within us."

It was the determination and conviction of Mahatma Gandhi and Nelson Mandela who fought for the freedom and got freed India and South Africa respectively from the British Rule. A great winner once said, "Winning is a sincere choice of thoughts, invincible determination and extensive activities." Get up, wake up, defy the odds, stop seeking approval from others and start achieving your goals and living your dreams to full satisfaction."

Are you determined in your venture? Whatever you have dreamed off, do you feel that people may like it? O young men and women, get up, wake up and determine something which you like the most. "Invincible determination is your decree of success." Hold it! Hold it! Hold it!"

DEDICATE YOURSELF TO BELL THE SUCCESS

"If you believe in yourself and have dedication and pride, and never quit, you will be a winner. The price of victory is high and so are the rewards."

—Paul Bryant

"Each day brings a fresh opportunity for you to set the standard of how dedicated and committed you are to your needs, wants, goals and relationships."

—Steve Maraboli

Dedication! Dedication! A great sacrifice for the goal. A full devotion for the cause. A need of every soul. A great passion for the goal. Are you dedicated to your goals? If not, be dedicated to your goals to help the needy ones, to contribute immensely in nation building, to have golden success in your cherished goals.

"Dedication is putting heart and soul to the work at hand." "Your dedication to the work will bring passion and enthusiasm in the journey of success. Only desire does not serve any purpose. The desire has to be blended with determination, dedication and discipline." If you go to the life stories of successful people, you will find that they were highly dedicated to their goals and only through their sheer will, dedication, hard work and perseverance they got success. All the winners in international and national competitions belong to this category. "Dedication to your duty, to your goal is real worship." "What are needed to be a champion? These are: desire, dedication, determination, concentration and the great will to win. History is a witness to this fact and it is applicable to every venture undertaken-be winning of love, winning of games, winning in business, winning in competitive examinations, and so on.

"Dedication is the deciding factor of your success in any chosen venture. If you are fully dedicated, committed, fearless and don't quit, success will be at your doorstep."

If you desire to become a master at any skill, you have to give total effort of your heart, mind, and soul working together in tandem and harmony. The speed of your success will be governed only by your dedication, commitment and your sacrifice. Irvin Stone said, "Talent is cheap; dedication is expensive. It will cost you your life."

The following stories showcase the impact of dedication on success:

Invincible Dedication Brings Glorious Success Despite Severe Adversity: At the age of five, Spencer West tragically lost his both legs. The doctor said, "Probably he would never able to walk." But the Canadian-born, thirty-one years old has defied all odds, knocking every barrier and obstacle in his mission of life. He climbed Mt. Kilimanjaro by spending over twelve months on extensive training with full dedication. In seven days, he climbed to the summit in which he covered 80% of trek by hand. What a dedication! Through sheer drive, determination, dedication and perseverance, Spenser West has demonstrated the world that nothing is impossible. His achievement is an inspiration to all.

The **theme** of the story is: "Through invincible determination, dedication, discipline and perseverance one can achieve unachievable and impossible goals despite severe adversity."

Strong Dedication Overcomes Shortcomings: Josef Manuel was short in height as compared to the other boys of his age and he was always bullied. Jiu-Jitsu is a tough martial art form in Brazil. He decided and was determined to be a Jiu-Jitsu winner to show that short height doesn't matter and started taking extensive training with full dedication. He became a very strong and tough Jiu-Jitsu player. He won many prizes and awards in national and international meets. He started a training center named Cutting Edge Brazilian Jiu-Jitsu where he became the owner and instructor.

The **theme** of the story is: "In the event of strong determination, dedication and hard work, shortcomings do not matter in the greater success story."

Deep Dedication Brings Excellence: It is a story from the epic Mahabharata. Ekalavya was fond of archery. Guru Dronacharya was the great teacher of archery during that period and he was giving training to princes of both the Pandavas and Kauravas. Ekalavya approached Dronacharya to accept him as his disciple for training in archery. Dronacharya refused to accept him as his disciple on the basis of his birth in a low caste. But, Ekalavya was determined and dedicated to learn archery. So, he made a statue of Dronacharya and practiced hard before his statue and became a great archer. What dedication and determination!

The **theme** of the above story suggests that: "Odds and obstacles don't matter if you are deeply dedicated to your great vision of excellence."

Judge yourself: Are you dedicated to your work? Oh men and women! Bring dedication in your life, in your dream, in your desire to accomplish your goal. "Dedication is your devotion to work delivering excellent result. Practice it! Practice it! Practice it!"

DISCIPLINE MAKES YOU A WINNER

"To enjoy good health, to bring true happiness to one's family, to bring peace to all, one must first discipline and control one's own mind. If a man can control his mind he can find the way to enlighten and all wisdom and virtue will naturally come to him."

—*Gautama Buddha*

"It was character that got us out of bed, commitment that moved us into action and discipline that enabled us to follow through."

—*Zig Ziglar*

Discipline! Discipline! Discipline! A decoration of life. A crown of every soul. A formidable weapon for success. A call of humanity. A life of rhythm. Are you a disciplined person? If not, practice it from the core of your heart to excel, to win, and to achieve success.

"In simple words, discipline is about maintaining responsibility, honesty, time management, positive attitude, and following rules, regulations, codes of conduct of a system, society, organization and life for betterment, irrespective of the situation." A preacher was asking questions to the audience. Do you know what the reasons of failure are? Why are people not achieving success? What stops them from achieving their goal? The reply from the audience was not satisfactory. The preacher said that they are failing because they are not disciplined in their lives. If you take the statistics of successful people in any field- sports, athletics, games, academia, business, medical, music, dance or movies, you will find that all of them were highly disciplined in their lives. (Refer Chapter 1, 5 & 6)

"Discipline is the soul of positive personality and formidable weapon to enable you to win in every venture."

Without discipline, our desire stands nowhere. There are many cases when people are not disciplined at work and the simple errors bring disasters. Many pilots have been found missing from cockpit to gossip with the air-hostesses. Many pilots have been found sleeping when planes are flying mid-air. Now some people talk on their mobile while driving. In India, the number of vehicles is one percent of the world while the number of accidents is ten percent and number of deaths is six percent in 2013. This is mainly due to not following the traffic rules- an act of indiscipline. A simple mistake due to not being serious about one's duties may bring disaster killing hundreds of innocent people including the person concerned. A proven survey suggests that more potential leaders fail because of inner issues like character, discipline, etc. than outer ones. When you are organized due to your self-discipline, you have the special power and a great will to prepare to win.

"Disciplined life is a very happy and balanced one. It makes you a better person. If you are not consistent in your approach and action in your daily life, it means you lack in discipline. Discipline demands sacrifice, self-control, no distraction, focus, following of rules of life, avoiding temptation, and followup ethics. An undisciplined person cannot achieve success in life." Many parents model discipline as a combination of time management, hard work, honesty, responsibility, character, persistence, and positive attitude regardless of the situation for their children to practice in life. Such children do much better in life. "Learning is not possible without discipline. That is why, in all learning centers-schools, colleges and universities, a great emphasis is given on discipline. Those institutions that ignore discipline they go in the bottom, and no good students go there as these become centers of cheating, abuses, fights, no teaching and no learning."

Discipline means deliberately aligning our energy with our ethics, values and priorities. With the help of mental practice, we can focus on the concerned matter as a task before us and let other temptations and distractions pass by. "Self-discipline demands from us that we should endure frustration, disappointment and pain in the service of higher goal as expected from noble citizens. In other words, being willing to push ourselves to the limits of our will and endurance, which is what is needed for success." H. Jackson Brown, Jr. advocated, "Talent without discipline is like an octopus on roller skates. There's plenty of movement, but you never know if it's going to be forward, backward or sideways."

Have you ever thought about the real meaning of strength and might? What is real strength? What is real might? Who is stronger- the young man who gives in to his rage and becomes physically and verbally abusive or the young man who remains calm and assured of his inner strength? Those who know to restrain their power are the mighty ones, as real might lies in control and discipline, in gentleness and mercy. "Discipline is the deciding factor of your destiny. Improve it! Improve it! Improve it!"

Self-discipline should not be harsh; rather, it takes the form of a quiet resolve or determination which then directs our choice. It allows us to make use of whatever power and capabilities have been given to us in the service of our dreams.

The following stories showcase the impact of discipline in our lives:

Strong Self-discipline leads to Goodness: In ancient Greece, Socrates was regarded as a great philosopher. One day, an acquaintance met him and said, "Do you know what I just heard about your friend?" Socrates replied, "Before telling me anything, I'd like you to pass a little test, called the Triple Test covering Truth, Goodness, and Usefulness." The man replied, "Whatever I have heard, it does not pass the Triple Test". So Socrates said, "There is no need to tell me." The story is the best example of self-discipline of Socrates.

The **message** is: "Not listening and not acting on any matter out of Triple Test covering truth, goodness and usefulness is the best example of self- discipline."

Undisciplined Youth Kill Their Destiny: Some youth due to ego problem and intolerant attitude fight with others on petty matters. As a result, either they get hurt or they hurt others or get killed or kill others. In any situation, there is a great loss in terms of person concerned, their family and finally the nation. Among such youth, some of them could be very talented.

Further, when any agitation goes against any government due to any problem, people become indiscipline and they destroy a lot of private and government properties.

The **theme** of the story is: "It is wise to have discipline in life for the growth of self, family and nation. Youth are the nation builders. They should realize that their families and nations have great aspirations from them. If they get spoiled, everything gets spoiled."

Defense Personnel are a Symbol of Disciplined Life: A good example of disciplined life, one can find in defense organizations (The Army, The Navy or The Air Force). In defense, discipline is the core parameter and without discipline defense organizations cannot achieve anything. All victories by the army, air force and navy personnel are the result of their discipline, dedication, spirit and bravery.

The **theme** of the story is: "It is a high degree of discipline and bravery that wins the battle."

Discipline Shapes Destiny: Former Manchester United manager Alex Ferguson says, "He owes his success to being beaten with a belt by his favorite school teacher Mrs. Elizabeth Thomson for a fight on the playground, which taught me to become a fierce disciplinarian. Mrs. Thomson was a fierce disciplinarian lady teacher and whoever was touched by her, their lives have been shaped." Though, the new adage- "Spare the rod, save the child" is prevailing instead of "Spare the rod, spoil the child." Discipline may be brought by persuasions, by practicing discipline by parents, teachers, and seniors, by making systems, policies and processes conducive for discipline and their honest implementation. Napoleon Hill opined, "Self-discipline is the first rule of all successful leadership."

The **message** of the story is: "Sometimes fierce disciplinarian acts shape the future of individuals for greatness."

For the overall development of a person, discipline plays a vital role. History has shown that it is the discipline, hard work and self-confidence that are responsible for the success of individual, family, state or nation. The importance of discipline and concentration may be understood from the news when Mike Tyson, an undisputed heavyweight champion, known for controversy, was knocked out by Buster Douglas in 1990; he said, "You can't conquer the world before conquering yourself." It is very essential to start developing self-discipline in a small way today in order to be disciplined in a big way in the near future. Note that a small plan taken seriously makes a big difference in life."

> *"Success demands 6Ds from you- Desire, Decision Direction, Determination, Dedication, and Discipline."*

[*Mathematically, Success(S) = f(6Ds)*]

Observe the following facts with reference to discipline:

- Mother cares night after night for her baby even though she is very tired.
- Teachers discipline students despite taking too much pain, pressure and absorbing their antagonism.
- Army, Navy and Air force units can't run and perform without good discipline.
- Winners are followers of discipline.

What are the messages?

Discipline improves love, duty, ethics, responsibility, performance and finally brings success, while indiscipline brings hatred, anger, chaos, anarchy and finally failures."

Some people misuse the word freedom given by the laws of a nation or an organization and get involved in indiscipline activities. Such indiscipline, indecent activities are observed in buses, trains, planes, cinemas halls, and fairs by undisciplined persons. Disciplined persons do not like such indiscipline activities and try to stop and as a result commotion starts, police men come and the troubles of undisciplined persons start.

"Discipline is the decoration of life and core of civilization. It helps you to lead a meaningful, glorious and successful life."

Excessive freedoms given by parents to their children sometimes spoil them and they are declared bad boys. They do not respect parents and elders and start fighting on street on simple issues and get trapped in problems. Bertrand Russell said, "Right discipline consists, not in external compulsion, but in the habits of mind which lead spontaneously to desirable rather than undesirable activities."

The old story about the race between tortoise and hare is well known to everybody from childhood. It is a lesson of discipline. Due to indiscipline hare lost the race.

*The **theme** of this story is old one: "Slow and steady wins the race and fast and indiscipline loses the race."*

Bertrand Russell opined, "Success isn't measured by money or power or social rank. Success is measured by your discipline and inner peace." Maintaining discipline in life is not easy. It is painful but regret is much more painful than discipline. George Washington opined the importance of discipline in army in a lucid way, "Discipline is the soul of an army. It makes small numbers formidable, procures success to the weak and esteem to all."

Ask yourself: are you disciplined? If not, be disciplined for the sake of yourself, family and nation.

STEPS TO IMPROVE YOUR SELF-DISCIPLINE:

Do the following to improve your self-discipline:

i. **Avoid excuses**: In general, people make excuses for their failure in meeting any requirement of life. Stop making excuses for not being self-disciplined. Make a list of reasons for not being self-disciplined. Find the solution to win over these obstacles and don't quit due to dispiritedness and desperation.

ii. **List the benefits:** There are various benefits to being self-disciplined. List them and read daily for auto-suggestions.

iii. **Identify areas of your priorities by starting small**: Identify five critical areas which are most important for your personal and professional life. First, your heart and soul are to be self-disciplined in these areas and then go on developing it in other areas too.

iv. **Organize your life**: With an organized life, you have a special power. You can walk with confidence and a sure sense of purpose. Your priorities are distinct which will help in its completion. Learn from nature to adopt an organized life.

STEPS TAKEN BY YOURSELF

After going through this chapter, I (as a reader) will do the following to practice determination, dedication and discipline in life:

i. _____
ii. _____
iii. _____

***

Chapter 4

Build A Positive Attitude

#THE 3RD MANTRA

POSITIVE ATTITUDE BRINGS PROSPERITY

"Any fact facing us is not as important as our attitude towards it, for that determines our success or failure. The way you think about a fact may defeat you before you ever do anything about it. You are overcome by the fact because you think you are."

—*Norman Vincent Peale*

"Nothing can stop the man with the right mental attitude from achieving his goal; nothing can help the man with the wrong mental attitude."

—*Thomas Jefferson*

WHAT IS ATTITUDE?

A great saint-cum-speaker was asked by a lady doctor from the audience in a symposium to speak to us of attitude. He replied: Attitude! Attitude! Attitude! An outlook towards anything. A psychological impact. A choice for diamond or dirt. A choice for positive or negative aspects. A life changer. A destiny shaper. Hey, men and women: 'Are you a victim of negative attitude?' If yes, it is a killer of your golden success. "Go for a golden destiny, grand living, golden success and greatness by practicing positive attitude in life."

"Attitude is the readiness of the psyche to act or react in a certain way (positive or negative) to anything. In other words, attitude is a positive or negative evaluation of people, objects, events, activities, ideas or just about anything in your environment. It is a psychological fact of the mind–body connection that affects our physical and emotional wellness."

"Attitude is a perception to see anything positive or negative. Positive attitude leads to progress and greatness while negative attitude negates your energy and places you at the rock bottom position- a failure."

ROLE OF ATTITUDE IN PERSONAL LIFE

In recent years, studies have shown that the positive attitude of a person plays a vital part in his success story and happiness. Those who have a negative attitude suffer a lot and always remain unhappy. William Jennings once said, "Destiny is not a matter of chance ... It is a matter of choice." As per a study at Harvard University, it has been found that in getting a job or a promotion, 85% of the time it is due to the attitude of the candidate and only 15% due to his/her knowledge and intelligence. As per the Standard Research Institute, the money you make in any venture is determined only 12.5 percent by knowledge and 87.5 percent by your attitude with people. Your attitude determines your relation with people. "Foundation of success in life is based on the positive attitude of a person like the solid foundation of a tall tower."

"Winning edge lies in the attitude, not aptitude."

Long back there was a belief that no runner can run a mile within four minutes. When Roger Bannister broke this record in 1964, many runners after that duplicated his feat. This was made possible due to their positive attitudes.

"Attitudes - positive or negative are contagious."

Your attitude is the primary vital force that will determine whether you succeed or fail in your chosen venture. "The difference among people in ability is very little, but that makes a big difference based on one's positive or negative attitude." As per a great consulting firm, the single greatest reason for firing an employee is their attitude problem (about sixty-two percent). Note that our attitude is an important asset. As per 1983 Companies Report on American Business, ninety-four percent of all Fortune 500 executives attributed their success more to attitude than to any other basic ingredient.

"Attitude and potential go hand in hand and shape your destiny."

"The impact of negative attitude is beyond imagination. It is impossible to estimate the number of jobs lost, the number of jobs missed, the number of promotions missed, the number of unsold items, the number of relationships ruined, and the number of marriages ruined due to a negative attitude."

"Your attitude determines your approach to life and finally your destiny."

Many times, adversity offers blessings. Adversity gets converted into prosperity by those who are rich in positive attitude. Abraham Lincoln, John Bunyan, Sir Walter Raleigh and Dante earned their respective greatness while facing great adversities. Martha Washington said, "The greater part of our happiness or misery depends upon our dispositions and not upon our circumstances."

"Your positive attitude can turn your adversities into great blessings."

"Leadership is more concerned with disposition than with position." "The greatest day in our life will be when we take total responsibility for our attitudes." "Many top companies of the world use the **five attitude areas** for appraisal when employees are being considered for an executive promotion. They are: ambition, attitude towards policy, attitude towards colleagues, supervisory skills, attitude towards excessive demands on time and energy."

The following **stories** showcase the importance of attitude in our personal lives:

What's Inside Your Brain that Matters, not the Outer Color: A chemistry teacher had planned to demonstrate the effect of the nature of gas to her students. So, she brought three cylinders of the same size but of different colors – black, blue and red, in which she had filled different gases. In the black cylinder, she filled nitrogen; in the blue cylinder, oxygen; and in the red cylinder, natural gas. All the cylinders had caps. One by one, she started creating sparks by opening the cap of the cylinders. The gas from the black and blue cylinders didn't burn while the gas from the red cylinder burned with a high intensity. One student asked the teacher, "Does only the gas filled in the red cylinder burn?" The teacher answered, "My dear students, it is not the color of the cylinder filled with the gas that burns, but it is the nature of the gas filled in the cylinder irrespective of colors, that burns. In the red cylinder, the gas filled is natural gas which has the characteristic to burn while nitrogen and oxygen don't."

The **morals** of the story are:

"It is what is inside our brain that matters and not the outer aspects like color."
"If our brains have a positive attitude, we will shine like stars and if we have negative attitude, it will spread darkness in our lives."

Different Attitudes Shape Destiny Differently: Two Shepherd brothers, Philips and David, residents of Germany used to keep each a 1000 sheep on their each ten acres of unfertile rocky land. Both were fond of playing the guitar, content and happy with their lives. When they were playing on their guitars in the morning, a wise man while passing along the road praised their music and sheep, and explained the importance of diamonds to them. He said, "If you have one kg of diamonds, you can purchase your own city, and diamonds are found in rocks."

The younger brother David could not sleep in the night due to his greed for diamonds, while elder brother didn't show any lust and was of the opinion to shape destiny here itself. David was disturbed and wanted to acquire diamonds. So, David sold his sheep and lands to his brother Philips and went in the search of diamonds. He toured Europe and never found any diamonds. He came to Egypt and toured there, but couldn't find any diamonds. By this time, he was very weak, frustrated, and all his money was exhausted, and so he jumped into the river Nile to end his life.

In the meantime, his elder brother Philips tilled the surplus five acres land for planting flowers. While watering the land, bright light from two stones sparkled like a rainbow and these two stones were declared as diamonds by a diamond merchant. He sold one of the diamonds, purchased two beautiful houses, two big cars and got a beautiful wife.

The **morals** of this story are:
- "Your attitude recognizes an opportunity."
- "With positive attitude you can feel that you are in the world of diamonds."

- "People always feel that the other side is greener without knowing facts and figures and it may prove worse."
- "There is no need to run after the brighter side as you can create the same brightness in your side."
- "Opportunity does not come always."
- "A right decision based on a positive attitude may give you success and a wrong decision made with a wrong attitude may place you in great danger and even kill you."

Any Giant Can be Beaten: There is a famous story in the country side of India to motivate the children based on a biblical story. There was a giant man named Kalia who was eight feet tall and looked very scary. People started fearing even his name. A young man just five feet tall and of twenty years named Hira was very scared of the name of Kalia. His elder brother Panna used to motivate him not to have any fear of Kalia and said, "Even being short you can beat the giant." Hira replied, "Don't you see he is too big to hit?" On hearing this reply, brother Panna said, "No, he is not too big to hit, but he is too big to miss." Hira got motivated and he killed the giant with a slingshot. What we observe is the same giant but different perceptions.

The **morals** of this story are:

- "The way you perceive anything that matters."
- "No giant is big enough that he can't be beaten."
- "No height is great enough that it can't be scaled."
- "No problems, no obstacles are big enough, that they can't be overcome by right attitude."
- Right attitude may shape your destiny while wrong attitude may kill you.

Vision, Intelligence, and Attitude Win the Race: As per Hindu mythology, Lord Shiva had two sons – Lord Karthikeya and Lord Ganesha. A discussion started between the two sons about who should be first worshiped. In order to solve this issue, Lord Shiva put a condition that: "Whoever first completes a round of the earth, he will be worshiped first." Karthikeya used his mode of transport "Swan" and started the journey. The swan is a very quick bird at flying, so Karthikeya was confident about winning the race. Lord Ganesha's mode of transport was the mouse which runs very, very slow. Ganesha thought that he couldn't win, so he used his vision, intelligence and attitude and he took four rounds of his father, Lord Shiva and mother, Goddess Parvathi and after that, Lord Karthikeya came after taking one round of the earth.

After a lovely discussion, Lord Ganesha said to his father and mother, "You both are my universe. I have first completed already four rounds of the both of you so I am the winner." After this discussion, Lord Shiva gave the decree that first Lord Ganesha would be worshiped.

The **morals** of the story are:

- "It is the vision, intelligence and attitude that win the race."
- "It is the speed of mind that matters in a success story and not the physical speed."
- "Your universe, your God in the real sense is your parents. They should be treated like God."

A great preacher was telling his audience about attitude: "Every morning comes with a new hope for everybody. It is your attitude which will decide whether you have to be in good mood or bad mood every day. People with good mood increase productivity, maintain quality and create a cool environment at the work place for their reputation, growth and excellence. God has sent us to remain positive in life, to enjoy every day with happiness and to make others happy irrespective of the situation."

Remember the following cutting edge truth of life and apply it in your life for success and glory.

"Life is 10% what you make it and 90% how you take it."

—*Irving Berlin*

Having a positive attitude always helps anyone in any circumstance, especially in a situation that seems challenging and daunting. Co-workers might make you feel like working alone is the best option, one's boss may frustrate one's life too, but one should have at the back of mind that no one is an island, besides, all these experiences are great lessons for us to learn from and to make us a better person. These circumstances will make you learn how best to relate and interact with difficult people in all spheres of life while maintaining a positive outlook and attitude. The more we live with a positive attitude, the more respect we earn from the society. "Positive attitude creates a cool environment leading to prosperity."

"The building block of your success, irrespective of your chosen field of pursuit is positive attitude."

Positive attitude applies to every sphere of life. Can an athlete be a good athlete without a positive attitude? Can vice-chancellors, directors, principals, professors, students, be good performers in their respective roles without a positive attitude? Can parents, teachers, salesmen, employees be good performers in their respective roles without positive attitude?Can presidents, prime ministers, chief ministers, ministers, MPs, MLAs, secretaries, officers, managers, CEOs and leaders be good performers in their respective roles without positive attitude?The answeris a big NO, and then what should be the mantra? It is the positive attitude that forms the foundation of your success. "The truth of the world is: You can alter your destiny by altering your attitude of mind."

Your Attitude Determines Your Approach to Work: Three stonecutters were cutting stones at a place. A Wiseman was passing through that place. He asked one stone-cutter, "What are you doing?" He replied, "Don't you see that I am cutting stones." The Wiseman asked the same question to second stonecutter. He replied, "I am earning my bread." The Wiseman asked the same question to the third stonecutter. He replied, "I am making a grand and beautiful monument which will be an asset for the future generations." See! For the same work, the three stonecutters have different attitudes. Obviously, the attitude of third stone-cutter is highly positive, while the first one is negative.

The **morals** of the above story are:

- "For the same work, people may have different attitudes-positive or negative."
- "Your attitude determines your approach to life."
- "People with positive attitude will increase productivity and bring the finest quality in their work."

Norman Vincent Peale once said, "You are not what you think you are. But what you think –YOU ARE!"

Yes! "I can change" philosophy is to be imbibed by everyone who wants to be a man of positive attitude. Ask yourself: "Are you ready to adopt this philosophy? What does prevent you from adopting it?" The words of Horace Rutledge beautifully portray the way, "When you look at the world in a narrow way, how mean it is! When you look at it selfishly, how selfish it is! But when you look at it in a broad, generous, friendly spirit, how wonderful you find it!"

ROLE OF ATTITUDE IN ORGANIZATIONS AND NATIONS BUILDING

The role of attitude in the building of organizations and nations is enormous. Why are some organizations and nations more successful, more organized and more prosperous than others? Why are government organizations and industries performing poorer than private multi-national companies? Why are government schools performing poorly compared to private schools? The main difference is the attitude of all stakeholders.

They are better and successful because the people of the organizations/nations have positive attitude, think effectively, create transparent and growth oriented systems and are highly sensitive to their duties for the progress of their organizations/nations. "In any organization or country, if the majority of everyday experiences are negative, the organizational developments will not occur." It is to be noted that people do not automatically get a positive attitude and become competent. Organizations/nations invest heavily in their most valuable asset – **people** as they are the game changers.

Since the last three decades, new concepts of Total Quality Management (TQM) and Total Quality People (TQP) have emerged. "TQM is a zero defect(defect free) product without any rejection (one rejection in one thousand) but the present Prime Minister of India, Narendra Modi has added a new dimension to it and it is zero effect (no effect on environment).

"TQP may be defined as people with complete knowledge, skill, character, integrity, good ethics, values, empathy and positive attitude." With these qualities one can be very good in knowledge, in skills, in maintaining quality assurance, in maintaining conducive environment, in maintaining peace and order, and will be highly productive. Organizations and nations train people on TQM and TQP through various means for their overall growth. Note that both –TQM and TQP, are mind-sets.

"Branding of any organization/nation is judged by the quality of people in the bottom of pyramid (about 70%)."

"It is the Total Quality People (TQP) that puts an organization/nation on the glorious path of prosperity, progress, peace, happiness, reputation and branding."

An organization or nation should have the following ethos for all round prosperity and growth in any form: "Driven by ethics, values and transparent systems; Powered by intellect, innovation and positive attitude."

Many top organizations/nations follow this ethos in different forms up to the satisfactory level.

i. **Multi-national Companies (MNCs):** MNCs from the very beginning keep their vision, mission, governance, systems, policies and practices in such a manner that spur growth and excellence, not of the companies only but also those of the human capital-employees. They train their employees inTQM, TQP and other aspects heavily, so that they not only become good and maverick people, but also people with high positive attitude. Such companies become great places to work, a beacon of hope for the people.

If you ask the top executives of MNCs about what would be the single factor that would spur growth, profits, and market share in their organization, the answer will be only one: "Change people's attitude towards positivity." If people are positive towards mission, vision, growth, profit, customer satisfaction, transparency, training on TQM and TQP, etc. of the companies, obviously the companies are bound to prosper, including the employees. The company earns a brand name, everybody starts viewing such companies as a beacon of hope and longs to work for such companies. The revenue of one such company is more than the GDP of many small countries. The same philosophy is true with nations.

However, due to the lack of transparency, wrong decisions mainly based on greed, and lack of innovation, even some MNCs fail within 30 years of their span.

ii **Non-MNCs**: In most of the non-MNCs, the mission and vision are just on paper. There is no training on TQP. The employees get instilled with a negative attitude and are ready to go on strikefor every small issue due to the lack of transparencies and values. Such companies are not able to attract the best talent and hence, profit and growth margin are low. Some companies miserably fail with heavy losses and are shut down resulting in unemployment.

The situation in Indian government companies is more pitiable except for those in the NavRatna and MahaRatna categories. There are many Achilles hills in the system. Just after ten to fifteen years, many companies are failing miserably with heavy losses due to the negative attitude of a majority of the employees, and no training on TQP. Due to being the government's companies they survive for many years by consuming taxpayers' money and finally get shut down. Employees lose their jobs and there is a great national loss.

Focus on the following facts for companies, organizations or nations about TQP as given below:-

"People are the greatest assets or greatest liabilities; care them, train them and motivate them for TQP, otherwise face the consequences."

iii. **Educational Institutions**: There are generally three stages in education system – primary, secondary and higher. After primary and secondary education, students enter into the higher education system. The quality of teaching in about 80% to 90 % primary and secondary schools in developing countries (like India) is highly pathetic and deplorable. In India, about 75% educational institutions are public and about 25% private and the condition of public institutions is poorer than private ones. Though infrastructure and sufficient qualified teachers (which are meagre) matter a lot, the attitude of teachers, officers, ministers, owners matter much more towards the future of children and the nation, than other aspects. "If the twelve years of grooming and conditioning of children in schools are poor, how can they perform better in higher education?" As a result of poor conditioning, some children follow negative approach while they are still the buds of their nations, waiting to blossom and to spread the fragrance of excellence.

The condition of the higher education system in most developing countries like India is also pathetic and alarming, except for about top ten percent of institutions, mainly due to the poor quality of intake of students, faculty, infrastructure; non-conducive environment; the lack of will; the greed of private owners;the lack of positive attitude of all stakeholders.

Not a single institute of India ranks below 100 in QS World Ranking of 2015 including IITs and IIMs. What a pity! Further, only fourteen institutes fall under the top 800 among the world ranking. The quality of students in IITs and IIMs is unmatched in the world. The faculty is also highly qualified. The infrastructure is comparable. Then what prevents our top six institutions to fall in the top fifty in the world? "The main reason is the lack of right will and right attitude of all stakeholders towards achieving the goals that they deserve. India's reputation will go high if they achieve all these which they can and deserve." "When India can send a spacecraft (MOM) in its first attempt to Mars, a record in the world, the falling of its top six institutions/universities under the top fifty ranks is not difficult if they can have a mission like ISRO."

Similar to this is the poor story of other developing countries except two or three leading institutions of four to five countries.

iv. **Nations:** All nations in the world are classified into three categories – developed, developing and underdeveloped. "It is not the God that makes nations developed, developing and under-developed." "It is the attitude of people (positive or negative) in the respective nations towards sensitivity of duty, responsibility, self-contribution, good governance, transparent systems, justice system, quality of education, quality research, innovations, quest for quality of life, equality, freedom, justice, fairness, ethics & values, policies and processes that make them developed, developing and underdeveloped. Obviously, the attitude of head of state, ministers, officers, and other stakeholders matter much more." With highly positive attitude in every sphere, a nation can become a developed one in a reasonable span of time. "On and average basis about sixty-four percent of the national wealth rests with the quality of human capital, and developed nations are on the top due to high quality of their human capital."

USA is on the top of the world, not by God or luck but by the American people, as God has created us to shine by our own efforts, by our own attitude, by our own governing system, by our own vision and mission. As per one estimate, the economic value of Indian migrants in the USA is close to USD 50 billion per annum in 2013. See the importance of quality of human capital. Is any nation ready to achieve the status of the USA? If yes, then develop quality of human capital, practice all good aspects of the USA and other top countries including your own in real spirit, in an honest manner and success will be at your doorstep in due course. It is not ten or twenty years of affairs but much more. Singapore, a tiny country became a highly rich country within thirty years by the efforts, attitude, governance, vision, mission and wisdom of its head of state Lee Kuan Yew.

WHAT SHAPES OUR ATTITUDE?

We have observed that attitude is a vital factor in the development and success story of a person. Since every human being is a different person due to the highly complex system of human mind, so many pertinent questions arise:

"Why are some people having positive attitude and others negative? Is there any way to change negative attitude into positive attitude?" Human brain gets fully developed by the age of eight years, so the attitude is also formed during this primitive age. However, attitude changes with the passage of time depending upon at least five parameters which can be abbreviated as **EEECP**. (i)Environment;(ii)Experience;(iii)Education;(iv)Circumstances;and (v)Personality.

i. **Impact of Environment**: Environment encompasses a big spectrum and so its impact on the formation of attitude is much. It consists of: home, school, work place, media, social environment, cultural background, religious background, political environment, geographical environment, etc.

In one home, you may find the parents and children well behaved, well mannered, courteous, considerate and peaceful while in another home, you may find a place full of abuses, fights and disturbance. It is due to the conditioning of mind in the primitive age.

Schools are the greatest learning centers, so the environment created by the principal and teachers give a great impact on the positivity or negativity of the students. "Socio-economic condition and genetic diversity affect the cognitive development of the mind of children." "An honest (positive) environment promotes good people to excel and bad people have tough time; while in dishonest (negative) environment bad people thrive and good people have tough time leading to the failure of organization or nation in the long run. This is the truth you can find in all developed, developing and under- developed countries."

"A hungry stomach or greedy mind can't listen to morals."

"A dishonest environment promotes a team of I I Cs – Conman, Crook, Crime, Corruption, Contradiction, Confusion, Conspiracy, Chaos, Cunningness, Charlatan and Critics of right actions."

ii. **Impact of Experience**: Experience enriches wisdom. A good experience brings a great feeling while bad experiences produce fear, doubt and hatred. All these affect our attitude. Our behavior is a function of experience gained from interaction with various people.

"Experience is a great modulator of attitude."

iii. **Impact of Education**: Education, both formal and informal, affects the formation of attitude. If educational institutions impart morals, ethics and value systems over and above of knowledge, skills and information, then it will have a positive impact on attitude. In the case of immoral practices (say copying, fighting, drinking, taking drugs, stealing, indiscipline, etc.), the impact will be negative. "Schools, colleges and universities are the main places where positive attitude among students may be developed through various modes of education including practicing of values by teachers."

"Educating mind in knowledge and not in morals produces problematic people of negative attitude".

iv. **Impact of Circumstances**: Circumstances play a vital role in shaping the attitude. Tragedies, in general, completely change a person's attitude. Even a very bad person's behavior can completely soften and he can become a good person. But it depends upon the type of tragedy. Sometimes, tragedies turn good people into bad people. You might have heard that many dacoits have changed their hearts due to certain circumstances. But certain situations have changed many good people into dacoits. Sometimes, circumstances lead to rebellion, suicide, etc.

Insult (verbal or physical) to a person sometimes creates a peculiar situation. "Insult leads to hatred and hatred leads to rebellion." So, while dealing with people, one should be very careful not to insult anybody. "All over the world, the rebellious attitude of persons caused due to insult persists for a very long time. Sometimes, it even shifts from one generation to the next."

"Circumstances create an emotional force which may shape attitude at a fast pace- either positive or negative."

v. **Impact of Personality**: Every person is born with an individual personality due to the complex system of mind. Personality in the majority of people is influenced by environment, experience, education and circumstances (EEEC) but in some cases, the effects of these four parameters, (EEEC) are the minimum. People born in the same family, brought up in the same manner as other kids, go to the same schools, do jobs at the same firm but their personality in the form of positive or negative attitude is different. These differences form the spice of life we all enjoy. Some people change their negativity to positivity, but some remain negative throughout, even after making all attempts to modify them. In a family of four children, it is possible that three may be of positive attitude and one may be of a highly negative attitude while all other aspects remain the same. Some persons don't change at all but their percentage is very low (say 0.0001%). "Attitude and action go together; so build a positive attitude for positive action."

WHY IS POSITIVE ATTITUDE SO IMPORTANT?

A person with a positive attitude is like a shining and all seasonal flower in the garden of success who can be recognized and spotted easily. Positive attitude offers enormous merits, both at an individual and organization level as given below:

At Individual Level

- Helping in becoming a good person, shining like a star.
- Helping in achieving all the goals under a time frame.
- Bringing happiness and prosperity in life.
- Transforming you into a man with a pleasing personality.
- Making you an asset to your family, organization, society and country as a good human capital and a great quality contributor.
- Enabling you to become a role model for others.
- Making you a charismatic person.

- Liberating you from the past to face the future.
- Speaking of your good character.
- Acting as the prophet for your better future.

At Organization Level

- Productivity gets increased.
- Problems and crises, if any, get solved.
- Quality of products gets improved.
- Working environment becomes cool and conducive for growth and excellence through enhanced team work.
- Loyalty of employees to the company becomes strong.
- Profit of the organization gets improved.
- Relationships between employees, customers and employers get improved through enhanced wisdom.
- Stress on all stakeholders gets reduced.
- Branding of organization is made possible.

If one possesses negative attitude, all the above benefits are gone and further other problems like bitterness, resentment and demotivation get developed. O men and women! Acquire a positive attitude in life to gain the above stated merits.

WHAT PREVENTS US TO BE A PERSON OF POSITIVE ATTITUDE?

When there are so many merits, why don't we change our attitude towards positivity? The answer lies in the subsequent lines. Human behavior is highly complex and unpredictable. In the first place, most of the persons resist any change due to the fear of unknown, the lack of confidence, the lack of experience and the fear of more work involved. "Generally, negativity comes from frustration, the lack of experience, circumstances and wisdom. Habit hardly dies down. Resistance to change is universal. It invades all classes and culture." To change from negativity to positivity is a challenging task. Benjamin Franklin said, "When you are finished changing, you are finished."

Rodolfo Costa said, "Learn to adopt. Things change, circumstances change. Never see change as a threat because it can be an opportunity to learn, to grow, to evolve and become a better person." We are the real winner when we control our mind. Our attitude is shaped when we can control ourselves, and then we will be marching towards our greatness. "Control of ourselves is the most powerful control we can ever achieve in the history of mankind."

There are various methods by which you can change your attitude towards a positive one as given below.

THE TWENTY-FIVE METHODS TO DEVELOP A MENTAL POSITIVE ATTITUDE

Hey, men and women! Do you have negative attitude? Have you suffered due to negative attitude? Did you hurt someone by your negative attitude? Are you being alienated from your friends and family members due to your negative attitude? If the answer is yes, then there is a recipe for you to develop positive attitude. In fact, a large number of persons in the world have more negative attitude as compared to those with positive attitude. "Positive attitude is your motivator and destiny maker. Build it! Build it! Build it!"

"The core and progressive attainment of positive attitude is optimism."

Similarities Between Manufacturing of Products and Manufacturing (Achievement) of Success

There are similarities between manufacturing of products and manufacturing (achieving) of success. Products are manufactured by three ways:

- Removing material
- Adding material
- Changing the shape of material

Similarly, success is manufactured (achieved) by three ways:

- Removing bad thought materials (negative attitude) from mind
- Adding good thought materials (positive attitude) in mind
- Changing the shape of thought materials (attitude) in mind towards positivity

"It is you, who has to identify which are your good thoughts (positive attitude) and which are bad thoughts (negative attitude) in your mind."

You can learn anything through the mind which weighs about 1400 grams- a most vital part of our body. It is the mind which gives the direction to the body parts to act in a certain way. So, to achieve success one has to remove the negative thoughts from the mind and add only positive thoughts in it and shape the attitude towards positivity. Aristotle said, "The energy of the mind is the essence of life. It is our attitude which brings in thoughts, and shows us the true outlook of life. Lots of patience is required to maintain a positive attitude. One must remember that we become whatever we think. So, we must give everything to prevent negative thoughts replacing from positive thoughts."

The following are the **twenty-five methods** by which one can develop a mental positive attitude:

Method 1: Only Use Positive Words While Talking

"Words can confer strength; they can drain it off; words can gain friends; they can turn them into enemies; words can elevate or lower the individual. One must learn the habit of making one's words sweat, soft and pleasant."

—*Artharva Veda*

Your words are highly valuable and have incredible power in both ways – positive or negative during interaction. They can shape your bright future, put you at the bottom of the pyramid of success, or may help you in maintaining your status quo. "Words used by human beings can act as the most powerful drug." Your words strengthen your beliefs which in turn create your reality – having positive or negative attitude. "Your consistently selected words represent your state of mind, character and disposition." Many people at high positions have spoiled their careers by using inappropriate words in an important meeting or address. "Gautama Buddha said," Words have the power to both destroy and heal. When words are both true and kind, they can change your world. "Are you ready to change your world for a bright future? It totally depends on your positive attitude and mindfulness. The world has witnessed a lot of riots and fights, due to the use of wrong and objectionable words during conversations among people leading to loss of lives and property. Be careful in selecting words. "The words consistently selected by you will shape your destiny."

"While dealing with people, speak only suitable words- sweet, soft and pleasant, and save yourself from unethical words as it may damage your future beyond imagination." Humans are not creatures of logic, but emotions. Avoid the 3Cs in your life: "criticizing, condemning and complaining." Watch the following lines:

"Words spoken speak of your personality."

"Your spoken words enable you to receive either kisses or kicks."

Remember the following facts of life and shape your attitude accordingly:

- "One word can change your life."
- "One word can change a conversation."
- "One smooth touch can soften a hot argument."
- "One angry word withheld, can save a relationship."
- "One interaction can shape your entire world."

Method 2: Focus Only on Positive Thoughts

Thought is the creation of the mind. Our mind, on average creates about 50,000 thoughts in a day- both positive and negative ones. You need to be a man of positive thoughts. You need to focus on only positive aspects of your life. Human beings have two choices: "Either you control the direction of your thoughts or let your thoughts control your life." "God has given us freedom to choose a life of greatness or a life of misery through our choice. It is the positive attitude that makes a person or society or nation prosperous, creates a suitable environment to live happily in peace." "Mind needs a good picture, happy moments to generate the feeling of confidence, positivity and encouragement."

Dealing with People is Like Digging for Diamond: A student asked an eminent industrialist who was addressing graduating students in a famous university: "How do you deal with people?" He replied, "Go to dig diamonds". To get 100 grams of diamonds, you have to remove several tons of dirt. While digging you don't care and concentrate on dirt but your mind is concentrated on finding the diamond entrapped inside the stone. Tons of stones are broken and dirt is removed to find 100 grams of diamonds. Similar is the way to dealing with people. "Everybody is having something positive and negative. One has to dig deep to find the diamond in his thoughts."

The **moral** of the story is: "People have both positive and negative thoughts. Positive thoughts are like diamond and negative ones are like dirt. It totally depends upon you what you search in yourself and others."

"You are born as a raw diamond. Process yourself through positive thoughts and become a renaissance man and shine like the sun to bring positivity in the world."

Wishes of Young Girls and Boys for life Partners-Full of Positive Attitude

Young girls wish and aspire that their life partners (husband) should have certain good qualities which may be coined as **SMART** where each letter stands for something specific.

S: stands for Smart; **M**: stands for Money spinner; **A**: stands for Attitude; **R**: stands for Royal; **T**: stands for Treatment

"Husband should be smart, money spinner and his attitude should be highly positive so that he can give royal treatment to wife."

Young boys wish and aspire that their life partners (wives) should have certain qualities which may be coined as **BEAUTY** where each letter stands for something specific.

B: stands for Beautiful; **E**: stands for Elegant; **A**: stands for Attitude; **U**: stands for Utopian/Ultimate; **T**: stands for Treatment; **Y**: stands for Yahoo.

"Wife should be beautiful, elegant in disposition and her attitude should be highly positive so that she can give utopian/ultimate treatment to husband and as a result he says yahoo."

See the importance of positive attitude in the wishes of girls and boys for life partners.

Methods 3: Thrash Negative Influences

"The negative thoughts generate heightened emotions of fear, anxiety, negative waves inside and outside the mind. Anger or envy makes us restless, confused and impulsive." It is imperative that you don't let negative thoughts and feeling overwhelm you when you are feeling down or surrounded in a negative atmosphere created by others. Even if it is only a few hours a day, push your negativity aside and focus on positive aspects in your life, otherwise your self-esteem will go down. "Majority of the miseries in a family or an organization or a nation is mainly due to the negativity of its people."

"Negative people keep on howling loudly, but positive people keep on shining silently."

"Negative attitude leads to destructive approach while positive attitude leads to constructive approach."

Instead of being optimists, many people in the world are pessimists, sceptics and negative. As a result, such people criticize others or the system no matter what. Even with the best work done, they will always find fault in that and criticize. They criticize everybody and every system and become the expert in criticizing. They also become rumor-mongers. On any issue, they get agitated after criticizing and try to smoke heavily and gulp ten or more cups of tea or coffee for relaxation. They spread negative messages to a colossal level like a contagious disease. In general, negative words are experienced like lethal weapons by the victim and he/she may react harshly.

Negative Persons Find Fault in Any Work: When Wright brothers invented first aero-plane and advertised to show its demonstration; many sceptics and pessimists were present in the demonstration. Some were saying it will not take off, but it took off. Others were saying it will fall down but it did not fall down. Some critics were saying it will not land but it landed smoothly. Even after seeing all the successful demonstrations, some were saying it is not safe to fly.

Lesson learned from this story is: "Ignore the negative attitudes of pessimists, sceptics and critics in realizing your vision, in seeking success, and in making contributions."

Some of the common negative attitudes of critics are:
- It is not possible. I can't do this work.
- The boss is a dictator, so there is no use in working.
- The governance of the organization is poor, so there is no use in working.
- Our colleagues are useless. The company will fail.
- The new product might be very costly and it will cease to function in a few days.
- Always spread false rumors. Always give excuses.
- He achieved promotion through wrong methods.

Such critics influence the positive attitude of other persons. Thrash such negative influence. Don't surround yourself with negative people. Avoid negative co-workers and simply wish them. Always have people around you, who are very enthusiastic, positive and determined, about their own success and contributions to the world. Don't be one of these critics. Don't allow yourself to become a negative person. Thrash all negativity coming in your way. For example, thoughts of hatred and anger can be controlled by generating thoughts of forgiveness, mercy and non-violence. Try to become grateful, avoid comparison, raise your self-esteem, believe in the way of nature and use mindfulness to calm yourself. "Bring out the poison from your mind and build your mental positive attitude."

"Negativity is a deadly disease which is detrimental to your success and glory."

Are you ready to thrash negativity? Practice for thrashing negativity. "Many people are born with talent in music, singing, sports, dance, acting, knowledge, leadership, etc.; but die without achieving anything due to the lack of vision, the lack of opportunity, the lack of positive attitude, the lack of support and the wrong conditioning. The world remains deprived from seeing many legends."

If you want to be musicians, you have to associate with musicians. If you want to be a player of a certain game, you have to be in the company of players of that game. If you associate with winners, you will also come out as a winner. If you associate with a thinker, you will be a thinker. If you associate with negative people, you will be a negative person. "Conditioning plays an important role in shaping the life of a person. Right conditioning makes you a positive person while wrong conditioning makes you negative person."

This world is very beautiful but it is also full of pessimists and critics. When you succeed in life, critics will try to pull you down. Here, you need to be very careful. These critics are petty people and you have to ignore them otherwise you will also come to their level.

"Negative people are like energy suckers, demotivator and a source of downfall. Be away from them."

Various Social Ills – Smoking, Drugs, Alcohol, and Pornography are Killing Talents and Promoting Negativity

Throughout the world, various social ills have cropped up and they are draining the energy of people and promoting negativity. They include the following:

Smoking: All over the world, every year, more than **six million** people die prematurely due to smoking, and the world loses a lot of talent.

Use of drugs by youngsters is increasing day by day. These are blood suckers, killers of talent and promote negativity. A lot of drug addicted persons die worldwide and these talents are wasted.

Use of alcohol by young, middle and old aged persons has become a fashion all over the world. Alcohol is the third largest risk factor for premature deaths and kills about **2.5 million people** worldwide, as per estimate of WHO.

Pornography is another social evil which is spreading like fire. This evil pollutes the mind and brings negativity in the thought process. A lot of time is wasted by the young generationon viewing this. Pornography promotes the sexual assault on women and crimes of other sorts.

The **message** is: "Social ills lead to their addiction; promote negative attitudes, wrong culture, and finally invite misery and death."

Are you ready to give up social ills? If yes, then don't hesitate to give up and save yourself, your talent, your family and your nation.

Method 4: Practice Positive Affirmation Regularly

Positive affirmation is one of the most popular positive thinking exercises. This method means you need to repeat a positive phrase to yourself **on a regular basis** like:

"I deserve to be happy. I will be a winner. I will achieve my goal. I will get a good job. I am worthy of love. I will nurse the wound. I will not curse the wound but I will take it as an experience. I will be successful in my venture, etc." Believing that these things are true and reminding you constantly of these can help give you a more positive outlook of life. These positive affirmations act as a morale booster and finally you will be a highly positive person which will help become you a winner. Are you going to practice this positive affirmation regularly? Get up, wake up and practice. Tom Hopkins opined, "Repeat anything often enough and it will start to shape you like that." Medical research has proved that two-thirds of all healing is done through Placebo-effect, mind and belief of the patient determines response to treatment rather than the actual medicine or surgery.

Method 5: Direct Your Thoughts Towards Positivity

This technique is invariably used by psychotherapists, to control thoughts when one starts to feel down or anxious. The technique is to create a happy thought, a positive image or give you positive feedback to keep bad feelings in check.

Imagine yourself sitting in a beautiful garden through which a stream is flowing, a lot of colorful fishes are swimming and birds chirping on the trees. Imagine yourself sitting with your friends in a hill station enjoying the beauty of the hills, where white clouds are moving and playing hide and seek. Tell yourself that you are the best of all; you are the same person whose achievement was appreciated by everyone; and even today, you can perform better. "Think of yourself that you were born to keep yourself on the winning curve."

"Imagining and observing natural beauty, happy thoughts and positive images bring freshness and positivity in life."

Method 6: Apply Soft Skills During Interaction

Soft skills are the great tool to please persons with whom you are interacting, and who are working for you. Thank those that make your life better and happier to get a positive boost for yourself. Thank God for any work that gets done. Thank others for even their small help such as telling you the direction and location of a place. Such habit will make you happy and bring positivity in life.

> *"Thanks giving habits create an aroma of great respect to the humanity, bring happiness, create cool atmosphere and enhance positivity."*

Method 7: Turn Adversity into Opportunity

> *"Every adversity carries with it the seed of an equivalent or greater benefit."*
>
> —*Napoleon Hill*

Adversity comes in our lives in many different forms. It may be layoffs on the job, overwhelming debts, failing marriages, meeting an accident, get handicapped, unexpected medical emergency, cheating spouses or friends, failure in business and during the events of losing someone who meant a lot to you. Even though, these situations can be devastating but life is an unending line and learning to cope up with these situations is a must for every individual. "It is a major part of our character that we all must develop to overcome adversity."

> *"Adversity offers golden opportunity for achieving grand success by giving lessons, bringing out your hidden potential and making you tough like steel to withstand."*

What is the immediate general reaction when one confronts with adversity? The obvious reaction is to put forward complaints so as to put the blame on yourself. We start to question ourselves on various factors, "Why didn't my luck favor? Why did this happen to me? What will happen to my future?" Perhaps God is not happy with me.!" These are the natural responses but one should never get disappointed. Adversities are short lived and a source of experience. They offer various new opportunities which are required to be grabbed. "It is the rough road that leads to the pinnacle of greatness." We should not forget that, "Tough times always ebb, but tough people always rise."

> *"When one door shuts down the Great God opens up another better door."*

There are various cases around you when people turned adversity into opportunity. For examples: A person lost his job and ventured to start a highly successful business. Often, such people dedicate their success to their first adversity. Adversity for them comes out as an opportunity and success follows. J. K. Rowling wouldn't have been a renowned author if she hadn't found solace in writing after separating from her husband on legal terms. In World War II, Japan was devastated by Americans. They took a vow in revenge to be better than America in many fields. We know the position of Japan today. Indira Gandhi used to say, "When I am down, and I am pushed down against the wall, my best comes out and I don't give up." John D. Rockefeller said, "I always tried to turn every disaster into an opportunity."

"Treat your problems as prosperity in offing. Nobody can snatch your choice of seeing adversity with the positive frame of mind. We can't control adversity, but we can choose to make life less difficult. We can't control the beauty of our face, but we can control the expression on it. We can't control the negativity of the world, but we can control the negativity of our mind. Such choices will offer blessings."

"*Treat adversities as small pebbles in the path of success."*

A Promising Positive Attitude Brings Laurels Despite Severe Adversity: W. Mitchell met a severe accident while driving his motorbike in 1979. Unfortunately he suffered multiple bone fractures and sixty-five percent body-burns. He recovered within six months and left hospital to join his three friends for a plane ride. When the plane was ninety feet above the ground level, it lost its control and dropped stone dead on the ground. The three friends came out unhurt while the lower back of W. Mitchell was crushed and he was paralyzed from waist down. But, Mitchell was a man of high positive attitude. Unlike most of the persons, he didn't give up and never lost his zest for living. He told his inner thought, "I could do five thousand things before my injury and now I can do four thousands things after been admitted. Why should I stop living just because of the one thousand things I lost and not live with the four thousand other things that I am still capable of?"

With his positive attitude and experience of great adversity, he became major congressional nominee, gubernatorial candidate, great businessman and renowned motivational speaker. Such greatness lies within everybody.

The **moral** of this story showcases: "Perceiving and responding positively and boldly to your adversities makes a great difference in your life and can turn you into an idol."

Indirect Offer of Adversity

Though, adversity looks like the greatest problem of life but it serves us in many ways as given below:

i. **Bringing out hidden potential**: When you face the challenges in the form of adversity and come over it, you emerge emotionally stronger and highly confident. Once you pass the first hurdle, you can also pass the next hurdle and the following because, you are emotionally stronger and better equipped to handle any situation that may come in your way. It is the adversities and challenges that bring out the best within us about which we are ignorant. "Only rough sea makes the sailor tough." Adversity reveals your unlimited hidden potential and helps you to turn into a winner. Merle Miller said: "Everyone has his burden. What matters is how you carry it."

ii. **Teaching to be grateful**: When everything goes well in life, people become egoist, neglect down trodden and even forget the Almighty God. After facing the adversity, egoism starts declining; people start respecting the downtrodden and get involved more in religious activities. They start to believe in the Almighty and start visiting religious places to attain peace of mind. Once they overcome the adversities, they become more grateful to God, to those who helped them, and start helping others going through the same phase and giving donations to religious places.

iii. **Offering better perspective ignoring petty problems**:   After overcoming severe adversities, petty problems coming in your daily life such as tap leaking, roof leaking, and electric power cut-off for few hours, harshwords by others, illness, wound, etc. don't bother you. You ignore them, get them solved easily and focus on the bigger aspect of life. Nothing should distract you so that you learn to focus on better perspective.

iv. **Teaching valuable lessons**:   When someone fails in any business venture, this adversity offers valuable lessons and experience. You can think to switch over new business venture where you can succeed using your past experience or you may turn loss making venture to a profit making venture through judicious correction of mistakes.

v. **Motivating for making decision to change your profession**:   Many people get bored by doing monotonous work while they have other better potential in them. This boring life (a low level problem) forces them to change their career for what is hidden better in them. Chetan Bhagat and Amish Tripathi, both IIM alumni and bankers resigned the monotonous job of bank and became famous authors because of their passion for writing.

vi. **Building confidence and self-esteem**:   Adversity can't be overcome unless and until you develop confidence and self-esteem telling your inner-self: "I can." Once you overcome the adversity, your self-confidence and self-esteem become many folds in capacity. This is called the winning outcome and you ride on the winning curve.

vii. **Opening a new door**:   If relationships between husband and wife or between boyfriend and girlfriend show signs of separation, another better relationship is achieved. Losing one job and gaining another are just the way of life. These are not the problems but are opportunities for better options based on statistical data obtained from all over the world.

viii. **Bringing compassion and humanity in life**:   When you face adversities, you always think what wrong I have done in the eyes of God due to which I was punished. These thoughts change you completely and you become more compassionate, more human, more spiritual and more law abiding person. Your methods of dealing with persons and situations get completely changed. You finally understand the difference between "Human Being" and "Being Human."

Method 8: Believe in Yourself

Believing in oneself is a great trait to possess for an individual. There is nothing more wonderful than believing in yourself and sewing your own successful story of the chosen goal. Give yourself the benefit of the doubt and believe that you will succeed in fulfilling your dreams.

"Believing in self makes you confident, courageous and tough like steel to accomplish great task."

All achievers in the world had this trait. Abraham Lincoln believed in himself that is why, even a series of failures didn't deter him from his mission. At the end, he succeeded and became the most famous President of USA. "Believing in self brings success and glory." This is eloquently expressed by Norman Vincent Peale when he said, "When people believe in themselves they have the first secret of success." Give yourself credit for your past performance to lift your sagging mood and achieve your future endeavors.

Method 9: Practice Self-hypnosis

Self-hypnosis is aprocess to tune the mind for better responses like tuning of a car. It brings about a highly conscious state of mind that is willing to follow instructions. This means you'll be more open to positive suggestions that will allow you to be happier and hopefully healthier in your life. It needs a constant practice in a calm atmosphere to tune the mind.

Method 10: Develop a Habit of Doing It Now

"You cannot escape the responsibility of tomorrow by evading it today."

—*Abraham Lincoln*

The habit of procrastination is prevalent in most of the people and it's a fact that very few people are proactive. Once you postpone your today's work for tomorrow, you are basically multiplying your work. Once work becomes more, you become perplexed and negativity starts to cover your mind and you start declining from your position. If you are interested to remain positive, proactive and energetic, you have to develop a habit of living in the present and start working on the same day. Don't postpone your work for the future otherwise disaster is waiting for you.

"The habit of procrastination forms the foundation of your failure."

The habit of procrastination is very common with negative people. Students are more prone to this disease. Most of the students say that they will start studying from tomorrow, but next day they again postpone for tomorrow and tomorrow comes one week before examination. Similarly, all negative people, all losers tend to postpone their work in the same manner and their plights keeps on multiplying and under the huge burden of workload, they find themselves declining ultimately leading to a failure in life. "Time will not delay for your delay." (Refer Chapter 10)

To develop positive attitude one has to say the two great mantras to yourself as auto-suggestions: "do it now" and "procrastination is disastrous" Are you ready to do it now? Get up, wake up, accept the challenge and do it now. God has sent you to perform, to meet His wishes.

Method 11: Show Gratitude for Blessings

Blessings and troubles are the two sides of the same coin. Blessings may be showing right direction, providing help, giving knowledge, overcoming adversities, getting desired success, becoming winners, etc. In all these blessings, many aspects such as God, help by your friends, your hard work and dedication are involved. So, it is always better to show gratitude to God and deserving people. There is no need to curse anybody or God for troubles. "With the attitude of gratitude you will remain very happy and cheerful and will be regarded as a very good person." Our habit is to complain instead of showing gratitude. We should thank God for whatever that He has blessed us with. We must be grateful to those people who help us to achieve even very small goal – say showing the direction.

"Feeling and showing of gratitude is the graceful gift and the heartiest offering to God and to the people who bless you."

Many religious persons daily thank God on each time they take food in the form of ritual. "We are getting many blessings which are hidden and for these we must feel grateful to the Almighty God and thank him daily."

The attitude based on "Count your blessings and not your troubles" will make you a highly positive person and success will be at your doorstep.

Method 12: Get Educated Continuously for Positivity

"To educate a person in the mind but not in morals is to educate a menace to society."
—*Theodore Roosevelt*

Positive attitude covers a wide spectrum of parameters which are confronted by various internal and external issues. Therefore, it is essential to educate people continuously for developing positive attitude. Question arises: why is there a need of continuous education for positivity? The answer lies in the fact that mind needs practice. Positive thinkers may be compared to athletes who build an inner reservoir of stamina through continuous practice that they utilize during competition. Similarly, positive thinkers build a reservoir of positive attitude by constantly educating themselves with good positive thoughts through attending workshop, reading books on positive attitude on regular basis. This education is needed as the mind is receiving negative issues almost all the time from internal and external sources.

"Education is the kindling of a flame to remove ignorance of all kinds – be in knowledge, skills, wisdom, morals, spirituality and positive attitude."

Our minds need holistic education to remain positive and to acquire leadership quality. The present educational system is failing to provide holistic education. They are engaged in providing information, knowledge and skills only. While there is a greater need to inculcate positivity, honesty, compassion, courage, character, responsibility, discipline, soft skills, ethics and value system among students. "Try to be an impeccable and affable person."

Education system must develop capacity for commonsense, judgment and wisdom to use these in work environment. Winston Churchill once said, "The first duty of a university is to teach wisdom, not trade; character, not technicalities." (Refer Chapter 11)

"There are many people in the world who are highly successful with very less formal education because they possess: Positivity embedded with qualities of 9Cs – Curiosity, Confidence, Consistency, Character, Commitment, Courage, Conviction, Compassion and Cooperation." It is like nine planets (old theory) of our solar system. Such people include: "George Washington, Christopher Columbus, George Eastman, Jane Austen, Mark Twain, Charles Dickens, William Shakespeare, Thomas Edison, Benjamin Franklin, Dhirubhai Ambani, Walt Disney and countless of famous and successful people who started from naught and reached unmatchable heights." "Greatness needs many qualities in a person and only higher formal education is not sufficient. Real life is practical life and it is different than student's life. School smart is not sufficient. You need to become street smart also."

"School smart will give you a better living. Street smart will give you a better fortune. Both will take you to the world of greatness."

So, the advice for you is to get educated continuously and acquire positivity imbedded with qualities of 9Cs for success and greatness. Jim Rohn opined, "Formal education will make you a living; self-education will make you a fortune." Are you going to be self-educated? Are you going to learn how to grow rice? Are you going to get educated for positivity regularly? Are you sharpening your axe regularly? Oh! Men and women! Get up, wake up and take the stride for acquiring positive attitude.

Method 13: Be Constructive in Approach

There are many situations in which you need to be constructive in your approach. During meeting, many suggestions are being asked. Any positive suggestions increase the work load on employees but yield great results. Being a positive person you should always place constructive ideas. Negative people neglect the good ideas involving increase in work load.

At every stage, your approach should be constructive. Don't criticize others. Don't criticize yourself. Even if you criticize yourself and others, make sure your approach is constructive which can allow you to grow and let others grow as well.

Get involved in some new things such as painting, new models, social works, etc., for a feeling of positivity.

"Any constructive approach reveals your mindset of positivity."

Method 14: Develop a Positive Self-esteem (Refer Chapter 6)

"Nothing profits more than self-esteem grounded on what is just and right."

—*John Milton*

Self-esteem has a wider perspective about self. Self-esteem is a mode of feeling about yourself in all aspects of life. Nothing is more important than how you feel about yourself. One can only deliver up to the fullest when he/she feels good and remains happy. When we are in happy mood, our relations with others are also very cordial. It is this reason that all the leading companies of the world try hard to make their employees happy for higher productivity, better quality, higher growth and better positive feelings. Eric Hoffer said, "Self-esteem and self-contempt have specific odors; they can be smelled."

"Reputation is your currency. Resolve to raise it to higher level."

When you feel happy, negativity does not arise in your mind. Only positivity prevails. If we say it is a world of decent, then there is conformity between your positive feelings and behavior. But, when we say it is a world of deceit, then there is non-conformity between your positive feelings and behavior.

Oh! God's best creatures! Are you enthusiastic to develop your positive self-esteem for the benefit of yourself and society at large? Come on, be a fragrance of society by developing your positive self-esteem and hence positive attitude. (See chapter 6)

"Self-esteem is a fragrance of self- respect and self- worth that can be smelled and acts as a great enhancer of positivity."

Method 15: Take a Break, Watch Movies and Enjoy Beauty that may Bring Positivity

Take a break from your busy schedule and watch movies which you like. This will change your mood. Even if you are down, watch your favorite movie which will bring happiness and freshness in you and your positivity will increase. At present, TV shows talks about all kinds of depressing news. Don't sit for a long period in front of TV. Take a break from news and read something which fascinates you. See beauty in every natural thing including your work for the feeling of positivity.

Method 16: Associate with Those Who Think Positively

"Like negativity, positivity is contagious. So find friends and family members who look on the brighter side of life and associate with them the feeling of positivity."

Even during a lovely discussion and chatting, try to discuss or chat positive aspects only. "If you wish to go for the higher ladder of success, always live in a company who are better than you. In the company of good people with big dream, you will also think in that direction. Benefit greatly from the positive attitude of others."

"It is the company which may make or break you; so choose right companion to excel."

Method 17: Look at the Big Picture in Life

Looking at the big picture in life has many dimensions. A person living in a village can't think beyond the top person of the village and its surroundings villages due to his lack of awareness. It is the travelling which gives awareness. It is always advisable to dream big and act accordingly.

"Think small, act small and become small. Think BIG, act BIG and become BIG."

In our life, many undesirable and de-motivating things happen on daily basis. Ignore these small happenings and look at a larger picture of life for positivity. Suppose you are a student. Don't limit your education. Think big and picture about acquiring highest degree from a reputed institution and landing in a top job or in a big business. All these rosy pictures will inculcate positivity in your mind. All over the world, there are many examples where people who are born in poor family, lived in remote areas but reached to the topmost ladder of success. This was made possible because they looked at the bigger picture of life.

"Don't belittle yourself. You are born as diamond to shine brilliantly in the word of success."

Method 18: Do Something Nice and be Merciful

God has sent us to perform. Do you want to feel better? Do you want to see others feel better? If yes, then the answer lies in your actions. Doing some nice works to those who are near or dear to you or to the needy persons so that they feel happy and wanted; such acts will uplift your mood. This is one of the bestway to remain happy and think positive. Be merciful and kinder and the world will reciprocate. Robert H. Schuller said, "If you treat people nicely, you will be probably treated nicely. The kinder you are to others, the more kindness you are likely to receive in life. It is the law of proportionate return." Remember, believe and act on the following philosophy: "Get absorbed in a good cause and miracles will happen. Life is an echo. You get back what you give."

"Nice deeds emit the fragrance of happiness, coolness and positivity from your soul and thereby touching and soothing every soul."

"Nice deeds are the greatest worship to God and great enhancer of positivity."

Method 19: Avoid Laying Blame

Blame game is a buzzword when something goes wrong. This is nothing but running away from the responsibility and is one of the sources of developing negativity and enmity. Don't play blame game where things go wrong. Accept the mistake and discuss with concerned persons to assure them that nothing will go wrong henceforth. Even after remaining highly careful, if something goes wrong – be the home or office, accept the responsibility. This will enhance your positive attitude.

"Blame game is an undesirable drama and negative approach to disown responsibility of a failed venture."

Method 20: Believe that Bad Days are not For Ever

Bad days are never permanent. Good days always finds place in the life of every individual. "Time is a great healer of pain and sorrow." Even if you're suffering with the grief of a lost loved one, remember that with the passage of time you will feel better. "Joy and sorrow are like the game of light and shade of life. Don't feel down for a long period over any tragedy. Console yourself, bring courage in your life and think that it was God's will. Recover from pain and sorrow as soon as possible and this is the true sign of positivity in oneself."

"Bad days are like the temporary shadow of light created by an event which you can change or absorb for better days, believing that time is a great healer."

Method 21: Keep Hope Alive, Request for Help, and Don't Quit

"In the presence of hope, faith is born. In the presence of faith, love becomes a possibility! In the presence of love, miracles happen!"

—Robert H. Sculler

You are born to win not to quit. Keep your hopes always alive. Life is full of struggle and one can only overcome obstacles when he has the capability to think how to overcome and win over obstacles. Giving up is a very easy option out of a difficult situation. "No matter how negative you're feeling; never let yourself quit pursuing something you truly want from the core of your heart." "No task is big enough which can't be accomplished." You need patience and perseverance to accomplish. You'll thank God and yourself in the long run for your decisions of not giving up and your positive attitude and courage will be stronger. "Never give up hope." "Blessed are the ones who have hope in the heart, for they shall see success."

"Success starts when you 'dare to admit you need help' under difficult circumstances. It has been observed that businesses got restored, students got graduated and relationship got healed through this humble and hopeful attitude."

"Giving up the mission which you have always dreamt of accomplishing, due to difficult situation is a cowardice act."

"Action, action and action should be the essence of your life. No pause, no stop and no quitting."

Method 22: Create Realistic Goals

"Knowledge without wisdom is a waste. One needs to be practical in life to succeed." Everybody has some limitations in ability, in potential and in the conversion of potential into meaningful result.

Of course, you're going to feel frustrated and dejected if you make your goals so unattainable that you can't reach them, no matter how hard you work. Create more realistic goals so that you can accomplish them instead of getting defeated each day. Unattainable and unrealistic goals will bring only frustration and negativity in your life. Be practical in creating your goals.

"Unrealistic goals are like demons to eat your wealth, health, happiness and peace."

Method 23: Choose Joy, Happiness and Smile

Every day is a new day. When you wake up in the morning, you have two choices: to be in good and joyful mood or to be in bad and miserable mood. Make the choice to be happy and you'll live a much more joyful life. "If you think that wealth, fame, relationships can provide you with eternal happiness, you are absolutely wrong. Richness will take more than money. Many rich people lost all hopes of life due to depression and anxiety, leading to suicide and death. Fame is also fleeting and it is very difficult and painful to cope with ebbing fame. Relationship is not permanent and even those who love you immensely will sometimes let you down. Happiness is not dependent on whether or not we have problems or whether or not we have material wealth. There are many people who remain happy even though they have many problems and are poor." True happiness lies in serving others and bringing smiles on their faces. "Therefore, joy and happiness is a mindset and the purpose of life is to remain joyful and happy under all circumstances." Follow "Italian Philosophy Poem" in life as given below (Source: 'Positive Attitude' by Robert H Schuller, Jaico Publishing)

"Count your garden by the flowers,
Never by the leaves that fall.
Count your days by golden hours,
Don't remember clouds at all.
Count your nights by stars, not shadows,
Count your life with smiles, not tears.
And with joy on every birthday,
Count your age by friends, not years."

After waking up in the morning, learn to say this to yourself, "I will work hard today, I will have fun time with my friends, I will laugh wholeheartedly with fellow friends and while returning back I will feel happy to see my work done and to realize that my good action during the day will bless me the sweetest night and peaceful sleep." This is called choosing joy and happiness and leading the best life possible. This is one of the best positive attitudes.

"The idea of smile is the greatest means of business interaction. Smiling makes you attractive and elevates your mood. Smiling relieves stress and brings positivity in life."

"Joy and happiness is the essence and purpose of life. Enjoy every moment of life and feel highly positive."

Method 24: Focus on Finding a Solution and Act as Peacemaker

Irrespective of the goals you assign yourself at any stage of life, some problems are bound to crop up in the way to realize the goal. Take your problem head on. Once you find a right solution, you'll be able to feel proactive and feel in control of your life. Further, your confidence and positivity will be enhanced. "Act as peace makers and bridge builders where there is a breach among people." "Blessed are the peace makers, for they shall be called children of God (Bible, Sermon on the Mount)."

"Finding right solution for a problem is a key to confidence building, positivity and happiness."

Method 25: Engage in Physical Activity and Meditation Daily (Refer Chapter 16)

Physical workout releases stress and refreshes your mood. It enhances positivity. Meditation brings peace to mind, reduces stress and brings positivity in life.

"Meditation is the art of living."

STEPS TAKEN BY YOURSELF

After going through this chapter, I (as a reader) will do the following to build positive attitude:

    i. _____
    ii. _____

***

Chapter 5

Practice Motivation For Yourself and Others
#THE 4TH MANTRA

MOTIVATION BRINGS NEW ZEAL TO SUCCEED

"Inspiration fires you up; motivation keeps you burning."
—*Stuart Aken*

"Motivation is the art of getting people to do what you want them to do because they want to do it."
—*Dwight D. Eisenhower*

A great business leader-cum-speaker was asked by a student from the audience in a symposium to speak to us of motivation. He said: Motivation! A zeal creator for action. A passion creator. An igniting agent for creating fire in the mind to excel. A motive force to succeed. You might have heard people saying: "He is a de-motivated person. He needs motivation. That person is a highly motivated guy. That's why he is successful." Judge yourself: Are you a motivated person? If not, get motivated, otherwise success will slip from your clutch. So, question arises: What is motivation? How should we motivate yourself and others?

WHAT IS MOTIVATION?

"Motivation is a driving force, a spark, a psychological impulse that compels or reinforces an action towards a desired goal." For example, hunger is a motivation that elicits a desire to eat and to get required food. In other words, motivation is the purpose or psychological cause of action and sustains certain goal-directed behavior.

"Motivation is the great driving force of actions to realize the desired goals."

Roots of motivation cover a widespectrum field in physiological, behavioral, cognitive and social areas. "The basic impulse of motivation is to optimize well-being, minimize physical pain, maximize pleasure, bringing out maximum hidden energy, maximize self-esteem, maximize self-confidence, maximize inner drive, maximize quality and maximize productivity." Motivation can also originate from specific physical needs such as eating, sleeping, resting, entertaining or sex. "Since motivation is an inner drive, so the inner conditions such as wishes, desires, goals activate us to move in a particular direction in behavior and accordingly, action is initiated in an emphatic manner to achieve desired needs." Broadly speaking, there are two types of main needs – **"basic and emotional."**

Once person's basic needs are met, then emotional needs occupy the place of great motivator. "Human behavior is guided by **pain or gain principle (i.e. self-interest)** in a very strong way." Every situation offers pain as well as gain. If the pain is greater than the gain, then it acts as de-motivator and deterrent to action. But, if the gain is greater than the pain, then it becomes a great motivator and action is initiated to achieve the desired goal. There are two types of gains – **tangible** and **intangible**. Tangible gains include monetary rewards, vacations, gifts, and promotion while intangible gains include appreciation, recognition, and self-worth, sense of fulfilment, responsibility, entertainment, belief and growth. Both types of gains are important in human life. "Motivation is your major motive force to excel. Accelerate it! Accelerate it! Accelerate it!"

"In doing any work, at least three things are required: ability, motivation and attitude. This trio works in tandem to realize the goal." The words of Lou Holtz elucidated the impact of these three beautifully," Ability is what you're capable of doing. Motivation determines what you do. Attitude determines how well you do it." Forced motivation doesn't work except temporarily as people want to do a good job for self-recognition.

NEED OF MOTIVATION

Since ages, human life has been very challenging. "Life is a queer mixture of drift and diffusion." Everyone wants to lead a good life which is fulfilled by physical and mental (inner) needs. To meet the requirements of good life, one has to choose a profession for living and has to be successful in that. In every profession, there is an intense competition. "Without success, there is a little gain, little pride in life; excitement and happiness, either at home or at work place remain at low levels. Life is engulfed with disappointment and quality of life gets a beating. As a result, desire to succeed takes a leading seat- a challenging role in human life." "The purpose of life is the most powerful motivator for the mankind in the world. Higher the purpose, higher is the motivation."

"Motivation forms the driving force in our lives and is the only weapon by which one will get energized with new vigor, new zeal, new passion and new resolve to work hard in order to succeed. Life is a movement and the movement needs a guide and motivation in the form of consciousness is the guide." Shiva Ji, a great warrior of Maratha region (India) was a man who believed in himself and self-motivated himself with the blessing of his guru and as a result, he won many battles and was hailed as one of the greatest warrior. Paton, chief of the US Army was a highly self-motivated person and won World War II. Zig Ziglar rightly said, "Of course, motivation is a not permanent. But then, neither is bathing; but it is something you do on regular basis." Motivation is not a one time affair. A constant motivation is needed in life surrounded by uncertainties.

Even in day to day work, many problems from family, friends, society, tragedies, offices, business, etc. appear before us. These problems appear as great obstacles and de-motivate us. To overcome these problems, we need to be motivated on daily basis like taking bath. Steve Maraboli once said, "The universe doesn't give you what you want in your mind; it gives you demand with your actions."

A question arises: what is the difference between **inspiration and motivation?** "Inspiration is a thought for motivation whereas motivation is an action of inspiration. People get motivated themselves. A motivator simply inspires people to motivate themselves. So, the mother of all motivations is inspiration." A person who doesn't aspire to excel is basically emotionally dead. Never lose your self-esteem, self-confidence otherwise, demotivation will creep in your mind.

"Motivation behaves like a fire which needs fuel all the time to keep burning, and the fuel comes from the belief of your heart and soul to excel, to succeed in your goals."

VARIOUS THEORIES AND MODELS OF MOTIVATION

Researchers from all over the world have done a lot of research on motivation and presented various theories and models. These theories may be grouped in two basic categories:

- Psychological theories and models
- Non-psychological theories and models

Out of more than nineteen theories and models placed under the first category, only three given below are prominent and these will be discussed here in brief with practical approach.

i. Intrinsic and Extrinsic theory of motivation
ii. Need theory –Maslow theory (intrinsic motivation)
iii. Incentive theory (extrinsic motivation)

Motivation can be classified into two types: **Intrinsic (internal)** motivation and **extrinsic (external)** motivation.

INTRINSIC (INTERNAL) MOTIVATION

"Intrinsic motivation is driven by an interest or enjoyment in the task itself. It exists within the heart and soul of individual acting as a strong driving force to succeed, to excel in chosen venture rather than relying on external pressure or a desire for reward. It is a self-motivation."

Intrinsic motivation is needed virtually on daily basis because of the enormous problems in life which act as a deterrent to achieve our ambitions. "Only through intrinsic motivation, we get energized, refreshed and ready to engage ourselves with full might and full vigor to achieve the desired goal." But there are many situations where intrinsic motivation doesn't serve the full purpose and external motivation is needed.

NEED THEORY- MASLOW THEORY

Abraham H. Maslow, a famous American motivation psychologist developed the hierarchy of needs, consisting of **five hierarchic classes.** It is an **intrinsic** motivation. As per Maslow proposition, people are motivated by **unsatisfied needs.** The need, listed from basic (lowest –earliest) to most complex (highest –last) are given below in hierarchal order.

- Physiology: hunger, thirst, sleep, etc.
- Safety/Security/Shelter/Health
- Belongingness/Love/Friendship
- Self-esteem/Recognition/Achievement
- Self- actualization

These five needs may be put in the form of a **pyramid,** the lowest –earliest one, and then Physiology will prove to be the foundation stone. If there are deficits on this level, every behavior will be oriented to satisfy this deficit.

As a matter of fact, if you haven't slept or eaten adequately you won't be interested in your self-esteem and self- actualization needed at fourth and fifth level respectively. Subsequently, second level comes which awakens a need for security. After securing these two levels of needs, people move to third, then fourth and finally the fifth –self-actualization, the top in hierarchy (the uppermost portion of pyramid). Need theory is an intrinsic motivation.

To satisfy all five needs, people generate intrinsic motivation to achieve goal. "Most of the people remain engaged in first three needs throughout the life and fail to reach the fourth and fifth level. One can think of a reason behind it. Their self-esteem and attitudes are so low that they don't aspire more than that and limit themselves. Moreover, even in meeting the first three, many of them suffer from frustration, anxiety and demotivation, and internal motivation doesn't work, so there is a need of external motivation."

A Great Desire clubbed with Internal Motivation Can Make You a Bright Star: Akshay Kumar, a famous Bollywood celebrity and son of a defense personnel, was a drop out from (10+2) class. He was more interested in sports and so his father sent him to Bangkok to receive training in martial arts after 11th class. He became expert in martial arts and attained a toned and flexible body. He served in a guest house in Bangkok, where he used to cook and train people in martial arts. After that, he came to India and got a service of Rs. 5000/- per month. Luckily, a gentleman noticed him and invited him for a photo shoot for an advertisement. He was paid Rs.21,000/- for this and then he thought: "It is better to do modelling to earn more in less time with recognition. "In this pursuit, he met hero (actor) Govinda who said," You look like a hero. Why don't you become a hero (actor)?" This advice gave a spark in him and aroused a desire of becoming an actor that motivated him to work hard.

It is due to his hard work that today, he is one of the highest paid actors in the film fraternity.

He was having at least first three level of desires fulfilled, the desire to achieve the fourth level, the spark in his internal motivation changed everything. Now he has also achieved top fifth level being the leading star.

The **moral** of the story is: "A great desire to become something special motivates one internally in a strong way for working hard with great zeal in order to achieve the desired goal."

Motivated by Intense Desire, the Tribal Girls Football Team Won Bronze Medal: The eighteen tribal girl footballers from the outskirts of Ranchi, Jharkhand (India), represented India in under-14football championship and won the Bronze medal in Gasteiz Cup, 2013 in Spain beating thirty-four other International football teams. The team had no proper facility to play football, no grounds and not even a coach. All are of them were from poor families who did household and agriculture works to run their houses.

How did they achieve this despite of the many odds against them? They already had the first three needs at the minimum level as per tribal life of India. But, they were eager to achieve the fourth need (self-esteem/recognition/achievement). The irintrinsic motivations were so strong to achieve something that it propelled them to work hard ignoring all hardships and obstacles of the first three needs.

High Degree of Internal Motivation Can Make You the Best Player: Indian women team won bronze Medal in 7th FIH Junior Hockey world cup held in Germany in 2013. Rani Rampal was adjudged the player of the tournament. She comes from a poor family. Rani lives in a small house in Shahabad town near Kurukshetra (Haryana, India). While Rani's father is cart puller, her elder brother is a carpenter. She used to travel two kilometers distance from her house to the Academy on foot. Later on, she purchased a bicycle. In the beginning, she was unable to purchase hockey stick and kits which were given to her by her coach.

But what helped her to achieve this feat? It was nothing but intense desire to achieve the status of a best player. Her desire created a high level of internal motivation and she worked hard ignoring all her obstacles coming in her way due to poverty. She was just meeting the minimum first three needs of a poor family of Indian condition, but her intense desire for fourth need (self-esteem,/achievement/recognition) did a wonder through high degree of internal motivation.

The **moral** of the above stories is: "A high degree of internal motivation can propel and passionate you at colossal level to achieve any unparalleled feat at the world level competition ignoring all hardships of primary level of your life."

Ponder over the following cases of achievers:

a. **Richest People:** Out of the world's **100 richest people**, today only twenty-seven are heirs and seventy-three are self-made. Of the seventy-three self-made, eighteen have no college degree and thirty-six are the children of poor parents. Out of children of poor parents numbering thirty-six, only poor conditions of nine are given (Source: Bloomberg.com/billionaires, Times of India).

- Larry Ellison was an orphan.
- Li Ka-shing was a welder.
- Leonardo Del Vecchio was an orphan.
- Amancio OrtegaGaona was a cab driver.
- John Fredriksen was an orphan.
- Sheldon Adelson was a farmer.
- Ingvar Kamprad was a rail road worker.
- François Pinault was a miller.

What some of them did or still do are: "Took right decision in investing during hard times, tried different business before the one that clicked, saw trends early, micromanage their companies, make one life-changing deal, ate with employees and bought ruined companies and nurtured them like babies."

What was common among them: "It was the intense desire to improve their poor condition and to achieve something in life. High degree of internal motivation propelled them to select business as their profession, worked hard on it, took right decision at right time, used the irskills and fulfilled their dreams."

Lessons learned from above achievers are: "Everyone is a potential billionaire. It is the unfolding of one's own potential by using internal motivation, working hard, selecting business as profession, taking right decision, using positive attitude and soft skills that makes one a billionaire and history maker."

Opportunity is not a regular visitor to you. It comes to you in the form of troubles, problems and crisis while you are engaged in your venture. You have to grab it. This has been beautifully expressed by the words of John B. Gough: "If you want to succeed in the world, you must make your opportunities as you go on. The man who waits for some seventh wave to toss him on dry land will find that seventh wave is a long time a coming."

b. **Competitive Examinations and Admission in India:** Among the Indian Education System, getting admission in Indian Institute of Technology (IITs), Indian Institute of Management (IIMs), All India Institute of Medical Science (AIIMSs), and Indian Law Universities (ILUs) is very tough. It is a dream of every student to get admission in these highly professional universities. Students join coaching classes, foundation and main course from 9th class for IITs, AIIMSs, ILUs, examinations. For entering into IIMs, students start preparing from 2nd year of their under-graduate course. Only those students who have potential, intense desire to compete, high degree of internal motivation propelling for doing hard work are able to crack these examinations.

c. **Competitive Examinations for Jobs in India:** In India, for getting top jobs in government sectors, students have great craze to crack Indian Civil Service Examinations (IAS, IPS, IRS, IFS, etc.) and Indian Engineering Service Examination (IES). Top students appear for these examinations. Students having potential with intense desire, and internal motivation as strong as steel, crack these examinations.

d. **Competitive Examination for Admission in USA:** In USA, students get admitted in higher education system through SAT. This is also one of the toughest tests as students from all over the world participate to get a seat. Only highly internally motivated students having potential crack this examination. Similarly, in other countries also, such competitive examinations are held and only those students compete and win who are highly internally motivated.

The **message** from above examples is: "A great dream, an intense desire, a high degree of internal motivation, the required potential, a strong resolve, hard work and a judicious planning can enable one to crack any competitive examination."

HOW WILL YOU MOTIVATE YOURSELF?

We have gone through need of motivation and theories describing causes of internal motivation. We have some degree of internal motivation on account of our needs and our desires but due to various obstacles and difficulties in the way, internal motivation loses its intensity. Hence, there is a need to intensify and energize our internal motivation.

How will you motivate yourself? The answer lies in the **auto-suggestions**. It is the only tool to intensify and energize our internal motivation. Auto-suggestions have been constantly used by athletes and players to motivate themselves. Tell yourself: "Do it now. I will succeed. I am fearless. I will win. I should not lose heart. I will work hard. I will be patient. This problem will go away. I am not inferior to anybody. I have competence and confidence. I am courageous, I will achieve good grade, and I will compete in competitive examination and get selected." Repeat all these words several times in a day when any fear, any doubt and obstacle comes in your way to success.

"It is to be noted that emotions are controlled through the combination of reasons and actions. When fears are unwarranted or harmful, they can and should be neutralized through auto-suggestions." "Auto- suggestions are your great tools to motivate yourself."

The other method is to acquire the habit of those **thirteen virtues** in the form of 'self-motivators' suggested by Benjamin Franklin in his book "Autobiography of Benjamin Franklin."

They are:(i) Temperance, (ii) Silence, (iii) Order, (iv)Resolution, (v) Frugality, (vi) Industry (vii) Sincerity, (viii) Justice, (ix) Moderation, (x) Cleanliness, (xi) Tranquility, (xii) Chastity and (xiii) Humility.

"Our internal motivation is our driver, passion, attitude and purpose of life." It has to be always energized, intensified and made meaningful using auto-suggestions through control of emotions and acquiring those thirteen virtues called self-motivators.

EXTRINSIC (EXTERNAL) MOTIVATION

Extrinsic motivation comes from the outside of the individual. It refers to the performance of an activity by a person in order to attain an outcome, whether or not that person engaged in that activity is also intrinsically motivated. Common extrinsic motivation includes **incentives or rewards** (for example, money or grades) for showing the desired behavior at work place or at home, and the **threat or fear** of punishment following misbehavior or non-performance leading to issuing pink slip at work place or **scolding of children** by parents at home. Another form of extrinsic motivation includes **competition** because it encourages the competitors to win and to beat others, though; one also enjoys the intrinsic reward of the activity. Further, a **cheering crowd and the desire to win a trophy** in games and sports also come under extrinsic motivation. When teachers/experts motivate students by motivational talk for better performance, it is an extrinsic motivation. When experts/bosses motivate employees by motivational talk, it is an extrinsic motivation. "Learn to motivate others using beautiful words, and better techniques of incentives."

INCENTIVE MOTIVATION THEORY

Incentive motivation theory is an **extrinsic motivation**as incentive is given by other person. It is based on the concept of giving **reward, either tangible or intangible** to a person after the occurrence of a good action (or behavior) with the intention of causing the behavior to occur again. This is done to associate positive meaning to the behavior. Field data obtained from the research show that, if the person receives the reward immediately, the effect is greater and decreases as delay lengthens. "Repetitive action-reward combination can cause the action to become a habit. If it is stopped, demonization starts."

The incentive motivation is very common at work places, schools, colleges and universities and even at home by parents to children. Further, incentive motivation is also given to animals to take work from them or to extract milk from cows and buffalos. Chinese companies started to send all employees in mass on pleasure trip to foreign countries in order to get energized, to get motivated.

Fear Motivated a Salesman to Meet the Target: Mohan was a salesman in a big company which sold consumer goods. He was given a target for every month. In the month of January, he met the target, but in February, he could meet just half the target. He got a notice from his boss that, either meet the target or get pink slip. Out of fear of losing job, Mohan took the tips from seniors, worked hard and he crossed the target in the month of March.

The **moral** of the story is: "Out of fear of losing job, people get motivated and work hard to meet the desired goal." But, it is a point to keep in mind that fear motivation is a poor technique of motivation.

Reward Motivated a Dealer to Meet the Goal: Vikas was a wholesale dealer of a famous paint company. The company announced a program that those dealers, whose sale would cross a certain number in a year, would get a ten days free tour to Europe with spouse. With this offer, Vikas got very motivated, worked hard, used all his strategies and crossed the number in a year. The company sent him to Europe and he was highly satisfied and happy for being rewarded for his work.

The **moral** of the story is: "Reward creates strong external motivation to meet the cherished goal."

Loyalty Benefits cum Performance Incentives to Employees Improve Productivity: The chairperson Savji Dholakia of Hari Krishna Exports Pvt Ltd of Gujrat (India) dealing with diamonds, started a loyalty program in 2011 and offered his 1200 employees, worth Rs.500 million in the form of cars, flat and jewelry in 2014 on the eve of Diwali Festival. The performance incentive of each employee was Rs.3.6 lakh (0.36 million). 500 employees opted for cars, 570 jewelry and 207 chose to become homeowners. Savji Dholakia got education just up to 4rth standard. He came to Surat in the search of a job without any money in his pocket in late 1970. He started a very small company of diamond by borrowing money from his uncle. At present, its net worth is Rs.6,000 crore (USD 01 billion), Dholakia doesn't treat his employees as workers but as shareholders. What a positive thinking, big heart, empathy, compassion, motivation, success, and leadership quality!

The **theme** of this story is: "Treatment of employees as shareholders, giving unparalleled performance incentive to employees, bringing the company at the top level and infusing an unimaginable rise in motivation among employees by a chairperson who rose from the stage of a very less educated poor man to a bright star reflects his true leadership quality."

During my service period as a faculty and head of three engineering institutions, I have come across at least two or three students every year who were de-motivated due to poor score in one semester or by other reasons. I used to motivate them, guide them for a whole year and all of them passed finally with flying colors with good pay package in campus placement. "Sometimes, one word of motivation leaves a magical effect on others beyond imagination."

SOME APPLICATIONS OF MOTIVATION

We have discussed the need of internal or external or both motivations at every stage and in every walk of our life irrespective of the profession. However, some practical applications of motivation may give a broader picture on it including the understanding of the various reasons of people lacking self-motivation.

a. **Employees Motivation:** All over the world, workers in any organization need something to keep them working. "Motivation is a powerful tool in the work environment that can lead to employees working at their most efficient level of production." In most cases, if the salary and normal promotion are given at reasonable time then, it is sufficient to keep them working for an organization but it should also be kept in mind that the individual is deserving of that promotion. It is necessary to motivate employees to work hard for a company or organization as without internal motivation, employee's quality of work and their productivity, decreases.

For motivating an audience, one can use **general** motivational strategies or **specific** motivational appeals with very exciting and energizing words. General motivational strategies encompass **soft sell** versus **hard sell** including personality type. **Soft sell** strategies, as the name implies include logical appeals, emotional appeals, advice and praise, while **hard sell** strategies encompass barter, outnumbering, pressure and rank. **Specific** motivational appeals include provable facts, feelings, rights and wrongs, audience rewards and audience threats suitable for audience who are being motivated. While motivating employees, the following human behavior concepts should be applied:

    i. **Involvement:** Involve employees in all parts of the process including ideas and suggestions. Apply team work, not hierarchy. The chairman of Reebok International (Paul Fireman) followed the concept of involvement of employees to overtake market share from Nike.

    ii. **Treatment:** Treat every person as an individual human being. Respect them and acknowledge their importance. Treat them as very important part of organization. All top MNCs treat people with dignity to motivate work force.

    iii. **Encouragement:** Encourage superior work, recognize it and reward it to get it repeated. People can't be forced to do an extraordinary job. They can only do it when they want.

In the Japanese Kaizen system for continuous improvement, the whole work force is driven by ideas and suggestions. American Airlines follow this. Boardroom Reports Company of USA follows the consensus management approach. Apple Computers follows non-hierarchical approach or the power of persuasion. Dwight Eisenhower practiced the power of persuasion for taming the fractious congress during his presidency of USA.

Every person wants some recognition. With this in mind, motivation through **recognition** programs has been designed to act as **motivators**. There are two types of recognition programs- **Conventional and Strategic.** Employee's recognition (**conventional**) encompasses about gifts and points to affect motivation of employees. A highly motivated employee may adopt ownership of an organization.

'**Strategic employee recognition**' is supposed as the most important program not only to improve employee motivation and retention but, also to positively influence work culture and financial situation leading to high productivity and profit. "**Innovation** is the key objective under the strategic recognition program for higher motivation, innovative products and processing better quality, higher productivity and profit." Innovation is not an easy job. It can't be achieved by simply ordering the employees. A better management of an organization having conducive environment and empowerment of employees will result in innovation by them over due course. On the basis of innovation, employees may be recognized honestly, which will motivate them. Many leading organizations use strategic recognition program for motivation.

iv. **Motivation in Education Field:** Motivation plays a crucial role in the field of education as learning is different than other works. General theory of motivation doesn't work in education field. The following methods may be adopted:
   i. Apply high internal locus of control and academic achievement by giving fraeedom to choose courses, methods and mode of study, choice in games and sports, choice in placement.
   ii. Situated motivation technique may be used by teachers and experts during classes by praising the students at proper time.
   iii. Fresher students in higher education system should be motivated with highly motivating words covering every aspect of education, life and placement during orientation program.
   iv. Try to avoid creating anxiety by giving bad grades, but do course correction for poor performance. Increase their self-esteem by improving their fundamentals of courses or put students on slow pace. It doesn't mean to lower down the standard of education but to improve it.
   v. Involve students in physical activity. "Exercise relieves stress, increases focus, concentration and motivationwhich results in better academic performance."
   vi. Healthy sleeping habit must be inculcated among students. The right amount of sleep will enable individuals to keep their motivation high to secure good grade in education.

v. **Motivation in Games**: Motivational models are the key to game design because, without motivation a player will not be interested in progressing further within a game. It is the job of coach and captain to motivate players. Jon Radoff has proposed a four quadrant model of game play motivation which includes: "cooperation, competition, immersion and achievement (CCIA)." Game-based motivation may be applied even in business houses.

ALERTNESS OF LEADERSHIP ON THE ON-SET OF DEMOTIVATION

"Emotional engagement of employees with the organization is the core element for the branding of an organization. On average, it is just thirteen percent. Every organization should try to improve this eighty-seven percent emotionally-disengaged employees through various measures." Once a person joins any organization, he/she passes through various stages of motivation and demotivation due to the passage of time, the internal and external forces. There are **six stages** of motivation and demotivation as given below:

1. Joining with high motivation to prove their worth.
2. Motivation becomes ineffective due to improper guidance.
3. Motivation regains effectiveness after training and refresher course.
4. Motivation starts turning into demotivation with the passage of time: This results in the decline of motivation level and the employee starts to find themselves surrounded by negative people, disturbing their thinking power. This is the **on-set of demotivation stage.** Leadership involving senior managers should be on high **alert** at this stage but only few organizations are able to tackle this issue."
5. Demotivation becomes effective: When employee learns fully the tricks of trade and gets totally accustomed with the group of de-motivated people, his/her demotivation becomes highly effective. They do just minimum work to avoid getting pink slip. "This is the worst situation for an organization when the percentage of such people is more than five percent. The final result is, "productivity starts decreasing." There is a need to correct these people and to bring them in **third stage** by the leadership of senior management and by using all the techniques of motivation and revising policies and processes."
6. Demotivation becomes ineffective: "When employee is not corrected at **stage four and five**, he becomes a rogue element and the employer has no choice but to issue a pink slip." In a well-managed and professional organization, very few employees reach fifth and sixth stage but in non-professional organizations, it is common and firing of employees' leads to strike and closure. In poorly managed government companies, fourth, fifth and sixth stages are common and since firing is not possible, company suffers huge loss, leading to its closure in the long run.

FACTORS RESPONSIBLE FOR DEMOTIVATION

Every person who joins an organization is highly motivated to prove his or her selection, right for the job and has the enthusiasm to shape the organization to a glorious path of success. But with the passage of time, some of them become de-motivated. It is necessary to know: What are the factors that lead to the stage of demotivation? The possible factors are listed below:

- Lack of direction given to employees.
- Non-conducive environment at work place.
- Work place politics involving many dimensions.
- Lack of motivational workshop and training.
- Incapable top boss; Public humiliation by boss.
- Non-transparent system.
- Rewarding non-performers.
- Insufficient promotion stages for a service span of thirty-five years.
- Lack of measurable objectives in the system.
- Faulty rewarding/promotion.
- Lack of incentives given to employees.
- Untimely salary payment.
- Unfair criticism of colleagues/boss/company.
- Hypocrisy of higher authority; frequent transfer.
- Poor standard of living and interaction.
- Responsibility without authority.
- Fear of failure and fear of unknown.
- Negative self-talk.
- Negative attitude and low self-esteem.
- Not achieving desired goal.
- Non-supporting family and friends.
- Poor working condition at work place.
- Irregular in completing target, either at work place or home due to procrastination.

"Happiness leads to motivation; however, it is a function of attitude of a person. Motivation is a mindset. It is a subject of commitment. In many cases, if de-motivating factors of a person get removed, he becomes motivated. There are certain people who remain motivated throughout life irrespective of all poor conditions and odds against them. Such people are great." "But some persons are such (though number is very less) who can't be motivated." Demotivation derails a dignified life. Get motivated! Get motivated! Get motivated!"

HOW TO MOTIVATE OTHERS?

"Human life survives on the interaction with others." It is imperative to know how to motivate others in a proper direction, sensing the mood of the person and in the most effective manner. "It is a fact that throughout life you play dual roles in which you motivate others and they motivate you. You take each role of: parent and child, teacher and pupil, salesman and buyer, master and servant in the process of motivation."

"The greatest motivating factors are positive attitude and belief." Positive attitude will take care of situations-good or bad and belief in yourself and others make the motivation either to self or to others more effective. "Once you accept responsibility and act, everything improves. You observe a sudden increase in the quality and productivity of the work, teamwork or relationship as nobody wants to fail."

Following are some steps through which we can motivate others:

- Give encouragement. We may say: "We know that you are going to succeed in this job, so we have committed ourselves and others to your success. We are here, waiting for your success. Do better goal-setting and planning. We believe in you."
- Give respect to improve theirself-esteem and confidence.
- Put them on training to develop skills.
- Make theirwork interesting.
- Put before them achallenge to improve themselves.
- Help them during initiation of work and give them theconfidence that they can now carry out and weare firmly standing with them at all stages.
- Use incentive theory of motivation to motivate.
- Provide opportunityfor growth in a transparent manner.
- Have the faith that they will change and get motivated.
- Give them the much neededconfidence.
- By constantly supporting them.
- By giving examples and reporting stories based on real incidents in anenthusiastic tone. Inspiring them to read motivational books.
- By promoting self –awareness by various methods to curb the destructive habit.

The truth of the world is, "Nobody can be changed by external motivation unless and until one wants to change himself by using his own internal motivation inspired by external motivation. External motivation acts as catalyst to activate internal motivation to do the job."

"Cozy life doesn't bring success. It is based on the law of nature. Success and greatness will only kiss you when you work relentlessly." This is beautifully elucidated by MaulanaWahiduddin Khan, when he said, "The laws of nature are greater than everything else. They are eternal: they cannot be changed. The law of nature in this regard says that it is not ease but effort, not facility but difficulty that makes achievers out of ordinary people. So, the future is full of hope and opportunity!"

A Great Motivator can Motivate a De-motivated Person to a Colossal Level to Accomplish a Greater Task

This story is taken from the great epic ever written and the holy book of Hinduism, Mahabharata. On the first day of battle, Arjun, a great archer became de-motivated by seeing his own kith and kin facing against each other and hell bent on killing each other. Mahabharata battle is supposed to be a righteous act. Lord Krishna motivated Arjuna, gave him wisdom, illustrated the righteous path, taught yoga and dharma and ultimately Arjuna decided to fight and won the battle. Each and every word of Lord Krishna said on the battlefield became, what now is regarded as the holy text of Hindu religion, Shrimad Bhagavad Gita written by Veda Vyas in Sanskrit and running eighteen chapters for the battle lasted for eighteen days.

The **theme** of this story is: "A great motivator citing righteous path, righteous actions, dharma and wisdom can motivate a de-motivated person to a colossal level to accomplish heroic and unparalleled acts of greatness."

Oh!Men and women! Are you de-motivated? Are you feeling low on any issue? Are you frustrated due to failure? There is no need to worry. You have the greatest tool of motivation. Are you using your internal motivation to excel? If it is not working, go for external motivation by a great motivator.

STEPS TAKEN BY YOURSELF

After going through this chapter, I (as a reader) will do the following to practice motivation for myself and others:

i. _____
ii. _____
iii. _____

***

Chapter 6

Develop Self – Esteem and Self – Confidence (2 Ss)

#THE 5TH MANTRA

HIGH SELF – ESTEEM MAKES YOU A STAR

"Never be bullied into silence. Never allow yourself to be made a victim. Accept no one's definition of your life, but define yourself."

—Harvey Fierstein

"To establish true self-esteem we must concentrate on our successes and forget about the failures and the negatives in our lives."

—Denis Waitley

A famous basketball player-cum-speaker was asked by a girl from the audience in a large scale symposium to speak to us of self-esteem and self-confidence. He replied in sequence: Self-esteem! A hidden treasure. A hidden pride. An obscured shining star. A great internal driver to excel. A booster of self-confidence. A booster of passion to excel. Hey, men and women! Are you a victim of low self-esteem? Why is it so? You are born to shine like stars. "Show your self-esteem in your decisions and actions and sail in the ocean of success like shining stars."

"Self-esteem comes from you what you think of you, not what other people think of you." Self-esteem could be high or low. High self-esteem is the road to success while low self-esteem will lead you to failure." Self-esteem creates a spark in your sleeping energy to achieve great success." "To have high self- esteem, you have to perceive yourself as a worthwhile shining star. All human beings are born as raw diamonds. How you polish yourself is up to you. High self-esteem gives internal drive to excel, to prosper, to succeed." "Self-esteem is your USP. Raise it! Raise it! Raise it!" Earl Nightingale said in one of her addresses to the audience, "We become what we think about."

"Self-esteem forms your reputation. Raise it to a higher level."
"Don't crush your inner desires. You were born to think high and achieve greatness."

Rise in Self-esteem Turned a Lean-Thin Boy into a Great Footballer

There is a craze in Kolkata for football (soccer). A weak, poor boy from the suburbs of Kolkata used to go to the field to play football but other children avoided taking him in their teams for his poor play. These were the same guys who used to make fun of him. After so many humiliations, his self- esteem took a leading role in his life and he decided to be a great player of football. He started exercising, running, dribbling and playing alone with football for hours together. Seeing his growing capability in every respect, the same boys started to request him to play for their teams. Later on, he was selected for the school team and in the following year, he was adjudged as the captain of the team. With his sole effort, his team won the gold medal in the state football championship. Due to his excellent performance, a leading professional team of Kolkata selected him in their team and within two years of play, he was selected as the captain of his team. Due to his excellent performance, the team remained the winner of National Football Championship for nearly ten years. He earned a lot of name, fame and money.

From this story, we get the **messages** that,

- "Once high self-esteem enters in your mindset, no physical weakness, no adversities are great enough that can't be beaten."
- "Recognize the bright star in your inner-self."

Poor Man Turned into a Great Businessman Through the Rise of Self-esteem

There was a very poor man who used to earn his livelihood as a daily wage worker. On any day, if he did not get work, he used to beg near the road crossing where cars used to stop on the red light. A businessman cum-great motivator was passingby in his car and suddenly, one tire of his car got punctured. He parked his car on one side and started to change the punctured tire. Immediately, the beggar came and started to beg. Seeing the beggar the business man told him, "Why do you beg? You can be a great businessman like me. Don't lower down your dignity. God has sent you in the world not to beg but to contribute and shine. If you help me in the changing this tire, I will give you five dollars." The beggar agreed to help and the businessman gave him five dollars and proceeded on his journey.

After the departure of the businessman from the scene, the self-esteem of the poor man got ignited and he started to follow his words. He worked hard and earned some money and then started selling some items door to door. Later on, he started a business which flourished greatly. Five years later, he attended a motivational address in a nearby city where that very businessman was invited as the chief speaker. After the address, the poor man went to the speaker and said, "Perhaps you don't recognize me but I recognize you." "Your words completely changed my life". He thanked the speaker for changing his life by igniting his mind about the value of dignity and high self-esteem.

The **morals** of this story are:

- "By recognizing the value of dignity and high self-esteem in real spirit, even a beggar can change his/her future and fortune."
- "It is the self-esteem which gives a high degree of internal drive to excel, to succeed, to prosper and to win."

Anybody can produce extraordinary result provided one believes in oneself. This has been well expressed in Bible, 9-23(Mark) "If you can believe all the things possible." Your mindset and your thought process plays a key role in achieving success. Ralph Waldo Emerson beautifully described this when he said, "A man is what he thinks about all day long." Human success is a mind game. Nobody in the world can stop you from achieving your dream if you have already decided to achieve it.

FACTORS THAT AFFECT SELF-ESTEEM

The following are the factors that affect self-esteem of a person:

i. **Boundaries of Vision**: Higher the boundary of vision, higher will be the self-esteem. The person who has all the time remained in villages, having seen only huts and simple houses and never travelled anywhere, what degree of self-esteem will he have? The adage: "A frog of well can't think of vastness of a sea" is true for self-esteem also. A tree on a brick wall can't grow big. A live watermelon kept in a small jar can't grow beyond the inner boundary of jar. The same is true with human self-esteem. The boundary of vision of Tata, Birla, Ambani, Narayana Murthy, Steve Jobs, Larry Page, Warren Buffett, Ford and Bill Gates were very big and so they built a great empire of industries/organizations. They belong to the category of the men of very high self-esteem.

The **message** is: "Self-esteem increases exponentially with the boundary of the vision."

ii. **Masked Laden vs. Openness**: Some people try to show false importance by pretending to be very busy. Some people speak too much lies to show off their past achievements, family status, contact with important people and so on. Such people adore mask to hide their poor self-esteem and low character. Whereas, there are some good and highself-esteemed people who are upright and are always ready to help the needy ones.

iii. **Auto-suggestions:** The quality of auto-suggestions plays an important role on self-esteem. If your auto-suggestions are positive and words like: "I will win; I am very good in games and studies; I am enthusiastic; I will overcome all obstacles; I will complete the work ahead of time;" obviously, it will create high self-esteem in you. But, if your auto-suggestions are negative, such as: "I can't win; I am weak in Math; I have poor memory; I can't compete;" are obviously going to put the person down in all his endeavors with low self-esteem.

The **message** is: "Self-esteem moves with quality of auto-suggestions."

iv. **Environment (Home and School)**: Environment at home and school plays an important part on the development of self-esteem of children. It depends upon the roots of family tree. If the roots are strong in culture, courteous in its manners, polite from its behavior and positive from its attitude, the children will imbibe good behavior and high self-esteem. If the family roots are weak where quarrels, fights, abuses are regular happenings in the family, it's quite obvious the members of the family would have low character and self-esteem. Similar is the effect of school environment on students.

The **message** is: "Positive environment promotes high self-esteem while negative environment promotes low self-esteem."

v. **Upbringing**: The type of upbringing of the children during primitive age affects on the formation of self-esteem. Even illiterate parents know that good values should be given to children. Those parents who possess high self-esteem, they try to inculcate the high self-esteem, confidence, courage and courtesy in their children. Parents of low self-esteem breeds low self-confidence due to their habits.

There are many dimensions in child upbringing such as:

- Children psychology, Manners, Behavior, Courtesy, Ethics, Values, Character, Career orientation, Sports, Music, Games, Culture, Mentors, Courage, Confidence, Motivation Individuality.

The parents during upbringing of children should give emphasis on above also. For all these, mentoring is needed and the best mentors to children are the parents themselves.

The **message** is: "Quality upbringing matters a lot and determines the type of man the child will become in his later years."

vi. **Education:** To inculcate good values, children should be educated on this line by teachers and parents. The impact of education in majority of cases on the formation of high self-esteem is huge. It has been observed that children taught on values, honesty, integrity, compassion, self-esteem and discipline imbibe good characters that last long.

"Educating children on values and high self-esteem by teachers and parents through their conduct is great way to contribute in nation building"

vii. **Comparison**: Human psychology towards comparison is highly venerable. There are three benchmarks – superior, comparable and inferior. If you say any person that he is superior to another capable person, he will feel motivated. If you say you are comparable, then he gets neither motivation nor demotivation. But, if you say any person that he is inferior to a capable person, he gets de-motivated and his self-esteem will go down. So, if you wish to compare, you should only compare for motivation, whatever the form may be.

"In fact, participation in any event is winning. Winners are declared only through participation. So, encouragement should be given on participation and not on comparison."

The **message** is: "Comparison, if taken as a benchmark of performance, then it is a de-motivating factor that will lower down the self-esteem."

viii. **Success or Failure**: Human psychology towards success or failure runs linearly. If you get success, you become highly motivated and your self-esteem becomes high. But if you fail, you become de-motivated and your self-esteem goes down. The adage here is quite simple, "Success breeds success and failure breeds failure" and it is true for almost all the cases. Even in sports and games, the win in a single match becomes the anchor and confidence to win subsequent matches and thus a winning start gives them the que over other teams. But, if a team gets defeat in one match, its morale and self-esteem go down if capability, confidence, strategy and morale of players are not improved considerably. "Success accelerates self-esteem and failure decelerates it." The coaches know the effect of defeat on the morale and self-esteem of players and accordingly they try to motivate and change strategies for winning.

When you fail, you have two choices before you: either internalize or externalize your failure. If you internalize, it means you are blaming yourself for your failure and lowering your self-esteem. If you externalize it to reject the defeat to win the next time, your self-esteem will remain stable and you will bounce back with more vigor to succeed.

"Rejecting failures improve your self-esteem."

One has to distinguish between failing and failure. Failing is not failure. Failure is quitting. Till you are not quitting, you have a full chance to succeed. "Hope is the bedrock of success."

The **message** is: "Success and failure just the two sides of a coin as motivational and de-motivational agents and that coin is always in your hands."

Remember the following expression of Benjamin Franklin which motivates us to raise our self-esteem on the account of failing, "I did not fail the test; I just found 100 ways to do it wrong." "Winners have unique characteristics. They are not afraid of losing like losers. They consider failure is a part of process of success. People who avoid failure also avoid success."

ix. **Expectations**: Expectations from child and from employees may act as a motivating or de-motivating factor, the way it is handled and reacted. Suppose a child scores four A's and one B grades in a test, there may be two types of reactions from parents. One parent may say congratulations for excellent result and the child might get motivation and high self-esteem out of it, resulting in good grades in subsequent tests. But if the parents neglect the good scores obtained and blame the student for one bad grade, then the child gets de-motivated and his self-esteem will go down resulting in bad grades in many subjects.

Similar is the story of expectations from employees by boss. If at any stage, the employees get scolding for one poor performance while he/she was excellent previously, it will de-motivate the employee and his/her self-esteem will go down.

The **message** here is also very simple, "Always appreciate children or employees even for one good performance to motivate and to raise their self-esteem."

> "People possess powerful potentials. Create passion in them for high self-esteem through motivation to excel and shine."

x. **Discipline:** (Refer Chapter 1 & 3)

> "If there is no discipline, there is anarchy.
> Good citizenship demands attention to responsibilities as well as rights."
> —*Joe Clark*

Discipline plays an important role in the formation of self-esteem. Discipline is a direction towards righteous path and loving firmness to mold yourself in a right way. It harnesses and focuses energy for great performance. "Your success swims or sinks in proportion to the degree of your discipline."

"If you are disciplined, you will work hard for the longer period and your performance will be better. It will increase your self-esteem. An undisciplined person doesn't work hard for a longer period, creates problems wherever he works ultimately leading to poor performance and low self-esteem."

> "Give wings to your self-esteem and you will fly on the winning curve."

xi. **Labelling by Sarcastic/Heroic Names:** Labelling any person by sarcastic name gives a damaging impression on the psyche of person. If you call any child stupid, fatty, dummy, ass, and dog and other cheap words will ultimately lead hasten his mentality to the lower end and he might become that.

In India, the caste system has created havoc on the psychology and self-esteem of those who are being called regarded as inferior and downtrodden due to their caste and creed. In USA and western countries, racial discrimination based on colors was present in the past (still present to some extent) and that affected the self-esteem of blacks. Now, they have equal rights and they are picking up. Being a black, Barack Obama has been the President of USA for two terms. Many Olympics gold medalists in athletic meets are blacks who not only win medals but set records and sweep the Olympic with flying colors. Sledging in sports in quite common these days and this helps in bringing down the morale of the opposite team. But if the person is designated with funny and heroic names, it rejuvenates energy and helps the person gain high self-esteem.

The **message** is: "Labelling any person by sarcastic name lowers one's morale, confidence and self-esteem unless one bounces back with new vigor."

xii. **Political System:** If the political environment is not conducive to growth, transparency and honesty, the morale and self-esteem of people go down. That is why, the people from good (honest) political environment having emphasis on transparent and honest systems lead to prosperity compared to political environment which are poor and filled with corrupts and hatred towards each other and ultimately leading to poverty and demotivation of the countrymen.

The **message** is: "Poor political environment promotes low self-esteem and gloom while good political environment promotes high self-esteem and self-confidence in life."

xiii. **Geographical locations**: If geographical locations are harsh and resources are less, there is a less chance of prosperity and growth. This situation dampens the morale and self-esteem of people. This does not always mean that these people can't achieve anything. Some people come out as huge personalities from harsh geographical locations. In prosperous nations, people in general, have high self-esteem.

The **message** is: "Poverty promotes low self-esteem and gloom while prosperity promotes high self-esteem and glamour in life."

xiv. **Tragedy**: Untimely death of kith and kin promotes gloom, sad emotion and low self-esteem for a longer period. Some people totally breakdown while some become much stronger after sometimes the incident. This doesn't really mean those people are emotionless but that they are too strong to give up easily. Time is a great healer. Internal and external motivations are needed.

The **message** is "Tragedy in life lowers down self-esteem for a longer period, but one should bounce back to regain high self-esteem to contribute in self-development and nation building."

xv. **Rare Individuality**: The psychology and attitude of some persons are such on which the effects of external and internal parameters promoting low and high self-esteem don't really matter. Either they remain with high self-esteem or with low self-esteem and external parameters play no role.

The **message** is: "Self-esteem of rare individual person doesn't get affected by any internal and external factors."

xvi. **Better Dress Sense and Body language-A Non-Verbal Communication**: A better dress sense promotes self-esteem. Clothes and body language absolutely reveal your power of self-esteem. A study on 'Silent Message' has demonstrated that about 55% of message delivery is based on visual- how we look and behave. Prof. Albert Mehrablan has given a rule of 7%, 38%, 55% for non-verbal communication representing their relative impact of words, tone of voice, and body language respectively while speaking. Further, a study by Harvard University says that the decision **not to hire** any candidate happens in the first fifteen seconds. "Better dress sense and your body language improve your self-esteem to a very high level."

THE EIGHTEEN METHODS TO BUILD A HIGH SELF-ESTEEM

The following eighteen methods may be used to build a high self-esteem:

Method 1: Just Get "First Success"

Many people have the potential but they are not career oriented and as a result they don't work hard and always take causal approach towards things. Consequently, they never get success. If by chance, either through external or internal motivation, they put some concrete efforts and get "first success", then after that, they don't look back. On getting the first success, their self-esteem gets increased, and they now know the taste of success. There are many such students, such employees, such players and such businessmen who completely changed their fortunes after getting first success.

The **message** is: "First success'acts as a motivating agent and brings complete change in the lives of many persons and they begin to observe a sudden rise in their self-esteem."

Method 2: Convert Adversity into Achievement

"History is full of golden wonders by many people who have changed their adversities into achievements. Disappointment due to adversity never touched them due to their very high self-esteem and willpower. They are beacon of hope, guiding star, great icon for the hope of mankind who can change adversity into a great achievement."

Give a thought on the high self-esteem of the following persons whose accomplishments were great despite of the fact that they had severe adversities in their lives:

- Arunima Sinha, a resident of Ambedkar Nagar (UP, India) and one leg amputee scaled the Mount Everest in 2013.
- Milton being blind wrote greatest poetry.
- Franklin D. Roosevelt working from wheel chair became four times president of US and proved to be the greatest world leader.
- Richard Branson suffering from dyslexia became a great businessman owning many big companies.
- Stephen Hawkins suffering from autism and always on wheel chair became the greatest aero-physicist.
- Stevie Wonder being blind became the greatest singer.
- Marilee Marlin who was deaf from childhood became a famous actress.
- Wilma Rudolph, paralyzed with polio proved to be the fastest woman on the earth, by winning 100 metres race, 200 metres race and 400 metres relay race in 1960 Olympics.

The **message** is: "If you have high self-esteem, no adversity can prevent you from reaching at the top."

When people with severe adversities can achieve greatness, why can't you without adversity? Have high self-esteem, colossal willpower to accomplish a great work."

Joseph of the ancient Hebrews was sold into slavery by his brothers; after thirteen years of slavery, he was sent to prison, even for taking highly right decision, but from the prison he was made in charge of an Egyptian kingdom due to his high positive attitude, self-esteem and leadership quality.

> *"If you possess high self-esteem, positive attitude, leadership quality, even severe adversities can't deter you to achieve unparalleled success."*

Method 3: Accept Responsibility; Acquire Competence, Act and Deliver

What is the rationale behind accepting responsibility and acting on it? This is because of the fact that many people who have low self-esteem are not ready to accept responsibility and give innumerable number of excuses for the same. If such people accept responsibility and start acting on it, certainly their behavior will change towards positivity. Their accomplishment will give them a high degree of satisfaction and their self-esteem will go high. "Domain competence and a combination of relevant knowledge and skills are an essential requirement to meet any responsibility." If you possess these, you can sharpen them further. If you don't possess, it is highly mandatory for a person to acquire these with great passion. "Competence is the core parameter to raise your self-esteem." Further, the productivity of nation and quality of life of people will improve with their efforts in meeting the responsibility. "Responsibility raises your self-esteem to achieve your cherished goals."

There are various situations where we have to own responsibility and work towards it. It is about, "to self, to family, to work, to society, to the environment and to the nation." All these responsibilities invite us to own them and act. We can help the needy ones. We can help the poor sick people. We can organize various awareness camps to aware people on stopping child abuse, drinking, smoking, use of drugs, harassment of women, misuse of resources and many other social and environmental issues confronted by our nation. Who will save this beautiful planet earth and humanity at large? It is we. By accepting responsibilities on various fronts enhance self-esteem and we can make ourselves an asset to the society and contribute to nation development at large.

The **message** is: "You can enhance your self-esteem by accepting your various responsibilities, acquiring domain competence and acting on these, till fruitful result is achieved. This will give you joy, happiness, confidence and satisfaction."

Method 4: Use Imagination and Intuition

> *"Imagination and intuition make up more than three quarters of our real life."*
>
> —*Simon Well*

Imagination and intuition are most valuable tools of minds which give birth to major scientific and technological discoveries. These offer happiness, joy, satisfaction and confidence and as a result, the self-confidence of such person increases to a higher degree. We have heard the blockbuster movie **Jurassic park** in which a lot of imaginations and intuitions have been used. The self--esteem and self-confidence of the all stakeholders got increased to colossal level. Henry Ford, educated only up to school level imagined a V-8 engine to give more power and speed for his dream car. His engineers told him, "V-8 car is impossible even working on it for one year". Again, he told them, "I want only V-8 engine and one day it was a reality." The self-esteem of Ford and his engineers turned sky rocketed. There are many fiction movies made in the past and some of them became partly or fully a reality.

The **message** here is: "By converting your imagination and intuition into reality, your self-esteem gets enhanced to higher level through the channel of happiness, joy, satisfaction and confidence."

Method 5: By Proper Conditioning

Sometimes, it so happens that by remaining unknown about the real fact you become enthusiastic and passionate to learn much more than your real originality under proper conditioning, and that helps you to develop higher self-esteem.

Proper Conditioning Improves Your Self-esteem

A person placed chicken's egg in the nest of pigeon out of curiosity. After hatching, both babies grew together. The chicken baby did not know that it was not a chicken but a pigeon, so it followed the foot path of pigeon and learned to live by their ways.

The **moral** of the story is: "By remaining ignorant about the fact of originality and with conducive conditioning, one can perform much better than expectations of one's originality due to high self-esteem."

Method 6: Diverting yourself towards Social Work during Low Self-esteem.

What is the way out when you are in trouble due to various mental pressures and are feeling low? As per famous psychiatrist you should divert your attention from daily routine work and get engaged in social works such as, "helping needy persons; giving roses to patients in hospital; doing service to God for one or two hours daily either at temple, mosque, church, or gurudwara as per your faith like a dedicated volunteer."

By this way, your mind will be working completely in new direction. The adage: "Be a true volunteer, help others and help yourself." By helping others, you will feel a sense of gratification which in turn will give you joy, happiness, and your self-esteem will be high. God has made you rich to distribute your wealth, God has given you knowledge to spread your knowledge, and God has made you strong to help the weaker like flowers spreading its fragrance without taking anything from others. "The importance of giving without any expectations is much more than taking."

If you are engaged in good social works and are being successful in bringing smiles on the faces of all needy and down trodden persons, you are doing the kindest work. James M. Barrie said, "Those who bring sun shine to the lives of others cannot keep it from themselves."

The **message** is: "Diverting oneself towards social works during personnel turmoil builds high self-esteem due to the feeling of gratification, self-worth, selfless contribution, happiness and satisfaction."

Method 7: Practice Warm Compliments

"Humanity is humility which must be humming with love, compassion, courtesy, grace, compliments, happiness, joy, welcome, respect, sincerity and obedience. These are not only jewels of human beings but tools to lead a beautiful life."

Compliments are one of the tools which we can use to make ourselves and others happy. Even for a minor help, you should give compliment to the helper by saying "thank you." Similarly, when we help anybody and one extends compliments, we must receive them with great gesture and smile. By this way, your self-esteem will improve due to happiness and good mood.

The **message** is: "Giving and receiving warm compliments improve one's happiness and mood which in turn raise our self-esteem."

Method 8: By Becoming Self-Disciplined

"It's easy to have faith in yourself and have discipline when you're a winner, when you're number one. What you got to have is faith and discipline when you're not a winner."

—*Vince Lombardi*

Self-discipline is a great tool to shape one's life. Every work goes smoothly and without any tussle of a self-disciplined person. People appreciate and respect the self – disciplined persons. Since all works of disciplined persons run smoothly, they remain happy, satisfied and successful. As a result, their self – esteem is high.

"Human civilization is not a world of jungle where might is right, but it is a world of humility, discipline, love, respect, cooperation and affection." Be a civilized person for your high self-esteem.

The **message** is: "Self-esteem increases with self-discipline."

Method 9: Have a Good Company of People with High Moral Character

The adage: "You are what company you keep" is true in every walk of life. Your association with type of people matters much. If you associate with the persons who drink heavily and use drugs, then naturally it will affect your psyche and you will find yourself following their footsteps, knowingly or unknowingly. If your friends and seniors are of high moral character, their good qualities will influence your psyche and you will also try to possess good moral character. Avoid association with negative people. George Washington once said, "Associate yourself with people of good quality if you esteem your reputation, for it is better to be alone than to be in bad company." "Note that all your association with negative people having poor moral character will always put you in trouble and on the ebbing curve of success, whereas association with good people with high moral character will lead you to a path of glory and make you successful resulting in your high self-esteem."

The **message** is: "Association with people of high moral character will raise your self-esteem and place you on the winning curve."

Method 10: Practice Repetitive Positive Auto-suggestions

Self-esteem is a mind game. Human mind is highly complex and it is divided in three categories: subconscious mind, conscious mind and super conscious mind. Major aspects happen in subconscious mind. Whatever input we give to subconscious mind, it is stored there and we act accordingly. If we give matters which will boost self-esteem, it will be received in subconscious mind and we will behave in that fashion. To boost this, always enrich your mind with positive thoughts like: "I can win; I can accomplish; I am good in every subject; I will crack competitive examination; I can meet any target; I." As a result, your self-esteem will become high and your depressed mind will be energized. Have you ever heard words uttered during a local war between two groups? One group says repeatedly – "Oh God! Help us to crush the enemies" and other group says – "Oh God! Help us in winning." Such words give motivation and increase self-esteem to a very high level.

The **moral** of this example is: "Self-esteem and self-confidence rise rapidly to a colossal level with repetitive positive auto-suggestions."

Method 11: By Bringing Happiness and Peace through Positive Thinking

Since self-esteem is an act of mind and so it may be conditioned accordingly as per need. What does paralyze human mind? These are bitterness, emotional bad feelings, jealousy, criticism, fight, quarrel, failure, fear, broken relationship, mental hurt, punishment and revenge. Unless and until these bitterness and gloomy feelings are removed from mind, happiness and peace will never come in mind and self-esteem will never rise and be stuck in the lowest stage.

You have to divert your thinking from gloomy atmosphere to inspiring atmosphere through positive thinking to make your self-esteem high by the following ways:

- Set your standard of life. Stop criticizing others.
- Be honest to yourself and towards the importance of life.
- See positivity in others and in every situation.

- Don't get impassionate on negative criticism.
- Avoid jealousy. Don't bear guilt and hold grudges.
- Adopt forgiveness, the best virtue of human beings.
- Believe in ups and downs in life and remove fear.
- Consider every situation as opportunity.
- Feel the appreciation on your every single contribution.
- Help others and be courteous.
- Enjoy the beauty of nature.
- Resolve to be happy in all situations.
- Take action without expecting the fruit of action.

Positive thinking on above mentioned aspects will give you pleasure and happiness which in turn will enhance your self-esteem.

The **message** is: "By bringing happiness and peace in your life through positive thinking, you can do wonders."

Method 12: Avoid Comparing Yourself to Others

Comparing yourself with others is a wrong step on your part. "Everybody is a different personality." You may be having some very good quality about which you are ignorant. You can always bounce back. Comparison will always de-motivate you and as a result your self-esteem will go down. Stop comparing with others, but instead, adopt the best quality of others.

Method 13: Replace the Habit of Perfectionism

In reality, nothing can be perfect. In the search of perfection, too much time is devoted and as a result, other works suffer. You can't complete the work in time, so demotivation creeps up in mind and as a result, your self-esteem will go down. Go for very good or excellent aspects as per need and choice. Don't chase shadow of perfectionism.

Method 14: By Having Patience

In execution of any work, constant effort is required for certain duration. During the execution period, some adversity may also crop up. So, patience is needed to achieve the goal. A gardener waters plants two, three or more months, then only flowers appear. Brian Adams once opined, "Patience creates confidence, decisiveness, and a rational outlook, which eventually lead to success." If you have a glimpse on the life stories of all achievers, you will find that all of them were men of patience. By developing patience, your held up work will be completed and your self-esteem will improve.

The **message** is: "Patience leads to success."

Method 15: By Being Internally Driven

In achieving goal, a lot of adversities and obstacles appear in ourway. One might lose his confidence, get irritated and quit. But there are some people who never give up. What really allows them to never give up? It is nothing but the internal drive for the cherished goal. We have to remain cool. It is our internal drive which engages us from the core of our heart to achieve the goal irrespective of countless difficulties.

An Internally Driven Person Outperforms: There was an internally driven principal in a leading government engineering college. Non-teaching staff used to abuse him during every year strike which used to last about a month. He used to listen to all abuses passed on to him very patiently and in the last, he used to give four or five jerks to his shirt saying that: "All your abuses like dirt have fallen down, come and have some tea."

Since the principal was internally driven from the core of heart to develop the academic level and the branding of the college, so he used to bear all abuses of non-teaching staff.

Once you are internally driven, you will remain happy, after seeing the output of your hard work. The philosophy is: "Enter the workplace with happiness every day and with a resolve that you will work hard. When you proceed for your home after working hours, feel happy to see the output of your hard work." This is called FISH! Philosophy and everybody should follow it religiously.

The **message** is: "By being internally driven, you will feel confident, patient and mission driven, which in turn will raise your self-esteem."

Method 16: By Broadening Your Vision

Travelling gives a lot of experience and knowledge and widens the vision in all fields of life. With these you may be able to set higher goals and solve all the obstacles in the way to achieve your goals. As a result of wider vision, success finds its way to your feet. And your self-esteem will increase. You have to believe in your potential and power for achieving greatness.

The **message** is: "Broadening your vision broadens your self-esteem."

Method 17: By Not Following the Crowd

Following the crowd doesn't offer any challenge and learning is less. The confidence level will be limited as it is not a path less travelled. If you want a high degree of confidence, a great achievement, reputation, name and fame, the only way is not to follow crowds and do something different and excel. This will raise your self-esteem to a very high level and the world will remember you, salute you. George Bernard Shaw elucidated, "All reasonable men adapt themselves to the world. Only a few unreasonable ones persist in trying to adapt the world to themselves. All progress in the world depends on these unreasonable men and their innovative and nonconformist actions." All entrepreneurs, inventors, innovators follow the path less travelled or totally unchartered path to achieve greatness.

The **message** is: "Doing something different from crowd produces innovation and excellence, which in turn, raise your self-esteem and make you successful."

Method 18: By Thrashing the Fear of Failure from Subconscious mind

"Failures are finger posts on the road to achievement."

—*C.S. Lewis*

The fear of failure is a great obstacle to high self-esteem. The characteristics of fear are peculiar. Once it enters in our subconscious mind, it starts affecting our high self-esteem and self-confidence. Only through external and internal motivation, we can thrash fear from our subconscious mind. Once fear is gone, you will regain your high self-esteem. "Fear floors your self-esteem. Thrash it! Thrash it! Thrash it!"

The **message** is: "By thrashing fear of any kind from your subconscious mind, you can regain high self-esteem and success will be at your doorstep."

CONVERTING OUR LOW SELF-ESTEEM CHARACTERISTICS INTO HIGH SELF-ESTEEM

Self-esteem (being low and high) promotes many characteristics among people. The following are the characteristics of people with low (**given without brackets**) and high (**given in bracket**) self-esteem. This will help you to evaluate yourself where you stand. "If you are plagued with low self-esteem, follow the **eighteen methods given above** for raising your self-esteem by converting low self-esteem characteristics into high self-esteem characteristics." Take any characteristic; the degree may vary from person to person.

Low confidence (High confidence); Arrogance – (Humility); Confusion – (Confidence); Aggressive to hide – (Assertive); Selfish – (Self-interest); pessimistic – (optimistic); Unwise – (Wise); Taker – (Giver); Greedy - (Reasonable); Touchy - (Sensitive); Argumentative – (Discusser); Lonely – (Solitude); Irresponsible – (Responsible); Unwilling to learn – (Willing to learn); Unconcerned about character – (Concerned about character); Criticism – (praise or no comment); Poor sense of freedom-(Discipline); Externally driven – (Internally driven); Enjoy vulgarity – (Enjoy decency); Non-believer in limitation- (Believer in limitation).

Benchmark yourself on a scale of ten for every characteristic. If you get less than eight out of ten for any characteristic, you require improvement on your part.

The **message** is: "If you have positive attitude, you can change your characteristics of low self-esteem into high self-esteem."

It has been observed that people take advantages of situation created by you, either by your incompetency or foolishness to lower down your self-esteem. This has been well expressed by the words of Eleanor Roosevelt: "No one can make you feel inferior without your consent."

Are you a victim of self-esteem? Why have you lowered down your self-esteem? We have come to this beautiful world to contribute something but we are not showing any sign of this due to low self-esteem. Get up, wake up from the world of low self-esteem, bring out your hidden potential on forefront, take a giant leap, and shine like stars for which you have taken birth on this beautiful planet. God would certainly be happy to see you happy and successful.

SELF-CONFIDENCE MAKES YOU A WINNER

"Believe you can and you're halfway there."

—*Theodore Roosevelt*

"Somehow I can't believe that there are any heights that can't be scaled by a man who knows the secrets of making dreams come true. This special secrets, it seems to me can be summarized in four Cs. They are curiosity, confidence, courage and constancy, and the greatest of all is confidence. When you believe in a thing, believe it in all way, implicitly and unquestionably."

—*Walt Disney*

Self-confidence! An off-spring of self-esteem. A natural vibrant energy. A capacity to move even a mountain. A sign and symptom of winning. Are you a victim of low self-confidence? Why? You are not born coward, but brave. Develop high self-confidence and win the world with your success and greatness.

"Self-confidence is the most important characteristic of self-esteem." "It is the self-confidence by which people can do anything, achieve everything and be something to the society. Norman Vincent Peale opined," Without a humble but reasonable confidence in your own powers, you cannot be successful or happy. "The entire challenging task demands a high degree of self-confidence. Note that self-confidence comes from knowledge and skills. If you know your job well, then you'll have the confidence to do it well." Tom Landry, the super successful coach of Dallas Cowboys said, "Anybody can be a winner if he wants it bad enough, strives for it hard enough, actively seeks it out by learning it all he can and working with all his strength. Of course, positive anticipation, feeding on good, clear, positive attitude is essential." Do you want to win? If yes, follow the sermon of Dallas Cowboys

"Self-confidence is the hallmark of inevitable success."

Ponder over the feat achieved by the following great and successful people in the world. What is common among them? It is to major the self-confidence:

- Mathew Webb, Thomas William Burgess, Henry Sullivan, Gertrude Elderly and others who crossed the English Channel.
- The great businessmen like Ford, Tata, Ambani, Bill Gates, Steve Jobs, Narayana Murthy and Mark Zuckerberg and all the other rich andhighly successful businessmenwho pillared an empire of their work.. They are icon of the world economy.
- AbrahamLincoln, after a series of failure in all ventures he undertook, finally became one of the highly respected presidents of USA.

"Among all great successful persons, the one thing common (excluding the other virtues) is self-confidence." They are believers. Lao Tzu said, "Because one believes in oneself, one doesn't try to convince others. Because one is content with oneself, one doesn't need other's approval. Because one accepts oneself, the whole world accepts him or her." Self-confidence is affected by many factors, but the most important one is fear. It is the fear of failure and the fear of unknown that may affect a self-confident person. But, if we handle fear very effectively through internal motivation, then the effect of fear gets nullified, and again we can achieve success. "Self-confidence is our morale booster. Improve it! Improve it! Improve it!"

Invariably, it looks that believers can do anything in the world. They are the builders in every field of human activities. Imagination, dream and desire alone, can't create development and success unless and until you have self-confidence and believe in your dreams. This has been well expressed by Napoleon Hill, who said, "Believers are the forerunners of civilization, the builders of industries, the creators of empires, the revealers of the beautiful benefits made available to us by the creators of all things."

Ways to improve self-confidence include: Planning and preparation, learning, knowledge and training, positive thoughts, being assertive, having experience, having hope and avoiding arrogance.

Hey, desirous men and women! Come on. Develop your self-esteem and self-confidence through the eighteen methods given above. Rekindle your inner fire and contribute. The world needs more self-confident and self-esteemed people to contribute immensely in making a difference. Join the glorious team of self-confident and self-esteemed people and be an asset to the society.

STEPS TAKEN BY YOURSELF

I will take the following steps to raise my self-esteem and self-confidence:

i. _____
ii. _____

***

Chapter 7

Build Character, Courage, Conviction, Commitment and Concentration (5 Cs)
THE 6TH MANTRA

CHARACTER IS YOUR CROWN OF GREATNESS

"Good is good and bad is bad and nowhere is the difference between good and bad so wide and as fateful as in human character. For character makes destiny in the individual and in the race."
—Edward O. Sisson

"Nearly all men can stand adversity, but if you want to test a man's character give him power."
—Abraham Lincoln

A famous woman seer-cum-speaker was asked by a student from the audience in a congregation to speak to us of character, courage, conviction, commitment, and concentration. She replied in sequence: Character! Character! Character! A buzzword on everybody lips. A crown of human beings. A road to success. A glittering reflection of light in work environment. Are you a man of character? If yes, you will shine like stars. If not, your future may be doomed. Build your personality embedded with excellent character to create a beautiful world to live in and let live in, to succeed.

"Character is an excellent combination of many moral and ethical virtues including: integrity, honesty, unselfishness, truth, responsibility, understanding, courtesy, loyalty, respect, caring, courage, tolerance, citizenship, conviction, fairness, fidelity and monogamy. It is a jewel in the crown of an individual. It is always reflected in our behavior and actions. "The light inside you illuminates your outside beauty." Character is the building block of success. The road to success is filled with twists and turns. It is full of pitfalls, waiting for you to fall. There is always a danger that your character may take a dip in that pitfall and so one has to be very mindful of the same. When you are advancing on the glorious path of success, many people will envy and criticize you and even your character would not be spared. Don't let criticism distract you from your coveted goal and your cherished dream." Character is your crown of success. Build it! Build it! Build it!"

"As the quality of steel is judged by the carbon content, the quality of a person is judged by character content." As per Russian proverb: "A hammer shatters glass but forges steel" is highly true in the case of character also. Judge yourself whether you are made of glass or steel. Be steel in character, courage and confidence. "The real beauty of human beings is not the physical appearance but character." "Character is the core virtue of human beings and if character is lost everything is lost." In fact, success, greatness can't come by following only one mantra but it is always a combination of many. Among many virtues, courtesy, though, looks very simple but it helps us in achieving great success without investing anything except some pleasant words. Simple words, say, 'thank you please,' may change your world.

"Success demands qualities of 12 Cs – character, courage, conviction, commitment, concentration, confidence, curiosity, competence, consistency, compassion, cooperation, and courtesy."

Mathematically, Success = $f(12Cs)$

Eleanor Roosevelt opined, "People grow through experience if they meet life honestly and courageously. This is how character is built. "It is the duty of teachers, leaders and people with power to inculcate the character among their citizens for the progress of society and nation." Developing good character is the foundation of leadership quality. Parents or mentors can give you good advice and put you on the right path, but the final formation of your character lies in your hands." Good character is not formed in one or two months. It is a slow process and passes through handling of your life's problems. It is created little by little, day by day. A high degree of persistent and patient effort is required to develop good character. Imbibe the philosophy, "Try to become a better person, not a bitter person."

"Practicing of **'truth'** plays an important role in character building." Note that character building requires careful steps in exercising truth. Truth takes many roles. The words of Friedrich elucidate this beautifully when he said, "Truth is the discipline of the ascetic, the quest of the mystic, the faith of the simple, the ransom of the weak, the standard of the righteous, the doctrine of the meek, and the challenge of the mature."

"Dealing with the circumstances of life tells you many things about your character. Crisis in life doesn't necessarily make character, but it certainly reveals it." "Your mode of action is your mode of character." Adversity in life acts as a crossroad that offers an opportunity to the people to choose one of the two paths: Character or Compromise. A person (leader) who goes along the character road becomes stronger and more daring to take up challenges of life. He finds it easy to deal with all kinds of crisis, adversities and problems and counter them to rise again and contribute. Mahatma Gandhi has shown to the world the power of truth and non-violence during India's Freedom Struggle. Martin Luther King Jr. once said, "The ultimate measure of a man is not where he stands in moments of comfort and convenience but where he stands at times of challenge and controversy." A great thought, a great reality.

Anybody can be positive, polite, graceful and kind when things are going smoothly in life. What differentiates people with an extraordinary character from the rest of us is how they respond when life presents distressing signals with a lot of severe problems. Such people of extraordinary character don't crumble or surrender to their fate but fight back with grace and win over. A wise person with extraordinary character shows a remarkable ability by remaining grounded when engulfed with severe problems in life. The foundation stones for golden success are: character, honesty, integrity, love, faith, loyalty and self-confidence.

"Character building is along standing habit covering all aspects of life starting from even small matters." The words of Albert Einstein elucidate this aspect very beautifully, "Whoever is careless with truth in small matters cannot be trusted with important matters."

Treating people nicely is the building block of character development. Treating any meek and weak person in rough, indecent and abusive ways signify that you lack in character and you require building it greatly as you know that such persons can't fight back. "Sometimes mind works on wrong path due to greed and it is the character which controls it. Character is that trait which holds everything together." Thomas A. Edison advocated, "What a man's mind can create man's character can control." The future of a nation depends upon the character of its citizens. If a nation houses majority of people with low and mean character, that country is bound to fail miserably. The words of Theodore Roosevelt justify this, "Character in the long run, is the decisive factor in the life of an individual and of nations alike."

"Freedom and progress of a country are based on the characters of its citizens. "Think about the reasons," Why were many countries of the world ruled by British?' The major reason was the lack of character, patriotism and national pride among people in the respective countries." "Character paves the path of progress for an individual, a family, an organization and a nation." In making of great scientist, the character is the core and not the intellect. Through good character one may easily achieve a respectable position. The great scientist Albert Einstein opined about this, "Most people say that it is the intellect, which makes a great scientist. They are wrong: it is character."

"Your **words** in public conversation matters much and what adjectives you use reveals your character. People make an opinion about your character based on your conversation." The words of Mark Twain elucidate this very beautifully, "A man's character may be learned from the adjectives which he habitually uses in conversation."

A lot of persons (past and present) are symbol of character. Mahatma Gandhi, Abraham Lincoln, APJ Abdul Kalam, Ratan Tata, Narayana Murthy, Nelson Mandela, Jawaharlal Nehru, Ambedkar, Franklin D. Roosevelt, profound CEOs, statesmen, doctors, scientists, professors, engineers, officers, businessmen, advocates, villagers, singers, actors and ordinary people from all over the world exhibited their best character and the world salutes them. "The greatness is exhibited when you choose character instead of compromise."

"**Tolerance** plays an important role in character building. Humanity survives on the acts of tolerance. Intolerance creates chaos, loss of lives and loss of properties."

"Tolerance exhibits the real character, the real wisdom, the real religion, the real ethics, and the real wealth of a human being."

Honesty is one of the important ingredients of character. Honesty not only relates to money but it covers every aspects of human life. Human life becomes fulfilling when honesty prevails in every segment of human activities. "Integrity, fidelity, fairness, monogamy, loyalty, responsibility are also the major ingredients in building the character of a person."

News of Taxi-drivers returning gold ornaments worth lakhs and crores, left behind by the passengers to the police station is a sign of an uncorrupt heart. This is a great sign of good character showing extraordinary honesty. The world salutes such honest persons. While we also can't ignore the reality of the other side of the same coin where houses and banks are looted for money out of greed.

The **moral** of this story is: "Character is much more worthy than illegal money."

Where do you stand on the scale of character? Ask yourself. Ask yourself honestly whether your words and actions match? If not, you lack in character. In the great epic "Ramayana" Dashratha (father of Lord Rama) once said, "Tradition of descendants of Raghu had been such that words of promise would be always met at all cost even if it was to sacrifice their own life." This is called character. King Dashratha, Lord Rama, Lord Laxmana, Devi Sita, Lord Bharatha exhibited character of highest order as per the epic. Mahatma Gandhi said, "Knowledge without character is a sin." King Satya Harishchandra of ancient India had exhibited an unparalleled example of character through his integrity, truth and honesty.

"Character categorizes your worth."

Hey, young men and women! Think over character building for the welfare of self, your family, the organization and nation at large. The world is in great need of total quality people (TQP) with good character. Join the world of people with good character to shine like star.

STEPS TO IMPROVE YOUR CHARACTER:

Following strategies may be adopted in real spirit to improve your character:

i. **Watch your cunningness**: Every week, spare some time to work on your cunningness, your lies, your cutting corners at work places, compromises made by you on decisions or duty, letting down people, use of abusive or bad language, dishonesty and cheating committed by you and the people you might have hurt. If you find yourself involved in these, then you require working on your own self not to repeat next time.

ii. **Find pattern in character weakness**: There is a pattern or particular areas where people show weakness in character – say female attachment, money involvementand personal matters. If it is true on your part, then improve upon these.

iii. **Repair character**:   For repairing character, you have to face the music out of wrong doing, apologize for this and solve created problems. It's rightly said that, "It's not about being better than someone else but about being better than your older self."

iv. **Rebuild character**:   Find your weakness and work upon it. Find patterns in your mistakes and adopt a method to rectify it. Give some time to improve yourself and start from naught. "Zero is the best figure for a new beginning." Rebuild your character by working on it.

v. **Consult saints or gurus, not swindlers**:   For repairing and rebuilding character, consult some saint guru of good character and not swindler saints who are in large number in modern age.

EXHIBITING COURAGE MAKES YOU A WINNER

"Being deeply loved by someone gives you strength, while loving someone deeply gives you courage."

—*Lao Tzu*

"You will never do anything in this world without courage. It is the greatest quality of mind next to honor."

—*Aristotle*

Courage! A sign of confidence. A winning criteria to navigate on difficult path. A sign and symptom of history maker. A weapon of great warrior. Are you a person of courage? If yes, you are a winner. If not, you need to acquire courage to succeed and to achieve greatness. "We are not here to make only history but write it."

Success in any venture starts with imagination, dream, desire and decision. What is it really that is preventing you to take decisions and actions on your dream? It is nothing but the lack of courage and the fear of failure. "Success in any venture is not the result of any miracle. It needs courage and confidence to decide, to involve, to do sheer hard work, to sacrifice and to overcome obstacles in the process of glorious success story. It is only the courage which will thrash fear from your mind. Courage is the resistances to fear." Steve Jobs ones said, "Your time is limited, so don't waste it living someone else's life. Don't be trapped by dogma - which is living with the results of other people's thinking. Don't let the noise of other's opinions drown out your own inner voice. And the most important, have the courage to follow your heart and intuition. They somehow already know what you truly want to become. Everything else is secondary."

Mahatma Gandhi, Bill Gates, Steven Spielberg, Grandma Moses, Rosa Parks, Steve Jobs, Abraham Lincoln, Oprah Winfrey, Narayana Murthy, Tata, Vasco da Gama, Ambani and Ford, Jack Ma, Masayoshi Son, each of these individuals stood up with courage to decide and act on their imagination, dream, desire and thinking and finally showed the world, "what courage can do." "Courage is a mindset. It's not about your physical health but about your mental status. Train your mind to be a lion instead of a goat." "Courageous are winners and winners are courageous." This is the truth of life. "Success is still determined by the old formula of ABCD: ability, behavior, courage and discipline."

"Courage is the core of all virtues. When you stand up with courage to follow your heart for anything, other virtues will accompany to give you a golden success in that thing."

"Success swims or sinks in proportion to your courage in the journey of life."

Fearful experience in life plays an important role in enhancing courage and confidence. In such a situation, one may curse one's fate but with positive attitude you may withstand boldly. Such experience of life will enhance your courage to a colossal level. Eleanor Roosevelt once opined, "You gain strength, courage, and confidence by every experience in which you really stop to look fear in the face. You are able to say to yourself, I lived through this horror. I can take the next thing that comes along."

Here are some success stories of the people who were able to swim across the English Channel out of sheer hard work and bold determination.

i. **Mathew Webb**: He became the first person in the world to cross the English Channel without the aid of artificial buoyancy. His first attempt ended in failure but on August 25, 1875, he started from Admiralty Pies in Dover and made the crossing in twenty-one hours and forty-five minutes despite the challenging tides which delayed him for five hours and a painful sting from a Jellyfish which welcomed him as an enemy during his journey. Such a feat is a testimony of colossal courage, confidence and determination. "Courage conquers over fear and yields success in your clutch."

ii. **Thomas William Burgess**: After his fifteen unsuccessful attempts, he started swimming on September 6, 1911 from Doves, Gris Nez and became the second persons in the world to successfully make the crossing in twenty-two hours and thirty-five minutes. There were eighty unsuccessful attempts made after Mathew Webb but it was Burgess who duplicated Webb's feat.

iii. **Hennery Sullivan**: He was successful in 7th attempt and took twenty-seven hours and forty-five minutes to cross the English Channel.

iv. **Gertrude Elderly**: She started her journey at Cap Gris Nez in France at 7:05 am on the morning of August, 1920. Her trainer was Burgess. She crossed in fourteen hours and thirty-nine minutes making first woman to cross English Channel breaking all previous time records.

After that, a lot of persons crossed the English Channel.

What is common among them? All of them were the persons possessing high degree of courage, and unflinching will to make an achievement in life and to become successful in their dreams defying all failures by overcoming all obstacles. These people are the beacon of courage, hope, aspiration, struggle and adventure.

The **lesson** here is quite simple: "Blessed are the honest, courageous, disciplined, kind, patient, persistent, adventurous and perspiring people for they shall inherit the earth."

"Achievement is the outcome of dream, courage, commitment, character, curiosity and activities."

Oh! Men and women! Today is your time to step up, take decision, develop courage, defy the odds, act wholeheartedly, stop taking approvals from others and begin achieving your cherished goals of life. Nothing is impossible in this world. "Courage is characterized by fearlessness. "Make this the slogan of your life and learn to fight fear and resist it. Bernard Edmonds advocated, "To dream anything that you want to dream, that's the beauty of the human mind. To do anything that you want to do, that's the strength of human will. To trust yourself to test your limits, that's the courage to succeed."

"Courage and fear lie inside you. Once fear dominates, courage takes a beating. But when courage predominates, fear gets a beating." Tell yourself: "What do you want to beat?" "Courage is your mental strength. Improve it! Improve it! Improve it!" To succeed in life and to accomplish, thrash every fear from your mind which is holding you back and let courage dominate your mind. "Be courageous and strong enough to turn tragedies into triumphs." "Our life shrinks or expands in proportion to our courage."

STEPS TO IMPROVE YOUR COURAGE

In order to improve your courage, one may follow these steps to improve it:

i. **Involve in courageous acts:** Involve in mountaineering, skydiving, and sea surfing and every other sport which has frightened you. Try them and come out of fear and be bold enough to do that and grow in courage.

ii. **Take bold step:** If you are thinking to change your career to satisfy your hobby, then do it. Don't think too much. Do what you love and success will come at your feet.

iii. **Face embarrassment:** Learn to listen to people. Face confrontation on the hands of your boss and family and work on it in amicable manner.

iv. **Forget fear in life:** Whenever you feel in taking up any challenging work, don't forget that it's just your mentality that's holding you back. Participate with much vigor to break past the barriers which are holding you.

Hey, men and women! Step up to thrash fear. Bring courage and keep it permanently in your mind. "The world of success is for courageous people. Join this world where life has a meaning."

CONVICTION BRINGS GREATNESS

"Never give in, never give in, never, never, never. -in nothing, great or small, large or petty – never give – except to convictions of honor and good senses."

—*Winston Churchill*

"He who stands for nothing will fall for anything."

—*Alexander Hamilton*

Conviction! A faith like steel. An unbreakable belief. A strongest driving power for action. An unshakable faith. A creator of passion. Winning criteria. Do you have conviction over anything? If yes, success will be at your doorstep. If not, you may be a looser. Have conviction in your work to get success in life.

"Conviction is the strongest faith in anything." If you are deviating from your belief due to internal and external forces, you must remember that it is only conviction which can bring you back. Albert Einstein said, "That deep emotional conviction of the presence of a superior reasoning power, which is revealed in the incomprehensible universe forms my idea of God." When you take a strong stand based on your conviction, the world salutes you to your strong resolve. In fact, human life becomes meaningful only when you have strong conviction in your endeavor and take a stand accordingly.

"If you have an unshakable conviction in your dream, decision, courage and action, nobody can stop your success."

"Conviction creates courage to conquer."

There are five kinds of people in this world as given below and you can easily judge who is a man of conviction:

- Those who make things happen.
- Those who watch things happen.
- Those who take credit of things happened.
- Those who wonder what happened.
- Those who obstruct things to happen.

Among the five types given above, first one is the man of conviction, second one is an indifferent person, third one is like an opportunist and cunning, fourth one is having zero conviction and rudderless and the last one is a man of negative attitude. Decide on what type of a person you wish to be. "You will miserably fail, until you impress your subconscious mind with the conviction you are a success. This is done by making affirmation that clicks better. Practice such affirmation which makes your conviction strong for your success.

Deep Conviction Brings an Unparalleled Success: Will Kellogg was a shy man, limited interests, and with average talent. He was working for his brother Dr. Kellogg at a salary of USD 87 per month. Dr. Kellogg was interested to improve the quality of food for his patients. In this process, both brothers started experimenting to improve wheat food, but by accident they discovered **"flakes"**. Will Kellogg had left a pot of boiling wheat to stand a little too long and as a result, wheat became tempered and Will rolled it into a flake. WillKellogg had a deep conviction, that it was a great discovery which could be mass-marketed as food. Will Kellogg tried to convince his elder brother that their accidental discovery was a promising one and it could be mass-marketed but his brother, Dr. Kellogg doubted his idea and refused to go for it. Ultimately in 1906, Will Kellogg decided to market the idea on his own which made him one of the richest men in America. His Corn Flakes are sold worldwide.

The **moral** of the story is: "A deep conviction in an idea carries a great driving power for action on an uncertain venture resulting in a great achievement."

A Great Conviction, Courage, and Sacrifice in Social Work Can Even Move Mountains: Dashrath Manjhi (1934–2007) was a simple landless laborer of a village called Gehlaur, surrounded by hills in Gaya District (Bihar, India). The villagers had to travel fifty-five kilometres. to go to the nearest town Atari Wazirganj block by long route due to hills for medical help, official works and marketing. His wife, Phalguni Devi died in the absence of medical help due to distance. Government refused to construct a road through the hill. So, he decided to create a wide passage through the hills for the villagers by which the distance could be reduced to 15 km. He started digging and cutting stones of the hills alone for days and nights together with the help of raw tools like hammer, chisel and shovel. In about twenty-two years (1960-1982), he single-handedly and by selfless hard work, carved a passage of 360 feet long, 25 feet deep and 30 feet wide through the hill for the villagers. In the beginning, villagers used to make fun of him by calling him crazy and mad. But, after about ten years, they started appreciating him. He is known as the **Mountain Man**. What a single handed gigantic contribution! What an unparalleled social service! What a colossal conviction!

The **theme** of the story is, "It is the intense desire and the Himalayan like conviction which can inspire you to do the impossible -such as cutting and moving mountain single handed for twenty-two years in social service."

Out of fear of failing, many people live a "life of quiet desperation." "All the time, some people recall their past failures and don't dare to proceed for any meaningful action. Such people can't possess any conviction for anything except the fear of failure." "A deep conviction in good things corrects many bad measures."

Most of the developed countries have certain **"Conviction in policy"** on which the prosperity of a nation depends. For example, USA has a conviction that it gives freedom, liberty and equal opportunity to grow to all its citizens and also to all brilliant, intelligent and competent persons born anywhere in the world irrespective cast, creed and religion. As a result, USA houses maximum brilliant, intelligent and competent persons in the world which made USA prosperous. Harvard University has a strong conviction in **"New Ideas"** on which the university banks and as a result, it is number one or number two ranked university in the world. MIT has unshakable conviction in **"Excellence"** on which the institute banks and it also ranks between 1st to 2nd positions in the world. French, in their political project, believe in tremendous **moral resilience** and in the values of the Enlightenment-secularism, tolerance, human rights or probity in public life. "Have you ever thought why US, UK, France, Germany, Japan and China progressed? If one major reason is taken into account, it is the strong conviction in their chosen parameters and religiously following that conviction in all actions which enabled their progress."

"What is the reason of poor condition of India (per capita income just about USD 1627 in 2014 even after sixty-seven years of independence) and of other developing countries? This country never had an unshakable conviction in any good thing in real spirit, though, philosophy is great, religious epics written before 1500 BC are great, sermons are great, constitution is great, people are intelligent and hardworking, but nothing is in action in proportion to the great capabilities. India never gave sufficient value to the intelligent, brilliant, honest, excellent and capable persons in real spirit." This is just one aspect. As a result, sycophants, toadies, flatters, thugs, encomiasts, parasites, boot- lickers, yes-man, criminals, crooks, and seamier are thriving and some highly capable and intelligent people are leaving the country for green pastures and except few competent people, rest are side-lined from what they deserve. "Just like IT sector, India is capable for giving its recognition in the world in other sectors provided Government and Indian people should have strong convictions in excellence in which our conditions are poor." Are we ready for this? "Conviction in parameters like quality, transparency, excellence, effectiveness, efficiency, intelligence, honesty, character, persistence, education, learning, research, innovation, freedom, fairness, responsibility, national pride and justice is needed in every sector by every citizen to create a great country to live in."

Apply this philosophy of conviction in these two main aspects – 'Governance and Development' **(GD)** which covers whole spectrum of any organization or any country and see the results. It will be amazing and mind-blowing and the world will salute you on your transparent governing systems, accomplishments, glory, contribution, development, inclusive growth, justice and success.

For prosperity, peace and pride, every country, every institution, every society and every person must have a strong, unshakable and unflinching conviction in good things and true actions are needed on that in real spirit. Infosys founded by Narayana Murthy and other six has a great conviction in its logo slogan which says, "Driven by values and powered by intellect". The company religiously follows it and as a result, its reputation in the world is very high. Started with a meagre amount of USD

250 in 1980, after thirty-three years (in 2013) Infosys's revenue rose to USD 8.2 billion. Apple Computers founded by Steve Jobs always believed in "Excellence in Innovation" and as a result it is one of the top companies of the world having cash reserve more than USD 150 billion in the bank in 2014 eclipsing the combined cash of Israel and Britain. See the importance of strong conviction in "Excellence in Innovation."

"In order to succeed, you need strong courage to discard disapproval by others. Most independent thoughts, ideas and strong action beyond the common measure are greeted with strong disapproval accompanied by skepticism, ridicule and violent outrage. In order to preserve anything exceptional, you require inner strength and unshakable conviction that you are hundred percent right." Are you ready to develop strong conviction in your new ideas to succeed, to change the world?

From the experience over ages, people have observed that genuineness of your conviction is only tested when you sacrifice something for that otherwise simply claiming your conviction is not the genuine one. For the freedom of India, many people like Shaheed Bhagat Singh, Raj Guru, Rajendra Lahiri, Ram Prasad Bismil, Ashfaqullah, Thakur Roshan Singh and Veer Savarkar sacrificed their lives as they have unshakable conviction in freedom of India so that the country could be free from the clutches of the British. E. H. Chapin advocated, "No man knows the genuineness of his convictions until he has sacrificed something for them."

Do you want success? If yes, then you must have a driving force in life for your cherished goal, and for that you must have conviction in good things such as character, empathy, innovation, dream, freedom, persistence, excellence, quality, justice, goal, new ideas, entrepreneurship, etc., then success will be at your doorstep. "A belief makes you strong; a doubt makes you weak; and a strong conviction precedes great action. Be a man of strong conviction and kiss greatness in life." The burning examples of conviction include: "the conviction of Nelson Mandela in the freedom of South Africa for which he spent more than twenty-six years of his life in jail; the conviction of Mahatma Gandhi in the freedom of India for which he struggled for thirty-two years; the conviction of Subhas Chand Bose in the freedom of India; the conviction of Abraham Lincoln in giving equal rights to blacks in USA and the conviction of all great men who have either sacrificed their life or their living to make this world a better place to live in."

Test yourself. Do you have conviction in anything you do? If the answer is NO, build it.

STEPS TO IMPROVE YOUR CONVICTION

Do the following to develop conviction:

i. **Begin with small acts**: Select only two good things which you like most and develop conviction in that. Work hard towards these in the light of strong conviction.

ii. **Do sacrifices for conviction:** Do sacrifices by giving your energy, time, and money, forgetting comfort and facing hardship to fulfil your cherished goal in the form of conviction.
iii. **Enrich your knowledge:** Read autobiographies of great people having strong conviction. Meet such people and take advices from them to develop conviction.

COMMITMENT BRINGS EXCELLENCE

"The quality of a person's life is in direct proportion to their commitment to excellence, regardless of their chosen field of endeavor."

—*Vince Lombardi*

"Desire is the key to motivation, but its determination and commitment to unrelenting pursuits of your goal- a commitment to excellence –that will enable you to attain the success you seek."

—*Marie Andretti*

Commitment! An unwavering promise made. A full surety of promise made to happen in reality at any cost. A game changer. A sign to achieve success. A powerful promise to move even the mountains. Are you a committed towards your goal? If yes, success is at your door- step. If not, your success is a distant dream. Be committed towards your goal.

People usually say: he has committed this, she has committed that. What does it mean? It means surety in the thing what has been committed to. "Commitment is the essence of ultimate secrete of surety. There is no going back from whatever committed. Commitment is the willingness to do whatever it takes to achieve success in life.-long working hours, too many sacrifices, etc."

"The degree of success with quality, depth and excellence in your chosen pursuits is directly proportional to your real commitment to these."

"There are four pillars of commitment: integrity, wisdom, honesty and reputation." If anybody backs on his commitment all the four pillars are washed away by the flood of deceit. People usually say such persons seriously lack in integrity, wisdom, honesty and reputation and once these four are gone, everything is gone. Remember: *"Reputation is your real currency; resolve to raise to new heights"* This philosophy should be your motto, and one way out of many to raise your reputation is to meet religiously all your commitments made. "Once you've made a commitment to achieve your cherished goal, then you'll follow through with relentless determination, persistence action and hence overcoming all obstacles falling in the way until you attain the desired result. This is called the power of commitment." "Commitment to your cherished goals is core criteria to your success. Strengthen it! Strengthen it! Strengthen it!"

The degree of commitment may be well understood by the lines given by Human G. Rockover: "When doing a job-anyone must feel that he owns it, and acts as though he will remain in that job – forever." "Commitment creates a magic in your mind. Once you commit yourself to something, you create a mental picture of what it would be like after achieving it and draw happiness from that imagination. Then, your mind immediately goes to work to realize it, like a magnet by attraction. Events, circumstances and opportunities will help bring a vivid picture in your mind about the reality which will bring joy of achievement." The words by W. H. Murry eloquently describe, "Until one is committed, there is hesitancy, the chance to draw back. Concerning all acts of initiative (and creation), there is one elementary truth, the ignorance of which kills countless ideas and splendid plans: that the moment one definitely commits oneself, then Providence moves too. All sorts of things occur to help one that would never otherwise have occurred. A whole stream of events issues from the decision, raising in one's favor all manner of unforeseen incidents and meetings and material assistance, which no man could have dreamed would have come his way. Whatever you can do, or dream you can do, begin it. Boldness has genius, power, and magic in it. Begin it now."

What a flow of magic from commitment! Commitment brings many valuable things in life such as personal growth; security of the job done; predictability of promises made, strong relationships between individuals and society; lasting of strong professional relationships; and growth of family, society, and organizations. "Without commitment, you cannot have depth and success in anything, whether it's a relationship, a business, a work, a duty or a hobby."

Commitment demands sacrifice in certain situations, values and ethics. Commitment to customer means giving quality service; commitment to marriage means fidelity; commitment to friendship means sharing joy, happiness, sorrow and maintaining confidentiality; commitment to decency means staying away from vulgarity and misbehavior; commitment to patriotism means sacrifice; commitment to society means responsibility and integrity; commitment to job means responsibility, dedication, integrity, and character; and so on. "Commitment to the philosophy of continual improvement is the key to reaching your potential and to achieve success in the journey of life." Margaret Mead said, "Never doubt that a small group of thoughtful committed citizens can change the world; indeed, it's the only thing that ever has." "Develop a culture of commitment to achieve goals."

IMPACTS OF COMMITMENT ON CERTAIN AREAS

There are various areas in which commitment is most important as given below:

a. **Commitment in Relationship**: There is a great importance of commitment in relationship. In fact, commitment is the bedrock, backbone and foundation of all types of relationships. It is said, "Love, above all things is a commitment to your choice. Don't break it." The bondage of love and respect in relationship has to be strong. "Love is 99.99% proximity in all aspects of human life."

"Benchmark yourself on every aspect of human life such as: How committed are you to winning? How committed are you to being a good friend? To being trustworthy? To being successful? How committed are you to being a good father, a good teammate, a good role model, a good husband? "If you score poorly, improve in all segments. Commitment of parents to love children is sometimes so exemplary that many mothers are donating kidneys to their children who have failed kidneys. But in recent years, bondage of love and respect in relationship has deteriorated due to materialistic world and high degree of self-interest. Few people are killing their girlfriends, spouses, mothers, fathers, sons, brothers, daughters and relatives. Perhaps, this is a new phase and it will go away and good sense will prevail but may be then it would be a little too late. People will return to the wish of Emma Bernstein, who said, "From the cradle to the grave, all I want is you."

b. **Commitment of defense personnel:** The ethos in defense services is all about commitment to the duties involved. Defense of a country without commitment is impossible. Civilian people can't imagine the degree of commitment shown by defense personnel. Just go through the following few examples of defense personnel showing their degree of commitment towards their work.

  i. The Indian army defeated the Pakistani army in Kargil War where the enemies were on top of the hill with full advantage of location whereas the Indian army had to crawl to reach the top in order to have a close fight against severe firing from top. Due to high degree of commitment the Indian army won the battle.

  ii. During World War II, combined army led by Paton won the World War II by defeating Germany and Japan through sheer commitment of highest degree.

  iii. During June, 2013, Uttarakhand (India) witnessed an unprecedented devastating flood which killed about 10,000 pilgrimages and locals and about 50,000 people got stranded at many places. It was the commitment of the Indian army and air force personnel who saved the lives of more than 10,000 people and rescued about 40,000 marooned people.

  iv. When tsunami hit Japan and devastated many cities, it was the Japanese army which rescued more than 60,000 people.

  v. During September 2014 when severe flood came in Jammu and Kashmir, it was the Indian Army, Air force and Disastrous Management Personnel who saved more than 8000 lives and rescued more than 30,000 marooned people.

Such stories of high degree of commitment of defense personnel are found all over the world.

c. **Commitment of Health Personnel:** Doctors and nurses from around the world take oath to serve the ailing persons in the best way possible by ignoring their comforts. Peter singer advocated, "Every profession will have its rogues, of course, no matter what oaths are sworn, but many health care professionals, have a real commitment to serving the best interests of their clients."

Ponder over the following serious accidents where doctors and nurses work relentlessly to save the patients.

i. Train and road accidents take place all over the world, some people die and some face severe injuries and some get minor injuries. Doctors and nurses serve the victims with high degree of commitment to save their lives.

ii. In poisonous liquor and fire tragedies, many people get seriously ill and it is the commitment of doctors and nurses which saves their lives.

iii. Earth quack victims are better served by doctors and nurses and their lives are saved due to the high degree of commitment that doctors and nurses exihibit to their patients.

d. **Commitment in Business and Entrepreneurship**: Business can't run without the commitment of two or more business persons involved in the deal. Though, the general conception (may be wrong) is that the majority of business people are dishonest, but there are some core values on which a business grows otherwise it will crumble. In big business deals, Memorandum of understanding (MOU) is signed which is nothing but a document of commitment. The companies follow this MOU in letter and spirit.

World over, many companies are known for their commitment.

There are **five golden rules** of entrepreneurship as given below in which one rule is commitment:

- Thinking is the capital.
- Enterprise is the way.
- Hard work is the solution.
- Commitment is the key.
- Passion is the driver.

Commitment to Entrepreneurial Idea Can Make You a Very Rich Person: Masayoshi Son was born in Japan. He moved to USA at the age of sixteen to study economics at University of California, Berkeley in 1977. "He made a commitment to a relentless schedule of One New Entrepreneurial Idea per Day." By the end of year 1978, he amassed over 250 such ideas. He set-up and acquired many companies. His personal worth at present is over USD 20 billion, the richest man of Japan, a 43rd ranker in Forbes billionaire index and a highly committed person towards his work of expertise.

The **message** of this story is: "Commitment to imagination of various new entrepreneurial ideas and acting on these relentlessly can make you a billionaire and an icon."

e. **Commitment in education**: Education is paramount important in human development and nation building. Knowledge and innovation (KI) is the currency of 21st century. When education is so much important, then one can think of what should be the level of commitment in this. Bob Beauprez has elucidated the requirement of commitment in his words, "Education is a shared commitment between dedicated teachers, motivated students and enthusiastic parents with high expectations".

There are many students, poor or rich, who are highly committed to their education. Some poor students travel more than ten kilometres daily on foot to go to school, work at home for living and even then they do much better in examinations. Lincoln had to travel a lot on foot to get books from library. Some teachers are also highly committed to teach students. But the number of such students and teachers is very less. The students who are not motivated and committed to their study, they perform poorly in examinations. The teachers who are not dedicated and committed to their duties, their students and institutions perform poorly.

"If any country or any state or any family wants to prosper, one has to invest heavily and to infuse commitment of highest order in all stakeholders in the field of education." In the top schools and universities of the world, all stakeholders are highly committed to quality and excellence. "A sensible government should be committed to these core elements called 4Es: Education, Equality, Employment and Empowerment in true sense."

f. **Commitment in games and sports**: Commitment is the key element in games and sports. Your commitment forces you to get up early from bed and go to stadium or training center, where you practice hard keeping in mind to excel. Since games and sports activities are very exhaustive and tiresome, without real commitment people may give up. It is only serious involvement, action, commitment and sacrifice will take you at a substantial position. Steve Maraboli said, "Intent reveals desire, action reveals commitment." Barack Obama opined, "A change is brought about because ordinary people do extraordinary things. This is only possible through extraordinary commitment of ordinary people."

Jayasurya, a Sri Lankan Batsman and one of the best to have played the game used to cover sixty kilometers to the stadium from his home by taking a train at 4 am for practicing in early days. Shooters have to practice hard with full concentration and this is not possible without real commitment. Similarly, all sorts of games and sports need a high degree of commitment, dedication, motivation, hard work, confidence and willpower to excel in respective field. A sports person who is not committed never see a champion in him. "The quality of your life is directly proportional to your commitment to excellence."

g. **Commitment in Music and Dance**: Music and dance, the most beautiful aspects of life are the reminiscent of dedication, commitment, hard work and sacrifice. Over and above the natural talent, these need high degree of commitment for daily practice for hours, proper food habits, sacrifice, and dedication. Watch the daily routine of great singers, great musicians and great dancers and you will be stunned to know their dedication, commitment and the sacrifices they make in order to excel in their profession. "Hardwork beats talent." Many talents have gone wasted away due to the lack of commitment and dedication.

h. **Commitment in Social Work**: There are many social workers who are highly committed to social service ignoring all hardships in their lives. Whatever they earn, they spend in social service and are always ready to extend manpower to needy ones. Mother Teresa is a living example of this.

i. **Commitment in general**: Commitment is needed in every profession, in every work for excellent result. Vince Lombardi elucidated it in very beautiful words, "Individual commitment to a group effort –that is what makes a team work, a company work, a society work, a civilization work." We move into action only because we have some degree of commitment to something.

"Productivity is directly proportional to the commitment of workers. If the productivities of industries, agriculture sector, corporate offices and government offices in respective terms are poor, it directly means persons involved are not committed to their duties." In Australia, the coal output is about two times more than India while employing half of labor force of India. In India itself, the plant load factor (PLF) is above 90% in all power plants run by NTPC whereas the PLF of power plants run by electricity boards in various states varies from 50% to 75%. What is the main reason that most of the industries run by government in any country go in red in a span of about 15 to 20 years with heavy losses? The main reason is the lack of commitment of all stakeholders due to various reasons. When many industries of U. K. were in the worst conditions due to the fall of commitmentsfrom employees, Prime Minister, Mrs. Margate Thatcher had to privatize these.

A Sheer Commitment to Duty Can Create Great Empathy

James Robertson (fifty-six years old) of Detroit (USA) walks thirty-four kilometres both ways, to his workplace after the bus ride up to bus terminal every day, for the last twelve years without a single absent on duty including shift duty, despite rain and snow. What a commitment to duty! After knowing his story which appeared recently in a Newspaper in January 2015, one university girl student, Evan Leady (nineteen years old) tried to raise USD 5,000 through donations online for his car and insurance and people poured around USD 90,000 to help Mr. James Robertson. What an empathy and cooperation for a highly dedicated person!

The **theme** of the story is: "It is the sheer commitment to duty even under adverse condition which energizes qualities like empathy and cooperation among people to help the committed person in an unprecedented way."

"There is no sure success without commitment." Commitment is a very pious word. For progress, success, and result, you need to be committed. "It is the commitment which separates the winners from the losers." The committed people are going to hang in and prevail, no matter what obstacles, what hardships they have to face. Losers need security and comfort; winners seek opportunity and challenges. Losers are non-committal; winners are highly committed. This is elucidated by the words of Mary Crowley, who said, "One person with commitment is worth more than 100 people who have only an interest."

STEPS TO IMPROVE YOUR COMMITMENT

Do the following to improve your commitment:

i. **Check your level of commitment**: People think that they are committed to something but their actions do not conform to commitment. It is necessary to spare sometime to validate your priorities. Are these in line with your commitment? If not, then improve. These are one of the indexes to measure the level of your commitment.

ii. **Find what's worth dying for**: Sometimes your thought reaches a level where you are compelled to do a certain thing irrespective of its consequences. Think over on your thoughts and watch whether your actions match your ideals. Find whether your ideals are worth dying for and always practice what you preach.

iii. **Adopt the Edison Method**: If you find difficulty in meeting commitment due to mindset, use the Edison method who used to announce his new ideas in press conference so that he could work hard to meet that commitment.

iv. **Make good planning**: Make a good and conducive planning about meeting your commitment.

Hey, men and women! Why are you non-committal to your cherished goal? Life is short. Contribute immensely through your commitment to your cherished goal, to your beloved ones, to your profession, to quality, to excellence, to environment, to your society and to your nation. "Make a real commitment and you can do wonders. God is ready to help those who are committed to good things."

CONCENTRATION ON GOAL BRINGS GLORY

"What do I mean by concentration? I mean focusing totally on the business at hand and commanding your body to exactly what you want it to do."

—*Arnold Parmer*

"Throughout my career, I have discovered and rediscovered a simple truth. It is this: the ability to concentrate single-minded on your most important task: to do it well and to finish it completely; is the key to great success, achievement, respect, status and happiness in life."

—*Brian Tracy*

Concentration (Focus)! A store of enormous power. A bowl of confidence. A quality like LASER beam. A full attention without distraction. Winning criteria. An excellent method to achieve success. An excellent way to complete all your pending tasks. Do you concentrate on your goal? If not, you will be a great loser. Commit to concentrate on your venture to succeed.

You might have heard people saying, "My son is not concentrating on studies, so his performance is poor in the class." "My brother, who is a businessman, is failing in his business because he is switching over from one business to another." What is the reason behind it? One of the major reasons for not getting what people want is the absence of concentration and focus on what is most important for the success. They have a habit to give priorities to things which are less important. No great accomplishment can be done without concentration, self-sacrifice, perspiration and doubt. Many people while realizing their goals gets involved in minor things and secondary activity and as a result, the share of involvement in the main goal is much less than required. Consequently, they fail miserably.

"Greatness is garnered by concentration."

"The four pillars of concentration are patience, sacrifice, inner happiness and perspiration." From the statistical data of achievers, it has been concluded that they make a conscious effort to stay focused and concentrated on those things that can really make a difference in their goals and lives and not on distraction agents. Then, what does prevent others to do so? This is because of the fact that many external effects coming in the ways such as minor problems, rituals, TV news, Internet, e-mails, Facebook, telephones, etc. side-track our focus and concentration from our main goal.

So, one has to sacrifice many things to concentrate and focus on goals. "You have to be very particular about time and energy management in aspects to other than the main goal such as relationships, sports, hobbies and commitments and the saved energy and time must be concentrated and focused on the main goal." Charles Dickens opined, "I never could have done what I have done, without the habits of punctuality, order, and diligence, without the determination to concentrate myself on one object at a time." There is a great power in concentrating on what you want in your life. By focusing on your health you can realize world-class vitality. By focusing on your project at hand, you can achieve greatness. The person who tries to do everything accomplishes nothing. Confucius said, "Person who chases two rabbits catches neither." Beware of chasing two rabbits at a time. You might end up earning nothing.

"Concentration on cherished goal creates intense power in the mind without any distraction which ensures great achievement with finest quality, with extreme beauty, and with excellent result."

Concentration or focus possesses enormous power. Concentrating or focusing electromagnetic waves (say the sun rays), through a magnifying glass, will set a living leaf on fire. Take the example of solar thermal power plant in which solar rays or solar energy are reflected through reflectors (also known as heliostats) and concentrated and focused on a central receiver (acting as boiler) where the normal temperature of sun rays about 15°C to 45°C reaches a value of about 1000°C after concentration and focusing. The power of LASER beam is known to us.

The same is true with human energy. When we concentrate and focus all our energy, resources and attention on a desired goal, success is achieved. This is well illustrated by the words of Chuck Norris, who said, "Whatever luck I had, I made. I was never a natural athlete, but I paid my dues in sweat and concentration and took time necessary to learn Karat and became world champion." Are you ready to concentrate on your goal to succeed?

"Practice your power of concentration on your chosen venture and get a powerful success in it."

"Laziness may appear attractive, but concentration on work gives satisfaction to the soul."

Consider the advices of coaches to players of various games. In these games, there are various techniques and specific positions. Coach asks players: "At which position and in which technique you have the best strength" Cultivate, nurture and give strength to that strength so from that position and technique you have the killing instinct. For example, Mahendra Singh Dhoni, captain of Indian cricket team, possesses great leadership qualities and plays the best cricket when he bats at the lower middle order as a finisher. So, the coach advises, "Concentrate more on this to give it a further strength in order to get sure success. In hockey, those who have strength in penalty corners, coach asks them to concentrate on this further to get killing instinct ensuring sure goal. Though, in every game, mental concentration is needed, but shooting, archery, golf, cricket, boxing are the games of more mental concentration. Bob Butera, the former president of New Jersey Hockey team opined, "What distinguishes winners from losers is that winners concentrate at all times on what they can do, not what they can't do." "Focus on your strengths and miracle will happen in the result."

The present world is highly competitive and jack of all trades and master of none are not going to help you much. It is always better to wear many hats, but it is too much difficult to manage all and getting constant success in all. It is advisable to concentrate and focus on one hat so that one shines constantly. Hobbies may be given some time for the sake of happiness. A player can't acquire excellence in football, cricket, hockey, basketball and baseball at a time as every game requires full energy and time for excellence. Daniel Greenberg said, "If you watch young children play, you will notice that they create games, character, situation, in which they immerse themselves, with intense concentration."

All over the world, wealth distributions have been studied by economists for most of the countries. The results show that in developed and in some developing countries, the wealth distribution is about 80/20, i.e. 80% of wealth is concentrated in about 20% people and about 20% of wealth is controlled by about 80% people.

First, it was studied on Italy by Vilfredo Pareto, an Italian economist in 1895. Later on, Dr. Joseph M. Juran coined it as 80/20 rule or the Pareto Theory.

This also means that bottom of the pyramid (about 80% people) are having average, below average or low income to lead their lives. Even in the game of team work, on any day, about 20% players click and produce 80% result. In general, 20% of any group produces 80% result.

What is the reason that in most of the cases 80/20 rule applies? It is because of the fact that only about 20% people concentrate and focus throughout life and give their best. The same principle can be applied in activities. If there are ten activities which demand your attention, concentrate on top two that will provide you about 80% result. In any company which produces commercial items, you will find that their 20% products give 80% turnover. As a result, many companies sell their low income verticals in which their strength is less. Willie Sutton said, "Success in any endeavor requires single-minded attention to detail and total concentration."

Entrepreneurship demands many skills but concentration is the most important one. Harold S. Geneen said, "The five essential entrepreneurial skills for success are: concentration, innovation, discrimination, organization, and communication (CIDOC)." The crux of the solution is that you concentrate and focus on your top (core) strength which will give you success in your cherished goal. "The depth of concentration is your key to success. Increase it! Increase it! Increase it!"

Music is like a flowing stream in a beautiful garden. Music adds beauty, joy, pleasure and meaning in life and can be learned and developed only through concentration. Paulo Coelho said, "Music for me, it demands full concentration."

Writing demands full concentration and full perspiration through long seating. Acting needs a lot of concentration to portray the character and live it. Those who don't practice many times and concentrate on the job, they fail miserably. Catherine Deneuve said, "You get involved with a character after spending a long time waiting, and this demands a lot of energy and concentration."

Are you poor in concentration? Here are the methods to improve it.

STEPS TO IMPROVE YOUR CONCENTRATION

Do the following to improve concentration:

i. **Meditate**: Meditation not only benefits the mind and body, but also the soul. It offers higher alpha waves, which are known to reduce feelings of negative mood, tension, sadness, and anger and increase concentration. You can improve your concentration power through meditation of about twenty to thirty minutes daily in a calm atmosphere.

ii. **Use positive attitude**: Use positive attitude to increase your concentration power.

iii. **Find the reasons and area of non-concentration**: Spare sometimes to find the causes and areas of non-concentration. Work on these to improve.

Hey, men and women! Are you willing to be victorious, winners and successful? If yes, then start concentrating on positive energy and focus it towards your goal by using your mind as concentrator, magnifying glass and laser beam. Your success is guaranteed.

"Apply 5Cs - character, courage, conviction, commitment, concentration in personal life as well as in governance and development (GD) of any organization or any institution or any country for 3Es-excellence, efficiency, and effectiveness and miracle will happen in the result."

STEPS TAKEN BY YOURSELF

From today, I decide to develop character, courage, conviction, commitment and concentration in my life. I will do the following to develop these:

i. _____

ii. _____

***

Chapter 8

Develop Passion, Patience, Persistence and Perspiration (4 Ps)
THE 7TH MANTRA

PASSION LEADS TO GLORY AND SUCCESS

"Passion rebuilds the world for the youth. It makes all things alive and significant."
—*Ralph Waldo Emerson*

"Great ambition is the passion of a great character. Those endowed with it may perform very good or very bad acts. All depends on the principles which direct them."
—*Napoleon Bonaparte*

A great industrialist-cum-speaker was asked by a fashion designer from the audience in an international conference to speak to us of passion, patience, persistence and perspiration. He said in sequence: Passion! A great internal fire for the goal. A strong motive force for action. An intense enthusiasm. A great motivator. An immense energy provider. A gateway to success. Hey, success seekers! Possess passion for your goals to prosper, to succeed and to achieve greatness in life.

You might have heard some parents say this innumerable number of time, "My son is very passionate about high-speed bikes; my daughter is passionate about fancy dress; my wife is passionate about enjoying the pristine beauty of nature." What does it mean? It means they are highly emotional and intensely enthusiastic about getting the things of their intense choice. Everybody has a passion to do something in his life. "Almighty God has put inside every person the potential to be passionate. One person with passion is greater than the passive force of hundred people who only have an interest." "Successful people in the world are the icons of passion." It is the passion for something which ignites us to accomplish our goals. "Passion is a pious, powerful, hidden fire in your belly to garner success. Ignite it! Ignite it! Ignite it!"

"If you possess passion for something, a high degree of energy is released to drive you till you achieve unachievable success."

"Human nature is such that every person loves something. We are shaped, conditioned and motivated to get what we love in an enthusiastic manner – This is our passion. If we ignore and become careless about a part of potential that God has put inside us as one of the virtue, we will be nowhere- a great loser. We have to find the reason behind our failure and stop the possibilities such as what grabs our attention, erodes our passion, arouses anger, utters strong words and involves in irrelevant actions which are detrimental to success. Many people intrigue with and bank upon their destiny. This is not going to help. Whatever possible from you to do, do it but accomplish it with all your might."

Note that, nothing significant can be achieved by any person without enthusiasm and passion. This is brilliantly described by the words of Lauren Conrad, who said, "There is never just one thing that leads to success for anyone. I feel it is a combination of passion, dedication, hard work, and being in the right place at the right time."

Be wildly enthusiastic to win the world of your domain. Spread passion while working which will motivate others. Go to the extra mile to motivate your co-workers, your juniors, your boss, and yourself. Ralph Waldo Emersion said, "Every great and commanding movement in the annals of the world is due to the triumph of enthusiasm." When you possess passion, there is nothing you can't do. "Passion is the mother of intense enthusiasm. Without passion no energy is released and without energy you have nothing."

Mathew Webb, Thomas William Burgess and Henry Sullivan crossed English Channel after first, fifteenth and seventh unsuccessful attempts respectively. Similarly, people engaged in other ventures, got success after many failures. What is the moral behind it? It simply suggests, "Most winners are just ex-losers but they were highly passionate about their goals and that is why they never gave up and succeeded." "When you add passion and emotion to belief, it will turn to passionate conviction which will allow you to achieve everything in life" It is said, "What generates passion and zeal in you is a clue to revealing your destiny. What you dream is a clue to revealing your greatness. What you love is a clue to revealing something you contain. What you speak is a clue to revealing your attitude and character. What decision and action you take is a clue to revealing your approaching success."

A great achiever possesses great patience and passion to achieve the position of a shining star in his or her pursuit. He has to ignite the passion to bell his dream. Every great dream is an imagination of a great dreamer. Always believe that you have the strength, the passion and the patience to become a star and to change the world. Are you ready to be passionate to change the world?

Take a glimpse of some successful people in certain fields like movie stars(Amitabh Bachchan, Shahrukh Khan, Angelina Jolie, etc.); singers (Lata Mangeshkar, Taylor Swift, etc.); musicians (A.R. Rahman, Eminem etc.); dancers (Madhuri Dixit, Hrithik Roshan, Helen, etc); sportsmen (Usain Bolt, Michael Phelps, etc.); games (Messi, Ronaldo, Tendulkar, Dhoni, Cook, Federer, etc.) who are the icons in their respective fields, with their quintessential style as a result of passion and enthusiasm.

"Successful people in any field are the reminiscent of passion, dedication, desire, conviction and hard work." "It is the passion that gives the leading edge to a profession." This is brilliantly described by the words of Martha Graham, who said, "Great dancers are not great because of their technique, they are great because of their passion."

"Life without passion is a life without spark. Passion is a fragrance of life. Passion emanates a glow from your face. It is a great motivator. It is your passion which will reinvent, recharge and reset you to regain your goal." This is elucidated brilliantly by the words of Henry Frédéric Amiel, a Swiss poet and philosopher, who said, "Without passion man is a mere latent force and a possibility, like the flint which awaits the shock of the iron before it can give forth its spark."

Your future is a reflection of your passion. No passion, no future. Great passion, great future. Remember, "The future belongs to those who have passion and greatwill to work hard." Hence, possess passion for your dream to garner success, to contribute greatly in the nation building.

Those who scaled the Mount Everest, those who crossed English Channel and those who sailed solo or as team around the world are the ones who are the living legends of passion, enthusiasm, courage, adventure and dream. See! How much difference is in the lives of such persons and ordinary persons? Many ordinary persons are fearful at every step whereas what they did it looks like unimaginable, fearful and impossible. It is due to the sheer passion and colossal enthusiasm of these great achievers. T.S. Eliot said, "It is obvious that we can no more explain a passion to a person who has never experienced it than we can explain light to the blind."

"What is the worst bankruptcy in the world? It is the man who lost his enthusiasm and passion. There is a direct relationship between believing and achieving. You must first learn to be a believer, if you want to be an achiever. You must follow your heart more than your mind." "But, if your belief is in wrong thing like terrorism under the umbrella of passion, then it will bring disaster and dooms day in the nation; so be careful about it." "Every great win in the history of the world in any field is due to the triumph of enthusiasm and passion. This is highly true with reference to civil right movement; freedom of a country; achievement of top players, top movie stars, top dancers and top companies of the world."

It is the passion of a person who fights against injustice, frees slaves, overthrows tyrants, brings freedom, brings quality in profession and does adventure. It was the passion and conviction of Bhagat Singh and Rajguru for the freedom of India that led them to fight against British even if it meant sacrificing their lives. It was the passion and conviction of Mahatma Gandhi for the freedom of India that led to freedom on 14 August, 1947. This is brilliantly elucidated by the words of Jim Butcher, who said, "Also known as passion, I said quietly. Passion has overthrown tyrants, and freed prisoners and slaves. Passion has brought justice where there was savagery. Passion has created freedom where there was nothing but fear. Passion has helped souls rise from the ashes of their horrible lives and built something better, stronger, and more beautiful." Are you going to have a great passion which can fulfil the dreams of Jim Butcher?

Passion Brings Success Irrespective of Age: There is no age of hope and passion. For becoming self-independent, an illiterate lady laborer of sixty-year old, Norti Bai of Rajasthan (India) living on daily wage learned reading, writing, and basics of computer –operations, typing, e-mailing and trained more than 200 girls.

What a passion of learning of an illiterate lady at the age of sixty!

The **theme** we learn here is very simple, "Passion shapes the destiny irrespective of age and background."

"Passion is a pure mind game. Passion opens every door of human life. Sometimes, it looks everything-guide, joy, pleasure, driver, grief reliever, achiever, winner and what not."

Passion rules us all. "Awaken your sleeping passion for your goal to lead a vibrant, beautiful, successful and glorious life."

STEPS TO IMPROVE YOUR PASSION

Do the following to improve your passion:

i. **Measure your fire in the belly:** Have you ever realized how passionate are you about your life and dream? Passion brings fire in the belly. Is it true in your case? If not, then believe in the power of passion and bring it in your life.

ii. **Back to childhood love:** What really fascinated you in your childhood? Remember and try to revive them now. This will bring passion in your life.

iii. **Be in the company of passionate people:** If you associate with passionate people, you will also be motivated and energized. If you associate yourself with less-passionate people, you will find yourself going in the same way.

iv. **Read biographies of great people:** Read the biographies of great freedom fighters such as Bhagat Singh, Mahatma Gandhi, Nelson Mandela and other great performers in other fields. This will bring passion, motivation and inspiration in your life.

v. **Use auto-suggestions:** By using auto-suggestions you can bring passion in your life.

Hey, sons and daughters of God! Do you desire to achieve your goal? If yes, then arouse your passion for your dream and success will kiss your feet. Follow the above methods outlined to improve passion for your goal. The Almighty God is ready to help you at every juncture.

PATIENCE MOVES MOUNTAIN

"Patience and diligence, like faith, remove mountain."

—*William Penn*

"Adopt the pace of nature: her secret is patience."

—*Ralph Waldo Emerson*

Patience! A pace of nature. A vast ocean of tolerance. A secret of success. A rhythm of life. Are you a person of patience? If not, you will be a great loser. Be a man of patience to win over the complex problems, to succeed, to achieve greatness, to win the world.

Have you ever given a thought about the way of God, the way of nature? Is there any hurry in nature? No. Nature is incredibly organized and has a definite flow and pace. "The Rhythm of life," an outstanding book of Richard Exley clearly shows that God has created us to lead a life of right balance like nature. "We must live in a rhythm and adopt the pace of God whose secret is patience."

"Patience being the greatest virtue of human being is the key to success and with its smooth touch, all problems vanish with time. For a patient man, no road is too long, no glory is too far, no mountain is too high and no task is too difficult."

"What are the reasons of people being impatient? There are many reasons; unprogrammed mind which resides in a materialistic world, greed to earn more, out of pace at one place creates pressure at another place, the lack of wisdom, the lack of meditation, wrong notion, wrong advice and other major reasons which keeps us down." The adage "Haste is waste" is entirely true in life but people don't learn or rather don't wish to learn. "Patience is the way of God – His great secret. Patience is needed in every sphere of life." "Humanity needs a more patient world." This has been brilliantly described by the words of Steve Maraboli, who said, "Think of patience, God has had for you and let it resonate to others. If you want a more patient world let patience be your motto."

We have to learn a lot including patience from our nearby garden. A gardener goes on watering plants for months but buds appear at their own time. "Everything has a pace and the result will take sometimes and it will come on time." "A garden is a grand teacher in many respects. It not only teaches patience, careful watchfulness, beauty, planning, industry, thrift, but also entire trust of the world.

"Being impatient means inviting waste, problems and delay." People undo themselves by impatience. In general, one of the most frequent causes of failure is in being impatient in waiting for results." English poet and play writer Thomas Shadwell remarked, "The haste of a fool is the slowest thing in the world." Basically, impatience is a headache and problems in waiting. "Patience is the route to prosperity, peace, and pride." "Believe in the power of patience which has the power to overcome very powerful obstacles smoothly to bell a great success. Possess it! Possess it! Possess it!"

All seasons –winter, spring, summer and rainy come on time at a particular geography. The spring will only come after the winter. A wise man said, "There is a time to let things happen and a time to make things happen."

"There is no need of hurry for anything at all. Go on working rightly at the right pace and you will get result on the right time. One shouldn't consider a patient man as weak. He has abundance of power." It is said, "Beware the fury of a patient man." Among blessings, we get many times pains and sorrows and our main weapon to deal with adversities is patience. Joseph Addison beautifully portrays this, "Our real blessings often appear to us in the shape of pains, losses and disappointments; but let us have patience and we soon shall see them in their proper figures."

Abraham Lincoln, former President of USA faced darkest hours of civil war when he wanted to give equal right to the black people. He ultimately won but it was his patience which took him to that victory. The message from Lincoln story is very simple, "Patience brings great strength to win over gigantic tides and troubles." By burning the candle at both ends doesn't give double light instead handling becomes difficult. How we should lead life in difficult situation is well expressed by the words of Dr. MervRosell, who said, "A good man, like a candle, must keep cool and burn at the same time." The words of Leo Tolstoy portray the period of Lincoln in a beautiful way, "The two most powerful warriors are patience and time." "The most secret code of success is imbedded in patience, a non-replaceable virtue. It takes time to bell a great goal."

"In almost all games and sports, there is a need for utmost patience and cool head. Though, some games and sports look aggressive, players have to be patient and maintain their composure otherwise instant reflection, judgment and strategies will not work." Mahendra Singh Dhoni, the captain of Indian cricket team (known as captain cool) is supposedly the best captain due to his patience, cool mind and great finishing skills. Steve Maraboli advised, "We must remember balance and moderation. Patience can be spiritually enriching and virtuous – but taken in excess, it turns to procrastination, the poison of inaction."

"It is said that patience comes through wisdom and wisdom comes through experience. So, one has to be very keen for experience." A saint said, "Patience is the companion of wisdom." For human being, patience is a great treasure. Acquire it and be rich in life. This was brilliantly elucidated by the words of Lao Tzu, who advocated, "I have just three things to teach: simplicity, patience, compassion. These three are our greatest treasures."

Hey, young men and women! Identify yourself! Are you impatient? If yes, immediately work out for this. "Go for meditation and calm your mind. Tell yourself that for any work I will not be in haste and I will adopt the pace of nature. Tell yourself at least five times a day that I have to maintain patience in all circumstances. Once you achieve some degree of patience, you will derive the benefits and your patience level will be multiplied. A cool head brings joy in life. Patience is a great leveler of pain and sorrow. Observe closely a patient man. Follow his footsteps. Your success is sure if you have become a man of patience."

PERSISTENCE GARNERS GLORIOUS SUCCESS

"A little more persistence, a little more effort, and what seemed hopeless failure may turn to glorious success."

—*Elbert Hubbard*

"It's not that I'm so smart; it's just that I stay with problem longer."
—*Albert Einstein*

Persistence! A conqueror of the world. A magical effect. An omnipotent tool for success. An unparalleled recipe for success. Practice persistence and miracle will happen in your life. Happiness will be hugging you and success, kissing you.

Have you ever realized the power of persistence? It is amazing and unbelievable. Throughout human civilization it has left a great and grand imprint on our success in any venture. "Consistence, persistence and perseverance are the greatest tools of human beings." It is said, "Goal is the path to success; persistence is the vehicle you arrive in." "Any great and difficult work can't be achieved without being consistent and persistent. Many geniuses couldn't achieve much due to the lack of persistence and consistence." This has been well expressed in the beautiful words of Calvin Coolidge, who said, "Nothing in this world can take place of persistence. Talent will not; nothing is more common than unsuccessful people with talent. Genius will not; unrewarded genius is almost a proverb. Education will not; the world is full of educated failures. Persistence and determination alone are omnipotent." "Practice persistence to be winner and a history maker."

"Talent alone doesn't take you very far. Talent accompanied with will, desire, patience, persistence and perspiration yield desired result. Talent in the absence of these things vanishes and even modest talent with those characteristics flourishes.

"There is a unique characteristic to persistent people who begin their success where most others quit in desperation. People get involved in their goals and want to finish work as soon possible. But every goal takes time for its completion, engulfed with many problems and hardships. Ordinary people quit when time taking is more and problems crop up, but a man of persistence sticks to his/her goal, faces all hardships with courage and patience and finally emerges victorious." "Persistent people are winners whereas others are losers." It has been observed that one person with commitment, persistence, and perseverance accomplishes more than the work done by hundred people with interest alone. "Persistence is your prime power to produce miracle in your success story. Practice it! Practice it! Practice it!"

"Persistence, perseverance and passion are omnipotent and possess magical effect yielding grand success, and enabling even mediocre to give scintillating performance surpassing meritorious."

Your overall growth totally depends upon your habit of persistence. A right mindset has to be created to adorn the virtue of persistence. There is no substitute to persistence. It is the most accurate weapon for success. It can't be supplemented by any other quality. Develop this habit and your life will be prosperous and joyful. "Passion, patience, persistence and perspiration conquer all things." "You will achieve success in proportion to your degree of persistence."

Remember the **mantra** of winning: "For winning in life you have to go an extra mile. Those who are not ready to go an extra mile, they fail in their goal. If you analyze the story of all winners, they worked longer, stayed longer, practiced longer, studied longer, swam longer, ran longer, planned longer, acted longer, sang longer, danced longer, etc. Only persistent people can take in this pain."

Ponder over the work culture of following categories of various winners who worked persistently and got glorious success in life:

i. **Movie Business People**: Movie business requires a habit of immense persistence among all stakeholders, especially actors, and actresses. Before filming any scene, they have to first think over the character, do hours of practice, sit hours for make-up and then act and film at suitable locations and go through many cuts consuming hours. Those who are persistent survive and reach at the top of the ladder. Stars of Bollywood such as Amitabh Bachchan, Shahrukh Khan, Aamir Khan, Salman Khan, Madhuri Dixit, Priyanka Chopra, Katrina Kaif, etc. and stars of Hollywood such as Angelina Jolie, Julia Roberts, Hugh Grant, Steve Martin, etc. rose to their respective heights due to their sheer habit of persistence and sufficient potentials. Those who lack in persistence fail after few attempts.

ii. **Businessmen**: Success in business demands a habit of persistence in founder/founders. Henry Ford was known as ruthless to follow his plans with persistence which fulfilled all his dreams. Tom Monaghan, founder of Domino's Pizza started with one store pizza parlor and raised it to a chain of several thousand stores worldwide by working persistently. Bill Gates, the founder of Microsoft and Steve Jobs, founder of Apple Computers are living legends of persistence.

iii. **Sportspersons**: In sports and games, there is need for persistence during practice and for remaining fit. Those who are inconsistent fail miserably even with talent. Top players of Tennis such as Roger Federer, Rafael Nadal, Serena Williams, Sharapova, Sania Mirza, etc. are the symbols of persistence.

iv. **Musicians and Dancers**: Music and dance demands persistent efforts in practice and developing new styles and to perfect them. Recall the life stories of famous musicians, singers, and dancers and you will find that they are the beacon of persistence. Take the example of A. R. Rahman, Lata Mangeskar, Asha Bhonsle, Ravi Shankar, Saroj Khan, Madhuri Dixit, Beatles and Nicole Scherzinger. They became masters in their respective field only through persistent effort in practicing and innovating.

"Mastery in any profession is the result of persistent efforts. If you have achieved some height in your profession and you stop working, you will lose your mastery in the profession. Mastery is a journey till your life." Pablo Picasso, the great artist became genius through consistent and persistent efforts for more than thirty years. The words of George Leonard showcase this beautifully, who said, "We fail to realize that mastery is not about perfection. It's about a process, a journey. The master is the one who stays on the path day after day, year after year. The master is the one who is willing to try and fail, and try again, for as long as he or she lives."

Success in respective venture and goal will be achieved at its own time provided you are committed to your goal and working hard persistently. A 100 m race just takes about 9.58 seconds to earn gold medal but it doesn't mean that the success for the winner is the job of a few seconds. To win a race, persistent practice of high degree and remaining fit takes years together. This is well expressed by the words of Denis Waitley, who said, "As long as we are persistent in our deepest destiny, we will continue to grow. We cannot choose the day or time when we will fully bloom. It happens in its own time." "Flaming enthusiasm, accompanied with toil, courage and persistence makes you a great winner."

Excellence and quality in any pursuit are the results of persistence. Both need time, perspiration, patience, persistence and will. Persistence and excellence are called twin sisters. One is associated with time, while other with quality. Those who believe in quality and excellence are not in hurry. They know that both will not come in hurry rather it is a mindset and only a man of persistence will achieve quality and excellence. Remember: 6Ps- "Passionate persistence with politeness produces progress and prosperity."

Following are the stories of failures due to the lack of persistence.

Lacking in Persistence Leads You to Failure: Many students who are not regular and persistent in their studies, either they fail in examination or get poor score in spite of their potential.

Some players of football, cricket, hockey, etc., do very well in the beginning in their games and get selected for national/international level matches due to their potential and performance. For one or two years, few of them remain out of form. Due to the lack of persistence in their practice they do not regain the form and are sent out of the team.

It is said, "If you wish to be victorious, successful and a true champ, you need to be consistent, persistent and patient." The adage: "Where there is no hope go to persistence" is highly true. Dale Carnegie opined, "Most of the important things in the world have been accomplished by people who have kept on trying when there seemed to be no hope at all." Have you heard, drops of water can make a hole in even hardest stone? Yes, it is true. "Persistent falling of drops at the same place makes hole even in hardest stones. It is called power of persistence." This is well elucidated by the words of Lucretius, who said," The drops of rain make a hole in the stone not by violence but by apt falling.

"Persistence accompanied with passion, patience, perspiration, perseverance and prayer pays with productivity, profits, prosperity, proficiency, perfection and peace". This is called (7+6) Ps of persistence. Practice this in life for glorious success.

Oh! Dreamers! Dreaming alone will not get what you want to achieve. Embrace persistence like you do with your beloved one. Put it in your habits. The Almighty God is with you being His sons and daughters. "Success, how difficult it is. Winning, how competitive it is. Achievement, how far it is. Excellence, how mind boggling it is, and quality, how time consuming it is. All are possible by the pleasant, peaceful stroke of persistence." Believe in this above expression and be a man of persistence from the core of heart for glorious success.

PERSPIRATION BRINGS GOLDEN SUCCESS

"Patience, persistence and perspiration make an unbeatable combination for success."

—Napoleon Hill

"Genius is one percent inspiration and ninety-nine percent perspiration."

—Thomas A. Edison

Perspiration! A habit of long working hours even in adverse condition. A great tool for success and glory. A recipe for becoming competent and successful. A game changer. A success provider. Do you perspire hard to achieve your goal? If not, success is a distant dream for you. Perspire enough on your chosen goal to succeed, to win, and to achieve greatness.

The adage "There is no substitute to perspiration (hard work)" is an eternal truth. Without perspiration nothing is possible. Even for eating the food prepared by someone, you need to keep the items on a plate. You need to use your hand or a spoon for putting the food in your mouth and you have to chew it. "It is perspiration in a chosen venture which makes you competent and successful."

"Just watch the ants. You will find them running all the time for food, for carrying food, for digging their homes. Hardly, you will find an ant sitting idle or sleeping. They are capable of carrying load about ten times of their own weight. If the things are too heavy, they have the concept of team work. They are highly capable of finding shortest route." "Nothing preaches perspiration better than ants."

"Just watch the fishes. They swim continuously with hardly any rest. Persistence and perspiration is their way of living. We have to learn from fishes." "You will achieve success in proportion to your degree of perspiration." Mere dreams or desires or wishes alone don't bring success. Mark Twain advocated "Thunder is good, thunder is impressive but it is the lightening that does work." Act like an athlete to perspire hard through daily practice in the most important domains of your life. There is a need to practice to get your greatness. The price of perspiration is always less than regret. "Greatness demands its price in the form of perspiration, sacrifices, difficult life."

"Passion, patience, persistence and perspiration (4Ps) are the founding and unshakable pillars of unbelievable growth, fullest happiness, glorious achievement, and unparalleled success. It depends upon you how efficiently, how judiciously, you use the symbiosis combination of 4Ps for the fulfilment of your cherished desire and goal, the way you want."

"If you want success, if you want to achieve something, if you want to accomplish anything worthwhile, you have to perspire (work hard)." This is expressed beautifully by the words of Thomas A. Edison, who said, "The three great essentials to achieve anything worthwhile are first, hard work; second stick to activeness; third common sense." In order to succeed, you must have firm resolves, tenacity and persistence. Be geared to work hard all the way. Never give up in the journey of success.

The Almighty God has given everybody twenty-four hours in a day. Your progress depends upon how well, how judiciously you utilize your time. Twenty-four hours in a day should be divided in two parts- twelve hours for professional work (students included here) and twelve hours for personal life. Some high position work demands more than twelve hours, so that time has to be taken from time allotted for personal life. In some cases, people work for sixteen to eighteen hours a day. Time is your money. Don't waste. It can't be recovered. A large number of people waste too much time and as a result they remain at lower ladder of life. One should develop long working culture from student life itself. "Perspiration is your prime faithful vehicle to take you to your destination to bell a great dream. Practice it! Practice it! Practice it!"

Take a glimpse of working hours of some top persons in their respective professions. Prime Ministers, presidents, chief ministers, chief secretaries, chief justice of any country work fourteen to eighteen hours a day. Former President of USA Bill Clinton, and former state secretary Ms. Condole Rice were called workaholics as they used to work for sixteen to eighteen hours a day. Present Prime Minister of India, Narendra Modi works for about sixteen to eighteen hours a day. Many chief executive officers (CEOs) of MNCs work for about fourteen to sixteen hours a day. Many chief secretaries of center and state level work for about fourteen to sixteen hours a day. If you ask these people about their working hours in student life and early stages of profession they will tell you (except some) that they were working about twelve hours a day. Even some labors (skilled and unskilled) work for fourteen to sixteen hours a day, however, their earning is less but much better than their counter parts who work less. "Your time is most valuable thing in life as whatever time is wasted it can't be retrieved." This has been well elucidated by the words of Brian Tracy, who said, "Your greatest asset is your earning ability. Your greatest resource is time." In a conference, Sardar Raunak Singh, Chairman of Apollo Tyres group was the chief guest. One student asked him a question: "What is the cause for the success of the Apollo Group?" He answered, "Hard work, honesty and God above."

Writing work starts with inspiration and passion but its completion is mainly perspiration. This is well illustrated by the words of Robert Fanny, who said, "It has been often said that writing is 99 percent perspiration and 1 percent inspiration. In my experience, this is true. But, in my opinion, it is useless without that 1 percent. It's like an engine without fuel – can't get anywhere without it or like a lighthouse without a light on top- doesn't guide anyone home or to safe harbor." In making a writer, a judicious combination of inspiration, perspiration and desperation matters.

Many people show that they are very busy but produce no output. Gossiping is the greatest time killer if it is not generating new ideas. This has been eloquently described by the words of Thomas A. Edison, who said, "Being busy does not always mean real work. The object of all work is production or accomplishment and to either of these ends there be forethought, system, planning, intelligence, and honest purpose, as well as perspiration. Seeming to do is not doing."

Remember: "Time is the most valuable, precious, and fortune maker. It is our currency. It is your wealth. Everybody gets twenty-four hours in a day but the proper utilization of time, the proper selection of profession as per choice, the judicious planning and putting sufficient perspiration make great difference in your life."

For three minutes of an item dance, the actresses of Bollywood charge anything between Rs.10 million to 30 million. In IPL T-20, cricket match, the income of the top players lies in the range of Rs.0.3 to 0.5 million per run. One minute sketch of Pablo Picasso fetches millions of dollars. It doesn't merely mean that a three minutes dance or one run or one minute sketch is leading to the earning, but the talent accompanied with much severe perspiration, passion and patience put during the past years in high earning profession to reach at present level of branding is earning this huge sum of money. The adage: "Rome was not built in a day" is applicable in different sense with all top earning people. They have built themselves at this level through sheer perspiration, passion, persistence, patience and talent in professions which are more paying.

"In service, scale is the limit while in business or entrepreneurship, sky is the limit. Again, variation in income comes from type of service, type of pofession and type of business (personal consultancy included) including its size. Further, variation in position and income in a particular profession comes with duration of perspiration per day, your talent, your patience, your passion, your strategies and your leadership quality." Data collected from all over the world suggest that: "behind every extraordinary achievement, there was an extraordinary effort." "Remember that the best among us are not more gifted than the rest. It is just little extra step each day they took which got added into weeks, weeks into months, months into years, and finally, they occupied the throne of extraordinary." "Taking extra step each day in your venture makes you an extraordinary person in the long run."

Hey, students! Hey, men and women! Get up from slumber, nobody dies out of hard work, enjoy working at the fullest level, and perspire too much in your chosen profession (including study). And you will find the success in your clutch, achievement in your hand, happiness will be prevailing in every hair of your body, you will enjoy life with your family and friends like never before and finally you will scream -YAHOO.

STEPS TAKEN BY YOURSELF

I (as a reader) will do the following to develop passion, patience, persistence and perspiration for achieving my goals:

i. _____

ii. _____

iii. _____

iv. _____

***

Chapter 9

Practice Cooperation, Harmony, Wisdom and Forgiveness

#THE 8ᵀᴴ MANTRA

COOPERATION IS A PRICELESS ASSET

"The only thing that will redeem mankind is cooperation."

—Bertrand Russell

"We all do better when we work together. Our differences do matter, but our common humanity matters more."

—Bill Clinton

A monk-cum speaker was asked by a student from the audience in a congregation to speak to us of cooperation, harmony, wisdom and forgiveness. He replied in sequence: Cooperation! Cooperation! Cooperation! A staircase to excellence. Many strong shoulders to support. Many hands to push forward. Many minds to create sizzling environment to grow, to excel, to enjoy, and to live happily. Is cooperation a buzzword of society? Is it a need of humanity? Yes, it is. Practice cooperation and success will be in your clutch.

Cooperation is a priceless asset and golden gift for human beings. Visualize the upbringing of children by parents. Though, it comes under the duty, love and affection of parents but it may also be clubbed under cooperation of parents with children. Similarly, children also take care of their old parents. In general, cooperation isa two-way traffic. At every stage, we need cooperation from spouse, children, neighbors, friends, relatives, parents. It is said that "Your best relative is your neighbor" and one should not keep bad relations with the neighbor as in emergency only they can help you. "Humanity thrives on cooperation." Extending cooperation to others is a mindset, an ethic and an act of humanity. This has been elucidated by the words of Bertrand Russell, who said, "Ethics is in the origin, the art of recommending to others, the sacrifices required for cooperation with oneself." Indian culture is great in the concept of cooperation. It follows the mantra of "Vasudhaiva Kutumbakam", which means "the whole world is our family and family members are respected and loved." This is the one form of great cooperation. Lance Armstrong said, "Anyone who imagines they can work alone winds up surrounded by nothing but rivals without companion. The fact is, no one ascends alone."

"The four pillars of cooperation are: love, respect, friendship and compassion." "For the progress of an organization and a nation, cooperation is the core element." Henry Ford portrayed this beautifully, "Coming together is a beginning; keeping together is progress; working together is success." At the society level, people form groups for getting cooperation. On international level, many countries have made some groups to cooperate with each other, such as European Union (EU), G-7 Countries, G-20, OECD, BRICS Countries, Arab League, South Asian Countries, etc.

"Cooperation creates sizzling atmosphere of brotherhood, friendship, progress and brings success and wealth; while non-cooperation brings evils."

"God has sent us for the sake of others and we are connected with many unknown souls in the case of need or no need." This has been well portrayed by the words of Albert Einstein, who said, "Each of us comes for a short visit, not knowing why, yet sometimes seeming to be a divine purpose. Many times a day, I realize how much my outer and inner life is built upon the labors of people both living and dead, and how earnestly I must exert myself in order to give in return as much as I have received and I am still receiving."

"From the birth to the death, we need cooperation and extend cooperation with each other as in the absence of cooperation our survival is not possible. During the delivery of a baby, cooperation from doctors and nurses are given to the extreme extent to the lady. In remote villages, the expert maids help in the delivery. Further, the lady undergoing pain has to cooperate with the doctors, nurses and maids. Though, it comes under the duties of doctors, nurses and maids, if the concept of cooperation is not embedded with duty, the result will not be effective. During upbringing of the child, parents give complete cooperation to their kids out of love and affection and the child also cooperates with parents by stopping to cry or by simply obeying his parents."

In schools, teachers and children cooperate with each other otherwise learning is not possible. After the marriage, the relation between husband and wife will last only on the basis of mutual cooperation, love, affection and respect. Maintaining other relations also requires mutual cooperation, love, affection and respect. Harmonious cooperation is not only a priceless asset, but a gift of God. You will receive it in proportion to your giving. In service, a lot of cooperation is exchanged among juniors, seniors and bosses; otherwise the work cannot be completed. For the survival and growth of any organization, any institution, any office, any industry, cooperation is always needed among employees and bosses. Orison Swett Marden opined, "No employer today is independent of those around him. He cannot succeed alone, no matter, how great his ability or capital. Business today is more than ever a question of cooperation."

Build social capital for getting cooperation. As per new research, social capital could be your greatest asset. Social contacts enhance the productivity of individuals, teams, families, communities, and organizations. In the absence of adequate social relationships, you will feel lonely, isolated and empty, resulting in many chronic diseases.

"Richness in social capital sails you smoothly in the world of success."

"In the case of road accident, if cooperation is not provided by the passers-by, all serious victims will die, as the police in general tend to arrive late in most of the countries. Once we get cooperation from others, we should extend cooperation to others in return and it comes automatically. In the case of accidental fire in a house, especially in villages where fire extinguishers are not available, it is the villagers who cooperate in extinguishing the fire. When train accident takes place, it is the nearby villagers or residents who help the victims immediately. Police and railway employees reach much later to the site."

In conduction of social functions and marriages, a lot of cooperation is extended by society including relatives and neighbors. When one dies, it is the society including relatives and neighbors who cooperate in smooth conduction of ritual as per religion. "In any game, no team can win without cooperation from all players and team spirit. No movie can be produced without the cooperation of all stakeholders. Even agricultural work cannot be completed without the cooperation of all family members or employees. A country's freedom cannot be protected without the cooperation of all units of defense and other stakeholders. A war cannot be won without the cooperation of all stakeholders. Wherever cooperation is not extended, the performance of that unit is extremely poor."

The **message** from the above cited cases is: "Cooperation is the core of human civilization and forms the backbone for peace, progress, prosperity and survival of human beings. In its absence, our existence is at stake."

Though, competition is supposed to be the best tool for growth sometimes, after certain stage, competition may lead to disaster. This is also well described by Franklin D. Roosevelt, who said, "Competition has been shown to be useful up to a certain point and no further, but cooperation, which is the thing we must strive for today, begin where competition leaves off".

Language also plays great role in extending cooperation to each other. If the same language speaking people live in a land of different languages, they extend cooperation with each other. A language is a unique vocal symbol which attracts social groups to cooperate. When North Indian Hindi speaking people go to foreign countries or South Indians go to foreign countries, or when South Indians live in North India, or North Indians live in South India, they cooperate with each other on the basis of language.

Cooperation is extended at international levels to the needy countries by United Nations. This was well expressed by Kofi Annan, who said, "More than ever before in the human history, we share a common destiny. We can master it only, if we face it together. That is why we have United Nations."

In containing terrorism, other nationals help in combating terrorism. Terrorism is a great threat to the world and it has to be contained or eliminated. This has been well expressed by Barack Obama, who said, "Where the stakes are the highest, i.e. the war on terror, we cannot possibly succeed without extraordinary international cooperation. Effective international police actions require the highest degree of intelligence, sharing, planning and collaborative enforcement."

The following story will focus on the failure of the persons lacking in cooperation.

A Non-cooperative Attitude is Harmful for Your Dream: A highly qualified professor was appointed vice-chancellor of a leading university. He was arrogant, anti- dialogue and was not in the habit of supporting employees and students even for good cause. As usual, various types of problems started to creep in the university and due to the lack of cooperative attitude towards the employees, nobody cooperated with him when a severe problem arose. A lot of problems remained unsolved which multiplied the problems in the university and finally the vice-chancellor had to leave the university.

The **theme** of above story is: "Cooperative attitude is a must to live happily in a society, to prosper in life, to run and improve an organization smoothly, and to bring harmony among societies, and among nations."

In concluding remarks, I would like to say that if you want to get success, happiness, and brotherhood, you have to provide cooperation to others, and in return, at least about 80% people to whom you have cooperated plus 20% others will cooperate with you in achieving your success. Any individual who is not cooperative will have to face a lot of problems himself and may fail. Any family in which its members are not cooperative among themselves is bound to remain at lower ladder of success. "Any organization in which its employees are not cooperative will remain at lower ladder of branding and success and even may fail. Any nation who is not cooperative with other countries is bound to remain a poor country with a lot of problems and even its survival is difficult." "The concept of cooperation is core to your success, well-being and prosperity. Nurture it! Nurture it! Nurture it!"

Are you a cooperative person? Have you ever realized the bad effects of non-cooperative attitude? If your answer is no, make a habit to extend cooperation to others. Humanity can't survive without cooperation. Hey, sons and daughters of the Almighty God! "You have been sent to serve not only yourself but more to others. In return, God will send a great team of people to help you, cooperate with you in your journey of success. Learn cooperation from ants which are its unparalleled symbol."

HARMONY BRINGS PEACE AND PROSPERITY

Always aim at complete harmony of thought and word and deed. Always aim at purifying your thought and everything will be well."

— *Mahatma Gandhi*

"In the end we shall have had enough of cynicism, skepticism and humbug, and we shall want to live more musically."

—*Vincent Van Gogh*

Harmony! A musical living at the same wave-length. An environment of happiness and joy. A bridge builder among people. A peace and success maker. Believe in harmony and create a harmonious culture among all existence to remain happy, to lead a peaceful life, to succeed.

Have you ever thought about the importance of harmony? You will realize it when you think over the working of a body of any living creature. All the elements of our body work in harmony with each other and due to this harmonious culture of our body, we are able to live, grow, work, feel happy, sleep well, remain in peace, show love and affection to others. There is harmony in nature. "Harmony with all existence offers you a highway of happiness humming with peace and prosperity. Nurture it! Nurture it! Nurture it!"

"Generosity, love, affection, respect, happiness, tolerance, human values, cooperation, ethics and forgiveness are the backbone of harmony." Thomas Merton advocated, "Happiness is not matter of intensity but of balance, order, rhythm and harmony." For your progress and well-being, you have to make peace with yourself. The key is to find the harmony in what you love." Relation between human beings depends upon cooperation and harmony. God is always helpful in this respect. Robert H. Schuller eloquently said," When God sees breach-He builds bridge! When He sees a scar-He creates a star." If you want to grow, you have to maintain the harmony with existence otherwise you will be ruined. This has been well expressed by the words of Sallust, who said, "Harmony makes small things grow; lack of it makes great things decay." "There is a direct relation between power of harmony and power of joy. Better harmony leads to better life." "It is the highest job of education providers to teach the concept of harmony to students who are the future builders of their nation." The words of Rabindranath Tagore elucidate this beautifully, "The highest education is that which does not merely give us information but makes our life stay in harmony with all existence."

"Your success will depend upon your ecosystem of harmonious culture with yourself, with others and with all existence as it helps in clearing the passage of success, in bringing peace and happiness in life."

For a glorious life to lead, one needs to believe in the Almighty God and remain in harmony with Him. The words uttered by Sai Baba gives a glimpse of that. Baba said, "The life ahead can only be glorious if you learn to live in total harmony with the Lord." Harmony is the call of nature. Except human beings, all creatures of the world live in harmony with all existence. "We have an obligation to live in harmony with creation."

CONSEQUENCES OF ABSENCE OF HARMONY

In the absence of total harmony amongself, family, society, culture, administration, politics, religion, cast, nations, etc., various kinds of clashes, violence, chaos and conflicts- a havoc erupts all over the world. These result in loss of thousands of innocent lives and loss of properties (private and government). Further, these create hatred, and hamper peace, prosperity, happiness, and growth of people including nations. Just recall the past and present clashes all over the world; we will realize the importance of harmony. The riots that erupted in India during partition in 1947, various riots till date; sectarian violence in Pakistan, India, Iraq, Syria, African continent, Europe, Russian federation, North America (liberation of blacks), South America, etc.; terrorism world over (the infamous ones including 9/11, 26/11, etc.); World War I, World War II, Vietnam war, Afghanistan war, Iraq war, India-Pakistan war, India-China war, Israel-Gaza war and other aggressions the world over taken place, created great havoc, loss of lives, loss of properties and unprecedented human sufferings. Internal conflicts within nations such as Libya, Egypt, Syria, Iraq, Ethiopia, Yemen, Nigeria, Pakistan, Afghanistan, Somalia, etc. brought unprecedented suffering to the people and loss of lives and properties.

The **message** from the above cited examples is: "The absence of total harmony brings unprecedented human sufferings, loss of lives, loss of properties, loss of progress, extreme hatred, loss of peace and loss of happiness."

Realize the suffering of humans, loss of lives and loss of properties on account of the failure of harmony. George Washington advocated, "Observe good faith and justice towards all nations; cultivate peace and harmony with all." Lysander said more emphatically, "Greatest of all crimes are the wars carried on by government to plunder, enslave, and destroy mankind." A great thought, a great observation!

Whenever happiness exists on the earth- be it region wise or period wise, it is due to the understanding of people about harmony. Such people are great. This was well expressed by Jose Marti, who said, "Happiness exists on the earth and it is owned through prudent exercise of reason, knowledge of the harmony of the universe and constant practice of generosity." The happiest people in the world live in Scandinavia, says UN general assembly's second World Happiness Report. It is based on **six key factors**: "GDP per capita, healthy life expectancy, someone to count on, perceived freedom to make life choices, freedom from corruption, generosity" (Source: Times of India, 11th Sept, 2013). Denmark tops the list, 2nd, 3rd, 4th and 5th position are occupied by Norway, Switzerland Netherland, and Sweden respectively. USA and UK rank at 17th and 22nd position respectively. India ranks at 111th position while last position is occupied by Togo. Based on the Happiness Quotients, one can imagine the quality of life of the citizens of respective countries. "Happiness is the main purpose of life, and every country should work on the six parameters to improve Happiness Quotients." "Happiness is a mindset and a simple harmony between a man and the life he leads. But, if the six key parameters of happiness quotient are better, the majority of people will be happier with better quality of life."

"Ecosystem of harmonious culture plays an important role in achieving the success in life. If you are all the time in the mood to fight with other people on trivial issues, your energy will be utilized in wrong things and mind will not be calm. You can't work hard, and can't give desired result." This has been well portrayed by the words of Cyril Connolly, who said, "The secret of success is to be in harmony with existence, to be always calm, to let each wave of life wash us a little further up the shore." Just watch Mother Nature. It is in balance and in harmony with others. Jaeda De Walt opined, "Harmony is about bringing things into balance and knowing how to go from the sunrise to the sunset. Mother Nature teaches to us, in so many ways, each and every day."

"Love is a great attractive force and a great bonding material among different souls. It helps in developing harmony. Valentine's Day(14th February) is celebrated to showcase the love to girlfriends, boyfriends, wives, parents and friends to spread harmony among near and dears." It is said, "Love is the binding force that allows chaos and peace to co-exist in harmony. Increase the intensity of love among human beings."

Hey, men and women of the world! Totally avoid inharmonious culture in your life as it yields unprecedented and heart breaking sufferings, a lot of loss of lives and properties. Bring an ecosystem of harmony with all existence which will be yielding a scintillating success, a happy and peaceful life.

WISDOM STEERS OUR LIFE OUT OF ADVERSITIES

"By three methods we may learn wisdom: First by reflection, which is noblest; second by imitation which is easiest; and third by experience, which is the bitterest."

—Confucius

"Knowing yourself is the beginning of all wisdom."

—Aristotle

Wisdom! Wisdom! Wisdom! A huge store of experiences. A great symbol of dignity and patience. An absorber of insult. A symbol of forgiveness. Knowledge of self. A proven recipe to lead a peaceful, successful and glorious life. A jewel in the crown. A capability of moderation. A problem solver. Do you lack in wisdom? If answer is yes, acquire wisdom through experience to overcome over problems, to win, to succeed. Wisdom is needed at every step of life.

"The importance of wisdom covers the whole spectrum of our lives at every stage, at every moment. Since ages our sages, great thinkers, philosophers, poets and wise persons had been giving sermons on wisdom based on their experiences, observations and rational thinking for the benefit of mankind."

Everyone should learn from his/her own mistakes and mistakes of others. Have a big storehouse of experience in the form of wisdom to guide you on the right path for achieving success and greatness. Albert Einstein opined, "Wisdom is not a product of schooling but of the life- long attempt to acquire it."

The journey of life is neither smooth nor cozy. You need experience, wisdom, intelligence, and understanding of self and others to sail in the journey of life. The words of great thinker Lau Tzu express this in a beautiful way: "Knowing others is intelligence; knowing yourself is true wisdom, mastering others is strength, mastering yourself is true power. If you realize that you have enough, you are truly rich."

"Wisdom is that virtue of a man which offers enormous patience, ensures a high degree of moderation capability, equips with better harmonious culture, absorbs insults, practices forgiveness, and steers the life out of grim situations. It comes from experience, observation and positive thinking."

SOME ASPECTS OF WISDOM

Here, some aspects of wisdom are being dealt with:

i. **On Honesty and Integrity**: Wisdom is our great guide dealing with honesty and integrity. Thomas Jefferson said, "Honesty is the first chapter in the book of wisdom." "In leading our lives, we face many odds, conflicts and it is our wisdom that steers our difficult lives and makes it smooth." If we reach at a crossroad of honesty and dishonesty, integrity and no integrity, it is our good wisdom that comes to our rescue. Socrates opined, "Wisdom begins in wonder." Honesty and integrity is the backbone of good character and golden success. Practice this in life for glorious success.

ii. **On Life's Wounds**: In leading life, one faces many problems, many wounds of all varieties may be inflicted upon you, and you have to succeed through these by remaining calm, maintaining patience. They will widen your experience and make you tough to face bigger adversities. Oprah Winfrey said, "Turn your wounds into wisdom." Insult inflicted upon a wise man doesn't disturb him or her. The words of Moliere express this very beautifully, which states, "A wise man is superior to any insults which can be put upon him and the best reply to unseemly behavior is patience and moderation."

iii. **On Suitable Career**: Many thinkers had given sermons on various aspects of life. For choosing suitable career in life, Ralph Waldo Emerson advocated, "Do not go where the path may lead, go instead where there is no path and leave a trail." Greatness will not be achieved when you are following the already travelled path. Follow the path less travelled. Do something different and innovate. Basically the practical knowledge to lead life in all circumstances is the real wisdom.

iv. **On Teaching Wisdom**: What should be the best way of teaching wisdom is well explained by Kahlil Gibran, who said, "The teacher who is indeed wise does not bid you to enter the house of his wisdom, but rather leads you to the threshold of your mind." If your mind gets the capability to open in all directions and starts thinking rationally, you will receive better wisdom. "A man of wisdom always shows a high degree of dignity during discourse and demeanor." The head of a state or an organization should always show wisdom; otherwise he or she will invite problems. "The only wisdom is, knowing you know nothing". So learn more to acquire wisdom.

v. **On Key to Winning**: What is the key to winning? It is never to quit: never, never, never and go for persistence. Quitting is a cowardice act. This has been answered beautifully by the words of Vince Lombardi, who said, "Winners never quit and quitters never win." People in general are in the habit of inflicting inferiority complex on others during table talks, games, competition but nobody can do it unless and until you allow either by remaining incompetent or talking in foolish manner. The words of Eleanor Roosevelt clearly advise about this which state, "No one can make you feel inferior without your consent." The aim of Roosevelt here is to warn you that you acquire sufficient wisdom and capability so that nobody dares to get you to feel down and you win. "Wisdom is your watchful agent to yield wise thoughts over any issue. Acquire it! Acquire it! Acquire it!"

vi. **On When to Speak**: There is also an advice about when to speak and how to speak. One has to be very watchful before speaking. In general, the philosophy is: "more listening and less speaking. Speaking in a highly effective manner and at appropriate time should be your mantra." Maurice Switzer opined, "It is better to remain silent at the risk of being thought a fool, than to talk and remove all about of it." Mark Twain advocated, "Whenever you find yourself on the side of majority, it is time to pause and reflect." On every matter, it is not wise to react as what you are seeing or what you are listening may not be fully true. The words of William James confirm this beautifully, which state, "The art of being wise is the art of knowing what to overlook."

vii. **On Anger**: It is utmost important to manage **anger** which causes thirty-six toxic chemicals to pour into our blood affecting health severely. One can do any unpleasant acts out of anger inviting more trouble. Many families and leaders, ruin their lives due to anger. "Anger is the greatest enemy of mankind." Control of anger is essential and it will come through your wisdom. Amish in Shiva Trilogy has said, "Anger is your enemy. Control it! Control it! Control it!"

viii. **On Greed**: Wisdom plays an important role in controlling **greed**. In the great epic Srimad Bhagavad Gita, 16.21, lust, anger and greed has been rated as a highly self-destructive habit and it says: "There are three gates to self-destructive hell: lust, anger and greed." The following story shows the consequences of greed.

Greed Leads to Self- destruction: Match fixing in cricket had been reported many a times. Recently, an investigation in IPL-6 of cricket was conducted in 2013 in which spot fixing episode was reported. The episode brought into light players who were involved with bookies by accepting a lot of money from them and balling to the tunes of the bookies. This is highly illegal and the police caught the involved players and the bookies. Board cricket control of India suspended the players involved and their careers came tumbling down due to greed. In the past also, many players of cricket from the world over were banned due to spot fixing.

The above stories carry a lot of truth and every person should take **lesson** from this truth. "Greed is the great vice and one should be generous instead of becoming greedy."

Learn more from the following lessons to avoid greed:

"Greed is a great demon with big belly and big mouth and always hungry how much ever you feed it."

"Most of our troubles arise from selfishness and greed at individual or national level."

ix. **On Lust**: Our wisdom suggests that lust is a very dangerous habit and one should avoid this. Lust is the poison of mind. It includes all bad habits such as stealing, overindulgence of sex, pornography, sex with other partners, child abuse, drinking, smoking, drug addiction, etc. "Lust kills human spirit, self-esteem, character, and greatness. Go for spirituality to be away from lust, anger, and greed."

"Lust enables one to enter inside the domain of destruction."

x. **On Tolerance**: With reference to **tolerance**, wisdom plays an important role to control it. The following stories suggest how intolerance is a damaging factor in life. We are living in a world of technological advanced jungle where people flaunt power through intolerant behavior and not through ethics and values. Voltaire said, "Discord is the great ill of mankind, and tolerance is the only remedy for it."

   a. **Intolerance Makes You Unsuccessful**: A businessman was going by his car on a business trip. On the way, he wanted to take snacks and tea in a hotel situated on the highway and so, he tried to park his car in the parking slot. One person was backing his car which slightly collided with the car of the businessman. On this small issue, the businessman started abusing and beating the person who collided with his car. Hearing the commotion, friends of the victim arrived and beat the businessman mercilessly. He was hospitalized for a month and he had to pay a lot of money as medical bill. Further, he could not get the order for which he was going on the business trip. Had he been tolerant, such situation could not have arrived?

The **theme** of the story is: "It is the capacity of tolerance that ensures your well-being, happiness, peace, progress and success."

 b. **Intolerance can be Dangerous to Your Life**: In TV channels and newspapers, news of road rage, street brawl and a big fight on petty issues leading to murder and severe injuries have become a daily issue. One can think of national, family and individual loss due to sheer intolerant behavior. During 2013, the number of murders in India summed up to around 36,581 due to various reasons in which intolerance is the main reason (Source: Times of India, NCRB, dated 18th Nov.14).

xi. **On Fulfilling Life**: "A fulfilling life can only be led when you find the purpose of your life, fulfil it by dint of hard work, and remain stress free. The quality of your fulfilling life will be proportional to the quality and greatness of your purpose of life." "The past mistakes can be removed by forgetting it. The present life can be made better by facing it boldly." Apostle Paul showed us three simple steps to live a more fulfilling life leading to glory and happiness.

Find your Purpose.

Forget The Past.

Face The Present.

Atharva Veda says on blazing your trail, "Do not be led by others, awaken your own mind, amass your own experience, and decide for yourself your own path...." The words of Albert Einstein elucidate on how to live beautifully, "Learn from yesterday, live for today, hope for tomorrow."

xii. **On Mistakes and Criticism**: With reference to mistakes and criticism, many wise people having high profile in the past admitted their mistakes and people appreciated this gesture. Criticizing opponents severely lowers down your image in the society. Though, sometimes, there is a need of criticism but it should be with dignity and respect. Dale Carnegie opined, "Be quick to admit mistakes and slow to criticize. Above all, be constructive."

xiii. **On Unity and Hard Work**: The story of old wise man having four sons who were fools and quarrelling with each other is famous. In order to teach them the importance of unity, the old man asked them to break the bundle of sticks. Nobody could do any harm to the bundle of sticks. But upon unbundling, they were able to break all sticks. Nobody could understand the lesson learned. The old man said, "When the sticks were united in the form of bundle you couldn't break, but when all sticks were separated, you could break them easily. This is called **"Unity is strength"** This is also true with all of you as you are separated due to quarrelling. The **moral** of this old story is: "Unity is strength and division is weakness." J. K. Rowling said, "We are only as strong as we are united, as weak as we are divided."

"Hard work always pays. There is no substitute of hard work. It is said that it can produce gold and diamond in your venture."

xiv. **On Harmony**: In great epic **Ramayana** of Hinduism, a big emphasis has been given on the acts of harmony in human life to lead a happy and glorious life. The epic in its Sundarkand says, "Wherever, harmony prevails, there are numerous types of enormous prosperities; but wherever, inharmonious situation prevails, there are numerous types of enormous troubles."(See also the earlier discussion.)

xv. **On Attitude Related to Luck**: Wisdom plays an important role in shaping our attitude related to **luck**. Whenever, any problem comes in our life, we blame our luck instead of the lack of our wisdom and sufficient efforts put in to realize the goal. If you do not run out after breaking of fire in a building, in the name of luck or God, the fire is not going to spare you. Ponder over the following story.

Luck Doesn't Help when You Don't Act Wisely: A big function was going on in a very specious hall. Suddenly, the fire broke out and people started to flee from the hall. One person was just watching the fire. His friends advised him to run from the hall but he did not leave saying that: "God will save him as he has full faith in Him." Outside the hall when news spread, one young man dared to rescue him. The young man reached to the person but he did not accompany the rescuer saying that God would save him. The rescuer came out disappointed after suffering mild burns. The fire-fighting personnel arrived but the person was dead by then.

When he entered the Heavens, he asked a straight forward question to the almighty, "I believed in you Lord but you did not save me". God replied, "I sent you one person but you did not listen to him and did not accompany him. I have given you brain to use it judiciously. It was your wrong mindset that killed you."

The **theme** of the above story is an old one: "God helps those who help themselves."

There are two paths in life;Path of **least resistance** (little work) and path of **high resistance**(hard work). It is your choice. Lazy and weak-minded people adopt the path of least resistance and are finally declared losers. Winners follow the path of high resistance. In the athletic meet for the various races, athletes prepare very hard for at least three years. Why don't they believe in luck? Whatever be the pursuits, losers always play blame game: "Sometimes, they say it is an unfair world or my start was wrong or my planning was wrong or I was unlucky. They do not say failure is a part of game and next time they will work harder and be winners."

Whatever inventions and new products we are seeing in the world are the output of imaginations, hard work, dedication and determination. American, European and the Japanese don't believe in horoscopes and stars but they are on the top. They have created their bright destiny.

"Luck shines on those who toil for years together to become worthy of luck."

xvi. **On Short-cut Attitude**:   Wisdom plays a leading role to guide us towards the short-cut attitude of human beings. It is a deadly disease. One cannot attain success, perfection, quality, and can even end up losing one's life. Many have lost their lives due to short-cute attitude such as crossing railway tracks instead of going through bridge. The following story gives a message.

Hard Work is the Only Solution, not Short-cut: A group of human resource (HR) personnel of many big companies held a conclave in which students of management took part. During one session, one student asked the chairman, "What is your message for future generation on short-cut attitude?" He replied, "There is nothing free and no short-cut path in this world, and you have to earn everything by hard work." The audience was extremely happy with this message as it applies in every sphere of life.

The **message** of this story is: "You have to pay the price for everything you get in life."

xvii. **On Opportunity**:   With reference to opportunity, wisdom plays a vital role to guide human beings on grabbing it. Opportunities always exist in the form of problems, crisis, and obstacles. Greater the problems, greater are opportunities. Grab it or lose it. The following story showcases this.

An Opportunity Graber Shines in the World of Success: In a manufacturing industry, severe labor, financial and other problems appeared and CEO had to resign. No other senior executive was ready to take the charge as the CEO during this crisis. One senior executive dared to take the charge. With his wisdom, knowledge and capability, he solved the crisis and turned the loss making company into a great profit making company. The acting CEO was declared a hero and was made CEO with three times salary and a lot of perks.

The **message** of the above story is: "There is no need to wait for big opportunity as it comes in the form of troubles and hard work. Opportunities may be compared to sunrise. If you are too late you will miss them."

John F. Kennedy said, "The Chinese use two brush strokes to write the word crisis. One brush stroke stands for danger; the other for opportunity. In a crisis, be aware of the danger but recognize the opportunity."

xviii. **On Ego**:   Ego is one of the poisons in the human mind. Ego manifests in our mind through many forms such as: pride of wealth, pride of knowledge, pride of beauty, pride of power, etc. With this ego people hurt other people- both mentally and physically, though, the form of each ego will vanish with the passage of time. "Eliminate your ego to flush out the poison from mind, cleanse your soul, and reach closer to God."

Our life runs with the help of wisdom. Oh! Men and women! Acquire wisdom through reflection, experience, and from the mistakes of self and others, and learn by reading good books. Many problems come in life, in the journey of your goal and you can overcome these only by applying your wisdom.

FORGIVENESS BRINGS DIVINITY

"Always forgive your enemies- nothing annoys them so much."
—Oscar Wilde

"The weak can never forgive. Forgiveness is the attribute of the strong."
—Mahatma Gandhi

Forgiveness! Forgiveness! Forgiveness! An imminent need of every soul. The gatekeeper of peace and harmony. An economy of the heart. The best solution of revenge. Is forgiveness an act of divinity? Yes, it is. Practice forgiveness to calm your mind and win the world.

The world is full of good and bad people. Life doesn't go alone. You have to interact and deal with people. Life is full of amity and conflicts. You can't save yourself from conflicts. Some may hurt you; harm you either deliberately or out of sheer pleasure. Here, the question arises, how you handle yourself in the situation created by a person who has hurt you or harmed you? You can go on to carry the grudge, anger and hatred against him or you can use your wisdom of forgiveness to calm yourself. "Grudge, anger and hatred against your enemy or opponent is not good for your health, for your performance, for your progress and for your happiness." This has been beautifully portrayed by the words of Hannah More, who coined, "Forgiveness is the economy of the heart --- forgiveness saves the expense of anger, the cost of hatred, and the waste of spirit." "Human beings have three powerful resources with them: love, prayer, and forgiveness, and they can help you to make a better world, to achieve greatness." Billy Graham opined, "Man has two great spiritual needs. One is for forgiveness. The other is for goodness."

Revenge taking phenomena in the case of conflict, and grudge against the enemy is highly common. If everybody is bound to take revenge, then what will be the result? Our well-being, our survival will be difficult. Harm against harm, hurt against hurt, beating against beating, eye against eye will ruin the society. The words of Martin Luther King Jr. advocated on such issue, "Darkness cannot drive out darkness, only light can do that. Hate cannot drive out hate; only love can do that." The revenge issue has been well addressed by the words of Kahlil Gibran, who said, "An eye for eye and the whole world would be blind." Hatred breeds hatred. It is the love that only can remove the hatred. The words of Gautama Buddha eloquently express this, "Hatred does not cease by hatred but only by love and this is the eternal rule." Follow the teachings of Buddha on forgiveness which are highly relevant in the present world.

"Forgiveness is the divine virtue of human being. It cools your anger, warms your heart, offers a chance to make a new beginning, and conquers over enemy."

The world knows that Mahatma Gandhi freed India from British Rule not by violence but by truth and non-violence. He preached that if anybody slaps on your left cheek, you offer him the right cheek and for another slap. He practiced this many times during the fight against slavery. This is a great act of forgiveness and also a great tool to demoralize the slapper. "Forgiveness is an act of divinity. Practice it! Practice it! Practice it!" Alexander Pope advocated this beautifully, "To err is human; to forgive, divine."

In general, people react to insult or to harm and that raises further tension. Instead of reacting, you can use various demoralizing methods such as requesting humbly for more insults or say thank you for your bravery and my experience. The words of Oprah Winfrey confirm this, "True forgiveness is when you can say, thank you for that experience." Confucius opined, "To be wronged is nothing, unless you continue to remember it."

"There is a wrong notion among us that continuation of resentment, anger and grudge against the enemies will kill or correct the enemies. This doesn't happen at all. Instead, continuation of resentment, grudge and anger will simply harm you by affecting your health, thought process, peace, prosperity and progress." Nelson Mandela advocated on this in a very emphatic way, and said, "Resentment is like drinking poison and then hoping it will kill your enemies." Anne LaMotte opined, "Not forgiving is like drinking rat poison and then waiting for the rat to die."

For healing the wounds inflicted upon individual, group, community, society and the world at large, forgiveness plays an important role. "The practice of forgiveness acts as a divine contribution to the healing of the world." Martin Luther King Jr. said, "Forgiveness is not an occasional act, it is a constant attitude." "All over the world, you will find that a simple petty issues –lewd remark on a young girl or a petty wrong on religious fervor are made such a big issue by warring groups that it leads to a great riot resulting in loss of hundreds of lives and unprecedented loss of private and government property. Whereas these problems could have been solved easily and amicably and finally forgetting the issue. Such cases exist more in the developing and underdeveloped countries. Ask those who have suffered the riots, the atrocities, the torture, the terrorism and think about their misery. The issue is that their sentiments must be healed and this shouldn't be repeated on them. Everybody has the equal right to lead a decent and peaceful life." Steve Maraboli opined, "The truth is, you let go, unless you forgive yourself, unless you forgive the situation, unless you realize that the situation is over, you cannot move forward." Nelson Mandela and Mahatma Gandhi are the great symbol of forgiveness.

The **message** from above cited examples is: "Forgiveness is the core virtue of human beings which offers freedom from bitterness and hatred leading to love, brotherhood, friendliness, harmony, peace, prosperity, and progress."

Hey, sons and daughters of the Almighty God! Think over the sufferings of human beings due to clashes and wars of small, medium and big level on the account of the failure of harmony and wisdom. Avoid the sufferings of human beings. Practicing of the wisdom of forgiveness, though difficult, is possible. This will soothe your mind, heart and soul; will bring peace and harmony in your life and finally the happiness and success will blossom in your life.

STEPS TAKEN BY YOURSELF

After going through this very chapter of the book, I (as a reader) will take the following steps on the 8th mantra to practice cooperation, harmony, wisdom and forgiveness in my life:

　i. _____
　ii. _____

***

Chapter 10

Avoid Fear, Procrastination and Bad Habits
THE 9ᵀᴴ MANTRA

FEAR DESTROYS HAPPINESS AND HAMPERS PROGRESS

"To conquer fear is the beginning of wisdom."
—Bertrand Russell

"Fear defeats more people than any other one thing in the world."
—Ralph Waldo Emerson

A great CEO-cum-speaker was asked by a student from the audience in a conclave to speak to us of fear, procrastination and bad habits. He said in sequence: Fear! Fear! Fear! A sleeping killer. A destroyer of happiness and progress. A great killer of decision making. The main source of failure. Are you fearful? Thrash fear. Be fearless to take decision, to succeed in your venture, to win the world.

The ghost of fear is hounding most of the people due to the fear of failure in their ventures and the fear of unknown. "Fear arises out of the lack of understanding, the lack of courage, the hope for something, inferiority complex and unfavorable prevailing situations in the region (say riots, terrorism, civil war, political uncertainty, recession, breaking relation, etc.). Fear destroys happiness, hampers progress and derails your decision process. In fact, fear is a mindset and it its highly harmful." The adage; "He who fears, he has already died without death." is highly true in all cases except a few ones. "Invariably, we fear for those things we want most." "Fear is not for brave but for coward."

"The fear of failure is the great impediment to success. Build courage against fear and focus on things we desire most, not things we fear."

"If fear is taken as a cautionary step, then there is no harm in fear as you have changed its form including its impact. No person can become prosperous without any fear (as caution only) and failure." Francis Bacon said, "Prosperity is not without many fears and disasters; adversity not without many comforts and hopes." "Life is a mixture of everything and in that mix you have to enjoy, laugh, weep, dream, desire, imagine, struggle, fear, fail, feel pain, feel sorrow, work, win and succeed."

Faith and fear are directly opposite to each other. "Faith breeds confidence while fear breeds confusion." The words of Joel Osteen have expressed this in a very beautiful manner, which say, "Faith activates God, fear activates the enemy." "Our greatest savior is God and when you have faith in God, there shouldn't be any fear. So, one is advised to convert fear into faith." It is said, "Don't cultivate fear as it will become stronger, but cultivate faith as it will give mastery." "Fear grows larger by nursing it. In general, when people want to learn new trade, some have faith in themselves and that is why they become the master of their trade. But, for those who have the fear of learning, they may fear that it is beyond their capacity and as a result fear gets stronger."

"If your subconscious mind is grappling with fear, you cannot do anything – neither, you can decide, nor you can work wholeheartedly. It is very essential to thrash fear away from your mind. You should always consider fear to be a sleeping killer. Ask yourself, "Why do I fear?" The feeling of fear is more fearful than fear itself." "In order to conquer fear, don't sit home as you will think about it. Go out and get busy in some pursuits. Being busy, your mind will be occupied and you will learn something." Those students who study very less, they grapple with the fear of failure during the examinations. Norman Vincent Peale said, "Action is a great restorer and builder of confidence. Inaction is not only the result, but the cause of fear." "Even if you are a poor learner in certain trade (field), stick to learning, give more time to learning that trade. Be persistent and certainly you will be the master of the trade gradually and great confidence will be generated within you." "Life is not meant to be feared, it is only to be understood. To remove fear, understand life more." "Dealing with people either at family, office, company, state, national or international level, you have to negotiate on many aspects. People use fear to bring the negotiation in their favor. It totally depends upon the courage of negotiator, weather you negotiate out of fear or not." John F. Kennedy said, "Let us never negotiate out of fear. But let us never fear to negotiate."

The Most Twelve Common Fears Include

The fear of failures/rejection.

The fear of poverty/losing money.

The fear of criticism. The fear of facing boss.

The fear of being unprepared. The fear of ill health.

The fear of making wrong decision.

The fear of loss of love of someone.

The fear of old age. The fear of losing prestige.

The fear of unknown. The fear of death.

"In all the fears, one thing in common, i.e. anxiety and as a result, it paralyzes the faculty of reasoning, destroys the faculty of imagination, kills self–reliance, undermines enthusiasm, increases procrastination and discourages enthusiasm."

The inferiority complex, the lack of courage and hope for something also cause fear. Fear arises when you admit inferiority complex. There is a relation between hope and fear. "Fear and hope grow with each other." It is very essential to remove fear from our subconscious mind. Chanakya advised, "As soon as the fear approaches near, attack and destroy it".

Ponder over the courage of the following groups of adventurous people who don't know what fear is. Adventure is only their mission.

i. **Among sea sailors**, either solo or in groups, some cross Atlantic, some Pacific, some Mediterranean, some Indian ocean, some travel throughout the world, they don't know what fear is. They dare to complete their mission of their lives and believe in adventure where life has some meaning.

ii. **Sea swimmers** who cross English Channel or other seas don't fear at all. They are adventurous and the world salutes them.

iii. **Mountaineers**, who scale the Mount Everest or other similar summits, believe in their mission. When your mission is adventure, courage occupies the place in mind and not fear.

iv. **Rafters**, who love rafting in challenging rivers where current is enormous, believe only in their mission. Fear doesn't come to them. They take pride in their performance.

v. Just recall those **explorers** who explored South Pole, North Pole, America, India, and other unexplored places. They were fearless and the world is proud of these fearless and courageous explorers. We salute them.

vi. People who ventured in **start-up companies** with innovative ideas like Bill Gates, Mark Zuckerberg or Steve Jobs after dropping from universities never feared about the failures of companies and they are at the top of the world.

The **message** from the above cited examples is: "Fearless people floor the fear of challenges, the fear of adversities, the fear of difficulties, the fear of failures, the fear of unknown and become victorious in their chosen ventures with enormous challenges."

Do you fear? Forget fear. Thrash fear once it approaches you. Have a spirit like the sea sailors, sea swimmers, explorers, mountaineers, rafters, innovators and you will succeed in any venture. Many people don't enter into business out of the fear of failure. People do not adopt adventurous activities out of the fear of life. In the training of the Army, Air force and Navy, the purpose of training is not only to make trainees competent but to make them fearless, courageous and confident to overcome any difficult challenges.

Benjamin Disraeli once opined, "Nothing in life is more remarkable than the unnecessary anxiety which we endure, and generally create ourselves." We must act, otherwise it will invite procrastination. Some people only work out of fear, out of worry. It is worth to note that worry doesn't help tomorrow's troubles but surely, it ruins today's happiness. "Nobody gets tired of a whole day's work but worry for a few hours breaks them, both physically and mentally." The words of John Lubbock express this aspect very beautifully, "A day of worry is more exhausting than a day of work." Tiredness is not due to physical burden but it is of mental burden – worry, fear and anxieties.

The worry of future is too common. We worry about the future of our children, about future promotion, about future home, etc. But the fact is we cannot do anything unless and until we do something. Unfortunately, more people worry about future than prepare for it. Bishop Arthur Roche said, "Worry is thin stream of fear trickling through the mind. If encouraged, it cuts a channel into which all other thoughts are drained."

You may have a lot of imagination for your life. It is very good but it should be consistent and well arranged for action. We should always be on guard against our imagination otherwise it may create worry for you. "Worry may be modelled as dark room where negatives are developed." As per Newton's Third Law of Motion, if you can't help yourself from worrying, remember worrying can't help you either.

"The approaching success may be slipped away due to worry and the fear of decision and action." Shakespeare said, "Our doubts are traitors, and they make us lose what we opt might win, by fearing to attempt." How much fear could be dangerous, one can guess? Fear can snatch your victory where you could have won. Hence, don't let your fears steal success from you and prevent you from pursuing your dream. "Fear is your enemy, Thrash it! Thrash it! Thrash it!"

Are you ready to destroy fear from today? Just join the club of fearless people and you will be bubbling with energy, enthusiasm and the world will embrace you, salute you. Read the stories of adventurous people and your confidence will improve against fear.

PROCRASTINATION IS A KIILER OF SUCCESS

"Procrastination is the seed of self-destruction."

—*Matthew Burton*

"Never put off till tomorrow what may be done day after tomorrow just as well."

—*Mark Twin*

Procrastination! A deadly disease to prevent success. A hindrance to success and glory. A self-destructive bad habit. Hey, procrastinator! Have you ever realized seriously that you are destroying yourself due to your bad habit of procrastination? Occasionally, you simply say, "I have a bad habit of procrastination." This is not a real realization but mere befooling and deceiving yourself. Real realization is one when you take a firm stand from today itself against procrastination.

"Though, procrastination is a common bad habit due to the seriously unrealized fact of this deadly disease, so success slips away from the hands of such procrastinating people. The worst aspect is that such people don't show any proclivity to stop the habit of procrastination. As a result, the world witnesses very less number of successful people." In taking food, in putting on good dress, in enjoying sleep, in enjoying entertainment, nobody procrastinates but only in doing work, the most important aspect of human life, they do.

"Procrastination is a self-destructive bad habit of putting off today's work for tomorrow, and of wasting the most valuable time, thus, allowing the slipping of golden success."

"What work or decision you put off until tomorrow, you'll probably put off tomorrow too, and tomorrow may never come. Success embraces to the man who does today what others were thinking of doing tomorrow or day after tomorrow. The lazier a man is, the more he is going to spend the next day with all sorts of excuses." "Procrastination is the prime killer of your success. Avoid it! Avoid it! Avoid it!"

When you are procrastinating, you might be thinking of enjoyment and lot of fun. But such thinking is foolish and very costly. Procrastination may be modelled as credit card. It may give lot of pleasure but only until you get the bill. If you dodge the problem, it will only get worse in the future. The words of William Hasley rightly pointed out this, "All problems become smaller if you don't dodge them, but confront them. Touch a thistle timidly, it pricks you, grasp it boldly, and its spine crumbles." It is said, "Procrastination makes easy things hard, hard things harder."

As soon as the work or duty approaches, you must embrace it and gladly do it. Don't hesitate in accepting it otherwise it will burden you further." It is said, "Every duty that is bidden to wait comes back with seven fresh duties at its back." "Time is a precious gift given by God and he has given twenty-four hours equally to everybody. Wasting of time wastes your life. So time has to be managed in a very systematic and planned way. A lazy person doesn't go through life, he's pushed through it by mother, father, spouse and boss. Such pushing to a lazy man is a daily business. You can't think of the completion of work by a lazy man and forget quality work from him. Procrastinators never have small problems because their waiting multiplies problems. They are poor time managers." Lord Chesterfield advised eloquently, "Know the true value of time; snatch, seize and enjoy every moment of it. No idleness, no laziness, no procrastination; never put off till tomorrow what you can do today." Are you ready to follow this great advice in letter and spirit in your life?

"Don't leave before the miracle of success happens otherwise it may slip away leaving you bewildered. Some people stop working hard during the final moments, expecting that success hereon is a guarantee but sometimes, success takes a halt and even slips." Heywood Broun opined, "The tragedy of life is not that man loses, but that he almost wins." Procrastinators wait too long to begin the work and when they finally are in the mood to begin, time changes the course of future. "It is worth to note that the race is not always to the swift but to those who kept on running."

"The key to success is to complete tomorrow's work today itself in advance with full concentration, with full enthusiasm and with all intelligence so that you may be better equipped for the future. This is nothing but believing in the concept of being proactive and sincere." I am a great believer in this concept. "Do tomorrow's work today itself and today's work just now" should be the mantra of life. "What is the best possible way to prepare for tomorrow? It is to concentrate with all your intelligence, all your enthusiasm, all your passion on today's work superbly today itself." That is the only possible way you can prepare for the future. "Future belongs to those who prepare for it much in advance and practice going an extra mile. Oscar Wilde opined, "Hesitation of any kind is a sign of mental decay in the young, of physical weakness in the old."

"Simply remaining busy will not lead you to success. The question arises whether you are simply busy or you are progressing. It is a question of activity versus accomplishment. You will succeed only through accomplishment. Suppose one is studying whole day but he neither understands anything nor remembers anything. What is the use of this study?"

Activity Doesn't Always Mean Accomplishment: Some youngsters have been found always roaming in the city without any work for hours on the bike and gossiping hours on tea stalls or some other place, killing their precious time without generating any idea. Though, they show their busyness but they are not accomplishing any work. They are killing their fortune. Their behavior is similar to caterpillars that will be moving around a circular disc for days after days and even die of starvation but will not move even five centimetres to take their favorite food pine needles kept inside circular path.

The **moral** of this story is: "Remaining active the whole day and not accomplishing anything will not bring success."

Mark Twain advocated about this aspect, "Noise produces nothing. Often a hen who has merely laid an egg crackles as though she has laid an asteroid."

"The world is witnessing a lot of evils in the society. Have you ever thought the reason behind this? Good men are not doing anything towards this. On some issues, they have reacted and change came but in the majority of cases, there is no accomplishment." If good men don't do anything to curb evil, it will flourish exponentially. Though, noble men were accomplishing work for themselves, it is also their duty to save the society as indirectly the evil will affect them. They have to pay the price of dodging their responsibility either indirectly or directly.

"Killing time is not only a murder, but it's a suicide of your dream, your goal, and your success in an unnoticed, unrealized way." When the real realization takes place the train of success is gone from the scene much earlier. It is very easy to dodge your responsibility and have fun but be ready to face the consequences of dodging your responsibility.

Two things in life always hammer our peace of mind: "one is unfinished work and other is work not yet begun." Unless and until you do some concrete efforts towards these, they will remain stuck. The eternal hanging on an uncompleted task is highly fatiguing. "Some people start work towards their goal with a lot of enthusiasm, but in the passage of time they develop timidity, procrastination and extreme carefulness, and as a consequence of these, they fail." The words of Margie Warrell express this aspect in a lucid manner, "Whatever actions you take, keep in mind that over the course of life, you will fail far more from timidity, procrastination, and carefulness than you will from just stepping up to the plate, and, as we say in Australia, giving it a bloody go!"

Hey, procrastinators! Are you ready to destroy your deadliest bad habit of procrastination which is killing your dreams! If yes, then the first step is to stop giving various types of excuses for procrastination. The second step is to bring realization in your subconscious mind that working twelve hours a day doesn't kill a person, but idleness and laziness brings all sorts of miseries and diseases. The third step is to motivate yourself to thrash the habit of procrastination. Fourth step is to install in your subconscious mind that God has sent you for contribution in the world, for enjoying the life through your achievement and bringing complete happiness in life. "Remove any type of fear from your mind through motivation and wisdom as fear is only in the mind and note that the sense of fear is a great killer of your health, happiness, dream and success. I assure you, once you decide wholeheartedly to move on to fulfil your dream, God will be on your side, driving your chariot of success like Lord Krishna was driving the chariot of Arjuna in the battle of Mahabharata." We, human beings cannot expect more than this from the Almighty God and you have to simply act.

BAD HABITS DESTROY DREAMS

> *"There is nothing more dreadful than a habit of doubt. Doubt separates people.*
> *It is a poison that disintegrates friendships and breaks up pleasant relations.*
> *It is a thorn that irritates and hurts; it is a sword that kills."*
>
> —*Gautama Buddha*
>
> *"Nothing so needs reforming as other people's habits."*
>
> —*Mark Twain*

Bad habits! A self-inflected curse. A killer of dream. A poison for friendship and relationship. Give up bad habits to shape your world, to succeed, to win.

You might have heard many people saying: Mr. X has failed in almost all fields as he has all sorts of bad habits and Mr. Y has got success in every venture because he has very good habits and is disciplined. If good habits give a great impact on life, then why do we go for bad habits? This is a very pertinent question concerning all and answer has to be searched out.

"Habits (good or bad) are formed as a result of conditioning, the company we keep, the prevailing conditions in the society we live, the boredom and the mindset of person." "We are the sons and daughters of the Almighty God and He sends us in the world as raw diamonds with a hope to lead a good life and shine in the world by shaping ourselves in the best possible manner. In spite of this, people are failing miserably due to many reasons and one of the reasons is bad habit." The effect of conditioning has been also observed in most of the creatures. Domestic animals get trained in particular ways due to the effect of conditioning. As per Asian proverb, "Good habits result from resisting temptation."

"Bad habits are the greatest killers of your health, your wealth, your progress, your dream, and national wealth."

"The cultivation of a habit is a repetitive action of anything." It is like ploughing the field, watering the garden, getting up in the early morning, doing exercise, learning bike, exhibiting honesty, and so on. It doesn't cultivate in a day. It takes time to cultivate a habit. Habits generate other habits like chain reaction. A preacher in a conclave was answering questions on the differences among discipline, inspiration, motivation and habit. He said, "What gets us to follow rules and regulations is discipline, what gets us started is an inspiration, what keeps us on track is motivation, and what makes it automatic is habit. The easiest thing is to pick up bad habits, so beware of these." Confucius elucidated this beautifully, "It is easy to hate and it is difficult to love. This is how the whole scheme of things work. All good things are difficult to achieve; and bad things are very easy to get." Are you going to love people instead of showing hate?

If we want to prepare a list of bad habits, there could be many. Some of them include: "coming late on duty, rising up late, doubt in the mind, non-seriousness in work, using abusive language, not bathing daily, drinking, smoking, taking drugs, excessive sex, relation with other women, pornography, chewing pan/tobacco/gutka, constant failing, indiscipline activities, stealing, lying, self-boosting, dishonesty, non-working attitude, procrastination, etc." These are also called "**social ills.**"(Refer Chapter 4)

"Your net worth is decided on the basis of habits, and society views you accordingly. Sometimes, serious bad habit can take your life too." Benjamin Franklin advocated, "Your net worth to the world is usually determined by what remains after your bad habits are subtracted from your good ones."

WHAT ARE VALUABLE TRAITS IN LIFE?

There are some valuable traits for human beings which everybody should inculcate and possess instead of bad habits. These include: "exhibiting high degree of courage in the event of adversity; choosing extreme happiness in the event of hurt; exhibiting high degree of self-restraint in the event of temptation; exhibiting good character in the event of despair; picking opportunity in the event of obstacles; showing strong conviction in the face of downfall of quality, excellence, and value systems; exhibiting self-esteem in the event of your respect and honor is at stake; exhibiting commitment in the event of remaining in loss; trying hard and bouncing back in the event of failure with colossal confidence; living free from bad habits instead of indulging in these; and showing forgiveness in the event of insult." "These valuable traits can't be possessed automatically but need a lot of mental and physical training for a long period so that these become a habit and enrich positive attitude." "How can you expect from a person who shows cowardice or dishonesty in small events can handle a big event boldly and honestly? This is not possible because he has never practiced honesty and boldness." "Sustaining in good acts and abstaining from bad acts are the great tools of success." Imbibe this philosophy in life to excel. You should sustain in the good acts and abstain yourself from all undesirable activities till these become your habits. Aristotle said, "Good habits formed at youth make all the difference."

CONSEQUENCES OF BAD HABITS

"Perhaps the people who have practiced bad habits, such as smoking, drinking, taking drugs, excessive sex with different partners, viewing pornography and abstaining from work are not realizing, in general, what they are doing with their lives. They are killing themselves; they are murdering their dreams and health." Many youngsters have lost their lives by using **drugs**. **Smoking** invites T.B. and life gets shortened by at least ten years. Many get lung cancer and **six million** people die prematurely worldwide. Excessive **drinking** of **alcohol** damages liver and kidney and about **2.5 million** premature deaths took place worldwide in 2013. They are killing the aspirations of their families and their nations. It is very essential for them to break bad habits and adopt good habits. But tragedy is this that most of them are not ready to break their bad habits. Carlos Santana said, "Most people don't have the willingness to break bad habits. They have a lot of excuses and they talk like victims." Yiddish proverb says, "Bad habits are easier to abandon today than tomorrow." Remember: "A change in bad habit brings a phenomenal change in life."

It is easy to develop bad habits and that is why bad habits are more than good ones. The truth is: "Bad habits are easy to develop but hard to live with; Good habits are hard to develop but easy to live with." "Good habits will lead to the pinnacle of success. All the top position holders in the world are having in general good habits. Those who developed any bad habit they had to pay the price and the world knows this." "Successful people own successful habits." It is said, "We first make our habits, and then our habits make us-good or bad."

Good habits always pay to those who practice these in their lives. Charles Dickens, a great advocator of good habits said, "I never could have done what I have done without the habit of punctuality, order and diligence, without determination to concentrate myself on one subject at a time". For the writer, this is the best way to write and complete a book.

"Discipline doesn't come by force in habits. In schools, discipline among students is maintained by strictness, by external compulsion and as a result, students, in general, don't imbibe the discipline. Only those students who want to be disciplined in life put this in their subconscious mind under a disciplined atmosphere." The words of Bertrand Russell elucidate this very rightly, which depict, "Right discipline consists, not in an external compulsion, but in the habits of mind which lead spontaneously to desirable rather than undesirable activities." The habits – good or bad you have developed, later on become your character. If character due to bad habits is gone, everything is gone. "Our habits change into our character." If we want to build a good character, a pleasing personality, and to be on the winning curve, we have to monitor our habits closely.

Imbibe the quote given by Mahatma Gandhi, who said:

*"**Your** beliefs become your thought,*
Your thoughts become your words,
Your words become your actions.
Your actions become your habits,
Your habits become your values,
*Your values become your **destiny.**"*

Just ponder over this above quote. It covers the whole spectrum of life. It starts from your beliefs and passes through your words, actions, habits, values and finally destiny. If your beliefs are negative and bad, your thoughts, action, habits, and values will all be negative and bad, and finally your destiny will be bad. If your beliefs are positive and good, your thoughts, words, actions, habits and values will be positive and good, and finally your destiny will be very good. Robin Sharma opines, "Happiness in life does not come from getting, it comes from being."

"Bad habits will belittle you."

"Use of drugs will bring 9Ds- "disaster, destruction, devastation, demoralization, distraction, disruption, disturbance, darkness, and derailment" in your life."

"Social ills will sink your dream in proportion to their adoption."

HOW TO BREAK THE BAD HABITS AND BUILD THE GOOD HABITS?

a. **Conditioning and Involvement in good habits**: The process, by which habits are formed, by the same process, bad habits may be broken and good habits may be formed. It is a well-established fact that anything we do repeatedly becomes a habit- either bad or good. Any type of learning comes by doing. Involvement is the learning. "Negative traits such as dishonesty, injustice, harm, indiscipline, crime, etc., are learned by doing first and then repeating it, leading to mastery in these negative traits. Good traits such as honesty, courage, fairness, transparency are learned by practicing them and scarifying many temptations." Like bad habits, good habits make you master in these traits after continuous practice but good habits need more practice than bad habits.

Go on practicing anything and your mind will be conditioned and it will be programmed in that way. Take the example of a child learning to ride a bike. There are four stages of learning – (i) **unconscious incompetence of learning**, (ii) **conscious incompetence of learning**, (iii) **conscious competence of learning**, and, (iv) **unconscious competence of learning**. The first stage represents the stage when the child doesn't know what to ride and how to ride while the fourth stage is the stage of full competency, conditioned mind and a programmed mind about riding the bike. The child can ride the bike without concentration, he can use mobile on the bike, he can even leave the handle and attempt stunts due to hard practice on the bike. Many domestic animals such as cows, buffalos, dogs, elephants and horses are taught many things by conditioning their minds through practice.

"We should practice on good habits enough to make these reach to the level of **fourth stage** and bad habits have to be unlearned and should be kept on **first stage** through practice."

b. **Self-realization**: Many people give up bad habits after self-realization of the consequences of bad habits. A strong determination takes a leading role to give up bad habits.

c. **Auto – suggestions**: These are the best tools to break bad habits and build good habits: Auto –suggestions should be only the positive statements. Say repeatedly the following **positive statements:**

Smoking, drinking, drugs, gutka, tobacco, pornography are highly bad and injurious to health and life spoilers. I will be away from these from today.

Dishonesty, injustice and indiscipline are bad habits. I will not involve in these.

I can change myself towards positive thinking.

I can sacrifice many things to acquire good habits.

Life means good habits. God has sent us to do good work in the world by following good path.

I have guts to break all bad habits. All bad habits are deterrent to my progress and health. I can and I will win over bad habits and will acquire good habits from today itself.

I am energetic, competent and courageous enough to tide over any bad habits and crisis of life.

Auto-suggestions Helps in Abstaining from Drinking Habit: A prominent person who overcame alcoholism after a long struggle is a glaring and eye-opener example. He was a heavy drunker and it was harming him in many respects. One day, he decided to get rid of this under a time frame. He used to say, "I can handle my liquor. I will cut consumption by one-tenth every month. I refused to accept that I am an alcoholic. All the time I procrastinated that I am not an alcoholic. I will honor my decision to cut consumption. In ten months' time, no alcohol will touch my month.

God will help me to get rid of alcohol." To the surprise of all, he didn't touch alcohol after ten months. It was his auto-suggestions that gave freedom from his bad habit of alcoholism.

Self-realization Helps in Abstaining from Smoking: A young man was a chain smoker. His wife was too perturbed by his habit. He was blessed with a baby boy whom he used to love immensely. One day, his wife told him, "If you are not caring for your health, at least show mercy on your son as smoke will harm the child." In one week, he gave up smoking due to the love for his son. Many people have given up smoking due to their love for their children.

The **message** from the above stories is: "It is the willpower, self-realization of consequences of bad habit, love for children and constantly using auto-suggestions that break the bad habits."

If anybody overcomes over bad habits, he/she should be praised and rewarded. Robin Sharma said, "Never forget that behavior that is rewarded is behavior that gets repeated."

If auto-suggestions and self-realization of consequences are unable to break habits (which rarely happens), one has to join some rehabilitation center where experts are available to break the bad habits. They also use auto-suggestions as one of the various methods that they suggest. "Bad habits are your enemies. Give up these! Give up these! Give up these!"

STEPS TAKEN BY YOURSELF

After going through this chapter, I (as a reader) will do the following from today itself to avoid fear, procrastination and bad habits:

i. _____
ii. _____

***

Chapter 11

Have Eagerness for Education, Learning, Research and Innovation
THE 10ᵀᴴ MANTRA

EDUCATION ELEVATES YOUR INTELLIGENCE

"Intelligence plus character – that is the goal of true education."
—*Martin Luther King Jr.*

"Education without values, as useless as it is, seems rather to make a man more clever devil."
—*C. S. Lewis*

An eminent scientist-cum-speaker was asked by a school teacher from the audience in a conference to speak to us of education, learning, research and innovation. He replied in sequence: "Education! A great tool to remove darkness from mind and to enlighten it. A great tool to sharpen intelligence. A wealth creator. A value provider. A great path to success. A development tool. An index of progress and well-being. A tool for getting knowledge, doing research and innovation. A civilization creator and promoter. An enlightenment tool. Are you eager to get quality education? If not, acquire quality education to shape your life for golden success, to shape your family for value creation, to build your nation for greatness, and to shape the world into a better place to live in."

GROWTH OF CIVILIZATION AND EDUCATION

In the beginning there was neither existence nor non-existence. The entire universe was unmanifest energy...."
—*Rig Veda (Hymn of Creation)*

"Growth of civilization is directly linked with the growth of education, learning, research and innovation (ELRI) which is possible only when order and liberty exist in the society." Will Durant said, "Civilization begins with order, grows with liberty and dies with chaos." If we give a glimpse to the early civilization till today, we will find the great importance of ELRI in the growth of civilization. Nelson Mandela said, "Education is the most powerful weapon which you can use to change the world." The data from all over the world show that the maximum number of uneducated and illiterate people live in poor, underdeveloped and developing countries. A poor country signifies that it houses a very less number of highly educated people.

"Education which promotes intelligence and quality learning clubbed with values is the first and foremost index of progress of a nation and humanity at large."

Education, learning, research and innovation are highly interrelated, so it will be dealt with in a unified approach.

As per anthropology, man appeared around **1.5 million years ago** in the form of **Ape-man** called **Anthropoids,** which means man-like animals (monkeys and apes) on the earth. Anthropoids took many thousands years to evolve into modern man (*Homo sapiens*).

After stopping to live on tree, man needed food to feed himself and also some implements to protect himself from wild animals. He used stones to make weapons – **the first major learning of man.** This period is known as the **Stone Age (5,00,000 BC-4,000 BC).** From Stone Age till 21st century there had been a tremendous development in all fields of human civilization due to growth of ELRI. In 21st century, this vast world has become a village. ELRI has produced a modern world with computers, laptops, Internet, smart phones, aeroplanes, ships, submarines, rockets, satellites, bullet trains, cars, air-conditioners, robots, etc. Man has landed on the Moon, sent space crafts into the orbits of Mars and Pluto. In medical and other fields, there is overwhelming progress. Human life has become very comfortable and highly modern due to the impact of advancement in ELRI. In the last fifty years, major development took place beyond imagination due to advancement in ELRI.

A BRIEF REVIEW OF ELRI

"**Education** includes teaching, reading, writing, speaking, training, self-study, tutorial, assignment, seminar, presentation, workshop, project, thesis, coaching, discourse, experiment, conversation, experience and observation." "In wider perspective, education covers learning, research and innovation but to give emphasis ELRI has been chosen."

"**Learning** encompasses all types of learning, i.e. knowledge, comprehension ability, creativity, critical thinking capability, analyzing capability, imagination, all types of skills, wisdom, discipline, ethics, values and spirituality."

"**Research** is the creation of more new knowledge by consuming the available knowledge."

"**Innovation** is defined as converting ideas into new or improved products, processes and services."

"**Learning outcome** is the core of education, research and innovation. If there is no learning, then it negates the education, research and innovation. For the best learning, one has to go for the best possible methodologies available in the world.

The responsibility, commitment, accountability and enthusiasm of all stakeholders will bring learning outcome."

THE IMPORTANCE OF "ELRI" IN THE MODERN WORLD

The largest economies in the past-from 1 CE (Common Era) to 1500 CE were India (no.1) and China (no.2) based on GDP in billion International dollars at 1900 prices. India was known as Golden Bird and Spiritual Guru. The first university of the world, Takshashila was established in India during 700 BC. Algebra, Trigonometry, Calculus, concept of zero, and numbering system were developed in India. The dominance of India and China started receding after 16th Century and more after the industrial revolution in Britain in 1760. British developed steam engines which were the beginning of major industrialization. They made schooling compulsory for children in real spirit. They raised the standards of the universities. They developed guns, ships, industries, science, technologies, and enriched English Language. They overcame oceans/seas by developing ships and became the king of oceans. With these developments, first they traded with more than half of the countries of the world and later on established British Rule on these countries including India. It is said that for about forty-seven years (1900–1947) under the last phase of British Rule, the growth rate of India per annum was almost zero percent. Few other European countries also ruled over some countries. It is said that in British kingdom, the sun never set. English language became the world language. British also settled in USA, Australia and New Zealand which were very-very less populated by original inhabitants. "A tiny country Britain ruled about half of the world due to the development of mainly ELRI." With the development of Britain, other European countries also started developing.

USA became a nation of migrants (after its discovery by Columbus) due to its vast areas and resources, and very-very less population of original inhabitants-Red Indians. Early settlers were British and other Europeans in large numbers. As a result, the language of USA became English. In the last 200 years, the talented people from all over the world settled there. They developed the best policies, processes and governance for all round development and growth including ELRI and as a result USA became the dream country to migrate. They adopted a policy of freedom, liberty and gave equal opportunity to all citizens to grow irrespective of religion, cast, creed and nationalities and as a result they become the world leader through the development of ELRI: "in science, technology, arts, culture, finance, management, warfare, medicines, unparalleled infrastructure, manufacturing, etc." Along with USA, UK, Germany, France, Italy, Netherland, other European countries developed. All development except a few in every field took place in USA, European countries, Russia and Japan. "ELRI is the mother of progress and development. Embrace it! Embrace it! Embrace it!"

Now the question arises: What are the reasons that did not allow Asian Countries (except Japan, China, Singapore and South Korea), African countries and North American countries to develop even 25% of developed countries? "The main reasons of lagging behind from growth, development and success by large number of nations are the lack of: quality education, quality learning, quality research, excellent innovation, good governance, good policies and processes and good justice system."

"The implementation of quality ELRI is a great tool for the human development." What is a nation? A nation is the summation of individuals living in a country. If every person gets quality education, quality learning and gets involved in research and innovation in one's work environment, naturally every person and every country will progress and poverty will vanish. "Creativity and critical thinking is the core of ELRI." Mahatma Gandhi portrayed, "Live as if you were to die tomorrow. Learn as if you were to live forever."

Learning is a great tool to remain abreast of current knowledge and skills. Learning activates your mind. It is a fitness tool for your mind. "Mind acts as a razor. If you use it, it will sharpen, otherwise it will rust." Henry Ford said, "Anyone who stops learning is old, whether at twenty or eighty. Anyone who keeps learning stays young."

In under- developing and developing nations, very less emphasis and attention are given on the education of women. People have very wrong notion. Women should be equally educated to men. In fact, it is said that if you want to improve your present and future generation, you educate woman.

The simple philosophy to move at the higher ladder of success is: "To learn more, to contribute more you must learn more." A great CEO once said, "Be so knowledgeable, competent, talented, and brilliant in your profession that your organization can't run without you. Become indispensable." "Investment in education, and getting knowledge and skills at the world-class level will be your smartest investment among all. Be a master in your profession and greatness will reach to you." Just compare an educated and an uneducated person. The valuable contribution is much more by an educated person than an uneducated person. Great success, high positions and greatness can be garnered only through ELRI. It is said, "When you know better you do better." Aristotle differentiated in a more emphatic way and said, "The educated differs from uneducated as much as living differs from dead." J. Krishnamurti opined, "There is no end of education. And it is not about what you learn in school. The whole of life, from the moment you are born to the moment you die, is a process of learning." About a dozen CEOs of top companies of the world are of Indian origins. This shows the capability of Indians.

"If a person is receiving education, it doesn't mean that he is learning each and everything and his thinking is getting wider. Education will not be a real education, till his thinking process gets increased." Margaret Mead said, "Children must be taught how to think, not what to think." "Education is not the filling of a pail, but the lighting of a fire in mind." Confucius opined, "Learning without thought is a labor lost: thought without learning is perilous."

In about 90% educational institutions worldwide - primary, secondary or higher education, our emphasis is only on giving information to children and memorization (called **rote learning**). It takes a leading role in learning. It is similar to putting human brain in a mold. This is a great tragedy of education system. "Education should provide elasticity to mind and an educated mind should be a house of imagination." Thomas A. Edison gave too much emphasis on widening of thought and enhancing capability of imagination through education system and said, "The most necessary task of civilization is to teach people how to think. The trouble with the way of educating is: it does not give elasticity to mind. It casts the brain into a mold. It consists that child must accept. It does not encourage thought or reasoning and it lays more stress on memory than observation". Teaching- learning process has to be on the line of advice given by Edison.

"Education removes ignorance. A true education promotes empathy in the receiver. It removes the darkness and brings light in the mind of the recipient. The purpose of education is to overcome ignorance in every walk of life, not to validate it."

Real learning in the absence of holistic education is not happening. Character building is equally important along with gaining knowledge and skills. "Education is not meant to prepare us for life but education is life itself." "In the materialistic world, the purpose of education has changed. The emphasis is to earn more so that more comfort in life will be achieved. There is no emphasis on how to live." John Adams advocated, "There are two educations: One should teach us how to make a living and other, how to live."

"There is a need to recast the purpose of education in real spirit all over the world. The child has to be developed in a holistic way covering every aspect of life such as intellectual, emotional, spiritual, ethics, values and physical. If holistic approach is not covered, then we will be producing educated conmen which will prove to be a menace to the society. That is why scams are taking place all over the world by educated people." Kevin Swanson elucidated this very beautifully, "Education is the preparation of a child intellectually, emotionally, spiritually and physically for life and for eternity." "Only teaching ethics and values will not work unless and until these are imbibed by teachers, students and parents in real life." Ken Robinson warned the society on our method of education and said, "Imagination is the source of every form of human achievement. And it's the one thing that I believe we are systematically jeopardizing in the way we educate our children and ourselves." Only getting 95% plus marks is not real education. "Great people of the world are hardly schools, boards/university toppers." APJ Abdul Kalam said, "The education system in the 21st century must be based on **Five Components**: "research and enquiry, creativity and innovation, capacity to use high end technology, entrepreneurship and moral leadership."

It is the learning of skills which help us to make a living. Begging, freebies, and donations are common all over the world in different forms. Giving something to anybody is not going to help him rather learning of skills will meet the living cost. Confucius said, "Give a bowl of rice to a man and you will feed him for a day. Teach him how to grow his own rice and you will save his life."

"Every child born is a gift to the humanity." Some are born with talent and some acquire talent. "Talent is the strength and capacity to do things in an extraordinary way with ease." Talent may be classified in four categories–**mental, physical, creative and charismatic.** Talent may be found in two forms-born talent and acquired talent. **Born talent** (though very less in number) has less scope in capacity building while in **acquired talent;** there is a good scope for capacity building. "Education must enthuse students for life. Students must be counselled to make them realize that the attainment of greatness is larger than mere marks and a holistic approach is essential. Confucius said, "He who learns but does not think is lost. He who thinks but does not learn is in great danger."

"For any country, human capital is the real wealth." According to World Bank's assessment for 192 countries, wealth distribution is as follows:

Physical capital on average accounts only for **16%** of total wealth.

Natural wealth on average accounts for **20%** of total wealth.

Human capital on average accounts for **64%** of total wealth.

Education is the instrument by which knowledge, skill and talent may be developed. "Only through quality ELRI, the value and worth of human capital may be enhanced." Knowledge is expanding at a rapid rate and it is very challenging to cope with the expanding knowledge. The following is the estimate of **information explosion**:

In 1900, information was doubling in every 100 years.

In 1945, information was doubling in every 25 years.

In 1994, information was doubling in every 10 years.

In 2004, information was doubling in every 1.5 years.

In 2012, information was doubling in every 11 hours.

This shows the importance of ELRI. "Any country that will lag behind in ELRI will be poorer." "The consequences of poverty are highly pathetic. One might want to sleep in the midst of fire but not in the midst of poverty. Poverty degrades a nation with all sorts of miseries."

The Supreme Court of India in Unni Krishnan Judgment (1993 SSC(1) 645) had given immense importance of education(Times of India, Dhananjay Mahapatra). It said, "Victories are gained, peace is preserved, progress is achieved, civilization is built up and history is made not on the battlefields where ghastly murders are committed in the name of patriotism, not in the council chambers where insipid speeches are spun out in the name of debate, not even in factories where are manufactured novel instruments to strangle life, but in educational institutions which are seed-beds of culture, where children in whose hands quiver the destinies of future, are trained. From their ranks will come out when they grow up, statesmen and soldiers, patriots and philosophers, who will determine the progress of the land."

FUNDAMENTALS OF IMPARTING QUALITY EDUCATION

Education ecosystem consists of **four sub-systems** namely: **physical** (infrastructure, labs, library, facilities, etc.), **intellectual** (teachers and students), **administrative** (principal, directors, vice-chancellors, etc.), **regulatory** (government, governing body, accrediting agencies, etc.). The all four sub-systems are **stakeholders** on which **quality education lies.**

Following are the **fundamentals** of imparting quality education:

i. Fundamentals of imparting quality education lie in "**Good** quality, responsibility, commitment, accountability, and vision of teachers and administrators;" in "**Highly** curious and committed students for learning, excellence and self-development;" in "**Highly** enthusiastic parents for excellence;" in "**Good** suitable infrastructure, facilities and conducive environment;" in "**High quality teaching (no spoon feeding)** through dynamic, progressive and market driven syllabus;" in "**Less memorization(no rote learning);**" in "**Sufficient** extra-curricular activities;" but, "**More in**: self-study, understanding, concept building, problem solving, discussions, debate, involvements, passion for learning, intellectual curiosity, conducive environment for quality learning, quality project, quality seminar, quality thesis, creativity, critical thinking, imagination enhancement, multidisciplinarity, skills development, character building, values building, inspiring, commonsense, wisdom, judgment, quality research, quality innovation, patent(intellectual property right) filing and leadership development."

ii. "**How** to teach is much more important than **what** to teach. Real learning will only happen through the holistic approach and **best teaching methodology** (smart class rooms, visuals, applications, fun, play, curiosity, experiments, interaction, imagination enhancement, debate, discussion, values, etc.) imbedded with **dynamic innovation** so that students will be the real human capital and will be able to solve any problem of the world- be it technological, scientific, social, innovative, religious, spiritual, artistic, medicinal, financial, humanitarian, developmental, and so on, making them **School Smart as well as Street Smart.**"

iii. Academic integrity is a must. Assignments, Project reports, Master's theses, Ph.D. theses, Innovation reports, and patent reports should be **critically checked** for real quality contributions **without any plagiarism.** Shoddier projects and research works are **black dots** on the institute/university and act as a poison for quality education. Regulatory bodies must regulate for qualities. Accreditation agencies must accredit schools/colleges/universities honestly to improve quality. It is the duty of all stakeholders to see that quality education moves on a **rising curve** on the glorious path of academic excellence.

EDUCATION SCENARIO

ELRI is a lifelong process. Let us ponder over honestly: "How had we been educated?How are our children being educated? What is the quality of ELRI prevalent in one's country? You will find that the quality of ELRI in underdeveloped and developing countries is in highly bad shape in about 80% to 90% institutions. In India, about 75% institutions are run by Government and 25% by private. The condition of public run institutions is more worse than private ones. In 10% to 20% good institutions also, only about 60% students are better equipped and intelligent but they need better grooming on the lines of top universities of the world. "Bad schools are poison wells, and so, children must be saved from such schools." Though, Indians have established their authorities in IT sector in the world and brought appreciable reputation of India back, but they are more capable than what they have achieved. They can do wonders if the mindset changes. In India, except technology and management streams, there is no emphasis on seminar, project, presentation, discussion, tutorial, debate, and assignments in higher education system. The height is that most of the students except from leading universities/institutes don't read books but only notes prepared by tutors or tiny guess papers. In engineering and management also, quality of projects and theses of about 80% institutions (expect their 05% to 10% students) are poor as they are mostly plagued by plagiarism and shoddy work. Texts books are being written by those who have hardly taught. Except leading institutes and universities, in major cases, dishonesty, irresponsibility and favoritism takes a leading role in clearing projects, P G theses and PhD theses. In large number of institutions, class engagement is negligible or even nil and students join coaching classes. "There is too much disconnection between teaching requirements and placement requirements." "Communication skill is very poor. Conversational intelligence quotient(C-IQ) is very poor. Critical thinking, creativity, comprehension, analyzing capability and imagination enhancement have got a beating while students can produce mind-blowing results if all the stakeholders take responsibility honestly." The situation in developed countries is much better but they also do not cover about 30% of student's population in terms of quality ELRI. Every parent has a desire to admit one's ward in Ivy schools, but Ivy schools are very less in number and very costly.

"It is worth to note that quality of education in higher education system can't be better if the quality is not better in secondary system and quality in secondary education cannot be better if quality in primary is not better. It is a cascading and cumulative effect." "Twelve years of poor schooling can't produce quality in higher education system."

"**During primary and secondary education,** a child should be proficient in reading, writing and speaking and must have sound foundation in chosen stream (mathematics, science, art, commerce, etc.) with analytical, comprehension, communication, creativity and critical thinking capability embedded with ethics and value system." But, in India, about 50% children of 5th level are not able to read the books meant for 2nd level. Rote learning is predominant at all levels. Globally, India stands 62nd on the skills measure (reading, writing, mathematics and science) in schools. In other undeveloped and developing countries, the situation is more or less similar except four or five countries. **"Spoiling student's career is a moral crime against one's nation as they are the nation builders."**

"The **purpose of higher education** is to develop the following **qualities** so that students can earn sufficient for living through a profession of one's choice and know how to live in a society giving valuable contribution to their nation and the world at large."

Sound subject knowledge (emphasis on concepts, originalities, fundamentals, understanding, etc.)

Sound skills (writing, communication, soft, technical, practical, entrepreneurship, social, etc.)

Sound capabilities (analytical, comprehension, creativity, experimentation, seminar delivery, project completion, critical thinking, commonsense, judgment, wisdom, passion for learning, intellectual curiosity, imagination, research, innovation, problem solving, extra-curricular activities- games, sports, music, dance, painting, debate, etc.)

Better leadership quality.

Better disciplined, ethics and values.

Better at being school smart as well as street smart.

In higher education system, there are some agencies which rank universities on the basis of quality selecting some key parameters. One of the most acceptable agencies is Q. S. World Ranking which ranks universities of the world on the basis of the following six key parameters having 100 points, each with different weightage.

Academic Reputation Score (weightage 40%)

Employer Reputation Score (weightage 10%)

Faculty -Student Ratio Score (weightage 20%)

Citation per Faculty Score (weightage 20%)

International Faculty Ratio Score (weightage 5%)

International Student Ratio Score (weightage 5%)

Q. S. World University Ranking publishes the ranking of 800 universities of the world. In 2015 rankings, number one and number two positions were occupied by

Massachusetts Institute of Technology (100 points) and Harvard University (98.7 points) respectively. USA occupied a major chunk in top rankings followed by UK, Canada, France, Germany, Switzerland and Japan. American universities continue to dominate the top rankings taking more than half of the leading twenty places, but there is much greater diversity beyond that. American universities represent about **a quarter** in the top 200. Noble laureates are also mostly from American universities and research centers, followed by Europe.

"Only fourteen universities of India (including seven IITs) figured in 2015 rankings among 800 universities – a disappointing performance despite great talent." What a loss of talent! No university of India occupies a rank within the top 100. IISc Banglore (in 2015 ranking) topped the list having 147 rank followed by IIT Delhi having 179 rank and IIT Mumbai having 202 rank. NUS, Singapore (a tiny country) occupied 12th position. Peking University (China) scored 41th position and Tsinghai University ranked at 25th position while Chinese University of Hong Kong occupied 30th position. Research, innovation and academic reputation are the main ingredients of university system which are very less in developing countries including India. In 2010, the number of Ph. D produced in India is 20,013 while USA produced 48,069 and China produced 48,978. India houses only four researchers per 10,000 working people whereas Kenya has six, Brazil has fourteen, China has eighteen, Russia has fifty-eight, and UK and USA top the table with seventy-nine researchers each.

Further, the quality of research and innovation output whatever coming out is also not up to the mark in India and other developing countries while they are much more capable. The five old IITs and IISc Banglore deserve a rank below fifty in QS World Ranking and all stockholders should think over it. As per news, most of these IITs are short of about 30% teachers due to the lack in quality of applicants. There is not a single highly reputed International Journal coming out from India which could have enhanced Indian reputation in research. "What a pity when India having 1.27 billion population houses eighteen IITs, nineteen IIMs, thirty-one NITs, four IIITs and more than 725 universities, 38,000 colleges and 28 million students enrolled in 2014!" "It is these Indian students who are giving extraordinary performance in universities, research labs, and companies of USA, UK, Canada, Germany, France and Australia. In IT sector, the reputation of India is on the top of the world. The economic status of Indians in America (about 6 million, 2% of US population) is the highest among all nationals. They are known as model minority. The median annual household income of Indian-Americans in 2013 was USD 100,547, whereas overall US median annual household income was USD 51,000. At the time of birth, children of every country are having more or less similar intelligence level (except extraordinary talented and undeveloped mind) but it is the environment, bringing up and grooming of children that matter."

"What does Q. S. World Ranking of Universities signify? It signifies that quality ELRI is one of the most important index of prosperity and development of a nation and so its people. It is due to this fact that all the discoveries in science, technology, liberal arts, commerce, medicine, management, military, etc., took place in those countries who occupy the major and top positions in Q S World Rankings of Universities. They first developed their countries and later on, they sold the new exciting products developed by them to other countries of the world and earned a lot of money and became highly prosperous." Just search who have developed all modern equipment, machines, systems, and products, and who are the winners of Noble Prizes and you will validate my above comments. The earning of educational institutes of USA from foreign students alone (8,19,644 students) are more than USD 22 billion (in 2014), followed by UK (4,88,380 students) due to high quality of ELRI.

MAIN REQUIREMENTS OF QUALITY IN ELRI

The following are the **main requirements of quality in ELRI**:

i. Quality infrastructure (academic building, laboratories, computational facilities, library, hostels, residence, playgrounds, canteen, offices, lush green campus, various facilities, etc.)

ii. Quality students (curious and committed students towards learning, excellence and quality especially for secondary and higher education, and taking the maximum advantage of opportunities around them; and at primary level, students are to be prepared to be curious and committed to explore the world for quality learning and excellence.).

iii. Qualified, competent, dedicated and committed teachers and administrators with a great vision, great responsibility and strong faculty development initiatives with proper students- teachers' ratio.

iv. Curious and enthusiastic parents for quality education, and excellence and helping institutes to grow, to excel.

v. Better policies, processes, governance, values systems, transparent systems, teaching methodology, examination and evaluating systems, yielding conducive environment for promoting and maintaining stringent quality in: teaching, learning, research, innovation, patent, entrepreneurship, skills development, ethics, values, leadership development, extra-curricular activities like games, sports etc., robust support system; and soft skills like presentation skills, communication skills, image buildings; etc. leading to creativity, critical thinking and excellence with accountability.

vi. Excellent and dynamic syllabus conducive for overall development of students based on needs of societies, needs of markets, and needs of nation building from primary to higher education intended for quality education.

vii. Emphasis should be given to quality assignments handed to students for submission by a prescribed date and time **without any plagiarism**; excellent seminar presentation; quality and innovative project work; discussion; debate; innovative and transparent admission system; innovative, transparent and robust examination system; and quality Master's theses and quality Ph. D theses **without any plagiarism.** These initiatives will help in: developing creativity, enhancing elasticity to mind, igniting mind, giving challenging problem solving ability, and enhancing research and innovative capacity." A critical and honest evaluation of submission of assignments, project work and Master's and Ph. D theses with strict action on plagiarism is needed by teachers. This is the core of quality education and students are capable of meeting the requirements if groomed properly from primary level. Students should take part in various National and International Level Competitions including projects. This is followed in all top best schools and universities of the world. Leading top ten schools and universities of the world may be taken as role models to develop schools and universities on those lines including one's best policies and practices.

viii. Try to fulfil the requirements of the six parameters of QS World rankings and their related sub-parameters to score maximum points in at least fourteen Indian institutes/universities which figured in 800 universities in 2015 rankings so that top six may fall under fifty and the rest eight may fall under 100 to 200 ranks as per present rankings. Similarly, universities of other countries may follow similar policy or their own policy.

ix. Excellent vision and mission of governing body of institutions including head of institutions, and respective governments intended for quality ELRI are needed.

x. Feedback of employers is vital (in the case of higher education system) to implement the suggestions for improvement.

xi. Alumni participation in institutions helps a lot in brand building (Harvard University is run by Alumni as their hearts bleed for alma mater).

xii. Real and honest accreditation of schools, colleges and universities by renowned agencies leading to quality enhancement and competitiveness at national level should be done with an eye on nation building.

xiii. An award should be initiated by leading universities to promote new and innovative business and social impact start-ups by their alumni and other students of respective country as done by Harvard University.

REASONS OF LAGGING BEHIND IN ELRI BY MANY COUNTRIES

What are the reasons for developing and underdeveloped countries to lag behind in imparting quality ELRI to their citizens? The **reasons** are many as given below:

i. Never realized the true importance of education learning, research and innovation and never fulfilled even 50% requirements.

ii. Governance was poor and some countries remained either under foreign rules or after independence there was too much turmoil, chaos, and the lack of sound policies, processes, fairness, justice system and their proper execution.

iii. Never allocated sufficient funds for education, learning, research and innovation in annual budgets like the top countries of the world. As per Human Development Index (**HDI**) of 2014, India ranks at 135 out of 187 countries. The top five countries include: Norway, Australia, Switzerland, Netherlands, and USA. HDI considers three aspects: "Life expectancy at birth years, Expected schooling years, and Per capita income on PPP basis in USD (Source: HDR 2014)." **Population** (1.27 billion on 11th July, 2015) is the greatest problem of India. It has about 17% of world population and its population density is about 12.5 times of USA. Consequently, increase in per capita income will be very slow. Per capita income of USA was about 34 times of India (USD1627), in 2014. Though, the high population may prove as a boon also if quality education and skills are given to youths which constitute about 65% of population but it is very-very difficult, though not impossible. "In India, only 3.5% of the workforce is skilled through formal education compared to 46% in China, 74% in Germany and 96% in South Korea. A massive skill development program is needed in India and other countries that are lagging in skills in real spirit."

iv. "There could be at least **Five Point Formulae for the progress of India with real action:** (a) Increase human capital through quality ELRI; (b) Reduce the growth rate of population through wisdom and awareness from about 2% to around 1%; (c) Give good governance through transparent and honest systems including good justice systems; (d) Do rapid development, create growth and enhance economy in all sectors leading to the creation of a large number of employment; (e) Ensure inclusive growth and well-being for all." "With above **Five Initiatives** India can regain its past glory of the **GOLDEN BIRD**." Similarly, other developing countries may use the similar policy based on their strength and shortcomings.

v. In about 80 % to 90% schools (in India, about 75% public schools and 25% private) of primary and secondary education, quality education was never started due to serious shortcomings in large number of existing teachers (about 50% to 60%) such as: "poor quality of teachers, wrong attitude of teachers, no commitment of teachers, no accountability of teachers, absenteeism of teachers from duty, involvement of teachers in politics and in other government works. Further, less number of teachers, poor infrastructure, rampant academic corruption, non-seriousness in majority of parents and insensitiveness of government/private owners" which resulted in poor quality of students entering in higher education systems that are already in bad shape due to all above factors which finally resulted in poor quality of graduates. "Though, there are serious pitfalls, but it doesn't mean that everything is bad in education sector. Some teachers are so good, so much dedicated and capable that they give their 100 % to the profession, to students and they are to be saluted. They are the real gurus. They could be role model for other teachers." In other sectors also, there are similar pitfalls which resulted about 70% population poor. Gross enrolment ratio (GER) in higher education system in underdeveloped and developing countries is much less (about 16.5% in India) as compared to developed countries (about 30% in USA). "Quality of about 80 percent graduates is very poor due to various reasons as cited above and they are not employable while they can do wonders if groomed better from schools to universities as intelligence of Indians are great." India allocates only 0.88% of GDP into science research as compared to US's 2.7-3%, China 2-2.5% and South Korea's 3-4% of their GDP. If you go inside the education system in India, you will be aghast to see the pitiable condition in about 80% to 90% educational institutions. It is a great national loss. Swaminathan S. A. Aiyar has said, "Absenteeism is a curse and crime against the poor. It is especially high for teachers and health staff in many states (of India)." In higher education institutions, things are not better except 10% to 20% institutions/universities, while they can produce wonders. Research output is very less while they can do much better. India remained the World Guru as the great epics Vedas, Upanishads had been written more than 3500 years ago in India and it can retain its past glory if all stakeholders work in this direction.

vi. Quality is not one year affair. Even one starts with quality from the primary level, to produce quality students from work force needs 15 to 20 years. In fact, many universities are selling degrees and killing talent while they can produce better result if they are quality conscious and believe in nation building.

vii. "Quality is a mindset. It should have been a passion and vision of all the stakeholders which did not happen till date in India in about 80% to 90% schools, colleges and universities." An institution, an organization and a nation are judged by the quality of students and teachers, quality of employees, and quality of people respectively in every respect under the bottom of the pyramid (about 70%). If the qualities of students in the bottom of the pyramid are good, qualities in the top of the pyramid will shine automatically."

"Solution lies only when all the stakeholders of every nation: will become committed to quality; will be made accountable; will have positive attitude; and will meet all the requirements for quality education, learning, research and innovation under a time frame through a pious national movement for glorious success in enhancing quality of human capital. Extensive training of teachers in real sense to improve their quality in all aspects and skill developments for the youths under transparent and accountable manner is needed in first place under a time bound mission at national level."

INNOVATION BRINGS ADVANCEMENT

Innovation! A new idea for the betterment. A new technology provider. An idea of a new beautiful product or system. A wealth creator. A solution provider. Are you an innovative person? If not, be an innovative person for your success, for your nation building.

In 21st century, innovation is a new buzzword worldwide. On June 7, 2009, U.S. President Barak Obama in his Cairo address said, "Education and innovation will be the currency of the 21st century."

As stated above, "Innovation is defined as converting ideas into new or improved products, processes and services." India's world ranking on global innovation index (GII) is low. Based on survey in 2014, India is ranked at seventy-six in the global innovation index. Switzerland tops the list. Even Malaysia (33), South Korea (16) and Singapore (7) are ahead of India. As per Nature Magazine data, domestic and foreign patents filed per million populationin India is at 17 compared to 4,451 in South Korea; 3,716 in Japan; and 541 in China. "It is the innovation culture that made South Korea in just three decades after 1950 Korean War as one of the top ten richest nations from one of the poorest nations of the world. South Korea follows a philosophy of 4 **R's** - Re-engineer, Reform, Restructure and Refocus."

Many innovative people especially from leading countries developed innovative products and started companies which became money spinners and created a lot of wealth; the enterprise value (**EV**) of some of them are more than the GDP (in USD billion) of many small countries. Such companies include: Microsoft (274.06), Google (325.5), GE (629.04), Apple (451.5) estimated on 30th March 2014 (Source: Internet, Google, Q Search).

"It is the innovations that put USA on the top of the world." MIT alone of USA made 150 fundamental technological innovations that have had wide –ranging impact, while in the last 60 years, not a single fundamental innovation came out from Indian universities or institutes. "Innovation converts knowledge into wealth. There is a need to recognize that knowledge (Saraswati) and wealth (Lakshmi) should co-exist. A glaring example of this co-existence is in the innovation of George White Sides of Harvard University. The market capitalization of his research based companies is overUSD 20 billion. Such academic entrepreneurship is missing in India and other developing countries due to the lack in quality ELRI."

R. A. Mashelkar questions: Indian genes express themselves in Silicon Valley, but not in Indus Valley. Why? Five percent of Indian in Silicon Valley has 15.5% companies- a leap forward, a great achievement. The answer by Mashelkar lies in the fact that India lacks a **"robust national innovation ecosystem."** This is also true in the case of many developing countries. Only research labs are not going to help much. Any country including India has to develop idea of incubators, technology parks, a conducive intellectual property rights regime, enlightened regulatory systems, academics who believe in not "Just publish or perish", but,

"Patent, publish and prosper," potent inventor-investor engagement, adventure capital and passionate innovation leaders." India incubated around 500 start-ups in 2014 while China did over 8,000. Indians contributions to patents filed globally accounts less than **01%** while China contribution went to **32%** in 2013. This poor performance in innovation is when Indian intelligence is rated high. Hence, a strong innovation ecosystem is the need of the hour.

Indians have the capability to excel if infrastructure, conducive environment, accountability and good governance are created. Paradigm shifts are occurring now in the field of innovation. Aurigo's innovative software is handling infrastructure worth more than 200 USD billion. Now, a lot of start-ups such as Flipkart, Snapdeal, Magicbricks, Housing.com, Ola, Quikr, Capital Float, Sweet Couch, Innoviti, Mobokon, Exploride, etc. are being started by Indians and Bengaluru is known as start-up capital of India. Kerala Government has started a start-up village in Kochi. By 2020, India may be one of the leading start-up countries of the world in the next decade. The major innovation in the next decade will be taking place in the areas coined as: SMAC(Social, Mobility, Analytics, Cloud Computing); SAIR(Sensor, Artificial Intelligence, Robotics); and 3DP(Three Dimensional Printers, a new era of manufacturing).

Follow the suggestions given by R. A. Mashelkar (president, global research alliance) in 2009 for India. Then the dream of the 21st century being innovative India's century will certainly come true. Other developing countries may follow similar philosophy. "India needs monumental changes not incremental changes in every sphere." "The responsibility of fostering innovation rests with the educational system, research laboratories, corporate and young minds interested in start-up."

"A large numbers of innovations are needed in policies, processes, methodologies and delivery systems in the government sector to yield better result under transparent system to reduce corruption and enhance productivity." Similarly, other developing countries have to take similar initiative. Franklin Roosevelt once said, "We cannot always build the future for our youth, but we can build our youth for the future". This is only possible through quality ELRI. And Roosevelt followed this relentlessly.

In order to succeed in life, follow the innovative path. Just keep on innovating in every sphere of your life. "Stagnation invites death." The fall of world share of Nokia mobile phone is one of the examples. "Growth, invention, and innovation sustain life." "All the best fruits are on the skinny branch. To enjoy the fruits, you have to innovate daily and relentlessly." Companies that do not innovate do not survive and that is why even 20% of the Fortune 500 companies fail within thirty years. The innovative company, Apple is on the top in the world. "The innovative mantra is: Keep challenging yourself to think out of the box, do better daily and be better daily."

John Wooden opined, "Young people need models not critics." In any field, to become a model is not easy. The fifteen Mantras cited in this book are needed and critics can't become a model.

"Make education, learning, research and innovation as the elixir of your life."

A PIOUS DUTY OF ALL STAKEHOLDERS

"The creation of a pearl inside an oyster is a miracle of nature. Taking a cue from this lustrous evolution, every educational institute – be a primary, a secondary or higher level should nurture, motivate and transform its students into gems, pearls and diamonds of human society, empowering them to gain leverage in the future and excel in every field of life like shining stars of the universe. Teachers, students, parents, governing bodies and governments should help and cooperate in this pious duty of nation building by bringing excellence and richness in human capital." Educationists should strive hard to enhance creativity among students. A strong culture is needed for enhancing creativity and spiritual leadership quality.

William Arthur Ward said, "Educationists should build the capacities of the spirit of enquiry, creativity, entrepreneurial and moral leadership among students and become their role model." In Indian culture, the importance of teacher is great, next to God. William Arthur Ward has classified the type of teachers in beautiful words which say: "The mediocre teacher tells. The good teacher explains. The superior teacher demonstrates. The great teacher inspires." In Sanskrit, there is a hymn, "Vikram Bhogi Basundhara(Winner rules over the earth)." "Resolve to be a winner through quality ELRI." "Be an accomplished person who is rarely available."

"Human capital, the major wealth of a country can only be enriched and enhanced by quality ELRI-education, learning, research and innovation."

Hey, brothers and sisters of the world! Recognize the importance of quality ELRI as it enables to bring progress, to bring prosperity, to lead a decent life, to succeed, to contribute in the world, to enhance intelligence, to acquire knowledge and skills, to make the world a better place to live in, to build the nation, to become a giver like nature. Do you have eagerness to get involved in quality ELRI? If answer is no, then please involve seriously in ELRI, otherwise you are bound to lead a pitiable life.

STEPS TAKEN BY YOUSELF

Either as education providers or as recipients, I will take following steps towards quality ELRI:

i. _____
ii. _____

***

Chapter 12

Do Goal-Setting and Planning
THE 11ᵀᴴ MANTRA

GOAL – SETTING FIXES GOALS OF YOUR LIFE

"Whenever you want to achieve something keep your eyes open, concentrate and make sure you know exactly what it is you want. No one can hit their target with their eyes closed."

—*Paulo Coelho*

"People with goals succeed because they know where they are going."

—*Earl Nightingale*

A great industrialist-cum-speaker was asked by a student among the audience in a conference to speak to us of goal-setting and planning. He replied in sequence: "Goal! Your soul. Your purpose of life. A cherished destination. A target to be achieved. A dream with deadline. Isn't it? Be proactive to set your goal to realize your dream."

After imagination, dream and desire, it is necessary that your goal must be set what exactly you want. Goals are unwavering dreams of life with a great passion, deadline and strong action plan. Your goals may be worthy and unworthy. Don't bring unworthy goal in your mind. It is highly imperative to set the exact goal as this will not give any room for drifting and dilemma. A ship can't reach the destination without setting goal prior to journey. Nobody boards a train or plane without knowing destination. The power of concentration is enormous. A simple magnifying glass when focuses the sun rays at one point on a piece of paper burns it, but when you move glass all the time, it will not burn. Winners are those who are highly focused. The focus should be like a laser beams -pin pointed.

"A great archer is known not by his bows and arrows but by his hundred percent accurate aims to the goal."

Single-Pointed Intense Concentration Achieves a Difficult Goal: Princes Pandavas and Kauravas, including Arjuna were taking the training in the art of archery under the great Guru Dronacharya as per the great epic Mahabharata. After completion of the training, Guru Dronacharya conducted a test of art of archery for his disciples (princes). He put a wooden bird on a very high branch of a tree. He told everybody to hit the "eye of the bird" (i.e. goal) by aiming their arrow. He called the first disciple (Yudhisthira) to aim at the eye of the bird. Guruji asked the first disciple to describe: "what you are seeing?" He said, "Guruji, I am seeing the bird, trees, you, my brothers and the sky." Dronacharya asked the first disciple to wait. He asked other disciples, turn by turn, to aim at the target and to answer the same question. Guruji was not satisfied with their answers. The last turn was of Arjuna. Dronacharya asked Arjuna to aim at the target and asked the same question. Arjuna replied "I am only seeing the eye of the bird." Guruji said, "Very good, now you shoot." The arrow went straight at high speed and pierced the eye of the bird.

The **moral** of this story is: "To achieve the goal, one has to focus like a laser beam, and only at the target. Such skill is possible through practice, patience, persistence and dedication."

Dedication to Learning an Art Brings Excellence: This is also a story from Mahabharata. The teaching skills of Guru Dronacharya for archery became famous all over India. On hearing this, Ekalavya, son of a lower caste came to Guru Dronacharya to learn the art of archery. But, Dronacharya refused to teach him on the issue of lower caste, as the learning for the art of weapons was not permitted for lower caste people at that time because they were meant to get involved in service work. He returned back and went to the forest and made a statue of Guru Dronacharya. He started practicing archery day and night with a burning desire in the front of the statue and after sometime, he became an expert in the art of Archery.

One day, all the princes of Pandavas and Kauravas went to the forest with a dog. On seeing Ekalavya, the dog started barking at him. He shot seven arrows and completely filled the mouth of the dog without harming the dog. On seeing this, all princes got bewildered on the expertise of such archery. They asked Ekalavya, "Who are you and who your Guru is?" Ekalavya replied, "I am Ekalavya and my Guru is Dronacharya". All the princes got surprised on hearing the name of Guru Dronacharya. From there itself, Arjuna went to his Guru and narrated the full story to him and said, "Guruji, you have told me that no disciple will be more expert than me in archery, but your disciple Ekalavya is more expert in archery than me."

For some time, Guru Dronacharya thought over and then with Arjuna he went to the forest to meet Ekalavya. On seeing Guru Dronacharya, Ekalavya touched his feet and said, "Your disciple is before you for your service." Dronacharya told him, "If you are really my disciple, then give me your right thumb in the form of offerings to your Guru." Immediately, Ekalavya chopped off his right thumb and offered it to Guru. On this, Guru Dronacharya bowed to him at his dedication to archery and his gratitude to his Guru.

Morals of this story are:

With your strong dedication and commitment to your goal you can get expertise in any art without physical presence of Guru.

Talent is not the authority of any cast or creed.

Dedication to learning of any art may be so strong that one can be ready to sacrifice anything (like right thumb) out of joy on the demand of Guru, but such demand may be viewed in the different way also.

Lacking Definite Aim in Business Brings Failures: "In business, sky is the limit whereas in service, scale is the limit." This aspect tempts everybody and thus most of the people want to enter into business world.

As every business entity needs specific specialties, a person without accessing ones capability and finance enters into such a venture where one is unsuitable, he or she is likely to fail miserably. Some keep switching to different businesses after every failure instead of staying to it for some time and correcting its mistakes. As a result, they lose a lot of capital and become bankrupt. "Failures are the distinct icon on the road to achievement." If one could have a definite aim to enter certain type of business as per ones capability, he or she could have succeeded in business.

NEED OF GOAL- SETTING

There is a need of clarity in goal-setting. Without goal-setting, one will wander aimlessly all the time. People of different categories could have different goals. A (10+2) or level 'A' passed students may have different goals. Students may like to go in engineering, medicine, liberal arts, science, agriculture, pharmacy, bio-technology, mass communication, management, architecture, dance, show business, music, games, sports, etc. as per their choice. Again, after graduation students have to fix their goals according to the best availability for jobs or business or post-graduation as per choice, potential and other factors. But without fixing a goal, they will be nowhere as strong focus is required to excel in any field. Franklin Roosevelt said, "To reach a port we must sail –sail, not tie at anchor –sail –not drift."

For sports persons, the goals have to be set and accordingly hard practice has to be done to excel. For example, 100metres, 200 metres, 400metres or 1000metres race, the time is already set for gold, silver and bronze medals at various previous meets – either at international or national or regional level. Accordingly, athletes have to practice to meet the goal of timings already achieved in previous meets and further to improve it. For different games, different records are already set and one has to meet otherwise he/she is out of game/sport. Similarly, for every profession, one has to set the goal and to meet this otherwise one can't excel and the survival is difficult. Goals offer something to shoot for and place our efforts focused. They benchmark our success. Mary Lou Retton of Virginia(USA) set her goal to be Olympic gold medalist in gymnastics and took coaching from famous coach Bela Karolyi of Romania for two and a half years. She was highly focused towards her goal and she finally won the Olympic Gold Medal in gymnastics for USA. Harvey Mackay said, "A goal is a dream with a deadline."

A ship can't reach the harbor if it is not fixed prior to sailing. A plane can't reach at a particular airport if it is not fixed prior to take off. A car can't reach a particular place if it is not fixed before starting. So in all aspects, goal-setting is needed and to achieve this strong focus is needed as per the degree of the goal. Mike Hawkins once opined, "Goals seem impossible only when you are not heading towards them." Similarly, Les Brown once said, "Your goals are the road maps that guide you and show you what is possible for your life." Many people don't set goals due to many reasons such as: a fear of failure, a pessimistic attitude, a lack of ambition, a fear of rejection, a habit of procrastination, a low self-esteem, and a lack of knowledge. Get up, wake up, overcome over the reasons that prevent you and set your goals for your bright future.

REQUIREMENTS FOR GOAL- SETTING

"Setting goals is the first step in turning the invisible into the visible."

—*Tony Robbins*

Goal- setting is not easy. It needs many qualities in you. The following are the major requirements for goal- setting.

i. **High ambition**: A high ambition is needed to set a goal to succeed. Your thinking has to be of a high order. Unless and until you desire to lead a good life and not be satisfied with the present status of life, then only you can have a high desire, high ambition and you will be able to set a better goal for your life. The policy of "high in ambition and poor in condition" is not going to work and is bound to fail but the policy of "high in ambition and rich in condition" will work. I have seen many persons; many organizations failing or remaining at lower ladder of success due to the former policy. Some of the daily wages workers don't go to work next two days if they earn sufficient amount to have food for a few days. Their ambition in life is very low. Their policy of "a bowl some rice is sign of a rich man for two days." They will not be rich because their ambitions are just a few bowls of rice. With low ambition you can't set your goal high and can't work hard.

"Set your goals slightly high enough than your potential, plan judiciously and don't stop till you see their physical reality."

ii. **An optimistic attitude**: Keep optimistic attitude you will see the things with a different approach. Since your attitude is not negative, you will be able to set your goal in the right direction. If you are free to see pitfalls or possibilities, a person of optimistic attitude will see only possibilities. Such persons will set their goals high in life. A person of pessimistic view can't set his/her goal as they are habituated to see only pitfalls.

iii. **Fearlessness about failure**: Franklin D. Roosevelt once said, "The only thing we have to fear is fear itself." Nobody can do any work if one fears about the failure of completion of work. The word **"Fear"** has to be deleted from the subconscious mind. You can't decide about your goal if you fear all the time about its success. George Bernard Shaw once opined, "You are going to let the fear of poverty govern your life and your reward will be that you will eat, but you will not live." Attack and destroy your fear of failure and fear of the unknown and take decisions on your goal.

iv. **Confidence for getting success**: Success will be at your door step once you decide your goal, having self-confidence in yourself about your success. "Initiating action towards goal is inching forward nearer to success." "The great barrier to goal-setting is low self-esteem and low self-confidence. The slogan of "Raise your self-confidence and set your goal "is to be adopted."

v. **Goal-setting should address many aspects**: Goal-setting requires knowledge. Every goal has a different setting. Goal-setting needs step-by-step details and one has to learn it. Goals may be: a long-term plan, a medium term plan or a short term plan. People are not clear about their goals. Your goal should address many aspects such as to-do list before you die, spending time with family and friends, fun in life either at work place or home or chilling places, vacation, tour at beautiful places, health fitness, fulfilment of hobby, etc., which may be coined by a word 'ARTISAN' where each letter stands for something:

A: stands for **achievable**. Your goal should be a bit higher than your capacity and capability. Unachievable goal will bring frustration and failure.

R: stands for **realistic**. The goal must be realistic but challenging. Here realistic means the project/goal should be under the industry/possibility norm.

T: refers to **timebound**. The goal-setting must be time bound so that it may be completed in time. Delay costs too much and is detrimental to the health of your project.

I: refers to **interesting**. The goal must be interesting to you and your family also otherwise you will not be able to give your 100%.

S: stands for **specific**. If the goal-setting is vague and is subjective, then it is very difficult to give direction. For example, one may say, "I want to earn a lot of money doesn't convey any concrete amount, but if I say I want to earn USD 100 million, then it is specific." "Without specific goal, you may drift from the path."

A: stands for **appealing**. Your goal must not be only appealing to you but to your stakeholders.

N: stands for **nurturing**. The goal has to be nurtured from the very beginning like a child. Your project is like your baby and it needs nurturing at every stage otherwise it will not take its concrete shape.

vi. **Don't fear rejection**: Due to the fear of rejection by people on the non-fulfilment of goal, many persons don't set goals. "Don't bother about views of others. Very less people are supportive to motivate you. Avoid fear of rejection, and decide your goal. You are the master of your destiny. Make your destiny boldly and path breaking."

vii. **High self-esteem**: If you have high self-esteem, you will be driven by your high spirit and which will help you in deciding the goal. With low self-esteem you can't think of setting a goal and hence there is no success. "A ship can't sail to its destination without generating full power."

viii. **Knowledge of goal-setting for big goals.** You have to learn the importance of goal-setting then only you will be enthusiastic to set your goal. "Most of the big goals, big challenges are achieved by setting series of interim goals." Dr. James D. Watson made a lifelong goal to find the cure for cancer. He set a series of little goals to achieve the great goal. In this process, he discovered the structure of DNA and many other little goals and finally an initial breakthrough in the cure for cancer. Nobody wants to fail. You will get your happiness by achieving small goals at a time.

ix. **Avoid procrastination**: Those who procrastinate can't set their goal in life and so the success is far away from them. Avoid the habit of procrastination which will help you to work hard and to set the goal.

x. **Balanced life**: Your goal must meet the *work-life balance* so that when you take action on this, you must balance your various seven aspects called *"seven stars of life"* like 'Constellation of Milky Way' such as: *"family, finance, physical health, mental health, social responsibility, entertainment and spiritual needs."* If you don't balance these, then your life won't have any meaning and how much you earn, how many high positions you achieve, these become meaningless in your life while meeting goals.

Balancing of life along with meeting goals is a great art. History is full of stories where people earning billions of dollars had committed suicide, went bankrupt, lived like a beggar or were sent to jail. Life means goal and goal means life, so it has to be highly balanced. In the act of balancing of the above seven aspects, wisdom plays an important role.

"Balancing of life while executing goals is a great art of living. You are meeting goals not for living but how to live. Give yourself time to live, love and laugh(3Ls)"

xi. **Hard work needed**: If you are not committed to do hard work, you will hesitate to make the goal. As per human nature, everybody wants to lead a good life but very few want to do work hard. Even for goal-setting one has to work hard.

xii. **Prioritize your Goals**: If you have many goals at a time, prioritize them and work only on one at a time with full concentration. Don't open several windows.

xiii. **Meeting values**: Goal is the starting point of success. Your goal is your purpose of life. Your values are also your purpose of life. One shouldn't ignore values while setting and executing goals. Our goal should be very high. If you aim for gold, even you miss, at least you get silver.

"Discipline, character, honesty, compassion and courtesy are the main ingredients of human value systems." While framing and executing goals, take care of human values otherwise goals avoiding these human values will bring disaster to the society.

Suppose somebody goal is to earn millions of dollars by looting a bank or stealing, it is not a goal; that is why, it is suggested that your goal must be consistent with human values. Dale Carnegie opined, "Set goals that are clear, challenging, and obtainable."

Hey, men and women! Do your goal-setting in the light of above facts with an open mind, in judicious manner fulfilling all its requirements.

PLANNING PAVES THE ROUTE TO SUCCESS

> "Give me six hours to chop down a tree I will spend the first four in sharpening the axe."
> —*Abraham Lincoln*

> "If you fail to plan, you are planning to fail."
> —*Benjamin Franklin*

Planning! A road map. A sharpened axe. A route to success. Isn't it true? Can you think your goal will be achieved without planning? Not at all. Be a great planner to materialize your goal.

Planning is the backbone for the execution of work. Planning is needed at personal, society, village, town, organization, institution, state and country level. In one way or other, every country/organization is having planning department. If anybody fails in executing his goal, people first of all say that his/her planning was wrong.

"Planning is the roadmap on which your goal will move for getting physical reality."

Planning is a roadmap in which even minute details are documented from start to finish choosing the means to achieve the goal in a time bound period. Without a plan, one will not know how to organize self, people and resources effectively. Without a plan, one can't lead with confidence or expect others to follow them and you will feel bewildered. And without a plan, you have little chance of achieving your goals or knowing when and where they stray away from their paths. Controlling the situation in the absence of plan becomes an exercise in futility. Too often, faulty plans affect the future of the goal. Planning is crucial. You must have a good one. Remember:

"Practice brings perfection. Perfection brings proficiency. Proficiency brings excellence. Excellence brings success."

Planning for every goal is different. For athletes, players, service holders, students, musicians, artist, businessmen, organizations, countries, etc. goals will be different and so the planning. Moon mission, Mars mission, Tunnel beneath English Channel, Eiffel Tower, all Metros, Sea Link, etc., got completed due to great planning.

In Japan, for any execution of work, a thread wise planning with minute details is prepared. These are presented before the experts and all suggestions and shortcomings are incorporated. This process is continued four to five times and final planning is made. After that, the execution is started at a rapid pace. Work is completed in time with top quality. Napoleon Hill opined, "When defeat comes, accept it as a signal that your plans are not sound, rebuild those plans and set sail once more towards your coveted goal."

In general, planning is classified in two main categories, - strategic planning and operational planning. Strategic plans deal with relationships between people at an organization and people acting at other organizations. Operational plans deal with people within one organization. For even individual goal, this classification is valid with suitable changes in two words- people and organizations wherever applicable.

McKinsey& Co. follows the **7S-Model** for successful strategy implementation to achieve desired goal. They are: Structure, Strategy, Systems, Style, Staff, Skills, and Super ordinate goals. Each S will be exchanging information with each other and affecting goal. The same 7S-Model may be applicable to individual goal with suitable changes in functions. Delhi Metro led by E. Sreedharan is a living example of excellent goal-setting and planning. The completion of rail line in three years from Beijing(China) to Lhasa(Tibet) covering about 1100km in which about 500 km is icy/frosty mountain through which liquid nitrogen flows inside the track to maintain the track temperature (a unique and marvelous engineering feat) is an excellent example of grand goal-setting and planning. Planning ahead and hoping the plans work out perfectly is the key to achieving some semblance of work-life-balance." In some cases, micro-planning is needed to achieve the goal."

DIMENSIONS OF PLANNING

The following are the main dimensions of planning for a project/goal.
- Mission statement of goal.
- Date of initiation of work and completion at various stages.
- Space hired/procured as per need.
- Man power needed. Finance involved.
- Banks which may finance.
- Documents needed by banker and its procurement.
- List of materials (books, kits, other)/machines needed and their procurement with name of agencies.
- Arrivals of materials (books, kits, others)/machines ordered
- Training taken if needed.
- Daily involvement/practice per hour.
- Resource people and their contact numbers.
- Interaction with experts in concerned field.
- Drawing if needed completed.
- Preparation of project report with minute details.

Four steps of achievement of goal given by William A. Ward are to be kept in mind:
i. Plan purposefully;
ii. Prepare playfully
iii. Proceed positively;
iv. Pursue persistently

Earl Nightingale said, "All you need is the plan, the roadmap and the courage to press on your destination."

Do you prepare goal-setting and planning for getting success? If the answer is yes, move as per guidelines given above. If the answer is no, don't proceed till you prepare goal- setting and planning to meet your goal. Have confidence in you. God is with you. Go ahead and win.

STEPS TAKEN BY YOURSELF

After going through this chapter, I (as a reader) will do the following to do goal-setting and planning for my venture.

i. _____
ii. _____

***

Chapter 13

Take Decision and Action
#THE 12ᵀᴴ MANTRA

DECISION IS YOUR DESTINY MAKER

"Don't go where the path may lead, go where there is no path and leave a trail."
—*Ralph Waldo Emerson*

"In any moment of decision, the best thing you can do is the right thing, the next best thing is wrong thing, and the worst thing you can do is nothing."
—*Theodore Roosevelt*

A famous CEO-cum-speaker was asked by a businessman from the audience in a symposium to speak to us of decision and action. He replied in sequence: Decision! Decision! Decision! A fortune maker. A seed of your destiny. A starting point of your success. A win over fear. A bold step towards success in waiting. Are you plagued with indecision syndrome? If yes, come out from the world of indecision. Take decisions with full confidence and shape your future for greatness. Take risk and shape your destiny. Remember the adage: "No pain, no gain."

Are you ready to take decision for your goal? Desire alone will not bring success. After goal-setting, one has to take decision about goal and act. "Enormous power resides within you like in a tiny seed and your decisions are the means to unleash that power." If you want to turn your dream into reality, you must take a firm decision. If you are not happy with the present position, you can decide to change. Firm decision carries a great force which can change your course of action. If you can dream and decide something, you can do it. "Risk-taking capability is a must for everybody who wants success in life."

"Decisions are needed at every step by individuals for one's growth and prosperity; by groups for their benefits; by leaders at various levels for the growth and success of organizations or institutions where they work; by residents for the welfare of societies (villages, towns, cities) where they live; by citizens where they reside to choose the right leaders or politicians to govern the country for overall progress and prosperity; by executives of government for implementing policies for the benefits of people; by judiciary for delivering judgments while upholding the laws and giving proper justice to citizens; by politicians for governing the country in right and transparent way, meeting public aspirations and taking it to a great height, and so on. "The seed of success lies in the firm decision."

Don't drift like a piece of wood in a river on the direction of current at every moment. Set your goals and dreams right what you really want. Becoming clear about your desire, dream and goal of your life, you heighten your awareness around what's most important. The better the awareness better is the choice. "Clarity creates success." Ralph Waldo Emerson advocated, "Once you make a decision the universe conspires to make it happen."

> "Decision is your destiny. Don it or derail it. It is your choice."

Every person in the world is free to make decisions for his or her life and also for his/her nation directly or indirectly. David Russell once opined, "The hardest thing to learn in life is which bridge to cross and which to burn." The right decisions are taken based on knowledge and experience. Abraham Lincoln, Margret Thatcher, Mahatma Gandhi, Jawaharlal Nehru, Vallabhbhai Patel, Churchill, Indira Gandhi, Nelson Mandela, Rattan Tata, Bill Gates, Steve Jobs, Ambani and Edison were having decisive power and as a result they did commendable works and the world salutes them.

> "Decision is the doorway to your dream. Dare to take decision, walk through the door and fulfil dream."

"For any ruling political organization decisiveness, capacity to frame good policy and transparent systems, capacity to face adversities, the ability to repulse country's enemies, capacity to take right fast actions on all fronts should be effectively threaded into its top leaders and in the political strategy to fulfil the promised made to the citizens. Further, its enormous resonance and vibrant ecosystem should be found in the warp and hoop of the party identity to govern the country effectively free from corruption and in transparent manner with high growth raising the reputation of country and meeting the aspirations of citizens." "Failing in taking decision and action means to place a country or an organization or an institution or an individual at low level of growth or at negative growth." "Believe in your decisive and delivery power and miracle in the result will happen majestically."

THE IMPACT OF DECISION

The impact of decision is enormous. We can't move a single step without taking decision. Our survival, our progress and our well-beings are based on our decision making. The following **stories** reveal the impact of decision:

A Bold Decision Can Paves the Way to Bring Racial Equality: Long back in USA, there was a racial discrimination. In 1855, Rosa Parks, being a black refused to give up her seat on a crowded bus to a white man. Her that bold decision changed the mood of USA and after that a lot of events took place against racial inequality that led to the foundation towards racial equality.

The **theme** of this story is: "A bold right decision taken by even an ordinary person changes the course of history of a nation."

A Bold Decision out of Conviction Can Change the Course of History of a Nation: Abraham Lincoln took an unprecedented decision to issue his famous 'The Emancipation Proclamation' which gave freedom to the enslaved black people of America in spite of knowing fully well its consequences. His friends, supporters and the majority of whites were dead against this. This decision cost his life in the end. For such bold decision one needs great courage and deep conviction.

The **message** from this Lincoln story is: "A bold and highly right decision changing the course of history of a nation against great opposition and the fear of being killed can be only taken by a man of great courage and deep conviction in the right cause."

A Deep Conviction Can't be Beaten by Poison: Socrates took a courageous decision to drink the cup of poison, rather than compromising his personal belief-right to freedom of thought and of speech.

A Strong Political Decision Can Give Birth to a New Nation: Indira Gandhi, former Prime Minister of India was a highly decisive leader who took a strong decision to free East Pakistan (now Bangladesh) from the occupation of West Pakistan (now Pakistan) by sending strong Indian Armies in 1971. East Pakistan was freed and became an independent nation, Bangladesh. History was created when she made 93,000 soldiers of the Pakistani army surrender as war prisoners that she later freed. It was her strong political decision that gave birth of a new nation. She is known as Iron Lady of India.

A Strong Decision Can Make You a Billionaire: Bill Gates took a strong decision to start Microsoft Company by dropping himself from Harvard University when he was a second-year student of Mechanical Engineering. This decision brought about a revolution in the world of computers and he went on to become the richest person in the world.

Decisive Power Can Change Your Destiny: Steve Jobs decided to start Apple Computers Company after dropping himself from graduation course just after six months, and the rest is history. There was a revolution of laptops, tablets, pods, and smart phones. The world salutes a great innovator.

"Every right decision will make you a winner while every wrong decision may put you in a disadvantageous position. So, it is essential to take right decision at right time and for this you must have knowledge and experience." In life, from the morning till you go to bed, you have to take decisions. Remember: "It is your decision on your dream which will shape your destiny."

In life, once you make decisions, you are supposed to take responsibility for them otherwise the decisions have no meaning. Many people take wrong decisions without knowledge and without analyzing. When things go wrong they blame their fate. This is a wrong attitude. If things have gone wrong, use your wisdom and energy to correct it or to minimize its consequences or change the action steps.

One of the great hindrances that people face for making true decision is indecision. What causes indecision? Obviously, fear! The fear of making the wrong decision! The fear of the unknown result!The fear of what others will think of. The fear is the greatest devil. "It has been observed that indecision offers higher price to be paid than wrong decision." Why, is it so? This is because of the fact that something will happen with any decision as compared to no decision. So, conclusion is: Any decision is better than no decision. Be bold, have faith and take a decision.

There is No Age Limit for Success: One of the important revelations is that: "Age is not a prerequisite for success. It is the decision and action and persistence efforts on it yield success." The achievements of following persons give a testimony of taking decision at very young age and its fruitful result.

- Shirley Temple was six years old when she became a movie star on "Bright Eyes."
- Magnus Carlson became a Chess Grand Master at the age of thirteen years.
- Pele soccer superstar was seventeen years old when he won the world Cup in 1958 for Brazil.
- Elvis was a Superstar by the age of nineteen.
- Jesse Owens was twenty-two when he won four gold medals in Berlin Olympic, 1936.
- Isaac Newton at twenty-four wrote "Philosophiae Naturalis Principia Mathematica."
- Albert Einstein was twenty-six when he wrote the famous Theory of Relativity.
- Alexander the Great by age of nineteen had created one of the largest empires of the ancient world.
- Marie Curie at the age of thirty-five, got nominated for four Nobel prizes in Physics.

Consequences of Indecision and Wrong decision: The progress of an individual, a family, an organization and a nation depends too much on decision. "The indecision and wrong decision plague the progress of an individual, a family, an organization and a nation." You will find this truth at many occasions in all stakeholders. Many students spoiled their career or worked at low key positions due to the wrong decision of streams. Many educational institutions, industries and companies failed or remained at low level due to indecisions and wrong decisions on many issues such as: "the choice of products; the adaption of innovation; the payment and selection of competent employees; transparency, values, ethics; commitment; quality; the branding of organizations; the happiness of employees; etc."

Many nations remained poor or fell in the category of failed states due to many indecisions and wrong decisions on vital issues like: "mode of governance(democracy, communism, dictatorship, kingdom, etc.); quality of governance; transparent system; polices; processes; national values; ethics; care and well- being of people; education, learning, research, innovation (ELRI); taxation; opening of economy to the world; defense; health of people; constitution; constitutional great institutions; country economics;terrorism; justice system; quality of governing body (politicians or dictatorship or king); foreign policy; reformation of policies; etc." For example, USSR failed due to communism and got divided into many countries. North Korea is struggling due to dictatorship. Many African countries remained poor due to indecision on ELRI. India could be better placed if the government could have opened economy at least ten years before, i.e. around 1981 and more emphasis could have been given on quality ELRI. India has not taken any concrete decision to bring the talented people in specific areas which are available in MNCs at higher positions of government even for short period, say five years like developed countries to give a great push in policies, systems, reformations and development. It is a must for a talent- starved government. Incremental change is not going to serve much purpose. "Many countries promoted terrorism and now they are the main sufferers." Many countries remained indecisive on terrorism issue. Similarly, there are many issues on which countries either remained indecisive or took wrong decision and they had to bear the consequences. Sudan, Somalia Afghanistan, Syria, Pakistan are some of the examples.

Indecision Can Put You in a Great Loss: A woolen cloth manufacturer in a particular year manufactured just about 30% of woolen clothes as per capacity of the factory. He could not meet the demand of retailers. On questioning by retailers he replied that, "I thought this year, the cold would be less in this winter season so I could not take risk and played safe." What an indecision and wrong decision! What a great financial loss!

Indecision Brings Failures: A student did not appear in 10th class board examination. His neighbor asked, "Why didn't you appear in examination?" He replied, "I thought I would fail, so I did not appear." What an indecision and wrong decision!

> *"No initiation from your side to change your world*
> *for betterment is a highly disappointing inaction."*

The words of Theodore Roosevelt showcase this, "It is hard to fail, but it is worse never to have tried to succeed."

Decisive Power of China is Mind-blowing: In the nation building, no country can beat China after opening its economy in 1980. It is due to fast decisions by Chinese Government and Chinese people at all fronts of development, taking quick actions, yielding very high productivity, and reducing manufacturing cost by lowering input cost. In the last **thirty** years, Chinese Government removed the poverty of

600 million people. Their infrastructures are unparalleled. Out of top global **2000 companies**, US secures first position having **564** companies, second position is occupied by China having **225** companies while India houses only **54** companies in 2013 report by Forbes. Out of first top ten positions, both US and China house **five** companies each. The great strength of China is manufacturing and infrastructures through a large numbers of SEZ and these were made possible by fast decisions and fast actions. It can acquire million acres of land in a week and can vacate one million people in a month. China currently has the world's largest high-speed rail network for bullet train. Seven lines support 300 km/h speed stretch over about 3000kilometres. They took fast decision on using technology in agriculture sector and production is very high.

Just ponder over the recent decisive power of China. China has planned to build an ambitious **13,000 km rail line** to operate bullet trains to America through Russia passing through a tunnel under the Pacific Ocean to reach the continental US via Alaska and Canada. The proposed line beginning from China's north east could go through Russia's eastern Siberia, the Bering Strait, Alaska, Canada, and then reach the contiguous US. After completion of the proposed rail line bullet trains will run at 350 km per hour covering the distance in two days. China has already started discussion with Russia. (Help Source: Times of India, 10th May, 2014). Similarly, individuals, industrial houses, educational institutes and other nations can take fast decisions and actions to achieve goals.

So, the conclusion is that one has to take right decision, and has to avoid indecision. If any right decision of that time becomes wrong decision after implementation, it should be corrected as soon as possible or the bad effect may be minimized. But any wrong decision is better than indecision as something will happen and if correction is made, its bad effects may be minimized to very low level.

Remember: "Any individual or any organization or any country is capable of doing much better provided right decision is taken on any issue and honest and sincere efforts in all aspects are made to realize it under a time frame."

Are you ready to take decision and change your destiny by converting it into realities? Hey, men and women! Get up from slumber; take decision for your goal. God is ready to help you and see you very successful person.

ACTION BRINGS SUCCESS AND GREATNESS

"Doing is a quantum leap from imagining."

—*Barbara Sher*

"It is the action, not the fruit of the action that's important. You have to do the right thing. It may not be in your power, may not be in your time, that there'll be any fruit. But that doesn't mean you stop doing the right thing. You may never know what the results come from your action. But if you do nothing, there will be no result."

—*Mahatma Gandhi*

Action (Work or Duty)! Action! Action! A message of God. An act of every soul. A call of humanity. A *dharma*(duty) of everyone. A step in bringing success at doorstep. A step in self-making and nation building. Making a dent in the universe. Making a difference in the world. Is it true? Yes, it is. Take action for your dream to make a great positive difference in your life, in your success story, in your nation building.

God helps those who act. Have you ever noticed that why some persons are successful and others are unsuccessful? The answer lies in the fact that successful people act and unsuccessful people don't. "It is the action that makes the big difference between performers and non-performers." There are a lot of persons in the world who imagine, dream and desire but don't act. What is the use of such imagination, dream and desire? It is nothing but befooling and deceiving oneself. "Nothing happens by itself." Behind every success, there lies decision, action, persistent efforts, perspiration, failures, getting up again and again after every failure with renewed vigor. Even the mightiest tiger doesn't get food automatically, but it has to run fast miles after miles behind its prey to catch. It was the action of Mahatma Gandhi that gave freedom to India. It was the action of Rosa Park who refused to give her seat to a white man and that sparked a civil right movement in USA. "The purpose of human life is to give an impact for making the world a better place to live in." Are you going to make a dent today? What contribution are you going to make today by your action? "The seed of success germinates with actions and it is fully bloomed with persistent actions." Are you going to act on your decision to bloom your success?

> *"Imagination, dream, and desire have no value if these are not converted into reality through fast decision and action."*

THE IMPORTANCE OF ACTION

By seeing the birds flying, many people from all over the world might have envisioned flying before Wright brothers, but either they took no action or did little about it. It was Wrights Brothers who took decision and action to fly like birds. Even before Henry Ford, people thought of concept of car but they did little about it and Ford put his heart and soul to see cars for mass production. "Success belongs to doers, not to on-lookers." Many people might have imagined about operating system for computers before Bill Gates, but it is he who took action and worked on it by dropping out himself as a student of second year of Mechanical Engineering from Harvard University. Similarly, a large number of people on daily basis imagine many things, but only a few take decisions and actions to see the physical reality. What is the main difference between achievers and non-achievers? The answer lies in action. "Courageous people with strong desire and positive attitude take action; others simply talk in the air and become on-lookers." "No goal is achieved by itself. You have to exert with all your might to accomplish your cherishedgoals."

> *"Action activates your life for betterment."*

All students desire to pass with flying colors and to confirm a seat in competitive examination for a good job. But the world knows who does that. It is those who take action on their desires, work hard wholeheartedly and persistently with judicious planning, have great confidence and passion to achieve their goals. "The door of success is opened by persistent actions."

"The audacity of hope, decision and action places you in the world of success."

In recent years, the career in games and sports has become very attractive due to bright future in it. Many youngsters long for it. In many countries, there is a great craze for certain games and sports. To excel in games and sports, you have to practice very hard, and to remain very fit and cool without any involvement in social ills so that your focus does not get distracted. World knows that how many people do all these. Many new comers get lost in the way due to one reason or other. The main reason is not meeting the required actions. Kahlil Gibran elucidated about the **importance of work** in his book Prophet, and he said philosophically, "It is to weave the cloths with threads drawn from your heart, even as if your beloved were to wear that cloth." "It is to build a house with affection, even as if your beloved were to dwell in that house." I know one lawyer practicing in high court. He was very hesitant to speak before judges. His legs used to vibrate due to fear. But, as a result of sheer practice about ten times at home, and reading laws books extensively with love to his mission, now he is a great lawyer. What did bring a great change in him? It is nothing but the required actions with love. "Success embraces to the firm believer and strong performer."

'**Action**' is fueled by at least **Five Qualities** which may be coined by a word '**PEACE**' where each letter stands for something special: **P** stands for Passion; **E** stands for Enthusiasm;**A** stands for Attitude; C stands for Courage; and **E** stands for Eagerness. But, in India including other developing countries, '**Action**' is hampered by at least **Six Bad Qualities** among majority of people coined by a word '**DANGER**' where **D** stands for Delay; A stands for Absenteeism; N stands for Negativity; **G** stands for Greed; **E** stands for Ego; and **R** stands for Red- tapes. Rig Veda says, "Wealth has to be won by glory." So earn wealth through glorious actions.

In every field of economy, there is a too much scope of high growth through fast decisions and actions in every country. In developing and underdeveloped countries, enormous development is needed. GDP of India is nearly USD 2 trillion in 2015. Just to remove about 70% poverty from India, GDP should be nearly USD 08 trillion in the next two decades. India is capable of GDP growth nearly 10% as it has achieved in the past. India is better in IT export but it has touched just USD 86 billion in 2014 which is less than 8% of world market. As per Indian strength, the share could go to even 20% of the world market. See the possibility of decisions and actions in IT sector alone. In India, tourist arrivals stand to about 6.8 million in 2014, whereas only 'New York Central Park' attracts about 40 million tourists. "There is enormous scope of tourism in India due to its beautiful landscape and historical monuments and only fast decisions and actions are needed to meet a target of 50 million tourists in a transparent manner with high efficiency and effectiveness by providing excellent facilities and making the tourist places world-class."

"India has enough coal reserves but the assigned companies don't dig out enough coal, and government has to export coal." What a pity! "Similarly, infrastructure, design, manufacturing, education, research, innovation, innovative start-up, energy, minerals, agriculture, health, housing, trade, defense, etc. offer enormous scope of growth through fast decisions and actions for both-individuals and any government. "It is your fast decisions and actions with passion, patience, persistent, perspiration, honesty, sincerity, integrity, commitment, and dedication which will enable you to bell your dreams, hopes, and aspirations."

"The harsh truth in the world is that you can have all the imagination, dream, desire, skill and potential, but if you don't take action honestly and sincerely, nothing will happen and all your strength will go in vain." We know that fossil fuels (coal, oil and gas) have high calorific value. If we don't take any action to utilize the hidden chemical energy, it will be kept imbedded inside the earth. Suppose a lot of water in the form of fountain is falling from a great height, so the use of this potential energy gets reduced to zero except beauty if it is not utilized in power generation. Suppose you are a salesman and you have to promote a beautiful and useful product. If you can't promote it well, people wouldn't know about it. "Action on your cherished dream with deep love is your dharma. Perform it! Perform it! Perform it!"

i. **The Importance of Consciousness on Actions**: It is the quality of our consciousness that decides our actions. Rig Veda says: "Knowledge is structured in consciousness (Richo Akshare Parame Vyoman)." Maharishi Mahesh Yogi said, "The quality of experience depends upon the state of one's consciousness." "A cheerful mind brings cheers in our every action. A miserable mind brings gloomy picture and there is no desire for any action." Second and Third Laws of Thermodynamics are also applicable to human lives. As per Second Law of Thermodynamics, if temperature increases in fixed heat energy, chaos or randomness increases (less entropy). Here, temperature is analogous to agitation or activities in mind. If agitation in mind increases, we do wrong decisions and wrong actions. If temperature decreases, chaos or randomness decreases (more entropy), so mind behaves in normal and cool manner, and consequently, our actions too. As per Third Law of Thermodynamics, if temperature decreases substantially low (much more entropy), orderliness increases much more similar to perfect crystals. Similarly, if human mind is more ordered, more settled and fresh, we feel highly positive, more perceptive, and more effective in action, and we don't do any wrong things.

"So, actions must be performed with a balanced mind to achieve success"

ii. The Importance **of Actions on Unchartered Path**: Many a times, it so happens that you are required to take action on unchartered path even if the end result is not clearly visible. "Any action requires faith in the doers." This happens especially when you decide to go on an unchartered path. Fun, excitement and challenges are involved in unchartered path.

Take the example of project landing on the Moon, mission on the Mars, Space-walk and experiments in space by NASA, USA; and Chandrayan (Moon Spacecraft) Project of ISRO of India which changed the scenarios of the world. India is proud of sending its spacecraft (Mangalyaan) on Mars under a program called **MOM**(Mars Orbiter Mission) and it has been placed on the Mars orbit on the morning of 24th September 2014 in the first attempt, the first country in the world who could do it with very less expenditure, just about USD 75 million and on the first attempt. Every Indian could be seen saluting the amazing achievement that India had just achieved. On this occasion, Prime Minister of India, Shri Narendra Modi was present at ISRO and said, "Today Mangal (Mars) has got MOM."Indian scientist made India proud. A basket of congratulations was given to them from all over the world. These are all the result of imagination, decision, goal-setting, planning and action. The scientists and engineers engaged in these projects deserve a great applaud and kudos and should be given more name and fame than the famous politicians. Robin Sharma said, "Do good and leave behind a virtue that the storm of time can never destroy."

"Going on unchartered path brings many excitements, new knowledge and products." While doing research on "Landing on the Moon" about 200 totally new products for the use of mankind were developed. This is the advantage of action on the unchartered path.

Napoleon Hill once said, "You must be willing to pay the price of success and that usually can be translated into terms such as: Sweat and strain, tears and toil, hope and hurts, brains and brawn." Sometimes, you may visualize that goals are difficult to be achieved. Under this circumstance, it is better to follow Confucius who opined once, "When it is obvious that the goals cannot be reached don't adjust the goals; adjust the action steps." Some people hesitate to take action. In such situation, it is advisable to follow the sermon given by Theodore Roosevelt which states, "Get action. Seize the moment. Man has never intended to become an oyster."

"Take action, accomplish your goal, contribute immensely and leave a legacy to shine forever."

Jackson Brown Jr. once said, "Twenty years from now you will be more disappointed by the things that you didn't do than by the ones you did. So throw off the bowlines. Sail away from the safe harbor. Catch the trade winds in your sails. Explore, dream and discover."

iii. **Wealth Creation and our Survival through Actions**: "Wealth is created only through actions. Even our survival and existence is on actions." We have to take actions in every field of our activities for survival. Can you survive without taking food and drinking water? You have to take the food from the plate and put it in your mouth and chew it. Oprah Winfrey advocated, "The ability to triumph begins with you, always." "Major wealth is created through business and entrepreneurship." People of those countries with quality ELRI and who imagined, dreamed and desired for getting involved in business and entrepreneurship and did appropriate goal -setting and planning and took decision and action with all other required mantras, finally reached at the top. Government and people of USA, UK, Germany, Japan, and France are the examples of such story. The Fourth President of USA once said, "The main business of American is business."

Recently, the mind-blowing rise of China is due to unshakable decision and action in the field of manufacturing, business, infrastructure, entrepreneurship, education, games, sports and others. The global dominance of the Chinese across the spectrum of manufactured products- from PCs to ships in 2011is given below, percentage signifies out of total produced in world (Source: Times of India, Bloomberg)

Personal computers : 320.4 million (90.6%)

Energy-saving lamps : 320.4 million (80%)

Air-conditioners : 109 million (80%)

Solar cells : 21.8 Gigawatts (74%)

Mobile phones : 1.1 billion (70.6%)

Ship building : 76.6 million mt. (45.1%)

Jack Ma, a school teacher of English Language, took decision and action for opening e-commerce company Alibaba which has become a very big company in 15 years. In 2014, Alibaba has provided 25 million jobs, there are 8 million merchants in the Alibaba ecosystem, and each has minimum three to four employees. The size of demand Alibaba has created in 2014 is about USD 500 billion and it is growing at 40%. See the result of decision and action.

"India was behind China (about 2 to 3 percentage point less) in growth in GDP for about 9 years during 2002 to 2011(between 6.7% to 9.3%); but during 2011-2013, it lagged behind due to indecision, wrong decision, lack of proper execution, lack of one party rule, corruption, and internal wrangling. The condition of farmers in India is deplorable due to the absence of proper policy decision for farmers. Suicides have become common among farmers. "For any country, per capita income of bottom of the pyramid (about bottom 70%) matters more and better decisions and actions are needed for inclusive growth as one in out of hundred million populations may be rich anywhere in the world."

The regular wage and salaried employment in India in which casual labors are not counted in salaried class in Word Bank Report (% of total) is abysmally low (15% during 1990-2000 and 17% during 2001- 2010) compared to other large economies USA(92% and 93%), UK (87% and 87%), Japan (81% to 85%), Germany(89% and 88%), Brazil (62% to 64%), Russian Federation (93% to 92%) (Source: Word Bank Report, 2014). This means in other large economies, casual labor percentage is very low (USA7%) while in India, it is very high (83%). What does it mean? It means salaried class job creation has to be increased by improving every sector of economies in a big way. For this, strong decisions and actions are required by all concerned, to increase the creation of salaried class jobs. Similarly, other countries have to think in this direction.

In the last 50 years, worldwide many people took decision to become entrepreneurs for innovative and other products and acted on these and they are now millionaires and billionaires and GDP of concerned countries got increased tremendously. Such examples are founders and co-founders of: Microsoft, Oracle, Apple, Google, Facebook, Accenture, SAP, TCS, Infosys, Softbank, Samsung, Sony, Siemens, GE, Boeing, Reliance Industries, Foxconn, Petro China, Alibaba, Airbus, IBM, HCL, Capgemini, Exxon Mobil, Berkshire and innumerable other people who started young and thought different, with a "never give up" approach.

iv. **Result of Actions in Politics**: In 2014 Parliamentary election of India, BJP led by Narendra Modi (three times chief minister of Gujarat and PM candidate) said some beautiful lines as slogans during his campaign, "Good Governance and Good Development" and another, "Better Days are about to Come". He acted and worked very hard addressing more than 450 rallies and through his excellent oratory power, he convinced the audience in these slogans to happen in reality, and the unique and extensive advertisement in medias (print, electronic and social) and other political moves changed the scenario in an unprecedented way that BJP secured 282 seats alone and NDA 336 out of 543 seats defeating all main rivals badly and was elected as the Prime Minister of India. Similarly in USA 2008 Presidential Elections, Barack Obama used the slogan, **"Yes, WE Can"** and through his oratory power and extensive advertisement through electronic and print media, he convinced Americans and became the President of America not only once but twice.

The **message** is: "The power of convincing people conquers the world of success."

v. **Importance of Actions in Religious Books**: In famous religious act of prayers namely Navratri of Hinduism and Ramadan of Islam, there is an instruction that even during fasting, you have to do your normal work otherwise God will not shower His blessings on you. See the importance of action.

In Shrimad Bhagavad Gita, the value of Karma (duty) is given much more importance than any other approach.

"You have only a right to perform your prescribed duty (action), but you don't have any right to expect fruit out of your action. Don't become the cause of the fruit out of your action and you shouldn't have any attachment for not even performing any action."

—*Shrimad Bhagavad Gita, 2.47*

Kahlil Gibran in his book "The Prophet" has given highly thoughtful words of wisdom about action on work with love: "Work is love made possible. And you cannot work with love but only with distaste, it is better that you should leave your work and sit at the gate of the temple and takes alms of those who work with joy."

In getting work done and delivery of output, it is essential that: "government should be less and governance should be more." This policy has yielded better result all over the world as fewer laws permit more works. This is well elucidated by the words of Colleen C. Barrett, who once opined, "When it comes to getting done, we need fewer architects and more bricklayers." Verify this philosophy in the development of any organization and state and see the truth behind it. There is a famous saying in Sanskrit about action (Karma/duty): (Yogh Karmasu Koshalam) i.e.; Expert workmanship is meditation or yoga. In action (duty), expertise is meditation (yoga). Expert workmanship can only be given by that person who knows the difference between right and wrong work, good quality work and bad quality work and working hard under state of balanced wisdom. Therefore, there is no place of wrong work in expert workmanship. Is it possible to have a choice that can create maximum happiness both for you and for those around you? Yes, it is. Such choice is the spontaneous right action that nourishes you and all those persons who are influenced by that action.

THREE LAWS OF PROGRESS

For the progress of an individual, a family, an organization and a nation, there are **Three Laws of Progress**. They are:-

- Law of good policy.
- Law of timely decision.
- Law of proper and timely execution.

Take the example of a successful person, a rich family, a branded organization and a developed nation. You will find that they followed these three laws of progress in true spirit. "If anyone or any organization, or any nation is failing or remaining at low level, means it is plagued by policy paralysis, indecision, wrong decision and wrong execution." I have observed many people, many organizations and many nations which are failing or remaining at low level of growth due to their failure in following these three laws of progress in true spirit. China, Singapore, South Korea, Japan have been following the three law of progress since more than last thirty years and as a result GDP and per capita of income rose very high. India has followed these laws during 2000 to 2010 and as a result growth was very high, 7.5% to 9.5%. India growth got reduced during 2011 to 2014 due to not following the three laws of progress. USA, UK, Japan, Germany have been following these three laws since more than fifty years. Many MNCs and industries such as Google, Microsoft, Facebook, TCS, Reliance, Alibaba, Foxconn, Apple, Bharti Telecom, Amazon, etc., have been following the three laws of progress in an emphatic manner. Many individuals, who followed these three laws, achieved great success.

"Your growth increases in proportion to your right decisions and right actions.

"Decisions and actions under capitalism can create highly unbalancing phenomena. The world's three richest persons own personal wealth greater than the GDP of thirty-four poor nations. So, suggestion comes to have Conscious Capitalism." Decision and action are required for conscious capitalism.

Hey, the best creature of God! Are you imagining something? Do you visualize your imagination taking shape? Are you ready to decide and act on what you have imagined and desired to give a concrete physical shape? If not yet, then think about it. "Are you doing justice with yourself? God has sent you to perform and contribute in the world for the benefit of humanity and you are cozy in your approach. You need to work on it."

> *"Action, action, and more action should be essence of your life. No pause, no stop and no looking back."*

STEPS TAKEN BY YOURSELF

Based on your imagination, dream, desire, planning and goal – setting, give a time frame within which you take firm decision to act on your dreams and list those action steps here.

i. _____

ii. _____

***

Chapter 14

Practice Values and Spirituality
#THE 13TH MANTRA

BE A PERSON OF VALUES TO SUCCEED

"If we are to go forward, we must go back and rediscover those precious values- that all reality hinges on moral foundations and that all reality has spiritual control."

—*Martin Luther King, Jr.*

"When I would like to do is to leave behind a sustainable entity of a set of companies that operate in an exemplary manner in terms of ethics, values and continue what our ancestors left behind."

—*Ratan Tata*

A great sage-cum-speaker was asked by a student from the audience in a congregation to speak to us of values and spirituality. He replied: Values! An act of divinity. A desire of every soul. A greatest tool for survival of humanity. A great quality of leadership. Is it true? Yes, it is. Be a person of values in every sphere of your life and consequently achieve glory and respect.

"Practicing values and spirituality is not only a quality of effective leadership but of all human beings. It adds beauty, flavor and humanity not only in leadership style but also in human living style and completes the real meaning of civilization. The secret of life is in practicing values which energizes us to spread the fragrance of humanity by doing righteous deeds and helping others."

WHAT ARE VALUES?

"Values may be defined as appropriate courses of actions conducted by people or the outcomes received by them. Values reflect a person's sense of right and wrong regarding the best policies, practices, and actions." Honesty, integrity, justice and excellence deserve admiration and these are the representative of values. People should be treated with respect and dignity is another example of the representation of values. Values not only tend to influence attitude and behavior but also act as an ambassador of a society or a nation. "Practicing values is the real humanity, real spirituality and real worship."

Norman Thomas said, "The secret of a good life is to have the right loyalties and hold them in the right scale of values." Authentic values in life are those through which we can live happily and can produce great deeds and thoughts for the humanity.

"We all have divine and devil in us. The divine in us makes us pursue goodness and values while devil guides us to pursue demoniac path- self-destructive ways." It is easy and pleasant to opt for demoniac path. Though, divine path is unpleasant and difficult in the beginning, but later on, it gives the real enjoyment, happiness, peace, success, greatness and glory. "Values are the virtues of divinity. Adapt these in your life." The basic difference between divine and demoniac is the knowledge. The divine is guided by higher knowledge and spirituality while the demoniac is influenced by greed, lust and ego. Barack Obama said, "The peace we seek begins in human hearts.

"Core values like character, honesty, integrity, justice, courtesy, respect, love, compassion and accountability are the foundation of success."

Values may be of two types –personal and cultural.

Personal Values: It pertains to what is good, beneficial, important, useful, desirable and beautiful for a person. Personal values are formed in childhood during three periods namely:

- Imprint period:- from birth to seven years
- Modelling period: from seven to thirteen years
- Socialization period: from thirteen to twenty-one years

Parents should be highly careful during formulation of values so that their children acquire good values in life. "Values engrained in subconscious mind during formulation period last for lifelong."

Cultural Values: Individual cultures develop their own values which their members practice in general. It is possible to identify the values of a society by noting which people receive honor or respect. In USA, the best athlete and players are respected more than a best professor or best doctor or best politician or best scientist. In India, politicians and Babas(Godly men) are worshiped more than others.

Value System: It is a coherent set of values, morals and ethics, adopted or evolved by a person, organization, society or nation as a standard to guide its behavior based on those beliefs to be performed in all situations. Value system might vary from culture to culture and by religion with emphasis on certain behaviors to guide morality. It is worth to note that in US, the national value system relates to the core beliefs of freedom and liberty.

Elements of Values: There is a long list of elements of values. It is up to the individuals, organizations or nations to choose own sets of values. The elements of values include: "Honesty, integrity, justice, fairness, excellence, compassion, character, kindness, gratitude, empathy, freedom, liberty, commitment, achievement, courtesy, friendship, knowledge, power, skill, appearance, cleanliness, generosity, justice, love, religion, wealth, creativity, philanthropy, family, patriotism, respect, wisdom, help, education, fun, health, money, beauty, identity, money, etc." "Out of this long list of elements of values, some **Core Values** are **Universal** such as: character, honesty, integrity, justice, gratitude, fairness, tolerance, respect, love, excellence, humility, compassion, freedom and friendliness." "Money is very valuable, but it can't buy most precious things in life. People with strong character, strong integrity, right honesty, right values, and right justice are not for sale and that is why some top constitutional institutions in the world are surviving."

THE IMPORTANCE OF VALUES

Do you know the importance of values? "The importance of values can be realized when people are subjected to pain, harm, loss, chaos, inharmonious environment, lawlessness, slavery, theft, disrespect, injustice, etc. as a result of the failure of values." "Values flow from top to bottom." It will be unfair to expect the adherence of values from an empty stomach. Many failed countries, failed organizations and failed families are examples of this. Newspapers are full of news every day about the bad relations among fathers, mothers, husbands, wives, sisters, brothers, neighbors leading to physical and mental torture, murders and even sexual harassment in the most pious relations. Tolerance has got a beating and on minor issue, people are killing other people. Fairness is withering away. Sexual harassment of girls and women including murder has become common. God knows where humanity is going in 21st century. "When values die, demoniac acts start."

What happened to Satyam Computers and its founders: everybody knows! What happened to Enron and its CEO: We know that too. Nobody can estimate the level of consequences of failure of values. Everybody knows the fate of dacoits, looters, rapists and murderers in the long run. "Power of Shame may be used to have some degree of values- fairness, honesty and integrity in the society." Stephen Covey opined, "Personal leadership is the process of keeping your vision and values before you and aliening your life to be congruent with them."

i. **Better Values Practiced by Individuals:** Importance of values can be realized from the good deeds of men of values. With the birth of child, everybody rejoice in happiness while the child in the cradle cries. However, by the death of a person, the story is the other way round. The dying person rejoices thinking that he led a successful life, contributed something to the world and made the world slightly better place compared to the time when he inherited it. The world cries on the death of person who practiced moral values, contributed immensely through right means and made the world a better place to live in. What scenario the world might have witnessed when Mahatma Gandhi, Jawaharlal Nehru, Abraham Lincoln, Winston Churchill, Eisenhower, Swami Vivekananda, Tagore, JamshedTata, Dr. Rajendra Prasad, Dr. Vishweshwaraya, Dr. Ambedkar, Dr. Kalam and Nelson Mandela left the beautiful earth, woven from their arms and harnessed by their work. Similar story is witnessed at society, city and village level when a good person dies. But when wrong persons such as thieves, dacoits, looters, murderers, terrorists, and scammers die, people rejoice due to getting rid of them.

Lord Rama, Lord Krishna, Prophet Mohammad, Guru Nanak, Jesus Christ, Gautama Buddha, Mahavira are known as persons of great values. Some are revered as Lord (God), some are as Prophet and some are as Guru as per religion. In every profession, there are many people who are the men of values and society respects them. Barack Obama said, "We are the strongest when we see the inherent dignity in everybody."

ii. **Better Values Practiced by Great Leaders**: Many leaders leading their organizations or institutions or countries have practiced values systems and as a result, the organizations or countries grew at a faster rate with a brand name in products, policies and practices which resulted in prosperity. Everybody wants to work with those organizations and to live in those countries.

TATA Son's group of industries led by Jamshed Tata in the past and Ratan Tata followed a set of values since its inception and as a result companies in every respect have brand name. Infosys led by Narayana Murthy banks on values. GE, Microsoft, and Apples follow strictly their core values and everybody wants to work with these companies. Abraham Lincoln, Winston Churchill, Mahatma Gandhi, Nelson Mandela practiced values system and their glory will shine forever. USA reached on the top of world and everybody wants to live there. Why? With other things, leaders of USA followed strictly some values of nation like freedom, justice, liberty, excellence, transparency in a judicious manner. It doesn't mean that USA has no pit falls. "All nationals should try to follow values to make their respective countries a better place to live in, to grow, to prosper, and to feel happy." "Adherence of values is valuable for your life. Adhere it! Adhere it! Adhere it!"

iii. **Belief and Behavior**: S. Radhakrishnan said, "Belief and behavior go together." If we believe in murder, race, and hate, the world will be in turmoil as our actions will be on that line which is happening today in many parts of the world by different groups. But, if we believe in universal values, obviously peace, harmony, brotherhood and understanding will grow in the world. "Be a great practitioner of values and heaven will be on the earth."

iv. **An Unparalleled Response in Gratitude for an Act of Compassion**: Dominique Harrison- Bentzen, a student of fashion (Britain) raised on- line £45,000 for a poor homeless person Robbie of Preston (England) on 4th December, 2014 for his house for the act of compassion shown to her by offering her the only money £3 to go home when she lost her bank card and with no money in the pocket. What a great compassion and gesture! What a high degree of gratitude! What cooperation! There are many stories of compassion and cooperation exhibited by people all over the world. We should salute people like these. They deserve our utmost respect and gratitude for being better than the rest.

The **theme** of the story is: "Values are valuable virtues of the humankind for the survival of humanity. Compassion and gesture exhibited on someone gets rewarded in gratitude, sometimes greatly by the receiver."

Do you feel attracted to follow your good values and make the world a better place to live in?

JUDGING VALUE SYSTEMS

Every society has made some value systems including core and universal values. Parents and seniors advise youngsters to follow these values to become a better person. If top position holders of every segment of society fail to observe value systems, then chaos prevails and downfall of the society starts. It is easy to judge whether values are followed or not. However, the following tips are provided to judge this.

i. **Seven Deadly Sins by Mahatma Gandhi**: Mahatma Gandhi has advocated **seven deadly sins** for the mankind not **to observe**. They are:

> *"Wealth without work*
> *Pleasure without conscience*
> *Knowledge without character*
> *Science without humanity*
> *Commerce without morality*
> *Religion without sacrifice*
> *Politics without principles"*

Each of these seven statements represents a deadly lack of values. Match each of these in real life of the people and you will find the consequences. The bombing at Hiroshima reflects science without humanity. Many CEOs of the companies or officers in government involved in fraud reflect "Knowledge without character" and "commerce without morality." In many countries, some politicians change their own party even after remaining in the parent party for more than fifteen years and criticizing vehemently the opposite party on all fronts in which they join. This is one of the examples of "Politics without Principles."

ii. **Parent Test**: When you are doing something either at home or at work or elsewhere, either alone or with some and if the values of your involvement are in question, then ask yourself: "If my parents were to see me doing this, would they feel proud of me and say "good boy" or say "die in a cup of water out of shame." " If you pass in **Parent test**, you are on the right path. But, if you fail, you lack in values and need improvement. For example, the news of sexual harassment of a girl by a young boy may be devastating for his parents.

iii. **Children Test**: When you are doing something either at home or at work or elsewhere, either alone or with some and if the values of your involvement are in question, then ask yourself: "If my children were to see me doing this, would they feel proud of me and hug me or would they hang their head in shame?" If you pass in **children Test,** you follow values. But, if you fail, you lack in values miserably and need to be corrected. For example, the sexual harassment of a woman by a male parent may be devastating for his children.

iv. **Society or Office Views**: The society in which you live and interact or the office where you work and interact, their views about your values matter a lot. Do they rate you a better person of values or do they consider you a rotten element of the society? Ask your close friends about the view of others about yourself. If it is good, you follow right path, otherwise you lack in values and need an improvement.

v. **Call outyour Inner-Self**: When you are in peace, ask your inner- self about your values. The answer of soul will always be correct. Every thief, every cheater and every conman knows what they are. "It is their high degree of self-interest and greed that do not allow them to become a good person." Inner- self always tells you to practice values. Are you listening to your inner-self? "Values are your virtues. Value them otherwise you will be devalued."

MORE LEARNING ABOUT VALUES

The following parameters may give more learning about values.

i. **Conditioning Effect**: Once you get involved in any wrong doing by breaking values, and if you get substantial benefits, you will repeat it and then it will become your habit and you may give a lot of justification to prove your wrong doing as right ones.

ii. **Declining Standard of Values**: It is currently under news that standard of values among people is on decline. Though, in the 'Facebook' and 'twitter' age, younger generation has shown some positive signal about values at many occasions, but these are not enough. More change is the need of hour. It is the value based seniors who have to show the right path to youngsters by acts and deeds and not by the mere advices. Shiv Khera opined, "Values and virtues are not hereditary; they are learned."

iii. **Means are not in Question**: The earning of money is very important as without this nothing moves but money is not each and everything. Many people earned a lot of money without bothering the right means. In the beginning, they might enjoy it, but later on they will be very sad and poor due to their inner feelings and problems from children, society and government.

Martin Luther King Jr. opined, "Our lives begin to end the day we become silent about things that matter."

The Supreme Court of India said (Source: Times of India, 4th Sept., 2013), "Those with ill-gotten wealth become powerful through "politics or religion" by grabbing land and then end up committing heinous crimes." The person who has earned money through hard work is the only person who can tell you the value of money. Total illicit trade value every year from almost every country is very high and unimaginable. Even after so many cheeks this is happening. It is estimated that a large sum of black money deposited by different nations in safe banks of the world ranges from 10% to 40% of GDP of respective countries. There is a too much political discussion in India on bringing back the black money. Nobody knows, in real sense, the amount of black money but in political discussion, the amount is huge (10% to 30 % of GDP).

iv. **Effort by Transparency International:** In order to promote values system and happiness in every country, Transparency International has selected six key factors to decide the happiness quotients of a nation. They include:

(i) GDP per capita; (ii) Healthy life expectancy; (iii) Someone to count on; (iv) Perceived freedom to make life choices; (v) Freedom from corruption;(vi) Generosity

India is at **111th** position in happiness quotient while Denmark topped the list out of 156 countries in 2012. Happiness is one of the important values of life. "Happiness makes people live longer and free from stress. It makes them more productive, boosts their income, and turns them into a better citizen." Whether you are an ordinary citizen or a leader of any level, this Happiness Quotient matters a lot. Think of improving it through the right means.

India ranks **94th** in transparency International **Corruption Index** 2012 which ranks 177 nations (Times of India, 22nd Dec, 2013).

v. **Extreme Greed Leads to Tragedy-Midas Touch:** The story to King Midas known as **Midas touch**is famous and told to children by mothers and teachers and found in children books. King Midas was a great greedy person having a lot of gold. His greed for gold went on increasing with the possession of more and more gold. One day, a stranger appeared before the king and said he could grant any wish to him. The king Midas, greedy of gold said to him, "I wish that whatever I touch should turn to gold". The stranger replied, "You will have the **GoldenTouch** starting from tomorrow morning with the first rays of the sun." The king was highly excited in the morning and touched his bed which immediately turned into gold. He got more excited and he touched a book, his breakfast, his glass of water, his lunch, hugged daughter and all turned into gold.

He was hungry and highly disappointed to see his daughter turning into gold. He started crying and begging to God to return his daughter and to take back his granted wish. The stranger appeared again and said, "It looks to me that you have become wiser than before and understood the bad effect of extreme greed." The stranger took back the granted wish and king Midas got his daughter back and other things in normal position. "Greed is a great hell and kills your life at large."

vi. **Life Saviors:** Tragedies and wars happen all over the world. Many good persons of values save the lives of many people who are either drowning, trapped under rubble in earthquake, trapped in train or bus after accidents, trapped in fire and so on. In some cases, the saviors have lost their own lives. The importance of the person who saved the other man is much more important than the person who brought him to this planet."

vii. **Efforts by Media**: Media freedom and their true reporting is one of the indexes to judge the value system followed in a country. As per the Annual Index of Media Freedom, 2014, Global press freedom has fallen to lowest level in over a decade, with India ranking 78[th](a fall by thirty-nine points in the run-up of 2014 election). In this release, China scored 84, Pakistan scored 82 and Sri Lanka 76 out of 197 countries. Media freedom depends upon government as well as media owners. (Help Source: Times of India dated 3rd May 2014).

viii. **Immortal Deeds**:

a. **Alfred Nobel** invented Dynamite and earned a lot of money. His invention was meant for the use in the development works. The invention proved to be a danger for the humanity if not used with caution and by a balanced mind. When he was alive, obituary news appeared saying, "Merchant of death Dynamite King died". He was shocked and from that day he started working for peace and useful research in chemistry, physics, medicines, economics and peace and gave his all earnings to start Nobel Prizes award for those who contributed in these areas through research in a better way. He is remembered by his Nobel Prizes which are awarded every year.

b. **Bill Gates,** Microsoft founder started Gates-Malinda Foundation by donating his 50% earning in philanthropic work to improve medical facilities in the world. Warren Buffett donated a high percentage of his wealth in Gates- Malinda Foundation.

c. **Ford** has started Ford Foundation to help poor and needy.

d. **Other Philanthropic Foundations**: All over the world there are large member of foundations of small, medium and big sizes to help poor and needy persons in different fields. However, much more philanthropic foundations are needed. Kahlil Gibran in his book The Prophet said about giving, "And there are those who have little and give to all. Those are the believers in life and the bounty of life, and their coffer is never empty. There are those who give with joy, and that joy is their reward."

e. **Good Deeds of Top Officials, Politicians (Rulers) and Persons in other Professions.** People appreciate those officials and politicians (rulers) who work according to values and ethics and improve the lives of citizens through good deeds. The contributions of top officials and politicians matter a lot in the improvement of conditions for the people in all respects. Such politicians consider politics as service to people and not a means to earn money. But politicians and officers with values are very less in number. "They should be sensitive to the problems of people otherwise poverty and miseries will never vanish from developing and underdeveloped countries."

f. **Exemplary Values and Ethics Exhibited by Rare Individuals:**Lawrence Lemieux was taking part in Olympic Yacht Race and was a strong probable winner. During race, he stopped his race to help a fellow competitor who was in trouble. The whole world got stunned to see this. His main priority was safety of fellow competitor and not the gold medal. Though, he didn't win the race but he won more without winning. He was honored by heads of states from all over the world. This is one of the exemplary examples of values and ethics.

VALUES IN POLITICS- A PATH FOR NATION BUILDING:

Politics is much more important than anything else as politicians frame the laws, policies and processes for the governance of a country and officials working under them execute these. "A good politics builds a nation while a bad politics destroys a nation."

Taking cues from what is happening in the world, there are **two definitions of politics**:

"Politics is the art of possibility to provide prosperity, peace and pride to people."

"Politics is the art of possibility to provide prosperity, peace and pride to politicians and befooling and plundering people."

The first one is based on values, ethics and principles while the second one is based on self-interest and greed. A country will be more prosperous in which the maximum number of politicians (ruling class) will be of first category, and will be more poorer if the maximum number of politicians will be of second category.

It is a choice for nation building or nation destruction by political class.

It is to be noted that execution under values and ethics is very difficult, but not impossible. In every country, some politicians or rulers are working on the first definition and present generation is striving hard to force politicians to act on the first definition. Many companies of the world are working on values and ethics and that companies are on the top. The other type of observation about politics is given by Ernest Benn, who said, "Politics is the art of looking for trouble, diagnosing it incorrectly and applying the wrong remedy." The other view of politics is given by John Kenneth Galbraith, who said, "Politics is the art of choosing between the disastrous and the unpalatable."

TWO WORKING THOUGHT MODELS

There are followers of two **Thought Models** in the world in daily life:

Thought Model of 4Ts: Tyag (Sacrifice), Tapsaya (Dedication, Penance), Tejaswa (Intelligence) and Tanmayata (Sincerity)

Thought Model of 4Cs: Chori(Stealing, Scam), Chalaki (Cunningness), Chugali (Criticism behind back), and Chaplusi (Sycophancy, Buttering)

The first thought model is derived from the abstract of religions and values while the second thought model is derived from selfishness and greed. You will find the followers of 4Cs much more in the world than the followers of 4Ts. J. Krishnamurthi said, "The ways of cunning are always complex and destructive." "An individual, a family, a society, an organization and a nation are laid on the path of progress, peace and pride by the followers of 4Ts while the followers of 4Cs downgrade everyone including himself and the nation in the long run or short span." However, the immediate benefits come from 4Cs but they have their own severe consequences and some people indulged in 4Cs are facing severely.

Are you a follower of 4Ts or 4Cs? Judge yourself. It is your choice and will decide the type of person you will become when you grow up.

The cumulative illicit financial outflows between 2002 and 2011 of top countries with highest measured is alarming (Source: Times of India, 22nd Dec., 2013, Global Financial Integrity). The amount varies from about USD 80 billion to USD 1000 billion. Every country has various strong multiple agencies to check these illicit outflows, but the bad news is, even then it is happening. The citizens of concerned countries could have been better in facilities and prosperity if tax on outflow amount could have been paid to respective government

MESSAGES ON VALUES FROM RELIGIONS AND RELIGIOUS BOOKS

"Every human being sees the world through a frame of reference-**myth** which is mainly fate, free will and the concept of God. Religions were started from the concept of God." All religions give great messages of values in life in different ways while dealing with the message of God. Dr. Sarvpalli Radhakrishnan said about religions, "Religions are rivers flowing through the zigzag ways to meet the same ocean."

Ponder over the following expressions on values, God and religions:

"Values may be viewed as the message of God to be performed by every human being."

"God may be modelled as the Supreme, Infinite, or Omnipotent Energy which is present in every particle of universe called God Particle."

"The belief in God arises from the incomprehensible mystery and manifestations of the infinite universe and the search of great savior from all sorts of fear; and different religions model God in their own ways meaning and meeting the same Truth."

"Religions are like branches of a tree emanating from the same Root and the same Trunk."

All epics of different religions be it: Hinduism, Christianity, Buddhism, Islam, Sikhism, Jainism have dealt with values in big ways in different manner but they ultimately teach you the same thing. One needs to go through them as per choice. "Misuse of religions for personal gains kills their very purpose: serving the humanity."

Oh, Men and women! Practice values in your life for peace, happiness, leading a good life and achieving success in your venture.

SPIRITUALITY IS HUMANITY

"You are the most spiritual things you can do to embrace your humanity. Connect with those around you today. Say, "I love you," "I am sorry," "I appreciate you," "I am proud of you," — Whatever you are feeling. Send random tests, write a cute note, embrace your truth and share it ….. Cause a smile today for someone else … and give plenty of hugs."

—*Steve Maraboli*

"Grace is in garments, in movements, in manners; beauty in the nude, and in forms. This is true of bodies; but when we speak of feelings, beauty is in their spirituality, and grace in their moderation."

—*Joseph Joubert*

Spirituality! A pious word. A peace provider. A values keeper. A humanity saver. A religious oriented mind. A feeling of divinity. Are you a spiritual person? If not, be a person to follow spirituality in real spirit to remain happy, to calm yourself to succeed in life.

The term "Spirituality" is referred to the matters of religion based on the concept of directives given by the Almighty God who is our greatest well- wisher, savior. With the deep belief in God, one may choose a right path in the journey in life. "Every religion gives the concept of God in its own way and sometimes, on the matter of religion, a great difference of opinion starts which may lead to a great loss of lives and properties." The universe has been created by Only One God whether by Big Bang or by Nature or Energy or something else, nobody knows. "Nature can make something from nothing." Rig Veda in Sanskrit says, "Ekam Sat Vipra BahudhaVadanti." It means: "Truth (God) is one, though the sages (religions/gurus) know it as many." Then, why do people fight in the name of religions? Swami Parthasarthy has opined, "Religion has been reduced to mere parroting of ideas picked up from preachers. Neither the preacher nor the pupil has gone through any research of truths of life. You must start thinking, questioning and reasoning with the truths of life." "Values and humanity are vanishing from religions as many groups are using religions for their interest and killing thousands and thousands of innocents and tormenting other weaker sections of the society, while religions are for the survival of humanity through peace, values and prosperity. "It looks like the great danger of humanity may be from religions which are just a belief, a concept of existence of God, way of life and are meant for serving humanity. "It is not an act of humanity to clash and kill others in the name of the same God who is our savior based on different beliefs."

"The real religion is humanity which helps us in finding the best way possible to live and let live."

But, at present, contemporary spirituality or post-traditional spirituality or new age spirituality is more in discussion. "Those who believe in new age spirituality define themselves as spiritual but not religious." They believe in the existence of different spiritual paths, emphasizing more individual spirituality. Swami Kriyananda says, "The real work on spiritual path is to prepare the mind for the ultimate transformation. To realize our oneness with the Infinite, we must surrender the ego itself."

"**Modern spirituality** centers on the deepest values and meanings for which people aspire to live in a blissful manner. It envisions the inner path, ultimate reality and the essence of ones being. Spiritual experience plays a central role in modern spirituality. It includes connection with larger reality; practicing values; comprehensive understanding of self; joining and sharing the feelings with other individual or the human community; living with nature, cosmos, divine realm and enjoying their beauty, splendor and fragrance." Many people follow the modern spirituality.

"Religion of spirituality is humanity; and religions of humanity are values."

Peter Russell said, "The essence of spirituality is the search to know our real self, to discover the true nature of consciousness." "Once we awaken to the true nature of self, many fears that plague our lives vanish. It helps us to become less self-centered, less needy of others for personal advantage, less concerned for recognition and less focused on collecting poison, and fewer egoists. As a result, we become happier, healthier and more loving people; and don't become a cause of suffering to others." "Spirituality, religion, and happiness are beneficial for health. In the domain of spirituality, success is measured by how efficiently, how effortlessly, we co-create, keep harmony with nature and know our true self." Deepak Chopra says, "The first spiritual law of success is pure potentiality-pure consciousness, a field of all possibilities and infinite creativity." Swami Vivekananda said, "Manifest the divinity within you, and everything will be harmoniously arranged around it."

"Acts like compassion, humility, empathy, selflessness, altruism, integrity, faith, hope, the experience of inner peace and forgiveness are the hall mark of spirituality." "In nutshell, spirituality teaches us how to become a good person in every sphere of life." "The rituals followed in religious acts are not spirituality." Praying to the Almighty God for goodness and wellness for all human beings is spirituality but not of the highest order as it involves desire." African value system says, "I am because you are, you are because we are." One can imagine the importance of African value system for the survival of humanity.

"One of the best forms of spirituality could be: Give yourself time to live, laugh, love and leave a legacy of spirituality and greatness (5Ls). Do good, be good and do the right thing. Show empathy, compassion, forgiveness, ethics, and values in the every walk of your life. Be courteous, honest and a good human being."

Do you practice values and spirituality? Have you ever realized the effect of any act of values and spirituality in your life? Do you know the effect of values and spirituality on success? If your answers are not positive, it means you lack in practicing values and ethics. Tighten your boots and get set for working towards spirituality.

Do the following to improve your values and spirituality:

i. **Start with small acts**: Choose your sets of certain values which you can start with in all your acts. Receive people with warm heart. Always use good and fit words as per occasion. In all your dealings, however small may be, do show honesty. Help others in need. Whatever promised to anybody, meet your promise even at your loss. Forgive those who harm you and don't use any harsh words for them.

ii. **Enrich your knowledge**: Read religious books and enrich your knowledge by teachings of religions concerning values and modern age spirituality. Have faith in it. God will show you path to lead a happy and prosperous life.

iii. **Consult mentors**: Consult genuine mentors who will show you the path of values and spirituality. Don't believe in rituals but believe in actual requirements of humanity.

STEPS TAKEN BY YOURSELF

After going through the 13th Mantra, I will do the following to improve my values and spirituality:

i. _____

ii. _____

***

Chapter 15

Develop Leadership Qualities
THE 14TH MANTRA

LEADERSHIP LEADS YOU TO GREATNESS

"If your actions inspire others to dream more, learn more, do more and become more, you are a leader."

—*John Quincy Adams*

"A leader is one who knows the way, goes the way, and shows the way."

—*John C. Maxwell*

WHAT IS LEADERSHIP?

A great CEO-cum-speaker was asked by a student from the audience in an international conference to speak to us of leadership. He replied: Leadership! Leadership! Leadership! A very charming, charismatic, exciting and challenging position. A store of responsibility, capability and wisdom. A gatekeeper of values. A hope of betterment and prosperity. A game changer. A bright hope for masses. A craze of every soul. A philosophy. Do you possess leadership qualities? If not, develop great leadership qualities for your success, organizational success, nation building.

You might have heard people saying: "What leadership qualities of the Prime Minister or the Chief Minister or the CEO or the Director who changed the scenario!" The word, leader or leadership is so common, thrilling and charming in general talk that everybody understands this in his or her own way and craves to become a leader. But understanding of leadership among people is very vague. It is imperative to define it precisely; however, you may have some idea from the famous quotes given above:

"Leadership is defined as the process of guiding and directing the behavior of people in the work environment."

—*Nelson and Quick, 2009*

"Leader is regarded as a weaver whose main task is to weave together different kinds of people into the fabric of society."

—*Plato*

Are you imagining, dreaming and desiring for your success? If yes, then what lies between you and your cherished dream? It is your leadership qualities and their proper execution. Dr. John C. Maxwell said, "Everything rises and falls on leadership." This is highly true, be a person, a family, an organization, a state or a nation. "Developing positive personality is a major step to develop leadership qualities." "Good leaders are made and not born. It is your desire, willpower and self-realization which can help you to become an effective leader. Good leaders develop a never ending process of self-study, education, training and experience." "Leadership is influence, attitude, and responsibility." Peter Drucker said, "Leadership is defined by results, not attributes."

"A great leader is one who inspires, communicates, leads, weaves and empowers people of a group, or an organization, or a nation to achieve a set of great goals, great vision."

Leadership is needed in every sphere of life. A father or mother is a leader in a house. A person leading a small team in any work environment is a leader. A village head is a leader. A captain of a team of players is a leader. Every politician is a leader. President, prime minister, chief minister, and ministers are leaders. Chairman, president, CEO and heads of different sections of organizations or companies are leaders. Vice-chancellors, directors, principals, deans and heads are leaders. Officers of government departments at various levels are leaders. Every leader has different roles and functions but the main purpose remains the same- leading the team (small or big) to meet the cherished goals. Ronald Reagan opined, "The greatest leader is not necessarily the one who does the greatest thing. He is the one that gets the people to do the greatest things." "The economic progress of any nation mainly depends upon the aspirations, capability, and values based leadership of its corporate, industry, academic, research, government and political sectors." Eric Hoffer opined, "The leader has to be practical and a realist yet must talk the language of the visionary and the idealist." Follow the advice given by Hoffer. "Leadership is your USP. Develop it! Develop it! Develop it!"

LEADERSHIP THEORIES

Basically, there are only two main theories of leadership.

i. **Trait Theory of Leadership:** In this, some leadership qualities such as intelligence, extraversion, fluency in communication and other traits reside in people and through these, they lead the followers. This relates to theory for born leader, and now, it is old.

ii. **Process Theory of Leadership:** In this, leaders are made through grooming process based on interaction through mentors and also through followers. In the beginning, this was called behavior theory, then situational theory came up and at present spiritual leadership theory, effective leadership theory and inspirational leadership theory are in current use. "The world needs more inspirational leaders to infuse inspirations in the work force."

TYPES OF LEADERS

There are four types of leaders which may be shown in the form of managerial grid on a scale of 1 to 9. They are:

i. **Authoritarian**: Strong on tasks, weak on people skills (9, 1)
ii. **Country club**: Weak on tasks, strong on people skills (1, 9)
iii. **Impoverished**: Weak on tasks, weak on people skills (Delegate and disappear) (1, 1)
iv. **Team** Leader: Strong on tasks, strong on people skills (9, 9)
v. Obviously, a group, an organization, a country requires more team leaders with inspirational, effective and spiritual leadership qualities.

THE THIRTY-ONE QUALITIES OF LEADERSHIP DEVELOPMENT

Following are the thirty-one qualities of leadership which are supposed to be developed and practiced by a person who dreams and desires for success in his life either as a leader from any position or as a worker in any profession. They are as follows:

1. Character (Refer Chapter 7)

> *"When wealth is lost, nothing is lost;*
> *When health is lost, something is lost;*
> *When character is lost, all is lost."*
>
> —*Billy Graham*

"Character categorizes your worth and it is the foundation over which all your qualities of leadership will be built upon and your success will depend." Good character is the core and building block of excellence, winning and success. It is one of the first and foremost qualities needed for leadership development. Albert Einstein said, "Weakness of attitude becomes weakness of character." "Character is the core of your worth, leadership, honor, and success. Build it! Build it! Build it!"(See chapter 7.)

2. Positive Attitude (Refer Chapter 4)

Positive attitude is one of the founding pillars of leadership development. In a broad perspective, it is the power of mind to see anything positive or negative. "Believe in the power of positive attitude and miracle will happen in your success, greatness and life."(Refer Chapter 4)

3. Responsibility

> *"The price of greatness is responsibility."*
>
> —*Winston Churchill*

Acceptance of responsibility is a sign of positive attitude. It is a stepping stone in the process of leadership development. Making excuses is a victim mentality while embracing responsibility is a sign of rising star. Whether you want to be a winner or loser, it totally depends upon your choice of acceptance of responsibility. If you accept responsibility from the core of your heart and work hard persistently to complete the job, then you are a winner and nation builder. "Leadership begins with the heart, not the head."

"Acceptance of responsibility raises the level of leadership and creates an intense hunger for the fulfilment of cherished dreams."

A good leader or even a promising ordinary person in any position embraces responsibility of house and work place alike without transferring it to spouse, children, parents, boss or co-workers. He faces happily whatever life offers, works hard to overcome obstacles and shows the world the adage: "Wherever there is a will, there is a way" is always true. Whether you want to lead a small or a big team, you have to give the best results. "Accountability is closely related with responsibility. If you accept responsibility, you have to be accountable." A leader has to take responsibility on transformational goals and a sincere commitment is to be made to achieve them. Mitt Romney said, "Leadership is about taking responsibility, not making excuses." "Most companies and institutions are uninspiring. Even in advance economies, about 33% employees are emotionally engaged, while the figure for East Asia is only about 6%. A 142-country Gallup study on State of the Global Workplace says that only 13 percent of employees worldwide are engaged emotionally at work, 63% employees are not engaged and lack motivation, and 24% are actively disengaged indicating unhappiness and negative attitude. This is very dismissal scenario and good leadership qualities are required to revitalize 87% of employees at the world level. It is the responsibility of leader to inspire employees by encouraging and empowering them to take the organization or nation at a great height." "Leadership is more concerned with disposition than with position." The greatest day in our life will be when we take total responsibility for our attitude towards people. "Responsibility is your reward in advance of successful leadership. Grab it! Grab it! Grab it!"

If you wish to be a leader, you have to work every day without escaping your responsibility, without postponing today's work for tomorrow and you have to give results. A famous line by Abraham Lincolnen capsulates this perfectly, "You cannot escape the responsibility of tomorrow by evading it today."

Simply telling your philosophy for achieving goals is not going to work. One has to embrace responsibility and accountability in the line of your philosophy. Your objective should be to cultivate responsible behavior. The words of Eleanor Roosevelt elucidate this beautifully, "One's philosophy is not best expressed in words; it is expressed in the choices one makes --- and the choices we make are ultimately our responsibility."

"The poor existing conditions at work place, at home, in nation or in personal life can't change to better unless and until we take the responsibility to make these better." Denis Waitley opined, "There are two primary choices in life: to accept the conditions as they exist or accept the responsibility for changing them." "By leadership one should mean complete responsibility for an organization's well-being and growth, and changing it for the better. "Real leadership is not about prestige, power or status. It is about responsibility and making the difference in existing system for betterment."

As a leader of your family, you have certain responsibility towards your children which they will carry forward with them for their future. A beautiful line from Denis Waitley encapsulates this very nicely, "The great gifts you can give to your children are the roots of responsibility and the wings of independence." Liberty is a word by which one gets attracted to have a thinking of free from any work, any responsibility. But, it is just the opposite. Liberty demands high degree of responsibility and many wise people know this. George Bernard Shaw said, "Liberty means responsibility. That is why most men dread it."

"Responsibility is the mother of success and you have to own it if you want to move to the higher ladder of success." The words of Michael Koda elucidate this nicely, "Success on any major scale requires you to accept responsibility – in the final analysis, the one quality that all successful people have is the ability to take on responsibility."

Adopting social responsibility is the need of the hour. As per our ancient Indian wisdom, our first responsibility should go to the community, the second should go to our family and third to ourselves. But, if the order is reversed, society will start degenerating like hell. "It has been observed that the societies are not destroyed so much by the wrong activities of mischievous and bad people but by the inactivity of the good and noble people to check them." A line by Edmund Burke expresses this beautifully, "For evil to flourish, good people have to do nothing and evil shall flourish". Further, Helen Keller opined, "Until the great mass of the people shall be filled with the sense of responsibilities for each other's welfare, social justice can never be attained."

"Attributes without actions behaving like thundering clouds without rains, don't make a leader but responsibility, actions and results do."

"It is your responsibility, real actions and excellent results which will raise your reputation."

Are you a responsible person? If the answer is no or partial, then you need to improve on responsibility.

For enhancing responsibility, adopt the following methods:

i. **Grab responsibility:** Wherever you get a chance, grab responsibility happily and work hard on it to complete it.

ii. **Make persistent efforts:** Sometimes, it happens that your responsibility is not being converted into realities due to many reasons. Don't get disheartened. Hang on there, do persistent efforts, use your experience and complete the job.

iii. **Be creative:** After missing deadline to complete a job or losing a deal or starting off the work at right time, you have to be creative in your approach and in your planning.

iv. **Find reasons of non-completion:** The reasons of non-completion of work may be many such as slackness on your and co-workers' part, incompetent team, wrong planning, old tools and many more. Keep in mind that in future, such mistakes do not happen.

v. **Empower yourself with better tools:** If everything from your side such as your high standard, your quality consciousness and positive attitude are good and still you miss deadline, then equip yourself with fresh knowledge and better tools.

vi. **Accept your shortcomings:** If the deadline is missed out due to your shortcomings, find it, accept it and improve your skills in every aspect so that next time you don't commit such mistake.

4. Charisma

"Attractiveness and magnetism of your personality is the result of your inner radiance."

—*Yajur Veda*

"Charisma is synonymous to the quality of a strong magnet." It is the ability to draw and attract people to you. Charisma is one of the indispensable quality of leadership. Many people think charisma is mystical and by birth. But this concept is wrong. Like other traits, this may also be groomed and developed. Obviously, some people get this quality by birth. All over the world many political and other leaders have got quality of charisma by birth but many honed this and became comparable or even better than those who inherited by birth.

"Leadership is the management of **5Ps-people, product, policy, process and profit.**" If people are well managed by your charisma, then they will take care of product policy, process and profit. This is true for any leader- be of companies, organizations, educational institutions, states or nations in their own senses. For example, with reference to nations, product includes all types of products produced in the country including services provided, and profit refers to GDP, per capita income, employment, prosperity and well-beings of people. For educational institutions, product refers to students, and profit refers to knowledge, skills and values gained by students so that they will better placed, lead a decent life and contribute better in the nation building following ethics and values. "Charismatic personality is the soul of leadership and core of success." Napoleon Hill advocated, "Developing pleasing personality is one of the most important rungs on the ladder to success."

Are you a charismatic person? If the answer is no, you need to develop it.

Do the following to develop and improve your charisma:

i. **Expecting best from people**: For developing charisma, put a "10" point on every person's head meaning thereby that everybody is capable to deliver the best performance. You expect best from them and in this pursuit; you love them, appreciate them, guide them and help them. As a result, they will love you and start attracting towards you. This is the first step of developing charisma and improves there on. Further, note that if you start kicking people, then they will also kick you with the same force as Newton's Third Law of Motion is valid everywhere. Jack Welch advocated, "The most important job you have is growing your people, giving them a chance to reach their dreams."

ii. **Testing your quality of charisma**: Watch people closely. Are people naturally attracted to you? If not, you may be having one or more roadblocks to charisma such as pride, insecurity, moodiness, ego, perfectionism, hate, cynicism, rudeness, impatience, and greed. Find the real roadblocks.

iii. **Improve on roadblocks to charisma**: After finding roadblocks to charisma, improve on your areas of weakness. Try to be a very good human being. It is the first step to overcome your roadblocks.

iv. **Focus on people instead on yourself**: During conversation with others, instead of focusing on yourself, focus your conversation on people concerning their welfare in every respect. Solve their problems. Everybody wants a good life.

v. **Give first good impression**: Whenever meet any person first time, try your best to give a good impression of yourself by all possible ways. Treat him as "10", remember his name and call him by his first name; focus on his or her hobbies, interest and intelligence and utilize their experience.

vi. **Help people to grow**: Share your resources with people to grow personally and professionally. Concentrate on (say) 05% people every year (the number will vary as per entity) to add value to them so that they grow exponentially. By this way, in a short period, your organization will be equipped with competent people. On national level, this concept may be applied on large numbers of people every year for making country prosperous. I am a great believer in helping people to grow. This is one of the great social services including nation building and you will draw happiness. "Practice the philosophy of- "helping people to grow" in your life and miracle will happen in prosperity of your organization and the world."

vii. **Make contact with large number of people**: Prepare a list of people whom you have met with their names, contact numbers, birth date, marriage anniversary date, interest, hobbies, expertise, etc. and send messages on important occasions.

5. Commitment (Refer Chapter 7)

Commitment is the core quality of an effective leader. You have to fulfil whatever promised at home, work place and society and never break your word.(Refer Chapter 7)

6. Courage (Refer Chapter 7)

Courage is one of the indispensable qualities of leadership. It is the courage that wins over the mighty and gigantic adversities and challenges in life. (Refer Chapter 7)

7. Conviction (See chapter 7)

Conviction is a strong quality needed for leadership development. It helps you to achieve your rights and your dreams, how difficult, how painful they are. "Conviction is enhanced by clarity of purpose and loving what one does." (Refer Chapter 7)

8. Concentration (Refer Chapter 7)

Concentration or focus on a task is the desired quality of leadership development. (Refer Chapter 7)

9. Communication

> *"Developing excellent communication skills is absolutely essential to effective leadership. The leader must be able to share knowledge and ideas to transmit a sense of urgency and enthusiasm to others. If a leader can't get a message across clearly and motivate others to act on it, then having a message doesn't even matter."*
>
> —*Gilbert Amelio*

Effective communication is the bedrock to successful leadership. Our quality of life is determined by the way we communicate with other people and with ourselves. "Communication is the bread and butter for any person who wish to excel in life. In any professional front, you will find that it is the best communicator or orator who succeeds in occupying the top positions in any organization. In politics, effective communicators occupy the top slots." "It is your oratory power which will enable you to achieve the top position." For political leaders, oratory power is the jewel in the crown. "The art of great communication is the language of leadership." All great leaders of world (past and present) have been great communicators. Barack Obama and Narendra Modi are great orators. Sometimes good communicators use such words that change your world altogether. A line from Zig Ziglar encapsulates this eloquently, "You never know when a moment and a few sincere words can have an impact in life."

"Communication skill, a jewel in the crown is the most essential and key to effective leadership for clear, impressive and effective transmission of message among people enabling personal as well as organizational success."

Have you ever analyzed the reasons of social reforms which took place in the past? It is due to effective communication. The words of Clay Shirky elucidate this beautifully, "When we change the way we communicate, we change society."

Developing communication skill is essential for every person to excel in life. Good communication skill will not only enable you to find a good job in a good organization but it helps in promotion too. Jim Rohn suggested, "Take advantage of every opportunity to practice your communication skills so that when important occasions arise, you will have the gift, the style, the sharpness, the clarity and the emotions to affect other people." Tom Peters opined, "Communication is everyone's panacea for everything."

Communication is the best way to create strong relations with others. It is worth to note that the success of your marriage, job and personal relationships depends greatly on your ability to communicate. Rollo May once said, "Communication leads to community, which is to understanding intimacy and mutual valuing."

"Success of a leader depends upon his/her true followers." True followers need clarity in communication by leader. People will not follow you if they don't know what you want, where you are going or what the message is. They follow a master and not someone who doesn't know what he is doing but someone who is in complete vision of his work. George Bernard Shaw said, "The single biggest problem in communication is the illusion that it has taken place." For an effective communicator, it is necessary that message should be simple and meaningful and focus should be given on the people with whom you are in communication. "It is to be noted that goal of all communication is effective action." If the communication is not precise, the actions by followers may be zero, partial or unsatisfactory. James Cash Penny opined, "The art of effective listening is essential to clear communication and clear communication is necessary to management success."

"A bunch of informational talks dumped on people is not communication. While communicating with people, it is necessary that you must give them **four jewels**-something to **feel**, something to **remember,** something to **think** and something to **act.** In the absence of any jewel, your communication will not be worthwhile effective." Dale Carnegie said, "Communication is built on trusting relationships." In a world religion congress meet at Chicago (USA), when Swami Vivekananda opened address with the words- "Brothers and Sisters of America," there was a great applause for about five minutes in the hall as nobody opened the address any time in the past with such highly intimated words. This address of Swami Vivekananda enhanced the image of India greatly.

Every leader needs Conversational Intelligence(C-IQ), a frame work for knowing the impact of conversations. Some conversations may trigger our lower level brain activity such as primitive instincts for fight, flight, freeze, appeasement; and other may sparks higher level brain activity, such as trust, integrity, strategic thinking, empathy and capability to process complex situation. If our brain is more connected to social connection, we will be more connected with people.

"Communication is the cure of all problems."

"Communication failure or vague communication poses a lot of confusion and creates a lot of rumor affecting the success of a leader and his organization." A line from C. Northcote Parkinson elucidates this beautifully, "The void created by the failure to communicate is soon filled with poison, drivel, and misrepresentation." Follow the following steps for learning to communicate well.

- Make communication a top priority on any issue.
- Be open by heart to other people.
- Create a receptive atmosphere for communication with others.

"If you feel from the core of heart that your vision is great, highly meaningful and fortune maker and yet people do not accept it, that shows that your communication skill are not effective at all." You need to improve it. Communication skill plays an important role in getting the fulfilment of your vision, getting a good job or promotion. "It is your communication skill that will inspire the people. So, imbibe inspirational leadership quality."

Do the following to improve your communication skill:

i. **Bring simplicity and clarity**: Collect letters, memos and directives, you have recently written and ponder over these. Are your sentences short and direct or are they vague and confusing? Are they having difficult sentences and with unusual words which are difficult to understand without the use of dictionary? "Note that simplicity; clarity and use of proper words in communication (either written or verbal) are assets, needs and jewels."

Recall your recent address given to followers. Were your sentences short with proper words? Was your message clear and distinct? Recall the faces of audience. Were they murmuring? Were their faces red? Develop the technique to write small sentences with most appropriate words in order to improve your potential in writing. Spend some time on writing on some selected topics.

ii. **Pay attention**: Pay attention when you communicate (either written or verbal). Your communication should address the people, not yourself; and material should be in simple sentence with precise message. Your message must address their needs, their desires, their troubles, their questions and motivational words to take the organization to a great height fulfilling vision. Meet people at their local work stations to know all these things for better communications.

iii. **Take feedback**: Consult trustworthy people to know the fate of your communication whether they are living with that or communication was vague and meaningless. Accept their views and rework for the future by equipping yourself in a better way.

iv. **Select suitable sub-headings**: Don't communicate (written or verbal) without some preparation. Whatever you want to communicate, first select suitable sub-headings, arrange this in sequence and write accordingly using proper words and short sentences. Judge its impact on the audience. If not, then revise it, practice the final write-up and then communicate. After some preparation and practice, your communication will be effective.

v. **Read books, newspapers and listen TV Conversation**: To develop communication skill, read a large number of fictions, autobiographies, motivational books and newspapers. Practice daily to write something to convey the message in more effective ways.

Whatever suggested above for improving communication skill is also true and applicable to students in their own references. "Students should start improving their communication skill from 7th class itself as they are the future leaders in making."

10. Competence of Self and People

"A competent leader can get efficient service from poor troops, while on the contrary an incapable leader can demoralize the best of troops."

—*John J. Pershing*

Acquiring self-competence and developing competence of people (employees) is one of the important qualities of a leader. In every work environment, you always need competent persons which are very less in number. As a result, we all praise highly competent persons –be craftsmen, technicians, engineers, doctors, professors, scientists, players, athletes, singers, artists, officers, business leaders, political leaders, etc. It doesn't mean that you need to be only like Pele, Bill Gates, Einstein, Ford, Tata, Lincoln, Messi or Ronaldo. Ron Suskind once said, "Competence is the immaterial residue of material actions. Confidence is the public face of competence." In order to acquire competency in your chosen field of interest, you must: "have high intention, make sincere effort, do persistent practice, keep improving, use your intelligence for excellence, inspire others, and do more than expected." The world is crazy for competent people. "Competent leaders including people at other positions are in short supply. Develop and grab the golden opportunity. Organizations and industries are searching for competent leaders." People are searching to find competent technicians to get work done with quality. People are searching for good teachers, good pleaders, good doctors and someone trustworthy to work with. Once you delegate any work to a competent person you have the confidence that the work will be completed nicely in record time. "Competency is the core of leadership quality. Acquire it through knowledge, skills and practice." Mark Twain opined, "Obscurity and competence: That is the life that is worth living."

For improving your competence, it is necessary that you apply SWOT (strength, weakness, opportunity, threat) analysis on yourself. Identify your strength and strengthen it further. Identify your weakness, overcome it and turn it into your strength. Identify opportunity and grab it. Identify threat and overcome it. SWOT analysisis a very good tool in personality and leadership development.

"Competence is your crown which is acquired with positive attitude, sincere effort, persistent practice and intelligent direction."

"Any organization, any institution or any nation, cannot progress unless and until they have a large number of competent, intelligent, imaginative and innovative people working for it." About 64% wealth of a country lies in human capital which is nothing but talent of people and talents are groomed through effective and quality education, learning, research and innovation (ELRI). If people are not talented, earning will be less and country will be poor.

"It is the people with the qualities of **5 Is-imagination, intelligence, innovation, initiative and integrity** that change the landscape of a family, an organization, a city, a state and a country towards success and glory." There are many examples all over the world to support this. For example, USA, its many cities, institutions, and companies; UK, its many cities, institutions and companies; Germany, its many cities, institutions, and companies; Japan, its many cities, institutions, companies; fall under the umbrella of **5Is**.

The principles which lie in developing competence of people are: giving value to people, commitment to people, integrity with people, setting standard for people, and influence over people. A leader is supposed to know some simple facts: everyone wants to feel worthwhile; everyone responds to encouragement; most people do not know how to be successful, and most people are intrinsically motivated. With these facts in the mind, the competence of people can be developed.

Speaking on the topic "Leadership in turbulent times" at Great Lake Institute of Management, Ram Charan, a management guru said, "China would emerge as the place where a lot of different industries would be anchored from." When one person from the audience asked," How long he expects China's influence to last? He replied, "You can have a lousy leader and everything will change." On future trends, he said, "Four trends (DISA) - digitization, Internet, sensors and algorithms- are going to change every function across every industry."

Have you ever thought about your attitude towards the way you do your work? Are you doing your work with great zeal, passion, fervor and love? Is your accomplished work of the high order and of excellence within the time frame? Are you aiming all the time to achieve excellence and quality irrespective of size of work? If not, then you are not working to achieve competence. You have to change yourself. You have to be constantly watchful on your way of working, attitude and intention. "Involvement with the core of heart is real learning which gives competence over a span of time. You have to be mindful about acquiring competence." Do you feel that you are competent enough in your chosen field of interest? If not, improve it.

Do the following to improve your competence:

i. **Reengage yourself wholeheartedly**: Detachment from your work is not the solution. If you have got detached from your work either emotionally or mentally, it is worth and necessary to reengage yourself with the core of your heart. Find the cause of your detachment and solve it. Plan judiciously to reengage in your work with full vigor, spirit and love. Practice hard and gain competence. Remember: "The involvement in the chosen pursuits with passion, zeal and love is real learning." Twelve hours of working per day wholeheartedly in any field over a long period with an intention to get competence is sufficient to gain it in that field.

ii. **Find the reasons of low standard**: Do you cut corners? Are you lazy? Is your current profession not interesting and challenging? Why don't you put heart and soul in work? If it is one of them or more, solve this through auto- suggestions.

iii. **Raise your benchmark**: Benchmark or standard is an index and mind game to judge the quality of output. If the standard of your output is ordinary or below normal, then it has to be raised slowly in two to three steps to achieve highest point "10". You have to resolve to yourself that: "I can, I will score like the best gymnast and get 10 out of 10 points."

iv. **Search five ways to improve**: As per shortcomings in achieving competence, search five ways and work hard on these religiously to improve your competence. There is no free lunch in this world. Believe in yourself: 'You can.'

11. Passion (Refer Chapter 8)

Passion is a vibrant energy. It is the core of glorious achievement. It is the passion which makes you a competent leader and professional. Passion puts fire in the belly to achieve unparalleled height in leadership irrespective of field of interest.(Refer Chapter 8)

"The road to success is difficult to navigate, but with sheer passion and hard work, any dream is achievable."

12. Self-discipline (Refer Chapter 1, 3 & 5)

Self-discipline is the core and key to leadership. It is a success ladder through which one reaches to the top of leadership. "Talent without discipline is like a well without water." "Discipline is the demand and decoration of life and its absence is the basis of differentiation between winners and losers. "Jim Collins opined," A culture of discipline is not a principle of business; it is a principle of greatness." (See chapters 1, 3 and 5.)

13. Relationship and Social Capital

"If civilization is to survive, we must cultivate the science of human relationships- the ability of all peoples, of all kinds to live together, in the same world at peace."

—*Franklin D. Roosevelt*

Developing good relationship and working with people amicably is an indispensable quality of an effective leadership. It is one of the aspects of people skills. "The human nature is such that if you love, respect and work with people; they will also reciprocate with more zeal and fervor." Without people skills, one can't be an effective leader. "In relationship, love, respect, and faith to each other are the keys but in its backbone honesty, integrity and sacrifice play main roles. Poor relationship skills will result in poor leadership qualities."

"Social capital is a great asset. For ascending to higher ladder of success, social contacts help immensely. Joining clubs and going to functions help in building social capital. Enhance your social capital for better relationship with a large number of people. Always treat people with respect. Be candid and speak truthfully. Note that we are happiest persons when we feel connected well with others as a part of community, friends, and well-wishers."

"Relationship ringing religiously and strongly in symbiosis rhythm with people is needed not only for leadership but more for human beings."

Even in personal life, relationship with spouse, children, parents, neighbors, friends matter much; otherwise your life will be sad, tasteless and lonely. The words of David Rockefeller elucidate this eloquently, "I am convinced that material things can contribute a lot to making one's life pleasant but, basically, if you do not have very good friends and relatives who matter to you, life will be really empty and sad and material things cease to be important." Anthony J. Angelo said, "Treasure your relationships, not your possessions."

Do you have good relationships with family, children, brothers, sisters, friends and persons (juniors, seniors) at your work place? If not, then improve it.

Do the following to improve your relationships:

i. **Go to basics**: If you lack in relationships, go to the basics of it. Read relevant books to know the importance of relationships and parameters that are required. Observe those people closely who are good in relationships. Attend some workshops on it and work accordingly. "Sacrifice, integrity, honesty, love, faith and respect are the basic fundamentals of human relationship." Develop these basic fundamentals.

ii. **Identify your shortcomings**: There must be some solid reason for your poor relationship skills. List all of them. Relationship demands time, attitude, inner feelings, love and respect. Do you lack in them? Improve on your shortcomings on daily basis.

iii. **Change your feelings**: Change your feelings towards adding values to your friends and relatives. Prepare a list and start doing some helps to them and then extend this at your work place with workers. Forget habit of hate and adopt forgiveness in your life for positive feelings for others.

iv. **Repair faded relationship**: Plan to repair the faded relationships with others and plan it for long-term. Instead of treating the world as deceit, treat it as the world of decent. This is also a way to mold the deceit people towards decent.

v. **Build social capital**: By enhancing your social contacts your relationship with large number of people will increase resulting in cooperation from them.

14. Listening

"Of all the skills of leadership, listening is the most valuable – and of the least understood. Most captains of industry listen only sometimes, and they remain ordinary leaders. But a few, the great ones, never stop listening. That's how they get word before anyone else of unseen problems and opportunities."

—*Peter Nulty*

Leadership is mainly people's skills and for that you have to listen to their problems failing which you have to face the music. Listening is one of indispensable quality of leadership. Peter Drucker once said, "About 60% of all management problems are the result of faulty communications due to mainly poor listening."

"Listening leads to connecting with people and knowing of problems, under- current, feeling, solutions, knowledge and skills that a great leader needs for effective leadership."

For a leader, listening has two main purposes: to connect with people and to learn. Listening in not mere for words but for knowing: "feelings of employees, meaning of their demands, suggestions for improvement, undercurrent of grievances, capturing heart and mind of people, politics running among employees and enhancement of knowledge." "Listening is one of the most important communication skills." The words of J. Krishnamurthy portray this beautifully, "So when you are listening to somebody completely, attentively, then you are listening not only to the words but also to the feeling of what is being conveyed, to the whole of it, not part of it." Without credible and sufficient communication including listening, the hearts and mind of others are never captured. Capturing of mind is the vital factor. As per Argentine proverb, "Who speaks, sow; who listens, reaps."

For a political leader, listening the public is very important. It is only through listeningthat you will know their problems and will solve their problems. "If you are not listening, it means you are not sensitive to their problems and nobody will vote for you." "Nobody is more persuasive than a good listener," said Dale Carnegie.

Are you a good listener? If not, you need to improve it. Do the following to improve your listening skill:

i. **Spare time**: Are you listening to your followers, voters, customers, competitors, mentors and regulators? If not, then you are not leading your organization or your team members or nation in right direction. Spare time for all fine segments and put it in your calendar and try to listen religiously.

ii. **Meet people at working station**: What are the problems, feeling of people, satisfaction levels and undercurrent going on which you can't have without direct meeting with people at their working stations? Connect with them. Along with the problems, they will also offer solutions.

iii. **Find factual and emotional contents**: From the conversation with people find the factual and emotional contents. Solve the problems and if need arises, revise the policy and process of management.

iv. **Use auto-suggestions**: To improve your listening skill, use your auto-suggestions in a big way.

15. Decisiveness (Refer Chapter 13)

"Decisiveness is the deciding factor to differentiate between a great leader and a lousy leader."

Decisiveness is one the important quality of a leader and jewels in the crown. An organization or a nation thrives on the decisive quality of a leader. "Indecisive leader is a great curse and a black dot on the face of an organization and a nation." (Refer Chapter 13)

16. Initiative

"Success depends in a very large measure upon individual initiative and exertion, and cannot be achieved except by a dint of hard work." -Anna Pavlova

Initiative is one of indispensable quality of a leader. The secret to getting ahead is getting started and opportunities will automatically appear with different options. Mary Kay Ash beautifully said, "There are three types of people in this world, those who makes thing happen, those who watch things happen and those who wonder what happened". A leader comes in first category. Leader means actions to make the difference for betterment. Without taking any initiative, leaders are simply workers and failing at the leadership position.

"The great leader is one who is bold enough on taking initiative, seizing the moment and making a great positive difference for betterment."

"Opportunity does not knock your door. You have to find it out. Many capable persons lose through never starting any work out of the fear of failure. A job well begun is half done." Zig Ziglar said, "You don't have to be great to start but you have to start to be great." Without taking initiative you can't make any contribution in your work place. Once you start, fear in your mind disappears and your other virtues help in the completion of work. When you believe in your venture in hand and use your imagination and initiative, you can make the substantial difference. Steve Jobs opined, "Let's make a dent in the universe."

Are you passionate to find opportunity, or do you wait for it to knock your door? Are you prompt in taking initiative? Have you ever taken significant initiative in your life? If not, you need to improve in taking initiative.

Do the following to improve your initiative:

i. **Identify reasons**: Identify reasons which prevent you to take initiative at your work place. Make a list and solve these.

ii. **Build positive sense**: Your problem of taking initiative is based on your mindset. Build positive attitude on taking initiative on works leading to your and your organization's progress. Always be prompt to take initiative on innovation related to product, process, policy, governance in the work environment.

iii. **Don't hesitate**: Be alert on lookout for opportunities in the form of problems. Don't hesitate but take initiative and after that your boldness will increase. Make a plan for taking one initiative in a fortnight or month.

iv. **Use auto-suggestions**: Use your auto-suggestions to improve upon your initiative problem and bring confidence.

17. Problem Solving

"If a person possesses a unique quality through common sense to sense the problems in advance, and solves the problems in a best possible manner, he is a great leader."

Problem solving quality is one of the indispensable quality of a leader. For what one is a leader when he can't solve a problem of his organization or nation. Whether it is home or work place or nation or anywhere in the world, problems are bound to crop up mainly due to four reasons. First, the complexity, diversity and self-interest are increasing day by day. Second, working demands constant interaction and cooperation with people. Third, it is difficult to control all ugly situations created by internal or external forces. Fourth, it is the outcome of any wrong decision taken by previous authority.

A good leader is one who is equipped to know some of the troubles in advance by just using his third eye and common sense. They solve the problem one at a time by remaining firm and grounded. Further, they solve problem by keeping the big picture of future in mind. "Most of the time problems appear in the form of opportunities. Gold shines only when it is heated in fire. Similarly, a leader is heated while passing through the problem solving difficulties and shines after solving them. Further, the problems give a chance to overhaul the policies and processes of system of governance." "A crisis offers a great opportunity to introduce an effective change in the system for betterment." Note that problems give meaning to life. "A leader is judged by the size of the problem they tackle." "Task problems are easy to solve but people problems take longer time. Problems associated with people should be solved at the lowest level as soon as possible through right attitude and right action plan."

"Thinking ahead of time, taking strong decisions in crises, getting your people to share a common vision, imagining of an innovation, solving people's problem and instilling a pride in every employ or citizen are a few traits for any leader." "A good leader must be ready to work in global business environment, in challenging geography from the political or climate stand point of view, and in diverse culture and must be capable, visionary and innovative enough to solve problems arising in the organization and to take the organization to a great height. Finding problem is a better method to solve problem with reference to developing an innovative product." John McCarthy, father of artificial intelligence used to say, "Finding and articulating the problem is half the solution. The other half is to solve it."

Do you have the capability of problem solving? If the answer is NO, improve your capability. Do the following to enhance your problem solving capability:

i. **Don't avoid problems**: It is wrong to avoid problems. Search problems either apparent or hidden in your organization, make a list, and plan to solve.

ii. **Develop TACT approach**: Though common method of solving problems is more or less the same, but a comprehensive method could be coined by the term **TACT** where each letter stands for something special as given below:

T-**Time**: – spend time to dig in deep to find the real issue behind the problem.

A-**Assistance**: – take assistance from a competent team which will study the problem from all angles.

C – **Creative**: – be creative to find multiple solutions and select the best.

T –**Tactful**: – be tactful in solving problems.

iii. **Consult mentors**: Discuss your problems with mentors who are expert in solving problems. They can give you some valuable tips.

iv. **Take training**: Take training along with your team of problem solvers by attending workshop through case studies:

18. Servant-hood

"A godly leader finds strength by realizing his weakness, finds authority by being under authority, finds direction by laying down his own plans, finds vision by seeing the needs of others, finds credibility by being an example, finds loyalty by expressing compassion, finds honor by being faithful, finds greatness by being a servant."

—*Roy Lessin*

Servant-hood is one of the indispensable qualities (more of attitude) of a leader. Good leadership begins with becoming good servant. Every religion of the world advocates serving the needy ones and it is considered as great dharma. The same is true with a leader. But some of the people at high positions lack the quality of servant- hood. They behave rudely with the needy people. You may find this scenario in most of the government organizations by some officers, assistants and peons. John C. Maxwell said, "True leadership must be for the benefit of the followers, not to enrich the leader."

If the junior staff is not helping the needy people, one can think of their officers and leaders. It is very difficult to even meet them. Their sensitivities towards helping the needy people have withered away. Sam J. Ervin Jr. advocated, "A person who is worthy of being a leader wants power not for himself but in order to be of service." "Leadership should be born out of the understanding of the plights of needy persons and not the comforts of elite groups."

The moral duty of a leader is to care of his people not for himself. The kingship (or leadership) of Lord Rama is famous for the welfare of people. There is a famous poem by Brewer for servant-leader as given below:

"Strong enough to be weak
Success enough to fail
Busy enough to make time
Wise enough to say "I don't know"
Right enough to say "I am wrong"
Important enough to be last
Planned enough to be spontaneous
Controlled enough to be flexible
Knowledge enough to ask questions
And leading enough to "serve (with love)."

Are you a follower of philosophy of Brewer with reference to servant-hood? Are you putting people ahead of yourself in respect of welfare and well-being? Are you keen to help your people from the core of your heart? If not, you lack tremendously in servant- hood. Act on the philosophy of Brewer and empathy and servant-hood will come in your blood.

"Servant-hood decides the quality of leadership."

Do the following to enhance your servant- hood:

i. **Know the importance of servant- hood**: Consult great leaders in whom servant- hood is filled in every drop of their blood. Read good books on this topic and acquire wisdom. This will change your attitude towards servant-hood.

ii. **Start with small helps**: Start small, help other people and make them feel wanted.

iii. **Know their problems**: The best way to know their problems is to mingle with them at suitable time. Talk to them; ask about their health and start knowing them. Make a list of their needs and wants.

iv. **Indulge in action**: Indulge in action to solve their needs and wants as now these are known to you.

v. **Strengthen servant-hood**: There are many social places such as temples, mosques, churches, community agencies where you can act as volunteer to serve people. This will strengthen your attitude towards servant-hood. "It is worth to know that in gurudwaras, great importance is given to shoe-keepers and floor washers."

19. Learnability (Refer Chapter 11)

"Learning brings the light of knowledge in your life from the darkness of ignorance."

Learnability is an important quality of a leader. It is human nature that if people achieve some position and status they start thinking that they don't need to learn anything further. "People are plagued by the status quo syndrome; which is a wrong mindset." If you want to grow further, you have to learn many new things – be the new technology, new human resource management techniques, new leadership quality, new marketing principles, new products, and new financial techniques, new soft skills, and new philosophy of leading life, new people skills, and so on. There is no age of learning. Maya Angelon said, "When you know better, you do better."

Knowledge is expanding exponentially. At every eleven hours information is doubling.(as per records of 2012). If you don't keep abreast of growing knowledge, you can't compete in the competitive market. If a leader wants to grow himself and his organization, he has to go for learnability. Ali Bin Abi Thalib said, "There is no wealth like knowledge, no poverty like ignorance."

Some leaders think that they have acquired status and earned a lot of money, and now there is no need to grow further and to learn any new thing. They are totally mistaken. In this world, nothing remain stagnant as either it is growing or decaying. If you don't grow, it is sure that you will go down. A great leader doesn't think in this way. He remains teachable and learns many new things for himself and for organizations. If you are not growing, and if your organization is not growing, it means you lack of learnability. "Spare some time to read something good each day, learn something each day." "Good books will flood your soul with hope, inspiration and motivation." Oliver Wendell Holmes opined, "A mind once stretched by a new idea can never return to its original dimensions."

Do the following to improve your learnability.

i. **Test your learnability**: When you do something, there is likelihood that you may commit mistakes. Do you admit your mistakes? Are you defensive?

Do you react or do you apologize if need arises? If the answer is no, then you need your learnability.

ii. **Learn every aspect**: Being a leader, you must have basic idea of every field of your organization or nation. Try to learn each of them- in brief and their new knowledge. Bring innovation in every aspect of your organization including new people skills.

iii. **Strengthen your area**: Be more competent in the area of expertise of your strength so that you may be the torch bearer in your area of expertise. Note that change is only constant.

iv. **Stretch yourself in new area**: For becoming emotionally, mentally and physical strong, it is necessary to stretch yourself in new field.

v. **Become avid reader**: Develop a habit of reading new concepts in leadership. Go through biographies of great leaders of the world and latest techniques in greatness, management and leadership. Remember, if you want to lead, you have to read.

20. Discernment

"Discernment is the intuitive ability and third eye to find the root cause of a problem."

Discernment is an indispensable quality of a leader. It is a great ability to find the root of difficult matter based on high degree of intuition and rational thought. It relates to accurate judgment about the complex matter based on intelligentsia, instincts and some experience. Discernment is the power of sensing accurately.

When a great leader shines, based on his ability of discernment, people either view them as lucky or as a fluke. But, it is not true. Really, they have the ability of correct judgment which is called discernment. Those who lack in discernment they fail miserably as their judgment of the matter doesn't reach at correct place and at correct time.

The ability of discernment is so much important that even one decision driven by discernment can change the entire course of leader's destiny and organization's growth. Mahendra Singh Dhoni, captain of Indian cricket team has the ability of discernment in the dynamics of game of cricket.

Do you reach to the root cause of matter? If not, you lack in discernment.

Do the following to improve your ability of discernment.

i. **Back to history**: Recall all past problems which you have encountered. Take a stock of your intuitive assessment of pin-pointing the causes of problems. Make a list of these and ponder deeply on these. This will enrich your experience and your discernment.

ii. **Consult great leaders**: Contact great leaders and listen from their stories of discernment. Analyze about how they think through their intuition.

iii. **Go through case studies**: Go through some top case studies of discernment. This will form your base for developing intuitive power and help you a lot.

21. Generosity

"To practice five things under all circumstances constitutes perfect virtue; these five are gravity, generosity of soul, sincerity, earnestness and kindness."

—*Confucius*

Generosity is one of the most important qualities of a leader. It is a great ornament not of only leaders but of all human beings. God has sent us in this world to shower generosity to needy ones. "Generosity comes from heart and soul of a person to give his or her time, energy, money, possession, and knowledge for the benefit of needy ones. The glory of a generous leader is like a fragrance of a flower which is bound to reach every corner. "Real generosity is characterized by doing nice for someone without being known as the person who did it."

"Generosity is the call of heart and soul for relinquishing possessive mind to give something valuable to needy persons remaining unrecognized."

In the domain of a generous leadership, an organization or a country offers too many opportunities for the individuals to grow further due to liberty given for the fulfilment of dreams. Arnold Schwarzenegger said, "The success I have achieved in body-building, motion pictures, and business world not have been possible without generosity of American people and the freedom here to pursue your dreams."

In the past, there were many kings who were too much generous for their citizens such as Lord Rama, King Bhoj, King Harishchandra, etc. Their main motto of kingship was to provide all types of welfare to their citizens. Wealth of a generous person never recedes rather it grows. Generosity gives too much satisfaction. Philanthropy is an act of generosity.

Are you doing something as a leader or as a person to add any type of value in the life of others? Are you giving energy, time, money, possession for the benefit of needy ones? Do you feel from the core of heart that you are a generous person? If not, then you lack in the area of generosity.

Do the following to improve your generosity.

i. **Initiate small acts**: You must be having something precious- your time, money, possession, talent. Identify the person who wants what you can give which will be beneficial to him. Start giving something to needy ones such as medical helps, jobs, promotion, advice and knowledge.

ii. **Donate religiously**: Donate something which you can do some highly needy workers for public welfare which will outline you for many years to come.

iii. **Consult mentor:** For involving more in generosity, consult some mentors who will show you the right path.

iv. **Act as mentor:** Once you achieve a high level of leadership, act as mentor to develop leadership at second level: They will be indebted to you.

22. Vision

"Good business leaders create a vision, articulate the vision, passionately own the vision, and relentlessly drive it to the completion."

—Jack Welch

Vision is an indispensable possession of leader. He lives and works for his vision to see this turn into reality. It is the vision which drives and leads him. Without a vision, leader is inferior to an ordinary worker. The vision of the leader must excite the minds and touch the hearts of employees. For a great vision, people will follow you to translate the vision into reality. It is the capacity of leadership that translates vision into reality. "Vision with strong action can change the world."

"Vision is the empire of the future and the soul of a leader. He or she inspires vigorously the power and energy of followers to transform vision into reality."

The power of vision is great. The organization which banks on great vision of its leader thrives, grows and lasts for a very long period. The words of Kenneth Labich elucidate this eloquently, "Don't underestimate the power of vision." McDonald's founder, Ray Kroc pictured his empire long before it existed, and he saw how to get these. He wrote the company motto- "quality, service, cleanliness and value – and kept repeating it to employees for the rest of his life." Now McDonalds is a household name. "While formulating vision and translating it into reality, a leader has to be a great innovator." "The success of a vision is determined by its ownership by both the leader and its people and working persistently to translate it into reality."

To see the effect of vision of great leaders, just go through the market cap of the following great companies on 12th December 2013 given in billion USD (Source: Bloomberg, Times of India). See the outcomes of vision of their founders and subsequent CEOs of these companies whose individual MCap (Market Capital) is more than the GDP of many small countries.

Apple : 499	Exxon Mobile : 423
Google : 357	Microsoft : 305
Berkshire Hathaway: 280	General Electrical : 273
Johnson& Johnson : 256	Walmart : 250
Nestle : 231	Petro China : 230

"When you are inventing the vision either for yourself or for your organization or for your country, it is very essential that your eyes should aim to stars, and while translating it, your feet should be on the ground." John Sculley said, "The future belongs to those who see possibilities before they become obvious."

Napoleon Hill said, "Cherish your visions and your dreams as they are the children of your soul; the blueprints of your ultimate achievements." It has been observed that the organizations which survive for the longest period are based on the very sound vision. They do not only give just high growth and create wealth but they also exhibit excellence, brand, values, and respect for others and make employees happy. They build a healthy culture in the organization to enhance team spirit such as rituals, celebrations, conversation, training, goal achieving, and storytelling. People call their vision as soul. "The progress, greatness, respects and branding of an organization or a nation depends upon the vision of its leader. "USA reached on the top of the world because their presidents had grand vision for the country and they worked religiously and relentlessly for this. UK, Germany, France, Japan are highly developed countries due to the great vision of their previous heads of countries. Recently, Chinese leaders have shown great vision and now China occupies second position in GDP (USD 10.4 tn in 2015) after US (USD 17.4tn) while GDP of India is USD2.1 tn due to average vision. All top MNCs, top 100 universities of the world, top research labs of the world are on the top due to the great visions of their heads and honest implementation. Tony Hsieh (CEO of Zippos) said, "Chase the vision, not the money, the money will end up following you." "Be obsessed for the extraordinary leadership to make a great difference."

"A great leader is judged by translation of his extraordinary vision into reality."

You can't find a leader without a vision. He can't survive what to talk of growing. Do you have any vision for yourself or your organization? Is your vision great or of ordinary type? Do you work hard to realize your vision or is it just for the namesake? If you find any fault, you need a great vision.

Do the following to design or improve your vision.

i. **Identify the level:** Consult your key employees and close friends. Ask them to speak unbiased and without any hesitation about what they think about your vision. If they appreciate it, then you are going in the right direction. If not, either you have to reconstruct it or improve it.

ii. **Document it:** A vision whether personal or of organization or of a nation should be well documented. Official copy should be in leader's office and at all important offices so that every body works for it. The personal one should be at home. If your vision is not aiming to greatness, then start revising it and work hard to achieve it.

iii. **Spend time:** Construction of a vision is not easy as it is the soul. Take a comprehensive view of your organization or nation and prepare it by giving a lot of time on it. Read it many times and judge whether it ignites you or not. Does it make your dream? Revise many times till it ignites and energizes you.

iv. **Go through case study**: Go through some case studies dealing with great vision of a leader and its realization. This will broaden your awareness about vision.

23. Security (of Position)

"Insecure leaders can't secure an organization successfully and their insecurity is a dangerous liability for the organization."

Security (of position) is a mind**set** of a leader. A great leader always feels highly secure about himself where as an ordinary leader always feels highly insecure about his or her position. Insecurity of position always hound hover around an ordinary leader due to the fear from capable persons. Insecure leaders are either bound to fail or remain at low level.

Leaders commit many personal flaws while leading the organizations and as a result they feel insecure. Insecure leaders are highly dangerous to themselves, their followers and the organizations because they will follow the path of safeguarding themselves out of the fear of losing positions by not inducting talented people, which in turn, will not help them anyway. Insecure leaders show common traits such as: taking more from people than giving them, limiting the talented people, not bringing capable persons from outside. And so, they limit the organizations from growth and excellence including them.

But, the story with the great secured leaders is the total opposite. They believe in themselves and learnability. They know their strengths and weaknesses and are highly polite. They reward and praise the best performers and don't get threatened. They try to do their best to bring the best to people from outside to achieve their vision and for all round growth of organizations. It is the security in the mind that enables them to reach their potential and achieve their great vision.

From the core of your heart, ask yourself whether you feel insecure or secure. If you feel insecure, you need to improve various qualities to grow your leadership.

Do the following to improve your security:

i. **Identify your level**: Ask your best friends, to tell your strength and weakness about your feeling of security. Write them and match with your inner feelings and place it on a scale of ten. If you score less than 8 out of 10 points, you lack in security.

ii. **Start with small acts**: Whoever does good work in your organization, acknowledge their contributions by praising in writing and giving small gifts. Since appreciation is one of the greatest gifts so you can gift to the deserving people.

iii. **Analyze critically**: "Your vision can't be achieved and your organization can't grow without the contribution of competent people at all levels." "You will grow only when your organization grows, so the feeling of insecurity is a wrong mindset." Work hard to make up your shortcomings, due to which you are fearful and feel insecure. Go for learnability to remove insecurity from your mind.

iv. **Consult mentor:** Consult mentor for professional help to overcome your security problems. Tell them the root of your problems and they will give you the solutions to all of them.

24. Honesty (Refer Chapter 1)

"No legacy is as rich as honesty."

—*William Shakespeare*

Honesty is the indispensable quality of a leader and it must be developed ignoring what other people are doing with every criticism that comes in the way. Honesty offers openness, reliability, genuineness and frankness. An honest person is always respected. "Honesty is in being and not in appearing to be." Many people are dishonest but they will show and talk in such a way exhibiting just the opposite of their character. Be aware of such people. "Honesty is a very wide term. It relates to money, to duty, to thought, to truth, to service, to decision, to opinion, to relationship, to humanity, to judgment, to discussion, to vision, to interaction, to dealing, etc."

"Honesty is the hallmark of respect, success, progress and great leadership."

King Harish Chandra of ancient India sacrificed his son while practicing truth. "Honesty is a habit, a strong instinct and a strong resolve. It requires firmness and commitment."

All over the world, dishonesty is spreading at a higher pace than honesty due to selfishness and greed. A dishonest person may earn wealth in a short period but any time he may be caught and be put in great trouble losing each and everything, nobody knows. "Dishonesty is the worst policy whereas honesty is the best policy." Many dishonest ministers, high officials and CEOs of companies from all over the world were put behind bars and lost everything of life-peace, prestige and respect.

There are many politicians, officers and other heads who are honest, but some of them are very careful and sensitive about their honesty and afraid of getting trapped in fraudulent issues. So, they do not allow any work to be done due to the fear of criticism on honesty and lodging of false complaints by opponents. As a result, they either go through the route of putting objections on files or not taking any decision. What is the use of such honesty which hampers the progress of a nation? "Leaders who take decision honestly and execute honestly should be awarded as they are nation builders. Pinpricking in the decision and execution on minor issues, even without any loss of exchequer, by opponents should be avoided as minor mistakes are possible, either due to emotions or hurry when goals are for the nation building, otherwise nobody will dare to take any decision." "Honesty followed by too much development is the need of hour in the nation building. The honest decision makers should be awarded."

Judge yourself where you stand on the benchmark of honesty on a scale of ten. Do the following to improve your honesty.

i. **Stop temptation**: "Don't see the bad done by people and get inspired to tread the easy path. Control your temptation. Always remind yourself that the road to success lies in honesty and hard work."

ii. **Make policies and processes conducive to honesty**: By making policies and processes transparent and conducive to honesty, there is a less chance of dishonesty. E-governance in real spirit without any loop-hole is one of the solutions.

iii. **Use your auto-suggestions**: To inculcate honesty, use your auto-suggestions by various ways such as: In all my dealings, I will be honest. I am a man of integrity. Greed will not touch me etc.

iv. **Read autobiography**: Read autobiographies of great people who were or are the icon of honesty. This will motivate you to follow their footsteps.

25. Integrity

"The supreme quality for leadership is unquestionably integrity. Without it, no real success is possible, no matter whether it is on a section gang, a football field, in an army or in the office."

—*Dwight D. Eisenhower*

Integrity is one of the best qualities of leadership. It inspires credibility, righteous approach and ownership. Many societies, many organizations and many nations are in bad shape and in poor condition due to the lack of honesty and integrity among majority of people. Leadership starts with the whole issue of integrity, credibility, responsibility and enthusiasm. "Integrity integrates all your good qualities leading to success and glory." Tom Cochrane opined, "Tragedy in life normally comes with betrayal and compromise, and trading on your integrity and not having dignity in life. That's really where failure comes." "Integrity builds trust and confidence."

When calamity comes at any place in the world, the integrity of people is judged in the best manner. Those who are not honest and not men of integrity, they start looting people instead of helping them. This is well expressed by the words of Samuel Richardson, "Necessity may well be called the mother of invention but calamity is the test of integrity."

The story of shepherd boy telling lie – wolf, wolf, and wolf is known to everybody. What happened to him when the real wolf came? It was the lack of his credibility that killed him due to non-support from others.

"Integrity is the life line, strength and the supreme quality of a great leader through which he or she thrives and succeeds in a dignified, honest manner."

Socrates said, "The first key to greatness is to be in reality what we appear to be." Credibility test can be judged only through integrity. The more credible you are the more confidence people place in you, thereby allowing you to lead, to influence them. Reverse is true if you are less credible. Integrity is well conceived in an ancient wisdom when it is said about something, "Don't ask the price, it is priceless." Scott Hamilton opined, "The high road is always respected. Honesty and integrity are always rewarded." Integrity leads to: trust building, high influencing ability, high moral standards, high reputationand dignified life, freedom from cleverness, and transformation of person to greatness. From the core of your heart, judge yourself whether you are a man of integrity or not. Are your words and actions matching all the time? Have you deceived any person? Are you telling the truth of product while selling it? If not, then you need to improve on integrity.

Do the following to improve your integrity:

i. **Be careful in small acts**: In all small acts, whether it is selling, dealing, administrating, or promising: "be careful about your integrity." Whatever you say, your action must match. Slowly, it becomes your habit and your integrity in society will improve.

ii. **Learn to say No**: If you feel that a certain request or demand from others can't be met, tell politely and humbly, "Sorry, I can't help you."

iii. **Learn the importance of integrity**: Read stories of great leaders and from their deeds learn the importance of integrity. Ponder over your experience concerning integrity. They will be guarding you against greed when you will try to sell your integrity.

iv. **Avoid temptation**: People around you may be taking immediate advantage on deceiving integrity. Don't join that club. Think yourself a horse of big race and decide on what is good for you."

v. **Use your auto-suggestions**: Always remind yourself through your auto-suggestions to be a man of integrity, what may come.

26. Sincerity

"The only guide to man is his conscience; the only shield to his memory is the rectitude and sincerity of his actions. It is very imprudent to walk through life without this shield because we are so often mocked by the failure of our hopes and the upsetting of our calculations, but with this shield, however the fates may play, we march in the rank of honor."

—*Winston Churchill*

Sincerity refers to the call of mind and heart in doing your duty honestly and making available in the service of one's family, society and nation gladly and voluntarily. Sincerity is the outcome of a disciplined life. It comes from the inner feeling. A sincere person, at whatever position is considered to be a gem.

"It is sincerity that makes the very least person to be more valuable than the most talented hypocrite." Progress and respect embrace sincere people very easily. Margret Mead opined, "Never believe that a few caring people can't change the world. For, indeed, that's all who we ever had."

> *"The first principle of life is to practice sincerity, integrity and honesty to lead a peaceful, progressive and glorious life."*

If you want to see quality work in any sphere of life, you will find that it is the job done by only a sincere person. This was beautifully stated by the words of Thomas Carlyle, "The merit of originality is no novelty, it is sincerity."

"A sincere person is darling of all and respected widely. If any work is assigned to a sincere person, be sure, it will be done with top most quality before time." The words of François de La Rochefoucauld acknowledge this nicely, "Sincerity is an openness of heart, we find it in a very few people; what we usually see is artful dissimulation to win the confidence of others." Confucius advocated, "Sincerity and truth are the basis of every value."

Ask yourself the following questions to test your sincerity. Do you accept any work gladly? Do you complete all your work before time with quality? Are you available gladly for helping others? Do you consider your work as burden? Are you regular and punctual in your work? If not, then you lack in sincerity.

Do the following to improve your sincerity:

i. **Accept any work gladly**: If you don't accept any work gladly and wholeheartedly, then you can't give heart and soul to complete the work with quality and before time.

ii. **Change attitude**: Sincerity is a mindset and hence there is a need to change your attitude for exhibiting your sincerity.

iii. **Be regular and punctual**: Start becoming punctual at reaching workplace. Do time management and put your heart and soul to finish work before time- be duty, help to family, society or else.

iv. **Learn from sincere persons**: Watch sincere persons with their approach to work, to positive attitude and to society at large.

v. **Use your auto-suggestions**: Use your auto-suggestions to become sincere person by repeating various slogans for the benefits of self and society at large.

27. Courtesy and Humility

> *"Rudeness is the weak man's imitation of strength."*
>
> —*Eric Hoffer*

Courtesy is the backbone of all virtues and a gift for treating others with warmth and respect. It allows you to maintain your dignity and treat others with dignity. It helps you to be considerate, responsive, and kind in your dealings with others. Hilaire Belloc said, "The grace of God is courtesy."

Courtesy is one of the best qualities of a good leader. Simply put, it is showing consideration to others in the best possible manner. It requires humility and is a main constituent of soft skills. Practice courtesy and manners on daily basis. Napoleon Hill opined, "Courtesy is not dependent on education, but on common sense."

"A courteous person is welcomed everywhere. Even a less sharp courteous person goes much further in life than a discourteous very sharp person. It is a little act but makes a lot of difference in life. Courtesy is one of the moral behaviors of persons. It costs nothing but pays much more." Courtesy includes saying thanks you for smallest helps in gratitude, talking nicely with persons, addressing with honorable words, giving seats to elderly persons, always greeting people with a smile and so on. Mahatma Gandhi said, "When restraint and courtesy are added to strength, the latter becomes irresistible."

"Courtesy, manner, politeness and gratitude go hand in hand and make you a great gem if you practice these." It is the exhibiting consideration, courtesy and good manners to all people that bring warmth and acceptance in any society, any meeting. Jacques Maritain advocated, "Gratitude is the most exquisite form of courtesy."

Courtesy, politeness and gentleman behavior offer many advantage than rude behavior. Rude behavior is a negative attitude. Nobody likes rude people. Rude people may get immediate advantage occasionally but, in the long run, it is a curse.

"Courtesy and communication open all doors to manage people with dignity which results in achieving success smoothly."

Courtesy is generally seen as a result of good upbringing. So, it should be taught from childhood. "It is worth to note that many brilliant and talented people have spoiled their own success due to lacking in courtesy, behavior and manner." Are you ready to develop the habit of courtesy?

Humility

"It was pride that changed angels into devils; it is humility that makes men as angels."
—*Saint Augustine*

Humility is one of the great qualities of leadership. It refers to showing yourself less infront of others to avoid arrogance and not to let others down. Confucius opined, "Humility is the solid foundation of all virtues." Instead of blowing off horns by yourself, if others blow your horns, these will go much further and your respect will spread. "A humble leader is a prerequisite for successful organization or nation." "Nothing commands more respect in the society than natural humility, humanity, integrity, compassion and sense of humor." C.S Lewis said, "Humility is not thinking less of yourself, it's thinking of yourself less."

"Humility is humbleness, angel's act, free from pride and ego and a great leader acts in this mode in all spheres of life."

Humility Exhibited Raises Your Reputation: The famous story of humility shown by a great ancient king is of highest order and an eye-opener. He was on a horse ride in disguised dress going through a hilly area where some laborers were trying to move a heavy rock to clear road block but failing miserably. The head of the team was standing by the side where the laborers were struggling to move the heavy rock. The rider asked the head of the team, "Why aren't you helping?" The head replied, "I am the head of the laborers and my job is to give order." On this, the rider dismounted and helped them to lift the rock and the rock got moved by his help and road became clear. The rider after mounting on the horse went to the head and said, "If next time your men need help, call the king of the state for this." After the rider left the scene, the head and his men found out that the rider was the king of the state and the head of team leader got ashamed heavily and repented on his attitude.

The **moral** of the story is: "It is the humility that matters in helping others irrespective of one's status. It makes you an angel, who helps the needy ones."

D. Shivakumar, Chairman and CEO of PepsiCo India Holdings Private Limited, a subsidiary of PepsiCo, Inc. said, "The main reason for why companies fail is arrogant leadership." Napoleon Hill elucidated, "Humility of the heart will attract more friends than will all the wisdom of mankind."

Ask yourself: Do you show courtesy and humility? If not, you lack in both. Develop both.

Do the following to improve your courtesy and humility:

i. **Take small steps**: Do some small acts every day in the area of courtesy and humility. As a result, your habit will change. Everywhere, there is an enough scope of exhibiting humility and courtesy. Only you have to be ready from the core of heart. It is a culture to be learned from childhood.

ii. **Associate with courteous and men of humility**: Being in the best company of courteous people, you will also work for courtesy and humility. Learn from them.

iii. **Use your auto-suggestions**: Use your auto-suggestions to get involved in courtesy and humility.

28. Empathy and Compassion

"Empathy is about standing in someone else's shoes, feeling with his or her heart seeing with his or her eyes. Not only is empathy hard to outsource and automate, but it makes the world a better place."

—*Daniel H. Pink*

Empathy and compassion are important quality of leadership. At this stage, these are needed more. In general, we never bother when we do any harm to others. We never think of his pain, agony and feeling due to the harm inflected. If the harm is done to you by others, you start behaving differently. It is very inhuman not to bother about feelings of others. Henry Ford opined, "If there is any one secret of success, it lies in the ability to get the other person's point of view and see things from his angle as well as your own. Siddhartha (Gautama Buddha) is well known for his compassion shown on injured swan by a hunter.

"Empathy is the feeling of pain, agony, insult, views and happiness of others as if these are your own and action on this line will spread humanity and bring smiles in the world leading to success."

There is a difference between sympathy and empathy in approach. Sympathy is: "I understand how you feel". It is worth to note that both are important but empathy is more important, and if you have empathy, sympathy will automatically come.

To check whether you have empathy or not, simply ask yourself: "How would I feel if someone treated me in the sameway." If your answer is in the line of others feeling, then you have empathy otherwise not. Develop empathy. Are you ready?

Compassion

"Wisdom, compassion, and courage are the three universally recognized moral qualities of men."

—*Confucius*

Have you ever realized how the purpose of human life is different than other creatures? If it doesn't involve moral values and other good qualities, then what the difference between human beings and animals is? How will a society survive? Compassion is not only the need of leaders but more of human beings. Lao Tzu opined, "I have just three things to teach: simplicity, patience, compassion. These three are your greatest treasures." If you want to see yourself and other people to live a happy life in a harmonious culture, then everybody has to practice compassion. The words of Dalai Lama express this in a very emphatic way, "If you want others to be happy, practice compassion. If you want to be happy, practice compassion." **"Spiritual intelligence** is now regarded as an important quality of leadership. It is defined as the ability to behave with wisdom and compassion, while maintaining inner and outer piece, regardless of the situation." It is practiced by business leaders like John Mackey, co-CEO of the USD11 billion company, Whole Food Markets.

"Lead by heart, not head; but use head judiciously to support heart."

Compassion Shown Can Change the Heart of a Dacoit: A great saint had a very smart horse which was famous for its speed. A dacoit made a cunning plan to steal the horse. He dressed himself as very old lame man with many wounds showing extreme pain and appeared in the way of the saint when he was on a horse ride in the morning. By seeing the old lame man in pain, the saint dismounted and mounted the old man on the horse to take him to his destination. Once the old lame man took the seat on the horse, he ran away with horse. On this, the saint said to the dacoit in a loud voice: "Don't tell this story of stealing of horse to anybody as in the future, nobody will show compassion on needy persons. Tell that the saint has donated the horse to me." The words of saint were hovering in the mind of dacoit in the night, and he couldn't sleep in the night. And, in the morning, the dacoit returned the horse to the saint, requested to pardon him and became his disciple.

The **theme** of the story is: "Compassion shown on even a wicked person changes his heart towards goodness."

"Compassion, being the core moral value of human life is the need for the survival and progress of humanity."

If you are lacking in empathy and compassion, do the following to improve in these:

i. **Take a vow**: Take a vow that from today itself you wouldn't hurt the feeling of others in any way. Wherever you get a chance, show your kindness on the suffering people and help them.

ii. **Enrich your mind**: Through reading books on empathy and compassion, enrich your mind with the feeling of empathy and compassion. Attend some workshops on empathy and compassion.

iii. **Use your auto-suggestions**: Use your auto-suggestions to improve your empathy and compassion.

29. Values (Refer Chapter 14)

Human values are one of the important qualities of leadership. Practicing of values in an organization or a nation led by a leader brings fragrance of heaven, happiness, peace and conducive environment at the workplace resulting in prosperity and growth to all stakeholders (See chapter 14). Some core values needed for a leader has been discussed in previous articles. "**Enlightened leader** practices values and brings creativity in work environment."

30. Soft Skills or People Skills

"Soft skills leave magical impression on others giving enormous benefits to the persons who are rich in these."

Soft skills are one of the greatest qualities of leadership. A leader can't go ahead without these. "Soft skills are behavioral competencies and relate to a person's EQ (Emotional Intelligence Quotient)." These are also called Interpersonal Skills or People Skills or Lady Skills. Soft skills include the following:

- Courtesy, manners, behavior, empathy, and humility.
- Communication skills, Integrity.
- Conflict resolution and negotiation personal skills.
- Creative problem solving skills.
- Strategic thinking, Team building, Team spirit.
- Resilience, Influencing skills, Optimism.
- Friendliness, Simplicity, Openness, Common sense.
- Relationship, Social grace, Social capital.
- Behavior traits such as attitude, motivation and time management.

"Soft skills are personal attributes that enhance individual interactions within and outside organization in a very amicable manner resulting in better job performance and career prospects." Unlike hard skills, soft skills pertain to person's ability to interact effectively with co-workers, customers and outside world in a magical, amicable and impressive way. "Soft skills are your soft-cum- shining charisma that creates magic on others resulting in grand success. Develop it! Develop it! Develop it!

"Soft skills form the foundation of success not only at leadership level but at any level. All your personal problems get solved if you are rich in soft skills." Soft skills compliment hard skills which are the occupational requirements of a job and many other useful activities. "It's often said that hard skills will get you an interview but you need soft skills to get the job." Theodore Roosevelt advocated, "The most important single ingredient in the formula of success is knowing how to get along with people." John Rockefeller stated, "He would pay more for the ability to deal with people than any other ability under the sun." "The single most quality of great leader is the ability to work with the people."

A survey conducted by Hay Group reveals that: "80% business and HR directors say that the graduates who do not develop people skills create toxic work environments and they will never be high performers." Further, Hay group says that: "The present HR leaders are worried about the quality of future leaders lacking in people skills." "For the admission in Ivy schools of higher learning in USA, a great emphasis is given on soft skills."

Soft skills cover a wide area: Ask yourself: whether you possess soft skills or not. Test yourself: how do you approach anybody? Do you feel that people get impressed with your behavior? Do you have influencing and negotiation skills? If not, you need to develop soft skills. "The single most quality needed for a great leader is People Skills." The top earner leader in 2013 is Larry Ellison of Oracle with people skills whose pay package was USD 96 million.

Do the following to develop soft skills:

i. **Choose some critical areas to begin with**: Develop soft skills slowly on some critical areas and watch people who are rich in soft skills. "Learn from ladies who are in general very good in soft skills."

ii. **Improve communication skills**: Improve your communication skills using proper sentences and words most suitable and appropriate. Before meeting people, prepare yourself with good soft and pleasing words.
iii. **Enrich your soft skills**: After acquiring some initial skills enrich yourself with all soft skills by attending workshop conducted by experts. A great practice is needed at every stage of interaction. All the time you have to be mindful about using soft skills at all interactions.
iv. **Use auto-suggestions**: Use your auto-suggestions to remind you that you have to develop these skills and work on them.
v. **Attend workshop**: Read books and attend workshop on soft skills and develop yourself accordingly.

31. Mindfulness

"The stages of the Noble Path are: Right View, Right Thought, Right Speech, Right Behavior, Right Livelihood, Right Effort, Right Mindfulness and Right Concentration."

—*Gautama Buddha*

WHAT IS MINDFULNESS?

There isa buzzword in the world of leading management schools to offer a course on mindfulness as it is one of the most demanding qualities (recently recognized) for a leader. The question arises: what is mindfulness?

Bodhipaksa defines mindfulness as follows: "Mindfulness is the gentle effort to be continuously present with experience." Here, gentle word means absence of pressure and tension in mindwhile remaining present with experience.

"Mindfulness means paying attention in a particular way; on purpose in the present moment, and non-judgmentally."

—*Jon Kabat-Zinn*

It is to be noted that purposefulness is core aspect of mindfulness. Here, purpose refers to staying with the experience of your activities: "May be your breath, eating, walking, conversation, study, yoga or a particular activity." If this happens, then you are actively shaping your mind to pay attention on purpose.

"Non-judgmentally refers to non-reactive state of mind. Right mindfulness is an emotionally non-reactive state as we don't judge that this experience is good or that one is bad. We don't get upset by any experience and so there is no scope of stress entering your mind."

Gautama Buddha said, "On life's journey faith is nourishment, virtuous deeds are a shelter, wisdom is the light by day and right mindfulness is the protection by night, if a man lives a pure life, nothing can destroy him." Practice of mindfulness is not only essential for leaders but it is also needed for everybody. It doesn't demand your extra time to practice this. Simply one has to understand it deeply what it is and just practice in life every day in all your activities. But, it is not easy to develop the quality of mindfulness as mind is always wavering. It needs a great practice over a long period clubbed with positive attitude, wisdom, yoga and meditation.

"Mindfulness is a living style by paying deep gentle attention on the purpose in present moment non-judgmentally leading to joy and stress free life."

The benefits of practicing mindfulness may be summarized as follows:

- It keeps you in deep attention and conscious awareness in present moment and as a result, your every activity brings excellent result.
- It helps you to monitor your mind non-judgmentally and to remain free from mental stress, depression by remaining happy, enthusiastic and vibrant.

All over the world, many people including top personalities- be in politics, business, spirituality, services, entertainment, journalism or any other field have committed mistakes knowingly or unknowingly or in anger or in emotion and suffered a lot out of fear. This is all due to the absence of practice of right mindfulness, even non-judgmentally. Thich Nhat Hanh opined, "When we are mindful, deeply in touch with the present moment, our understanding of what is going on deepens, and we begin to be filled with acceptance, joy, peace and love."

Do you practice mindfulness in your life? What prevents you to practice? Knowing so many benefits of practicing mindfulness, why are you hesitating to practice it? If you practice, do you feel that mindfulness has not come in your habit yet? What is your level of practicing mindfulness? If you are not mindful in your all activities, it means that you don't practice it.

Do the following to practice mindfulness:

i. **Test yourself**: During eating, walking, discussing, working, taking decision, praying and doing yoga and meditation, checkup yourself, that whether your mind paying deep gentle attention in your present activities or not. If answer is no, you need practice of mindfulness.

ii. **Start with small beginning**: Select three to four activities first. Concentrate your mind on these when you are doing these selected activities. Always remind yourself that I have to pay deep gentle attention non-judgmentally in the present moment on that activity. After success in these activities, select other activities along with the already selected activities and practice mindfulness. Automatically, it will come in your habit. Practicing mindfulness and yoga will bring wonder in your life.

iii. **Use your auto-suggestions**: Auto-suggestions are the best tools to remind you to practice mindfulness in all your activities. Remind yourself that you are here to achieve.

iv. **Put a name plate of mindfulness on your table**: By putting a name plate of mindfulness on your table, it will remind you that you have to be mindful in your activities and enjoy it.

Hey, young boys, young girls, men, women! Getup from slumber and acquire leadership qualities to bring success in your life and help in the nation building. You are born to bring change in yourself, others, society and nation for betterment and excellence. God is waiting for you to fulfil your dreams and the dreams of your nation for meaningful and glorious life. Are you ready?

STEPS TAKEN BY YOURSELF

After going through this chapter (14th Mantra), I (as a reader) will take the following steps to develop the thirty-one qualities of leadership.

i. _____
ii. _____

***

Chapter 16

Maintain Stress Free Life and Good Health
#THE 15ᵀᴴ MANTRA

BEAT THE STRESS TO REMAIN HAPPY, HEALTHY

"Pain is relatively objective, physical phenomenon: suffering is our psychological resistance to what happens. Events may create physical pain, but they do not in themselves create suffering. Resistance creates suffering. Stress happens when your mind resists what is ….. The only problem in your life is mind's resistance to life as it unfolds."

—*Dan Millman*

"Adopting the right attitude can convert a negative stress into a positive one."

—*Hans Selye*

A famous doctor-cum-speaker was asked by a businessman from the audience in a health congress to speak to us of stress and health. He said in sequence: Stress! Stress! Stress! A horrible mental and physical load. An emotional outcome. A response to bad life's happening. A health and wealth destroyer. A great enemy. Is maintaining stress free life and good health a mantra of success? I say, yes, it is one of the most important mantra. Be stress free for better health, to enjoy life, to achieve success.

What is the use of high position, enormous wealth when life is full of stress and health is poor? Life is supposed to be best led when one is free from stress, maintains sound mental and physical health, remains happy, and practices values and spirituality in life. Without good health how can you work hard, how can you meet deadline, how can you enjoy life and how can you help your family and others? These questions and real situations in life demand that we should have a stress free life and good health. Ultimately, Health is Wealth.

WHAT IS STRESS?

"Human life is not governed by logic but by emotions. Our life in this modern world is full of challenges, competitions, hassles, uncertainties, frustrations, love, hate, fear, greed, ambition, happiness, deadlines, demands, dreams, disputes, deceits, success and failures." As a result, everybody goes through these events and in many cases, he/she gets highly affected and feels threatened. These cause pressure, tension, worry, emotion and our nervous system responds by releasing a flood of stress hormones, including adrenaline and cortisol that enable body to arouse for emergency action and finally generates stress in life. For many people, stress is so common place that it has become a way of life.

"Stress may be defined as a normal, emotional and physical response to events that make you feel threatened or upset your balance in some way in your life affecting both mental and physical health." In the event of sensing danger, whether, it's real or imaginary, our defense system of the body kicks into high gear in a rapid automatic process which is known as the "fight or flight" reaction, or the 'stress response.'The words of Natalie Goldberg express this aspect beautifully, "Stress is basically a disconnection from the earth, a forgetting of the breath and stress is an ignorant state. It believes that everything is in emergency. Nothing is that important, Just lie down". Hans Selye opined, "It's not stress that kills us, it is our reaction to it." Lou advocated, "It's not the load that breaks you down, it's the way you carry it."

"How do you meet challenges? It is the stress response which helps you to rise and meet challenges. For example: during presentation at work, it keeps you on toe to deliver better; it drives you to study hard by leaving watching TV during examination; or it forces to present yourself in better form in an interview." "The story of beneficial effect of stress is limited. Beyond a certain point, stress doesn't offer help. Instead, it starts causing major damages to our health, our mood, our productivity, our relationships, our behavior and our quality of life."

"Stress in inevitable in life but, it is our choice to allow it to affect us or not. Change the situation or reaction of your stressful thought process towards positivity and make a choice to be happy in present moment through mindfulness."

WHAT CAUSES STRESS?

A lot of different events are responsible in causing stress. They include factors such as fear of something dangerous to emotional like worry over family, job, unfaithfulness, broken relationship, emotional hurt, job loss, loss in business, failing to achieve goals, consequences of past mistakes, etc. The situations and pressures that cause stress are known as **stressors**. In general, stressors are considered negative. However, there are positives events also that put high demands on you, or force you to adjust which can lead to stress. These positive events include: "getting married, buying a house, going to college first time, receiving a prize, or arranging a function."

Causes of stress may be classified into the following two categories:

a. **External Causes of Stress:** There are many external factors that cause stress. They include the following main factors:

   i. **Danger of life:** There is a common response to danger in all people and animals. When we are afraid that someone or something may physically hurt us, our body naturally responds with our enormous energy so that we will be better able to survive the dangerous situation either by fight back or flight away. This is known as 'survival stress.'

ii. **Heavy work load, too busyness and fatigue**: The stress is caused by heavy work load; too busyness and fatigue builds up over a long time and can take a hard toll on your body. It may also be due to our failure in time management or not taking adequate rest and relaxation. In the modern world, this can be one of the hardest kinds of stress to avoid because people feel this is out of their control.

iii. **Major life changes**: In real life, sometimes unexpected happenings occur such as untimely death of parents, spouse death, children death, meeting serious accidents, job loss, etc. which completely changes our life. It is very challenging and difficult to cope up with new situations. The mental agony caused by this creates heavy stress and sometimes breaks the person.

iv. **Relationship difficulties**: Relationship is a very tender issue and good relationship demands love, affection, respect and space for everybody. A bad relationship with parents, spouse, friends, children, relatives, neighbors and colleagues, boss, etc. develop stress and sometimes people take a very harsh and wrong step out of frustration.

v. **Financial problems**: Finance is the core to lead a happy life. Financial problems may arise due to many factors such as: loss in business, loss in agriculture, loss of job, deceit by partners in business, theft, unable to repay loan, etc. The financial problems develop a constant stress on mind and in many cases people do not come out with mental agony and embrace suicides. A large number of suicide cases have been reported due to financial problems every year. J. K Rowling said, "Poverty entails fear and stress and sometimes depression. It meets a thousand petty humiliations and hardships. Climbing out of poverty by your own efforts that is something on which to pride yourself but poverty itself is romanticized by fools."

vi. **Children and family problems**: If the children and family don't cooperate with you, it will lead to stress. The children may be inert type and may not take any interest in study, job, work, or business, then your stress is bound to develop. If the spouse is dull or of fighting nature or non-cooperative, the stress is bound to build up.

vii. **Environmental hazards**: Environmental hazards such as noise, crowding, pollution, transport jam, etc. cause stress on you.

b. **Internal Causes of Stress**: "In general, people worry about things in which they can't do anything about or worry for no reason at all. This is an **'internal stress' caused by emotions** and it is one of the most important kinds of stress to understand and manage. It is a stress that people cause themselves without any reason, or they can't control. It is also known as **self- generated stress**. Some people are habituated to generate self- stress. Some people become addicted to the kind of **'hurried and tense lifestyle'** that results in causing stress." "Many people remain calm and stoic under all circumstances as they manage their emotions very well. They possess high emotional quotient." **Internal stress** is caused by the following factors:

- Inability to accept uncertainty in life.
- Inability to control emotions.
- Unrealistic expectations in every venture.
- Attitude of perfectionism.
- Pessimism view of life and always fearful for even minor things, past bad experience and unknown future.
- Negative self –talk; Lack of assertiveness.
- Lack of wisdom; Habit of procrastination.

"It is worth to note that what causes stress depends, at least in part, on your perception of it." Something that is stressful to one person may be an enjoying factor for others.

SIGN AND SYMPTOMS OF STRESS OVERLOAD

Stress overload always develops some signs and symptoms. The following are the common warning signs and symptoms of stress given in four sub-headings.

i. **Cognitive Symptoms**: Problems of memory loss; Inability to concentrate; Poor judgment on any issue; Negative thoughts on issue; Anxious or racing thoughts; Worrying all the time; No interest in fun; Fall of intelligence.

ii. **Emotional Symptoms**: Moodiness and irrational; Irritability or short temper; Agitation or inability to relax; Feeling overwhelmed; Depression or general unhappiness; Sense of loneliness and isolation.

iii. **Physical Symptoms**: Aches and pains in body; Diarrhea or constipation in general; Nausea or dizziness; Chest pain and rapid heartbeat; Loss of sex drive; Frequent colds; Tiredness/Fatigue

iv. **Behavioral Symptoms**: Sleeping too much or too little; Eating less or more; Isolating from other responsibility and no interest in work or socialization; Using alcohol or cigarettes or drugs to relax; Nervous breakdown habits; Procrastinating or neglecting responsibility; Increased absenteeism from duty.

It is worth to note that these signs and symptoms may be due to illness also, so always consult a doctor to know the real reason and accordingly take the necessary measures.

EFFECTS OF CHRONIC STRESS

Our body acts like metal. Metals break after yield stress, so similar is the story of our body. The human body doesn't distinguish between stress, either caused by physical pressure or psychological pressure. When you are stressed due to various reasons your body reacts very strongly in a way of life or death situation. "In the event of a lot of responsibilities and worries, you will face all the time emergency stress. The more your body's stress system is in active mode, the harder it is to shut-off." From the observations, it has been found that long-term stress can lead to serious health problems. Chronic stress caused by long-term stress can affect every system of our body seriously as given below:

- Raising blood pressure. Creating any type of pain.
- Causing heart disease. Affecting digestive system.
- Causing sleep problem. Creating diabetics problems.
- Creating obesity. Causing various autoimmune diseases.
- Causing infertility. Speeding of aging process.
- Creating skin diseases like eczema. Causing vitamin D deficiency. Causing depression.

THE FACTORS THAT INFLUENCE YOUR STRESS TOLERANCE LEVEL

"The impact of stress level varies from person to person. Some people stand up after many punches where others crumble at the slightest problems and frustration. Some people are fond of heavy work load and busy schedule, and they enjoy the hard work and thrive on accomplishments, while others hate hard work and want to lead a cozy life." The following factors influence your stress tolerance level:

i. **Support network:** A support of any kind helps to a stressed person. A strong network of supportive friends and family members acts as an enormous buffer against your stresses of life. They may help you in many ways- such as taking care of family, extending financial help, motivating and helping in completion of work, giving you wisdom to calm down, etc. A strong network is only possible when you maintain a better quality of relationships and widen social capital. On the other hand, if you are more lonely and isolated, you may breakdown due to excessive stress.

ii. **Attitude and mindset:** "Some people have optimistic attitude and positive mindset towards stress overload. They are stress resistant people. They love challenges in their lives, have a strong passion for success on their work, have a strong sense of humor, accept the change and obstacles as a part of their lives, and believe in the power, or purpose of life." "On other hand, people with pessimistic attitude and negative mindset get affected by slightest stress and feel perplexed resulting in nervous breakdown." Dale Carnegie said, "Tame your worries and energize your life."

iii. **Confidence and sense of control:** If you have confidence in yourself and possess quality to influence events in your favor finally and persevere through challenges in spite of all odds, it becomes easier for you to withstand stress. But, if you are not confident and your sense of control is weak, you will be highly vulnerable to stress.

iv. **Emotion control capability**: If you are poor in dealing with your emotions in the events of sadness, anger and fear, you are highly vulnerable to stress. "The ability to control your emotions in balance by remaining calm, smooth and tough helps you to bounce back from stress. It comes from wisdom, positive attitude and meditation." "Richness in emotion control capability is the prime factor to control stress"

v. **Awareness and preparation**: If you know the reason of stress, and how long it will last such as surgery, you will take the stress as normal events. Awareness reduces stress.

vi. **Genetics**: Genetics involved in our body structure also decides the tolerance level of stress. As a result, the tolerance level concerning stress varies from person to person.

STRESS MANGEMENT

The conception that stress in life is out of control is completely wrong. You can always control the stress in your life. "The simple realization that you're in control of your life, is the foundation of stress management." The fundamentals lie in managing stress is to take charge of all aspects of your life such as: your thoughts, your emotions, your schedule and your approach in dealing with problems." The **various steps of stress management** are given below:

a. **Identification of Source of Stress in your Life**: "The first step towards stress management is the identification of source of stress in your life."

In order to identify the true source of stress, observe closely the following:

- Your habits; Your emotions; Your attitude; Your excuses
- Do you consider your stress temporary phenomena whereas you were all the time stressful?
- Do you consider that stress is your integral part of life or is it a part of your personality?
- Do you blame others for your stress or is it a normal thing?
- Do you get agitated once stress gets creeping in your mind or you don't bother?

It is necessary to accept truly the role you play in creating or maintaining the stress based on the above facts otherwise your stress will be out of your control. Do the following for stress management:

b. **Start Writing Stress Journal**: A stress journal is an important document that can help you to identify your regular stressors in life and the way you can deal with them. Whenever you feel stressed of minor, medium or major nature, write down in your journal stating causes, your feeling, your reaction to stress and level of stress on a scale of ten points. This will help you to identify patterns and common themes.

    c. **Ways for Coping with Stress**: It is very essential to choose the right ways to coping with stress. In general, coping ways with stress may be **healthy or unhealthy, helpful or unproductive**. Many people, out of ignorance or for immediate relief, opt the unhealthy ways of coping with stress. The following are the ways for coping with stress:

        i. **Unhealthy Ways of Coping with Stress**: There are many unhealthy ways of coping with stress that are given above in **Behavioral Symptoms** such as smoking, drugs, drinking, etc. These unhealthy ways may give you relaxation for small period but they are very harmful and add more problems in your life. You can't imagine the consequences of these unhealthy ways on your health. This may lead even to death.

        ii. **Learning Healthier Ways to Manage Stress**: There are many healthier ways to manage stress but they all require change- **either change the situation or change your reaction**. Further, the response to stress varies from person to person, so there is "no one size fit all" solution exists, hence different strategies and techniques are to be experimented to overcome stress. "The fundamental in controlling stress lies in focusing on what makes you feel calm and in control of self."

Dealing with the stressful situations by **healthier ways** is represented by **4As** as given:

Change the situation	Change your reaction
i. **Avoid** the stressor	iii. **Adapt** to the stressor
ii. **Alter** the stressor	iv. **Accept** the stressor

STRESS MANAGEMENT STRATEGIES:

The healthy ways of various stress management strategies are mainly based on **As** given above. The following are the main **Six Strategies**, of stress management (Help Source: Melinda Smith and others write-up on website: helpguide.org/mentalstress-sign.htm and general awareness, doctor's views)

Strategy 1: Avoiding of Unnecessary Stress in Life

It is to be noted that not all stress can be avoided; however, their impact may be reduced to a bearable limit. Further, it is not advisable to avoid a stressful situation that needs to be addressed for the self or the organization. The following solutions come under the first strategy as given below:

    i. **Learn the skill to say 'no'**: Everybody has its own limit to accomplish tasks. So, it is advisable to know your limits and stick to them. Refuse to accept added responsibilities in a dignified and courteous way when you are close to your limits. Accepting more than your limits are a sure shot inviting stress in your life.

ii. **Learn to avoid people who stress you out**: There are many people who are stress creators for others. Beware of them. Limit the time spent with them.

iii. **Control your environment in the best possible manner**: Sometimes, the environment in which we have to work may create stress in some people such as traffic jam, evening news, shopping, etc. Search the alternatives. If noise agitates you, search for a serene place.

iv. **Avoid hot discussion topics resulting in anger and emotion**: There are certain topics such as politics or religion that are considered hot and some people get agitated and become emotional during discussion. Avoid such topics from your discussion if it agitates you. Further, avoid totally personal remark on any person during conversation as this is source of agitation.

v. **Trim your to-do list**: When your plate is full of tasks, distinguish these between "shoulds" and "musts". First you complete musts. If shoulds are possible without stressing yourself, do these, otherwise drop them entirely based on your analysis of schedule, responsibility, and daily tasks.

vi. **Avoid long sitting at a stretch:** It is advisable to work hard but avoid long seating, or long standing at a stretch. Take a break of five to ten minutes at every two hours. This will reduce your stress overload.

vii. **Learn the art of focus**: Focus on one issue at a time. Don't keep several windows open at a time as it is a great cause of stress.

viii. **Avoid thinking on past mistakes, present problems and future uncertainties**: Think always positive and don't think on past mistakes, present problems and the fear of unknown future as these create wrong emotions and stress. Take each day as a gift of God. Try to live with good and bad happenings in the same way. Look more at the good happenings and get busy in good work.

"No problem is worth for all the worry in the world."

Strategy 2: Alter the Situation in a Happy Mood

In the case, if you can't avoid the stressful situation, try to alter it. It is necessary to figure out what you can do to change things so that the problem doesn't arise again in the future. This is based on the philosophy of changing the way you communicate and operate in your daily life – be at workplace or at home or at society gatherings: The following are the solutions under the 2nd strategy:

i. **Give vent to your feelings instead of bottling them up**: There is a limit of storing up the resentment in mind and beyond that limits, resentment starts building up leading to heavy stress. If resentment is generated within you due to something or someone, it is advisable to communicate your concerns in an open but in a very respectable and courteous way. If you don't voice your feelings, resentment will build up and the situation may worsen. One day, it may burst which may cause more damage to you.

ii. **Be ready to compromise**: If you have resentment with someone on some issues that may bothering you, it is advisable to change your behavior and be ready to compromise with that person, shake hands and hug each other. There is no point in building up the grudge and stress rather the wisdom says is to compromise. "Carrying grudge is your great killer. Avoid it! Avoid it! Avoid it!" "We have come for short period on the earth, hence show love and respect to each other and compromise instead of carrying grudge."

iii. **Bring assertiveness in life**: Due to less assertiveness and cozy approach all the scheduled tasks get delayed and as a result worry and stress develop. Be more assertive in your life. Don't take a backseat in your life rather handle the problems head on. Do your best to prevent the stress. If examination is scheduled, get rid of your chatty roommate. Limit the discussion and gossiping period as there is no end of these.

iv. **Be a better time manager**: As a result of poor time management, many works get delayed and you can't stay calm and focused. Consequently, stress will creep in your mind and body. It is advisable to plan ahead as per your schedule so that you don't over extend yourself in the completion of work. This will help in removing your stress and you will enjoy your work.

v. **Acquire competency**: It is possible that due to the lack of competency you are not meeting the target. Identify your areas of poor competency and take training to overcome. Being competent, you will able to meet deadline and stress will not creep in you.

vi. **Alter stressful thought process**: If your mind is generating stressful thought process due to any reason, alter the thought process by being positive and happy, ones using your wisdom and mindfulness. William James advocated, "The greatest weapon against stress is our ability to choose one thought over another." Be cool and act swiftly during a crisis. In general, most people spend far too much time worrying about things that never occur. Ask yourself, just one question: "How likely is this thing to happen anyway?" The answer from you will take away your worry.

Strategy 3: Adapt to the Stressors with Positive Attitude:

If you're not able to avoid stress or alter the situation, the other strategy is to adapt to the stressors. This will regain your sense of control by changing your expectations and attitude. The solutions under the 3rd strategy are given below:

i. **See the problem in a positive frame**: Any problem or situation which is agitating you and developing stress in you may be viewed from a more positive perspective. When you get angry, thirty-six chemicals pour into your blood. Your heart rate shoots up. Blood rushes to your face generating heavy stress. Suppose traffic jam agitates you, adapt it by utilizing that period in listening favorite music, or connecting with your friends, or reading your favorite book. Consider the problem as the one which you can't change, so it is better to adapt and enjoy. "Be calm on any situation which agitates you." Say to yourself this will also pass. Ponder over what Sydney J. Harris, said, "If a small thing has the power to make you angry, does that not indicate your size?" So, it is advisable not to become angry at all on any matter irrespective of its size. Have a good temper and an amazing temperament.

ii. **View the problem in the big picture**: View the stressful situation in the big picture instead of in a narrow one. Ask yourself how important it will be in the long run. Will it matter in a month? A year? Is it really worth getting upset over it? Why am I killing myself on such situation? Is sky falling on me? If the answer is no, adapt the situation, and utilize your energy and time elsewhere or happily in that. "Consider every adversity as a golden opportunity for yourself as it is the truth of the world."

iii. **Adjust your standard suitably**: Many people believe in perfection for topmost quality. It is a good habit but with too much workload if perfectionism is followed, other works get delayed and that generates stress. Perfectionism is a major source of avoidable stress. Stop setting high standard for yourself and others which are failing you. Set a reasonable standard for yourself and others and learn to be happy with good enough. If perfectionism is the need, then reduce your workload. Amir Khan, actor of Bollywood is known for perfectionism, but he takes only one movie in a year.

iv. **Focus on your positive quality**: In the event of feeling low, depressed due to stress overload, don't feel so, as you have many other better qualities in life. Appreciate your better qualities to upswing the sad mood. Say to yourself, "I was not born to feel sad but happy. I was born to shine like stars." Bring your positive attitude in action to adapt the situation and uplift your sad feeling by remembering and using your positive qualities.

Strategy 4: Accept the Things You Can't Change in a positive frame:

Some painful situations in life that generates stress are unavoidable. You can't prevent or change stressors such as death of a loved one, a serious illness, natural calamities, bad people's behavior, or a national recession. In these situations, the best option is to cope with the stress and accept the things as they are in a positive frame, consoling you as God's will. This is well supported by the words of David Richo, who said, "When we oppose, we resist reality, and life becomes an endless series of disappointments, frustrations and sorrows. Once we learn to embrace and accept, we find real happiness."

A man was having daily hot arguments with his sixteen years old son who used to come late at night. But the moment he accepted, he felt better. "Acceptance of unavoidable situation is the real wisdom. Practice it! Practice it! Practice it!" The words of Deepak Chopra conform to this, "Nothing brings down walls as effectively as acceptance." In general, people are unhappy because they want other people to react the way they want, and all situations should be according to their likings. This creates stress. The following solutions may be tried under the 4th strategy:

i. **Don't try to control the uncontrollable**: Many situations acting as stressors in life are beyond our control, such as death, illness, natural calamities, bad behavior of some people, or recession or legal case. It is not advisable to try to control the uncontrollable stresses as there will be wastage of energy and the stress will be compounded to see the failure in controlling them. "Happiness lies in the unconditional acceptance of everyday situations, which generally makes us sad, angry and stressful."

ii. **Consider challenges as golden opportunity**: The saying, "What doesn't kill us makes us stronger" is highly true in real life. Whenever you confront with major challenges in life, consider these as golden opportunity for personal growth. Accept the challenges, embrace them and solve them intelligently and judiciously. This will enrich your knowledge and experience and enhance your self-esteem, self-confidence and personal growth.

iii. **Practice forgiveness**: The world in which we live is not perfect but imperfect. "Nothing is perfect." Anybody can commit mistakes which may act as stressor for someone. Learn to let go of anger and resentments. Try to practice forgiveness by making free yourself from negative energy and move on your future venture. "Forgiveness is the best virtue of human being. All your sufferings will vanish the moment you forgive people for their mistakes." (Refer Chapter 9 on forgiveness.)

iv. **Share your feelings with close person**: Sometimes, the effect of stress is severe and under that circumstance you are advised to consult a therapist or your close friend and share your feelings. By sharing your agony about stressful situations, your problem will be lessened and you will appreciate your decision of accepting the stressful situation. Doctor's therapist and friends will make you understand that making yourself stressful is not going to solve your problem but to increase it.

v. **Do the 24 hours test**: In the beginning, just for twenty-four hours, try total acceptance to whatever happens in real spirit. Nothing will disturb you and your mind will be calm. After this test, you will realize the **'Power of Acceptance.'** This doesn't mean that one should accept abuse, oppression all the time and become slave.

vi. **Don't chase shadows**: Everyday situations disturb us. Some may be looking charming from outside but a deep sad from inside. Stop chasing shadows as they may be looking beautiful when you are far from them. Don't believe in mirage and don't run after it.

Strategy 5: Give Yourself Time for Fun and Relaxation:

Over and above of positive attitude, take- charge approach and acceptance of things, you can reduce stress in your life by nurturing yourself in many ways such as fun and relaxation. "Fun and relaxations are the great tools to reduce or nullify stressors as these are recipes for energy booster and freshness in life." When you make fun with friends and spouse, a chemical is released in your mind which makes you fresh and energetic. Relaxation recharges your tired and stressed body and mind. You may practice the following to recharge yourself.

- Spend time in nature and enjoy its beauty.
- Call some good friends for fun and chatting and enjoy the fun. Get a message of fun from friends.
- Sweat out tension with a good workout.
- Take a long bath (with warm water in winter).
- Play with a pet for some entertainment and fun.
- Work in your garden to enjoy the growing of flowers, the beauty and diversion of mind.
- Curl up with a good book for relaxation.
- Listen to favorite music for relaxation; Watch a comedy picture for laughing, entertainment and relaxation.
- Meditate with mindfulness for recharge.
- Take a small break for relaxation.

Note that nurturing yourself is your main work and responsibility. The following solutions are proposed under the 5th strategy:

i. **Set aside relaxation time in your daily schedule**: Set aside rest and relaxation time in your daily schedule. Be firm for this schedule and don't allow other obligations to encroach. Mind it, this is your time to take a break from all responsibilities and recharge yourself. The set aside time may be judiciously used for fun and relaxations (choose the healthy ways from above list).

ii. **Get connected well with others for social capital**: It is a highly advisable to connect with good people, friends and mentors. Spend time with them who will not only help you in your personal growth but support you when you are heavily loaded with stress. A strong support system is a must which will buffer you from the negative effects of stress and tension.

iii. **Do something on your hobby to enjoy every day**: It is very essential to make time for leisure activities that brings you joy – whether it may be playing musical instruments (such as flute, piano, harmonium, table, guitar, etc.), working on your bike, laughing with friends, watching comedy film, or playing with children.

iv. **Develop sense of humor:** Humor is a great stress reliever. It rejuvenates mind. You may create jokes; tell jokes among friends, laughs even at yourself and with others. Laughing is a great tool to reduce stress in many ways.

v. **Take a long break at least in a year:** It is necessary to take a two weeks break at least in a year for relaxation and enjoyment forgetting completely the work. By this way, you will recharge and rejuvenate yourself.

vi. **Neither brings office or work place matter at home or home matter at work place:** There is a common habit that people think or discuss office matter at home most of the time. Avoid this otherwise, neither will you relax at home nor will you give full concentration to your work at work place.

Strategy 6: Adopt a Healthy Life Style to Enjoy Life:

Resistance to stress can be increased by strengthening your physical health. Adopt a healthy life style which will reduce your stress in life. (**See "Key to Good Life is Good Health," given below.**)

George Burns advocated, "If you ask what the single most important key to longevity is, I would have to say it is avoiding worry, stress and tension. And if you don't ask me, I'd still have to say it".

KEY TO A GOOD LIFE IS GOOD HEALTH

"There are six components of wellness: Proper weight and diet, proper exercise, breaking smoking habit, control of alcohol, stress management and periodic exams."

—*Kenneth H. Cooper*

"Take care of your body. It's the only place you have to live."

—*Jim Rohn*

The old adage: "Health is Wealth" had been and will remain great mantra since birth of civilization. Further, it is rightly said, "A healthy mind resides in a healthy body." If you want to enjoy life, the first and foremost requirement is to maintain good health, to remain fit. Can you achieve success without good health unless and until you are highly gifted? The fact says it is not. "Good health provides vitality and energy which are highly needed to achieve career success, excellent relationships and many other goals in life." "Getting world-class fitness is the smartest move. Remaining fit will make you happier and more value creator." "Good health is your crown, your real wealth as well as national wealth."

Though, there are no guarantees but here **fourteen Health Tips** are being proposed. It is also recommended to consult expert for maintaining good health. "The key to maintaining good health lies in food, we take; water, we drink; air, we breathe; body, we maintain; mind, we maintain; the cloth, we wear; the surrounding, we maintain; and the life style, we adopt." If Europe looks glamorous now, that's because it became hygienic first. Today, nobody can believe that Stockholm, Paris and London were ones 'plague spots.' Improving hygienic condition first, any city like Paris may be made glamorous and free from contagious diseases.

1. Eat Right and Proper Food

Eating of right and proper food with appropriate calories, protein and vitamins is a must as major diseases start from food. Eat food rich in Omega 3 fatty acid such as fishes (seafood), fruits, leafy vegetables, beans, dairy, grains, cereals, eggs, walnuts, and lean cuts of meats. Limit the intake of salty and highly fattening foods. The greater varieties of colors in food (vegetables and fruits) are supposed to be better because they contain different types of antioxidants which strengthen our immune system and slow the aging process. Fresh food is the best, frozen is second best, and the least nutrients are canned fruits and vegetables which should be avoided. Don't avoid breakfast, as your stomach remains empty after last night dinner. Take rich breakfast as this will keep you fresh and energetic for the whole day. Don't eat heavily; instead eat small diets many times (say six to eight). Use fibers as far as possible in your meals as it helps the digestive system. It is said that oil is to machine and fiber is to digestive system. Don't consume junk foods. Reduce coffee and sugar intake. Take dinner early, say between 7 pm to 8 pm.

2. Do Exercise

Exercise is a must. One must do exercise to remain fit and healthy. It burns fat, calories, and tones the muscle. It improves your blood circulation, your heart rate, your respiration, your mood and boosts neurochemical serotonin level (happiness molecule) in mind. We need three types of exercise: flexibility, aerobic and strength training. The minimum time for exercise is recommended by expert for about 15 minutes (brisk) or 20 minutes at normal speed every day. However, 45 minutes of exercise (normal pace) every day is the optimum." You can opt for gym if you can spare time and money. Moderate intensity cardio-vascular workout is a better choice for many people. The cheapest and simplest exercise is walking every day for at least 15 minutes (brisk) or 20 minutes(normal speed) while 45 minutes (normal speed) is optimum.30 minutes brisk walk daily reduces or even cures mild depression. If you are young, you can jog but after 50, you can opt either brisk walking or normal walking. Those who have blood pressure; they should not opt for neither jogging nor brisk walking but simply normal walking. After 60, normal walking is recommended by expert." Physical inactivity increases the risk of Alzheimer's by 82% and invites heart and diabetes ailments."

It is worth noting that physical activity is a great way to release stress. "The consumption of junk foods, smoking, heavy drinking, wrong life styles, physical inactivity and stress are damaging the health of youngsters in a big way all over the world." May youngsters have become the victims of heart, sugar, kidney and liver problems even at the age of thirty. In India, more than 70 million people suffered from diabetes in 2014. In China, 90 million and in USA, 30 million, while the world accounts for 400 million patients of diabetes. "Diabetes affects heart, kidney, eyes and feet." Control your body-mass balance. "No matter how busy you are or how much workload is on your shoulder, a good workout make you feel energetic, happy and positive." "Give at least one hour every day on your body for remaining fit and thirty minutes on reading to rejuvenate your mind."

3. Brush, Floss and Bath

Brushing of teeth after dinner and in the morning is recommended by better brush and tooth paste for good health of teeth. Brushing time should be between three to five minutes. Flossing is removing of food particles trapped between teeth and gum line. Brushing doesn't remove every piece of plaque. Those who don't floss regularly have much higher chances of developing an oral disease such as gingivitis. So, it is recommended that by using string, you floss after every meal. "Bathing with clean water daily refreshes you. It kills all germs. In winter, warm water may be used. Long bath relieves stress."

4. Reduce Stress

A lot has been suggested on stress management strategies, given above which may be followed.

5. Smile and Laugh

Smiling and laughing are the best tools to get relief from stress. They are the signs of true happiness. "Smiling makes you attractive, improves your mood by releasing serotonin in mind, relieves stress, boosts immune system, lowers blood pressure, and improves positivity." "Whenever, you feel that tension is building up in your neck, or your mind gets in slow mode, stop and just smile. You'll instantly feel relieved from your worries." Remember a funny movie which you have seen, or laugh about a ridiculous joke your friend told you, or tell that joke to your friends and laugh. The philosophy behind this is that you just take some time out of your busy schedule to laugh and flash that beautiful smile, not artificially but in real sense. This is the only tool of instant relief from stress.

6. Drink More Clean Water

Our body is made of about 50% of water. Water consumption keeps us hydrated and helps to flush our toxins from our body. Drink about 2.5 to 3 liters of clean water or clean water with lemon every day to flush your toxin. It is worth to note that there is large number of water borne diseases and so be careful about clean water. It is unfortunate that a large number of people from all over world are not getting clean water even in 21stcentury and children are the main victims. Developing and underdeveloped nations including India are not able to provide clean water to their citizens and are suffering various water borne diseases.

7. Get Some Sunshine

Our body needs vitamin D and sun rays provide natural vitamin D. So, it is advisable to get some sunshine preferably every day for about at least half-an hour before 9am. The sun also assists in releasing endorphins, a secretion from the pituitary gland that provides energetic feeling.

8. Sleep Well

A full eight hours of peaceful sleep is the requirement for good health. Those who get good sleep for eight hours are fortunate. If eight hours seems a little more for many busy persons, then one may opt for six hours. It is worth to note that God has designed sleep for every creature of the universe. For human being, it is recommended that they should sleep by the left side. Further, the old adage is still true: "Early to rise and early to bed, make a man healthy, wealthy and wise."

9. Wash Your Hands with Clean Water

Diseases are most easily and frequently transferred via germs which stick to hands. So, it is necessary to wash our hands continuously during the day to kill 90% of germs with hot water and antibacterial soap or antibacterial hand gel or clean water. Washing of hand is very essential after use of latrine and urinal, and before tea, breakfast, lunch, returning from work and dinner. After urination, hands should be washed by clean water.

10. Maintain Personal and Domestic Hygiene

Better hygiene up-keeping is a necessity for better health management. Personal hygiene includes up-keeping of your body and clean clothes. Take necessary steps for proper bathing, brushing of teeth and cleaning of hands, eyes and face. The cloths which you wear should be clean. Every room of your house, kitchen, bath rooms and immediate surrounding should be neat and clean. By this way, you will be exposed to less germs and remain healthy. Water logging anywhere is a place where germs originate. Avoid water logging near your house and hence keep yourself safe.

11. Avoiding Intake of Hazardous Substance

Tobacco, alcohol and narcotic drugs are hazardous substances. People get habituated and drug addicted by starting in general first as fun. These are killers of your health. These give temporarily relief from stress but they completely spoil your health. Be away from such hazardous substances.

12. Breath Clean Air as far as Possible

Many diseases start if we breathe polluted air. The air quality of many metropolitan cities of the world especially India and China has become poisonous due to air pollution caused by vehicles, thermal power houses, and industries. PM2.5 is very dangerous for health. One must try to breath clean air as far as possible otherwise you are inviting all types of health problems originating from lungs and eyes.

13. Regularly Check Your Health

Test for blood pressure, sugar, hemoglobin, serum creatinine, lipid profile, TLC& DLC (during severe cough and cold) should be done at least twice a year after forty and accordingly, living style should be adopted.

14. Yoga and Meditation

Yoga is the physical, mental and spiritual practices or discipline which originated in ancient India (Vedic period) before 3500 years with a views to attain permanent peace and physical well -being. The word Yoga has been derived from Sanskrit word **"Yuj"** which means "to unit or integrate". The Yoga sutras of Patanjali defined Yoga as the 'Stilling of the changing states of the mind'. Yoga has also been defined as **"union."** "A practitioner of yoga can achieve the union of breath and body, the mind and muscles and most importantly union of the self with the divine. Our body, like any good and complex machine, can run best if it adheres to the principles of nature." "The minimum time for Yoga and meditation is about 30 minutes and 15 minutes respectively; however, the optimum time is 60 minutes and 30 minutes respectively."

Yoga sutras of Patanjali are famous. Patanjali is widely regarded as the compiler of the formal Yoga philosophy known as Astanga Yoga (Eight limbs Yoga)from his 29th Sutra of the second book.

Art of Living organization defines Yoga as follows:

"Yoga is about harmonizing the body with the mind and breath through the means of various breathing techniques, Yoga postures (asana) and meditation."

Indian monks beginning with Swami Vivekananda brought Yoga to the West in the late 19th century. Since 2001, the popularity of Yoga has risen at a rapid rate. Yoga is now the universal language of spiritual exercises in U.S crossing many lines of religions and cultures. Every day millions of people practice Yoga worldwide to improve their health, to reduce stress and to improve overall well-being. In India, Baba Ramdev has done a commendable job by awakening the masses about Yoga by giving training to more than 200 million people in camps in over two decades. Millions people have got cured in some ailments and found medicated help through yoga.

The following **basics of Yoga** should be adhered.

i. Practice Yoga in the morning with empty stomach after your daily ablutions on a Yoga mat spread on an even surface, preferably in an open space facing the east or north. Start should be done chanting OM at least five times which produces a unique vibration and soothing effect in mind. Finish flexibility of body and postures of body first in sitting, laying and standing positions, and then start breathing techniques followed by meditation.

ii. Keep your mind calm, happy and refrain from anger, irritation, and tension.
iii. Don't practice Yoga in haste, avoid force or jolt on any kind either during flexibility or postures or breathing techniques.
iv. It is necessary to take into consideration your age, physical and mental condition, flexibility, capacity, and environment.
v. Avoid practicing Yoga when you have fever, cough, cold or are unwell.
vi. Keep a gap of 15 minutes between the end of Yoga session and before your bath or breakfast.
vii. The highest form of Yoga will be when we lead a very moral, ethical, disciplined life over and above the various techniques of Yoga leading to a balance of mind and eternalness in life.

The following are the **potential benefits** for adults after regular practice of yoga:

- It improves allround fitness, mental ability, and mental concentration, inner peace, immunity and energy level.
- It increases brain GABA levels and has been shown to improve mood, reduce anxiety and improve positivity.
- Hatya Yoga (postures, breathing and meditation) makes it beneficial to those suffering from heart diseases. It reduces low back pain and asthma.
- Yoga decreases stress, depression, insomnia, pain, and fatigue and increase ability to control anxiety.

Note: It is to be noted that Yoga must be learned by an expert otherwise some physical injury may be possible. There are now varieties of Yoga. There are many individuals and groups from all over the world offer training on Yoga. The book written by B K S Iyengar titled **"Light on Yoga"** detailing 200 Asanas and 14 types of Pranayma is a classic work published in 1966 which has been translated into more than 17 languages. Iyengar version of Yoga is currently the most practiced in the world. All organizations and individuals have their websites which you can visit for information. "As per one estimate in 2014, the size of the Yoga industries in USA is around USD 27 billion with about 20 million practitioners, as American is famous for making any idea into an industry." Ancient Indian idea, Yoga is now a great industry for fitness and well-being. **21st June** has been chosen as **World Yoga Day** by UN on the advice of Shri Narendra Modi, current Prime Minister of India.

MEDITATION

Though, meditation is an integral part of Yoga but in recent years, many people have separated meditation from Yoga due to its vastness. They practice meditation more. "Meditation is not a technique but a way of life."

Walsh –Shapiro (2006) said, "Meditation refers to a family of self-regulation practices that focus on training attention, and awareness in order to bring mental process under voluntary control and thereby foster general mental well-being and development and or specific capacities such as calm, clarity and concentration."

By Art of Living, "Meditation is that form of exercise which gives you deep rest." "The rest in meditation is deeper than the deepest sleep that you can ever have. When the mind becomes free from agitation, is calm and serene and at peace, meditation begins." ParamhansaYogananda said, "Meditation is deep concentration on God or one of His aspects or your breathing."

The benefits of regular and correct way of meditation are as follows:

- It offers a calm mind, good concentration, clarity of perception and improvement in skill.
- It improves skills and talents, provides unshakable inner strength and acts as mental hygiene.
- It gives the healing ability to connect to an inner source of energy, provides relaxation and rejuvenates the mood.

In this competitive world, stress is catching everybody and harming enormously. Meditation is a necessity. Some people do Yoga and meditation for two hours daily. "The training on Yoga and meditation must be taken by expert at least for five days but one month is the best."

If anybody wishes to embark on the path of meditation, it is essential for the seeker to understand the nature of mind. A typical feature of the mind is ever-fluctuating like monkey and generates about more than 50,000 thought processes covering past, present and future. This is because of the fact that mind is under the constant sway of the three qualities: **'sattava'** (purity and light), **'rajas'** (passion and activity) and **'tamas'** (inertia and darkness). The mode of meditation is only in **sattava,** so one has to practice for bringing mind in this mode.

Are you interested to lead a stress free life and to maintain good health? In general, people start exercise, Yoga and meditation for a week or maximum a month and leave practicing the techniques but this is not going to help you. Meditation is the way of your life. Get up, wake up and resolve to practice the various strategies mentioned for relieving stress; do yoga and meditation; and practice various tips for maintaining good health. Regularity is must.

Follow the following facts:

Stress is your enemy. Control it! Control it! Control it!
Exercise, Yoga and Meditation are your well-wishers and fitness tools. Practice these! Practice these! Practice these!

STEPS TAKEN BY YOUSELF

Based on the strategies mentioned to maintain stress free life and good health, I (as a reader) will do the following to practice these strategies from today itself.

i. _____
ii. _____
iii. _____

***

"Successful people treat failures as festivals and turn tragedies into triumphs."
"The power of persistence places you in the world of golden success."
"Human life and progress is the management of mind"

THE END

CPSIA information can be obtained
at www.ICGtesting.com
Printed in the USA
FSOW02n2026161017
39991FS